Advanced Windows™
Programming

Martin Heller

John Wiley & Sons, Inc.
New York   Chichester   Brisbane   Toronto   Singapore

Library of Congress Cataloging-in-Publication Data

Heller, Martin, 1951—
    Advanced Windows Programming / Martin Heller.
        p.   cm.
    Includes bibliographical references and index.
    ISBN 0-471-54711-5
    ISBN 0-471-55172-4 (book/disk set)
    1. Windows (Computer programs) 2. Microsoft
    Windows (Computer program) I. Title
    QA76.76.W56H45 1992
    005.4'3dc20   91-35881
                                      CIP

Printed in the United States of America
10 9 8 7 6 5 4 3 2 1

Printed and bound by Malloy Lithographing, Inc..

For my family:
Claudia, who thought it was a stupid idea;
Aaron and Rita,who only wanted to look on me;
and Tirzah and Moriah,
who may eventually stop arguing
long enough to notice

About the Author

Martin Heller develops software, writes, and consults in Andover, MA. You can contact him on BIX and MCI Mail as **mheller**, on CompuServe as **74000,2447**, and by mail care of John Wiley & Sons.

Martin is a contributing editor and regular columnist for *Byte Magazine* and the author of half a dozen PC software packages. He has been programming for Windows since early in the Windows 1.0 alpha test period. He has baccalaureate degrees in physics and music from Haverford College as well as Sc.M. and Ph.D. degrees in experimental high-energy physics from Brown University.

Dr. Heller has worked as an accelerator physicist, an energy systems analyst, a computer systems architect, a company division manager, and a consultant. Throughout his career he has used computers as a means to an end, much as a cabinet maker uses hand and power tools.

Martin wrote his first program for a drum-based computer in machine language in the early 1960s. No, not assembly language, machine language. The following year he taught himself Fortran II, and wrote mathematical programs in that language throughout high school.

In graduate school Martin wrote hundreds of programs in MACRO-9 assembler for a DEC PDP-9 computer, and hundreds more Fortran IV, APL, and PL/1 programs for an IBM 360/67. For his Ph.D. thesis he analyzed 500,000 frames of bubble chamber film taken at Argonne National Laboratory and helped take other data at Fermi National Accelerator Laboratory.

At New England Nuclear Corporation (currently a DuPont subsidiary) Dr. Heller developed an automatic computer data-acquisition and control system for an isotope-production cyclotron using Fortran IV+ and MACRO-11 on a PDP-11, with additional embedded 6802-based controllers. When the company acquired a VAX, Martin wrote one of the earliest smart terminal programs, in assembly language for the PDP-11 running RSX-11M.

At Physical Sciences Inc. (PSI) Martin developed a steady-state model of an experimental fuel cell power plant (under contract to the U.S. Department of Energy) in BASIC on a TRS-80 Model 3, and designed more advanced plants in BASIC on an early IBM PC. He developed a DOT-compliant crash sled data analysis program and a brake-testing data-acquisition, control, and analysis system in compiled BASIC for General Motors; he also developed the suite of programs that allowed General Motors to successfully defend itself against a government action over X-car braking systems.

Martin designed and developed MetalSelector, a materials selection and materials properties database program, under contract to the American Society for Metals (currently called ASM International), still in compiled BASIC. He designed EnPlot for the Society's graphing needs, intending the program for Windows 1.0, and put together a team of programmers to write it in C. When Windows 1.0 started slipping its schedule, Dr. Heller and his team implemented EnPlot for DOS instead of Windows.

Martin responded to the ongoing needs of the materials properties community by designing and implementing MetSel2 (at PSI) and later MatDB, in C for DOS, and EnPlot 2.0 for Windows (in both cases as an independent consultant). EnPlot is currently at revision 3.0 (and counting), and runs under Windows 3.0 and above.

While still at PSI, Martin designed two statistical subroutine libraries in Fortran for John Wiley & Sons. **Statlib.tsf** was a time-series and forecasting library, and **Statlib.gl** was a device-independent graphing library built on the GKS graphics standard. Both packages are now out of print.

As a consultant, Martin has worked with several companies to develop, design, and/or debug Windows applications. His latest solely developed program is **Room Planner**, a meeting and conference layout system for the hospitality industry.

Contents

· · · · · · · · · · · · · · · · · · · ·

Preface

· ·

Advanced Windows Programming was written to show the Windows developer
the essentials of writing *real* Windows programs. Up until now the only ways to find
out this information have been to program Windows for a couple of years, to look
over the shoulders of experienced Windows developers, and to ask questions in a
computer conference; the best such have been BIX (the Byte Information Exchange), CompuServe and GEnie. The material hasn't even been covered in course
work, except at Microsoft University and one specialized school in—of all places—
Iceland.

While the title says Advanced, this book will be of equal benefit to beginning
Windows programmers. A good set of prerequisites would be:

- A strong working knowledge of the C programming language, with a
  firm understanding of pointers and structures.
- A good grasp of Intel segmented memory architecture.
- A more than passing acquaintance with Microsoft C, including the **near**
  and **far** keyword extensions.
- Some familiarity with the Microsoft Windows application program interface and message-passing model. This can be achieved by reading
  through the Microsoft Windows SDK (Software Development Kit) *Guide
  to Programming* manual, and Charles Petzold's *Programming Windows,
  Second Edition* (Microsoft Press, 1990).

To compile and run the examples in the book or companion disks as presented,
you'll need Microsoft C V6.0 or later, the Microsoft Windows SDK V3.0 or later, and
Microsoft Windows V3.0 or later. If you don't have Microsoft C, you can still use the
programs from this book: Appendix 2 explains how to adapt the code for Zortech
C++, Appendix 3 explains how to do the same for Borland C++, Appendix 4 covers
the use of Watcom C, and Appendix 5 covers Quick C for Windows. You'll need a
PC capable of running all of this, of course; a minimum configuration would be an
80286-based PC with 640KB of memory, a hard disk, an EGA display, and a mouse.

Note that the companion disks have contents that don't appear in the book, and
vice versa. This is strictly a matter of space and practicality. Some material is best
presented as it is here, in print; other material is best given in executable form. If you
bought the book without the diskettes, you can order them using the attached card.
Some, but not all of the contents of the companion disks are also available on BIX
for downloading.

Once you've got the prerequisites under your belt—C and a little exposure to Windows at the introductory level—*Advanced Windows Programming* can help you get over the rather formidable mental barrier to writing Windows programs. There's a *big* difference between writing a 500-line program in small model that does nothing but draw monochrome pictures on the screen, and a 5,000-line multiple-module program in mixed model (medium model plus global allocations) that deals with color, palette management, printers, fonts, the clipboard, and dynamic data exchange. Don't feel that you have to know every little thing about Windows before you start: the value of this kind of book is that you'll pick it up and gain fluency as you go, as long as you have enough background to follow the exposition.

In *Advanced Windows Programming* I cover the process of developing *real* Windows programs, as opposed to toy examples. After some introductory matter, the book revolves around a single major application to display device-independent bitmaps, and a number of smaller test fixtures to help us develop our modules.

We start, innocuously enough, with a look at the SHOWDIB example program from the Microsoft Windows Software Development Kit (SDK). We add capabilities: more file formats, some image processing algorithms.

Then we add editing capabilities using the Windows clipboard, demonstrating useful functions like dragging regions, handling global memory larger than 64K, and implementing undo functions. We continue by investigating DDE and OLE client, server, and remote execution capabilities. Along the way, we deal with the problems unique to large-sized Windows programs, such as memory management and modularization, and problems that occur only when two Windows programs interact.

We take an intermission from our bitmap display program—which by now has grown into something of an image-processing program—and discuss different ways to debug Windows programs. We'll emphasize techniques for solving actual problems, in some detail, and we'll deal with the lovely problems that come up when the debugger makes the bug go away, or the debugger kills the program before the bug we're looking for can express itself.

We'll digress further, and talk about edit controls. We'll demonstrate how to customize edit controls by responding to various messages in a dialog box, and how to customize further by subclassing. When we've taken this as far as we think reasonable, we'll reimplement the edit control ourselves and enhance it to handle multiple fonts, point sizes, and text attributes.

Finally, we'll add our custom edit control to the bitmap display program and use it for adding titles to an image. A little tuning, and we—author and reader—will have built a fairly interesting application that is useful in and of itself, and open to further enhancements by the reader. Just as icing on the cake, we'll go on to talk about how we'd port this application—or less ambitious Windows applications—to Presentation Manager, X-Windows, DOS, and the Macintosh.

I couldn't have written this book in a vacuum. I am deeply indebted to the many Windows designers, developers, technical writers, and support people at Microsoft; to Charles Petzold, whose fine book provides a solid foundation on which mine builds; to Diane Cerra, Terri Hudson, and Katherine Schowalter at Wiley, who prodded me to turn a vague idea into a substantial volume; and to Claire Stone, who designed the book's layout and helped me over the hurdles of desktop typesetting. I thank my beta readers: John Butler, Michael Geary, Lee Hasiuk, Kyle Marsh, Jean-Marc Matteini, Barry Nance, Bill Neuenschwander, Dan Rubin, John Skiver, and Carl Sturmer, as well as Wiley's two anonymous reviewers.

I also thank the many programmers on BIX who contributed examples, made suggestions, or helped to test and debug my software, including Marc Adler, Mike Geary, David Jones, Barry Nance, Dan Rubin, Bill van Ryper, Jay Slupesky, Anders Thun, and Bert Tyler. I thank Dana Hudes for contributing some fine photographs, and Steve Rogers of Kodak for scanning the images. And finally I thank my wife, Claudia—because.

In which we present a general
introduction to the more advanced
Windows programming concepts,
such as interprocess communication, memory management, subclassing, and superclassing.

Introduction

· ·

In the beginning, C programmers write (or copy) **hello.c**, for which the
specification is to print the words "hello, world". The ordinary C version of this,
which works perfectly well in Unix, DOS, OS/2, and any number of other text-
based operating systems, is simply:

```
#include <stdio.h>
main()
{
        printf("hello,world\n");
}
```

Kernighan and Ritchie tell us that getting this program entered, compiled,
and run is the "big hurdle" to getting started as a C programmer; "everything else
is comparatively easy."

The equivalent "hello" program for Microsoft Windows (found in Chapter
1 of Charles Petzold's fine introductory book, *Programming Windows*) amounts
to three pages of text—some 80 lines of code—in three files: **hellowin.c** (the
C language source code), **hellowin.def** (the module definition file), and
hellowin.mak (the "make" file). Getting "hello" for Windows running is
another big hurdle—but not so big a hurdle as understanding everything that
goes on to make it run. An even bigger hurdle for beginning Windows

programmers is to venture beyond the manuals; the barrier here is as formidable as was the dreaded map designation *terra incognita* to fifteenth-century sailors.

Consider this book your Baedeker, your guide to unknown lands, written by one who has explored their blackest depths and returned to tell the tale.

Real-World Programs versus Toys

Nobody ever said **hello.c** was useful—other than as a learning tool. Neither is the "Hello, Windows" program. But there is more to a Windows program than there is to **hello.c**; Petzold's **hellowin**, the Windows SDK **generic** program and other readily available small examples do valuable service as templates. You'll never have to reinvent the obligatory parts of a Windows program: just copy an example, change the names, and start adding functionality.

Still, the programs you'll find in the Windows SDK and in other Windows programming books are mostly short, easily digestible examples—which also makes them toy programs. They sometimes do useful things, such as enumerate your fonts or take a window snapshot, but they don't generally push any of the size limits on Windows programs.

On the other hand, real-world Windows programs often do push the limits. What do I mean by "real-world"? Why, something genuinely useful. Word for Windows, the word processor I'm using to write this book, is a good example. Its executable, **winword.exe**, is almost 900KB of code and resources. Its dynamic link libraries add up to another 900KB. It has 500KB of data files, 350KB of document templates, 250KB of import and export filters, and a 400KB help file. It isn't big just to be big—it is big because it does a lot of different things.

There is an ethic among some programmers and Sixties counterculture types: *small is beautiful.* We must emend that specifically for computer software: given two programs that do the same thing at the same speed, we prefer the one that uses the fewest system resources. Small programs that don't do much or take a long time to run don't qualify as beautiful. But small programs that do one or two things elegantly may qualify as *good hacks.* There's a satisfaction in writing a good hack that you don't often get from writing a big potpourri of a program; but there are techniques needed for big programs you just won't find in little ones.

Back to Word for Windows. It's got several megabytes of code. Normally, the sum of a program's static data, stack, and local heap can't exceed 64KB. Can you imagine that Word for Windows would be possible if there weren't a way around that restriction?

A big program can't blithely assume that any global memory blocks it needs will be allocated successfully—the sheer size of the program almost guarantees that it will have to deal with low memory situations. Word for Windows can't require that every font available for your printer also be available for your screen: if it did, Microsoft would be swamped with returns of the product from people without enough disk space to build all those screen fonts. It can't assume that every file it reads will be in the format it expects to read, or it would crash every time it did an import. It can't arbitrarily limit itself to a "reasonable" number of fonts—the dozen fonts that might be reasonable at a secretary's workstation would hardly make a dent in the hundreds of fonts needed by a desktop publishing shop.

It has to deal, instead, with the real world—or as real a world as exists on personal computers. And the ways Windows programs deal with these real-world issues and problems is the major subject of this book.

Other Windows books concentrate on short programs because they're easier to understand than long programs. And, perhaps, because they're easier to write than long programs. We don't have that luxury: to show the problems of size and their solutions, we need to work on a big program. But for comprehensibility, we'll explain fragments of code in small chunks; and for reliability, we'll test them in small chunks with little test fixtures. Not all of our test programs will necessarily be Windows programs: when possible, we'll test our functions in a more controlled environment (plain DOS or OS/2) before bringing them into the multitasking mayhem of Windows.

I learned some of the techniques covered in this book the hard way: I worked them out for myself in the course of developing Windows programs. Other techniques were supplied by Microsoft, and still others were shared with me by other Windows developers. I'll do my best to give credit where credit is due—but I hope that the originators of some of the tricks that I present will forgive me, since their names have been lost as their hacks have been passed orally from programmer to programmer.

A small admission: while I advocate carefully testing functions and program fragments outside of the program they will eventually be part of, I don't always practice what I preach. Lots of times, bending to time constraints, I'll write the code once in its final resting place, quickly check that it works as expected, and go on the next pressing matter. I usually get away with such shortcuts; but, when they backfire, the time spent to isolate and repair the problem can be costly. You'll have to decide for yourself how much insurance (in the form of bench testing) you want to buy, and how much risk you can afford to take.

Memory Management Issues

Microsoft Windows isn't really a single environment. Depending on how you want to count, it is either three or five different environments in version 3.0. That count goes down to two different memory environments in Windows 3.1, at least under DOS. (The NT Windows environment is so different that we won't try to cover it here.)

Windows Memory Modes

To begin with, Windows 3.0 can run in real, standard, and enhanced modes. Windows 3.1 drops support for real mode, and runs only in standard and enhanced modes.

Real mode in Windows 3.0 is similar to Windows 2, and can use three memory modes itself: no EMS, small-frame EMS, and large-frame EMS. EMS stands for Expanded Memory Specification; it is also called LIM (for Lotus-Intel-Microsoft, the companies who specified the standard) or banked memory. You might want to check to see what memory mode your copy of Windows is using: to do so, pull down the **About** box from the Windows Program Manager's **Help** menu (Figures 1.1 and 1.2).

With no EMS in real mode—the *basic* memory mode—Windows has very little memory available for applications; it is dead certain that you won't be able to run two big applications simultaneously, and that an application big enough to be useful will constantly be discarding and loading code segments. If you want to stress-test your application to see if you've done your segmentation well, use this mode. You can force real mode without EMS by starting Windows 3.0 with the command line:

```
WIN /R /N
```

On a machine with more than 640KB of memory, **HIMEM.SYS** (which comes with Windows) makes an extra 64KB of memory available to Windows

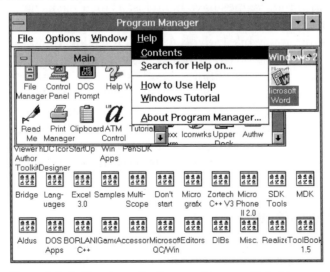

Figure 1.1. Pulling down the Program Manager Help Menu

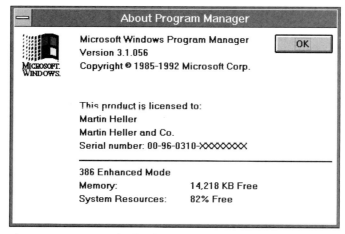

Figure 1.2. Memory display from Program Manager

through the use of the infamous A20 memory-addressing control line. (A20 refers to the pinout designation on the chip.) Basically, enabling A20 lets Windows use a quirk in the 80286 addressing scheme to reach the "High Memory Area," which resides just above the 1MB mark. Because of the way PCs are designed, only 640KB of RAM is mapped below the video adapters and ROM areas; additional memory is mapped above the 1MB line. To *really* stress-test your application for low memory situations, disable **HIMEM.SYS** temporarily and force Windows into basic mode—you're just about guaranteed to see segment motion, segment discarding, and segment loading. **HIMEM.SYS** is normally installed by the Windows 3 setup program; to disable it, edit your **CONFIG.SYS** file and reboot.

Small-frame EMS mode improves things somewhat for a single application: much of its code and data can be *banked*, or put into *expanded* memory. To get expanded memory in an 80286-based machine, you need a special expanded memory board (such as an Intel AboveBoard) that has bank-switching hardware. On an 80386- or 80486-based machine, you can emulate expanded memory using **EMM386.SYS**, which comes with Windows. You'll find instructions for installing **EMM386** in your Windows manual. You can also emulate expanded memory with third-party memory managers like 386-to-the-Max and QEMM.

You'll need to test your application in both EMS modes to ensure that it works correctly with bank-switching. To force small-frame EMS mode, start Windows 3.0 with the line:

```
WIN /R /E:999
```

Large-frame EMS mode gives each application its own banked memory, but leaves less low memory for each application than small-frame mode. The mix of low and banked memory is adjustable: vary the **/E:xxx** parameter on the

Windows command line to see the effect. Running Windows with the **/R** switch and without the **/E** switch will generally get Windows into large-frame EMS mode. Many commercial Windows applications will either fail to start or crash during operation in this mode, since most dynamic link libraries can't be banked and the low memory gets used up quickly. Unless you've marked your application for protected mode only (using the **/t** switch to RC) you need to test your own applications in large-frame mode to find out where the bank line needs to be set: you'll undoubtedly hear from customers who can't run your application because they're running Windows in large-frame EMS mode, and you'll need to know what to tell them.

Windows 3.0 standard mode uses the protected mode of the 80286 in much the same manner as does OS/2 1.x. Segment motion in this mode is handled by updating the segment descriptor table; the CPU uses the segment descriptor table to map segment handles to actual memory addresses. Handling the memory mapping in hardware improves the speed of Windows; even more speed improvement comes from the larger available address space. All the memory in standard mode is the same kind—you don't have any such thing as banked memory to worry about. The net result is that programs running in standard mode do a lot less discarding of segments than programs running in any of the real modes; the reduced disk activity and the reduced segment motion overhead combine to make standard mode a faster environment for Windows programs.

Standard mode allows one DOS session to run as a full-screen foreground task, but suspends the DOS session when it is in the background. This is fine on a 286, but doesn't use the full capabilities of a 386. Windows 3 enhanced mode, on the other hand, uses the advanced memory mapping modes of the 80386 to provide demand paged virtual memory, multiple DOS sessions, and some multitasking of sessions. If you've got a 386 box and enough memory ("enough" being theoretically more than 2 MB, or realistically at least 4 MB of RAM), enhanced mode will allow you to use disk as additional "RAM," run several DOS sessions at the same time you are running several Windows programs—and even run windowed DOS sessions. While the multitasking offered by Windows 3.0 in enhanced mode isn't as good as the multitasking offered by OS/2, it is good enough to let you run compiles while you edit, and play solitaire while you download.

Memory Use Guidelines

Every real application must be prepared to run out of memory and other system resources. Anytime you allocate or lock a memory block, you must check to see if the operation succeeded, and bail out cleanly if it hasn't. Unfortunately, this will clutter your code—but that's the price you pay for having a robust program. Paranoia in the proper places is a virtue: as you write Windows code, assume that each allocation might fail, or might succeed only at the expense of forcing the Windows kernel to go through a lengthy series of discards and moves.

In real mode, you can't leave memory blocks locked longer than necessary, either: you need to be nice to the other programs on the system. If you write a program that's a memory hog it'll slow down the user's whole Windows system, and your program will get a bad reputation. The price of following the rules for real mode is that your application may be a tad slower because it has to lock and unlock memory blocks all the time.

On the other hand, Windows uses the memory mapping hardware in standard and enhanced modes. If your program really needs a lot of memory, you might want to mark it protected-mode only with the **/t** switch to the resource compiler. If you limit your program to protected mode, the guidelines for memory usage are relaxed a bit: you can allocate and lock down all your memory when your program is initialized, and unlock and release it all when your window is destroyed. But don't allocate fixed memory blocks: these are different from movable blocks that have been locked, and might cause some fragmentation. Realize, too, that limiting your program to protected mode will limit your market to people with machines that can run standard or enhanced mode Windows on their computers. While that may not be much of a problem in the future, it will certainly keep you from selling your program to the huge installed base of 640K machines.

If you want, you can allow your program to run in all modes but optimize locking for protected mode. What you'd do is use the **GetWinFlags** function to determine the memory mode and set a global variable for your program. In protected mode you'd only lock a block once when it was allocated and release it once before freeing it. In real mode you'd unlock the block anytime it was not needed, and relock it whenever it was needed.

If you want to require Windows 3.1 to run your program, you automatically restrict your program to Standard or Enhanced mode: support for the three real modes was dropped in Windows 3.1, specifically to make life easier for developers. That doesn't change the marketing situation: somebody with an 8086 won't be able to run your programs. But it at least reduces the explanations you'll have to make—you can blame Microsoft—and it might even encourage people who want to run your programs to upgrade their machines rather than yell at you to support real mode.

Why Medium Model?

I advocate building most real-world Windows programs in the medium memory model. Small model is too restrictive, and compact and large models will not perform well in real mode. Medium model itself would be too restrictive because of the 64K limit on near data, except that you can augment the model with far data pointers and global heap allocations.

If you are building protected-mode-only programs, or programs that require Windows 3.1 or later, the arguments for medium model are somewhat weaker. In this case, large model programs may perform satisfactorily, although it is easier to get multiple instances of a medium model program than multiple instances of a large model program. I advocate medium-model multiple-instance programs rather than large-model Multiple Document Interface programs because they are faster, easier to maintain, and work better with DDE and OLE.

Unless your program is so small that all your code will fit into 64K, you'll need multiple code segments, which is the default in medium model. You can control the segment names explicitly with the **-NT** switch to MSC; in this way you can combine several object modules into a single segment. But most of the time, your problem wont be that segments are too small—it'll be that segments are too big. For dividing the functions in a module into multiple segments, you can use the **alloc_text** pragma in MSC. We'll discuss segment-size optimization and tuning at some length later on.

The default function call in medium model is done with long (far) code pointers. Far procedures are safe, but not efficient. When you're developing a program you should stick to the safe defaults; you can later optimize your code by changing those far functions which are called only within a segment to near procedures. If you switch to near procedures too soon, you may find that it's a burden to keep track of them when you tune your segmentation. Get things working correctly first; you can make them fast afterwards.

In order to access data on the global heap from medium model, you'll need to use far data pointers. This isn't especially hard—you just use the **LPSTR** type (defined in **windows.h** as **char _far ***) for strings on the global heap, or similar **_far** pointers for other data types.

Far data can get tricky when you need to use library routines. In the medium model almost all C library routines are built with far code and near data. The exceptions are special memory and string routines prefixed with **_f**, such as **_fstrcpy()**; these model-independent far functions were added in MSC 6.0 to support mixed-model programming. You don't usually need to use these functions from Windows, however; instead, you can use Windows kernel functions like **lstrcpy()**.

Many of the more specialized C library functions don't have far equivalents. You can do one of three things when you need to use one of these functions: roll your own far version from scratch, make a far version that does nothing but copy its arguments to local variables and call the library function, or copy the arguments to local variables before calling the library function. In practice, the last option turns out to be more convenient than it sounds, since where there is one library function there are often a string of them.

You may not want to bother with making far versions of library routines or copying variables at all. That leaves you with the alternative of using the large memory model, which will give you coding convenience at the expense of runtime performance and a probable restriction to a single instance.

Using Huge Pointers

What happens when you need to handle an memory object bigger than 64KB? Microsoft C handles this sort of thing with the huge model, which is just like the large model except that pointers are constantly being normalized (that is, reduced to the segment: offset combination with the smallest offset). In Windows, huge memory blocks can be allocated with **GlobalAlloc()**; if you want to work with a huge memory block, simply use a huge pointer and cast the result of **GlobalLock()** to match:

```
BYTE huge *hpB;
HANDLE hmem;

hmem=GlobalAlloc(GMEM_MOVEABLE,300000L)
hpB=(BYTE huge *)GlobalLock(hMem);
```

Huge blocks are not well supported. Since Windows routines generally expect far pointers—not huge pointers—you have to limit what the Windows functions do so that they don't inadvertently access data that straddles a 64K boundary, which would fault out in protected mode. For instance, you can read your I/O blocks into a huge buffer, but you have to do it in, say, 32KB pieces. In real mode, you dont have to worry about segment protection violation errors—instead you have to worry about your allocations failing.

It is not a good idea to declare large global or static arrays in medium model, since they will be near data; it's hard to keep the total of your local heap, stack, and static data below 64KB if you blithely declare big static buffers. Use the global heap: that's what it's for. Even in large model you'll find that support for huge static arrays is limited; in some versions of Windows, it doesn't work at all.

Interfacing with Other Programs

> *No man is an island, entire of itself; every man is a piece of the continent, a part of the main; if a clod be washed away by the sea, Europe is the less, as well as if a promontory were, as well as if a manor of thy friends or of thine own were; any man's death diminishes me, because I am involved in mankind; and therefore never send to know for whom the bell tolls; it tolls for thee.*

> *John Donne,* Devotions upon Emergent Occasions, *1624, no. 6*

No Windows program is an island, entire of itself; every Windows program is a piece of the continent, a part of the main. Each Windows program constantly receives (and should respond to) messages from the system, from itself, and from other Windows programs.

Being part of a larger system is quite different from being the center of your own universe. For a new Windows programmer, it requires a different way of thinking, a broader view of what a program is and does. And it requires the program to support many different mechanisms for exchanging data with other programs.

The easiest exchange mechanism for a new Windows programmer to grasp is probably file exchange, since file I/O in Windows is similar to file I/O in any other system. While hardly a real-time protocol, file exchange has the virtues of being asynchronous and fail-safe. It is asynchronous in the sense that one program writes the file, and later another program reads it. It is fail-safe in the sense that the information is not lost if the second program fails to read it on the first try; the file still exists for another attempt. The worst problem with file exchange is the multitude of different file formats that need support.

File Formats

In this book we'll deal mainly with text and bitmapped images. Every word processor in the known universe seems to have its own proprietary file format; conversion programs that preserve text formatting while translating between different word processing file formats have a thriving niche. For our purposes, word processing files won't matter: we'll deal only with unformatted ASCII text, and Rich Text Format (RTF)—and only a subset of RTF, at that.

Bitmapped images are another matter. Since our major application will be the display of color images, and since image formats are far from standardized, we'll support several of the more common formats: Microsoft's DIB/BMP format, CompuServe's GIF, ZSoft's PCX, Truevision's TARGA, Aldus's TIFF, and NASA's VICAR. The code to support all these formats—each of which has many variants—can be found on the book's companion disks, along with sample image files you can use to test the code. We'll discuss the formats and the code briefly when we come to the file I/O section of the book, but it would be prohibitive to list all that code here—and it would take you months to type it all in.

The only real requirement for two programs to exchange data in files is that they have a common file format. All too often, that is a least common denominator—perhaps an unformatted ASCII file to transmit text (which loses *all* of the formatting information) or a GIF file to transmit an image (which is restricted to 256 colors). But if the programs have a high-information format in

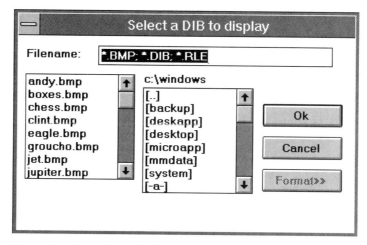

Figure 1.3. Open file dialog box

common—RTF for formatted text, or DIB for bitmaps—you may be able to work a single document back and forth freely between two programs, using the special capabilities of each program to enhance the result.

From the importing program's point of view, problem number one is finding the file. Windows programs have a standard open file dialog: older programs use a single list box for files and directories, and newer programs use separate list boxes (Figure 1.3). The file list box is generally linked to an edit control for the filename. Standard code to run such a dialog box can be found in the Windows SDK; the code generally relies on the **DlgDirList()** Windows function, which in turn uses the **LB_DIR** Windows message. Attribute bits in the **wFiletype** argument to **DlgDirList()** control whether the list box is filled with filenames, subdirectory names, or both. With the Windows 3.1 SDK, you can call the common dialog function to open a file instead of copying the code from an example program.

Once the file is found, the next problem is identifying the file format. The file extension (e.g., **BMP** in the figure) may indicate the general format, but then again it may not: a user may have set the extension at some point without really knowing the format. A robust program can't rely on the extension, although it can use the extension to make a first guess at the format.

If your program can't rely on the extension, what can it rely on? The user? Not for primary information: the program needs to look into the file and identify whatever unique signatures identify a given format. You may want the user to confirm the program's guess: algorithms for identifying file formats may not always be reliable. But neither is the user guaranteed to be reliable.

OK so far: your program has found a signature, and the user has verified the selected file format. Your program still can't be sure it's reading the format it thinks it sees, and further can't be sure that the file is uncorrupted. Paranoia has to dominate the file reading code in order to protect the program from dying ignominiously when it encounters incorrect data. At the same time, you don't want the program to refuse to read otherwise correct files because one or two bits are unexpected—that would cause the user endless frustration.

We'll return to these issues over and over. You want your program to be totally bulletproof; at the same time you want it to be pleasant to use—not a nagging, whining pest.

Clipboard Transfers

The Windows clipboard is a system facility for exchanging data in memory; it is also useful for editing purposes within a single program. Think of the clipboard as a global holding area that can hold one block of data—of arbitrary size—in multiple formats.

In **windows.h** you'll find definitions for the standard clipboard formats:

```
/* Predefined Clipboard Formats */
#define CF_TEXT          1    //Ordinary ANSI text
#define CF_BITMAP        2    //Device-dependent bitmap
#define CF_METAFILEPICT  3    //Windows Metafile
#define CF_SYLK          4    //Multiplan Spreadsheet
#define CF_DIF           5    //Data Interchange Format
#define CF_TIFF          6    //Tagged bitmap format
#define CF_OEMTEXT       7    //OEM character set text
#define CF_DIB           8    //Device-independent bitmap
#define CF_PALETTE       9    //Palette
```

The additional predefined formats **CF_OWNERDISPLAY**, **CF_DSPTEXT**, **CF-_DSPBITMAP**, and **CF_DSPMETAFILEPICT** are used to control the clipboard display window.

Beyond the standard formats, well need to work with a few formats defined by convention only, and accessed by their names as strings:

```
wCF_RTF      "Rich Text Format"    (used for formatted text)
wCF_LINK     "Link"  (used for DDE)
```

The names **wCF_RTF** and **wCF_LINK** are not **#defined** anywhere in the Windows include files: they are variables. I have added the leading w to indicate that they are variables of type WORD, but kept the trailing CF_<format name> to make it clear they are clipboard formats.

There aren't standard names for putting PCX, VICAR, Targa, or GIF formats on the clipboard. We'll avoid trying to set a standard by converting these formats to DIBs and doing our editing and file exchange using the CF_DIB format.

To access a predefined format on the clipboard, you ask for it by number (i.e., CF_TEXT, defined as 1). To access any other format, you register the name and then use the handle supplied by the registration routine to access the name. So, somewhere in your initialization routine you could register RTF with the statement:

```
wCF_RTF=RegisterClipboardFormat((LPSTR)"Rich Text Format");
```

Later on, when you want to retrieve RTF from the clipboard, you can use the saved handle:

```
OpenClipboard(hWnd);
hRTFdata=GetClipboardData(wCF_RTF);
CloseClipboard();
```

If there were no RTF data on the clipboard at the time, the handle **hRTFdata** returned by **GetClipboardData** would be **NULL**. Otherwise, you could lock down the RTF data memory block and read the data. When we discuss DDE, we'll see that it uses the same formats as the clipboard.

Real-world Windows applications need to support multiple clipboard formats. When copying information to the clipboard, copy it in all formats that make sense, starting with the most detailed and ending with the most generic. If all these formats are too much of a burden, then use delayed rendering: send **NULL** data handles to the **SetClipboardData()** function, and be prepared to supply the actual data for any of the posted formats in response to a **WM_RENDERFORMAT** message.

You'll want the clipboard application to have something to display even if you post a private format. One way to handle this is to supply a **CF_TEXT** entry that describes the binary data; another is to use a display format (**CF_DSPTEXT**, **CF_DSPBITMAP**, or **CF_DSPMETAFILEPICT**); a third is to take full control of the clipboard with the **CF_OWNERDISPLAY** format.

When your program is reading the clipboard, it will specify the format it wants on any given **GetClipboardData()** request. Assuming that the posting application has placed the formats on the clipboard in richest-first order, the correct strategy for choosing a format is to enumerate the available formats, and take the first appropriate format from the list.

The clipboard is invaluable when the user is editing a document, and for transferring items between documents. Its drawbacks are that the copied data is not automatically updated if the source changes, and that the user has to do too much manual labor when transferring any substantial amount of data.

We'll come back to clipboard handling in Chapter 4. Don't worry too much if clipboard formats aren't totally clear to you right now: try to push on and understand how the clipboard relates to DDE.

DDE Transfers

DDE is Windows' principal mechanism for interprocess communication. The Microsoft Windows Dynamic Data Exchange (DDE) protocol defines a method for communicating among applications that takes place as applications send messages to each other to initiate conversations, to request and share data, and to terminate conversations. Although DDE transfer is more difficult to set up than clipboard data exchange, it has several advantages.

In the *hot link* form of DDE transfer, the *server* application sends data to the *client* application whenever the data changes; this guarantees that the derived form of the data (perhaps a table in a word processing document) will always reflect the current state of the original data (perhaps a spreadsheet). A variation of this, the *warm link*, notifies the client when the data has changed, but sends the data only if the client wants it; this enables the client to control the rate at which it receives data. A simpler mechanism, the *request*, is equivalent to a single copy operation from the server and a single paste operation to the client, without the need for the intermediate step of putting the data on the clipboard.

You might think that DDE transfers simply pass global memory blocks among applications. Actually, Windows applications don't necessarily share an address space, so the DDE kernel code takes care of copying memory blocks between address spaces. For this reason, there is a special flag, **GMEM_DDESHARE**, to use when your application allocates global memory for DDE transfers. The OS/2 Presentation Manager implementation of DDE is simpler, since support for "giveable" memory was built into the operating system kernel.

DDE also supports a back channel transfer, the *poke*. And *execute*, perhaps the most intriguing DDE mechanism of all, allows one application to control another.

DDE was developed for Microsoft Excel; for a long time, the only applications that supported DDE were Excel and a few demonstration programs (all of which seemed to have something to do with stock tickers). Since the advent of Windows 3 made simultaneously running multiple applications practical, it has become *de rigueur* for "real" Windows applications to support DDE exchange.

DDE supports a *client—server* architecture in which both client and server programs carry on multiple *conversations* with other applications. Each conversation has a *topic* and may include multiple *advisories*, each of which refers to an *item*. The application is responsible for keeping track of ongoing conversations and advisories; conversations are uniquely identified by the window handles of the client and server.

A tricky point: there is a good reason for both the client and server to create a unique window for each conversation. You might think it would be enough for only one application to have unique window handles. But suppose one application used its main window handle as identification for a DDE conversation, on the grounds that the other window handle should be unique? And then suppose two such applications tried to talk to each other? Oops. Applications that want to support DDE properly have to create *object windows* to guarantee that each DDE conversation will have a unique identifier.

DDE Remote Control

The DDE execute facility can be the basis for remote control. In the early days of DDE the only example of this was the famous **FISH** demonstration; using DDE execute commands from Excel, you could activate a submarine that would torpedo the fish.

With so many applications supporting DDE these days, you can do somewhat more useful things with DDE execute: for instance, you can control the Packrat personal information manager from Word for Windows, to find documents easily. A WordBasic macro makes this look like any other operation in Word; the fact that it invokes and controls another application is neatly hidden.

As you might expect, DDE execute is most useful if both client and server applications have macro languages. The server needs to respond to simple commands; the client application needs a language with control structures, the ability to manipulate strings, and commands to support DDE.

DDE is useful, but it can be difficult to set up. Both applications have to run simultaneously, or in a fixed order (with one invoking the other). The person who sets up the DDE transfer—or writes the macros to do so—has to know both applications in some detail. And DDE links are fragile: restoring a link between two documents depends on one application storing the complete path of the other's document. Reorganize your hard disk, or e-mail the document to someone with different directory structures, and remaking the DDE links between documents can be a painful process.

The DDE Management Libraries (DDEML)

Starting with Windows 3.1, the preferred method for implementing DDE in an application is to use calls to DDEML, rather than issuing DDE messages. While the concepts for using DDE via messages and DDE via ML are similar, the implementation looks quite different to the application.

DDEML is restricted to protected mode: the DDEML client and server libraries are written for protected mode only. You can use the DDEML libraries shipped with the Windows 3.1 SDK with applications that need to run under Windows 3.0, but only for enhanced or standard modes. (You'd have to ship the DLLs with your application.) If you want your application to use DDE in real mode, you will have to use the old method of sending messages. On the other hand, DDEML can help you insulate your application from the details of interprocess communication; it ensures that your DDE implementation will be consistent with other applications; it supplies some string and data management services; and it supplies a server-name function.

OLE: Object Linking and Embedding

Microsoft's OLE specification is one attempt to overcome the problems with DDE links. The OLE linking libraries are built on DDE, but insulate the application from the gory details. OLE embedding attempts to fix the "fragile link" problem by putting a copy of one application's data in a *container* in the other application's document. The second application doesn't need to know how to edit the first application's data—only how to display it. For editing, one application invokes the other transparently.

OLE makes it easier for the user to generate complex documents, without having to know a lot of gory technical details. On the other hand, it is yet another set of functions for a real Windows application to support. And there are still problems: you can have automatically updated linking, or unbreakable embedding, but you can't have automatically updated, unbreakable links. Microsoft hopes to address the fragile link problem in the future with an improved file system.

You can use the OLE libraries instead of or in addition to the DDEML libraries. You should use DDEML if your application needs to support simultaneous links for many items, especially if the items are updated frequently. You should use OLE if you want persistent embedding and linking of objects, rendering of common data formats, server rendering of specialized data formats, creation of objects and links from the clipboard and files, and activation of embedded and linked objects.

You should also use the OLE libraries if you want your application to support New Wave. This may be the clincher—if you write to OLE, you can make your application work with other OLE programs, with programs that support basic DDE, and with New Wave.

New Wave

The HP New Wave environment is, among other things, another way to fix the "fragile link" problem—and it does a lot more than OLE, improving automation with *agents* and supporting networked operation transparently. New Wave uses a central database to resolve names: the intelligent link manager relates New Wave names to file system names. In many other ways the New Wave architecture is similar to the OLE architecture.

New Wave is implemented as a layer on top of Windows. The New Wave Office window is a "root" object that owns all New Wave tools and objects. Tools are resources (like printers), represented on the desktop as three-dimensional icons. Objects are data (files) of specific types (applications), which may in turn contain other objects.

People familiar with the old Xerox Star, or with the Apple Macintosh, will immediately find New Wave easy to work with—much more so than Windows itself. You throw things away by dragging them to the trashcan (and later you can root through the trashcan or empty it). You put files in folders by dragging them to the folder icon. You put folders in the file cabinet by dragging them to the cabinet icon. You print a file by dragging it to the printer icon. You open a folder, file, or any object by double-clicking on its icon.

In fact, New Wave 3.1 recognizes and supports OLE applications. Once you add interprocess communication to your program using OLE protocols, your application will act like a full-fledged New Wave application when it runs under New Wave.

The Oral Tradition Codified

A number of useful Windows coding techniques have been passed from programmer to programmer over the years, but not explained well on paper. In this section, we touch on the most important of these. If you find any of them difficult at first, feel free to skip them and perhaps tackle them later: some of the concepts can be slippery.

Subclassing

Windows is, as an architecture, highly object oriented. The system arranges windows in a hierarchy of parents, children, and siblings, starting with the desktop (background) window. Each window is an *instance* of a *window class*, and each window class has a *window procedure*. The address of the window procedure, and the style bits that control the appearance and some of the behavior of window, are kept in the window data structure. Each window instance *inherits* its properties from its window class.

If you have two windows that should have similar, but not identical, behavior, you can make one window a *subclass*. The first window would use the default properties of the window class (established when the class is registered); the second window would supply its own behavior for selected messages, and pass all other messages up to the class window procedure.

The subclassing methodology is obvious once you understand it; but it is not something most Windows programmers could invent without seeing it first. I learned the technique originally from the service that preceded Microsoft Online when I needed to handle the TAB character in multiline edit controls within dialog boxes. (Subclassing is no longer necessary—and no longer works—for this case since the behavior of TAB in dialog box edit controls changed in Windows 3.) Other Windows programmers seem to have learned about subclassing by word of mouth: it is a classic case of oral lore that now needs to be written down. There actually *is* one example of subclassing in the Windows 3 SDK, but it isnt really explained: in the example TTY, you'll find a subclassed window derived from the class "Stdio."

By the way, you may encounter a warning against subclassing controls elsewhere in the Windows SDK manual—in the introductory section that explains the term. The warning doesn't really apply to the techniques described in this section: it applies more to subclassing standard control *classes*—a dangerous technique that changes the behavior of all controls created from the master, not just the behavior of one window instance.

I used subclassing in a slightly different form when I designed the user interface for Symbolics' PC/Macsyma: half a dozen dialog boxes that are minor variations on a theme share a single dialog resource and a long common dialog procedure, but each have their own, very short special-case dialog procedure that calls the common dialog procedure for most messages. It isn't easy to create class hierarchies in ordinary C, but it is possible given enough motivation.

You can make windows that are subclassed from system window classes: this is a powerful way of producing variations on existing behavior without a lot of work. For instance, you might want to have a subclassed window based on an edit control, which looks up each word typed in a controlled vocabulary. Conceptually, you'd do this in three steps.

Step one is to create the window with the **edit** window class. Step two is to replace the windows procedure long word with the procedure instance of your own window procedure. Step three is to intercept key stroke messages within the new window procedure, checking the previous word against the vocabulary list whenever a space character is seen. If the word did not match, the window procedure would generate an error message and return; otherwise, the windows procedure would pass its arguments on to the original class window procedure:

```
case WM_INITDIALOG:
// subclass edit control: make subclass proc instance
lpfnNewEditProc=MakeProcInstance((FARPROC)NewEditProc,hInst);
// tell Windows to call our subclass proc first
// this call replaces the Window Procedure function pointer
lpfnOldEditProc = (FARPROC)SetWindowLong(
                            GetDlgItem(hDlg,TEST_IDD_TEXT2),
                            GWL_WNDPROC,
                            (LONG)lpfnNewEditProc);

<code intervenes here>
}
```

```
LONG FAR PASCAL NewEditProc (HWND hDlg, unsigned iMessage,
                                        WORD wParam, LONG lParam)
{
switch (iMessage) {
   case WM_CHAR:
      if(wParam==' ') {                //we are drawing diagrams here
            if(CheckPreviousWordTyped()) {
                  PutUpErrorMessage();
                  return FALSE;
                  }
            }
      else
            break;
   default:
      break;
   }
// CallWindowProc is specifically for the sort of daisy-chain that
// subclassing requires: let the old procedure handle all
// messages that fall through to here
return CallWindowProc(lpfnOldEditProc,hDlg,iMessage,wParam,lParam);
}
```

Superclassing

While subclassing is a good way to change the behavior of one window, it can become a bother if you have many windows that need to be subclassed. In this case, it is more convenient to create a *superclass* of the base class, and make each window an instance of the superclass.

You register a superclass like any other window class, only you copy most of the parameters from the base class. In the window procedure you pass any unchanged messages to the window procedure for the base class, in much the same way as our subclassing procedure. The example from which the routine below was extracted appears to have originated with Ed Mills of Microsoft.

```
BOOL InitSuperCls(HANDLE hInst)
{
  HWND hEditWnd;
  WNDCLASS Class;
  /* Now we start to do the superclassing. */
  /* We only create this window to be able to get information out
     of it. */
  hEditWnd = CreateWindow((LPSTR)"EDIT",
        (LPSTR)" ",
        WS_CHILD,
        0, 0, 0, 0,
        (HWND)hWndMain,          /* parent */
        0,                       /* use class menu */
        (HANDLE)hInst,           /* handle to window instance */
        (LPSTR)NULL       /* no params to pass on */
        );
```

```
    /* Get the stuff we need to save from the class, and make our new
class. */

    /* Save this for use later in our new window proc. */
    lpEditWndProc = (FARPROC)GetWindowLong(hEditWnd, GWL_WNDPROC);

    /* Register the new super class to the standard edit control.
    We make it the same as the original except for the new
function, hInst, and class name. */
    /* Note that we must be very careful about the window extra bytes.
       If our superclassing procedure doesn't need them, the code given
       here is correct. If we want to use them, we musttake note of how
       many bytes the standard control procedure uses, add ours to
       cbWndExtra, and access them after the standard control's bytes
       since it will access the bytes starting at zero. */
    Class.style        = GetClassWord(hEditWnd, GCW_STYLE);
    Class.lpfnWndProc  = SuperEditWndProc;
    Class.cbClsExtra   = GetClassWord(hEditWnd, GCW_CBCLSEXTRA);
    Class.cbWndExtra   = GetClassWord(hEditWnd, GCW_CBWNDEXTRA);
    /* We want to use our instance here so that our WndProc will run
on our DS, and so that the class will be destroyed when the        last
instance terminates. */
    /* Note: Classes are destroyed at app exit time by searching the
       list of classes looking for any classes with the current
       hModule. (Derived from hInst.) Hence, to get the class "SuperEdit"
       destroyed, we must set its hInst to our own. The internal class
       structure actually stores hModule rather than hInst. (This gets
       converted by RegisterClass().) */
    Class.hInst        = hInst;
    Class.hIcon        = GetClassWord(hEditWnd, GCW_HICON);
    Class.hCursor          = GetClassWord(hEditWnd, GCW_HCURSOR);
    Class.hbrBackground    = GetClassWord(hEditWnd, CW_HBRBACKGROUND);
    Class.lpszMenuName = NULL; /* It doesn't have one. */
    Class.lpszClassName    = (LPSTR)"SuperEdit";
    /* We don't need it any more. */
    DestroyWindow(hEditWnd);

    if (!RegisterClass( (LPWNDCLASS)&Class ) ) {
      /* Initialization failed. Windows will automatically deallocate
         all allocated memory. */
      return FALSE;
      }
    return TRUE;
}
```

Custom Controls

You might want to think of a control as just another window class—albeit one that may have rather elaborate behavior. The standard Windows text control does nothing but display text in its window, but the edit control knows how to respond to mouse clicks (by setting the I-beam cursor), mouse drags (by highlighting text), arrow keys (by moving the I-beam cursor), and keystrokes (in most cases, by entering the character as text).

There are a few special considerations for controls that may not apply to other windows. For one thing, you have to worry about the name space: that is, the control's class name can't conflict with the class name of any other control.[1] Another issue is that controls are generally DLLs, which can't use any standard C library functions that assume that SS==DS. Finally, controls work by responding to private messages—not by direct function calls. A control in Windows is very much an "object" in the sense that it has reusable code and private data.

To make a control known to the dialog editor you need to implement a few special functions: the **xxxInfo()** function, which tells the dialog editor about the controls in the library; the **xxxStyle()** function, which lets the user edit the control style; and the **xxxFlags()** function, which interprets the window class flag bits. You also need to install the custom control on the system, so that the dialog editor knows to load and use the custom control's DLL.

The following fragment of code, from the Windows 3 SDK example file rainbow.c, illustrates the three helper functions needed for a control DLL to work with the Windows dialog editor. The **rainbow** control seems to be derived from Kevin Welch's **spectrum** control, which was first written up in the July 1988 issue of *Microsoft Systems Journal*.

```
/* RainbowInfo() : HANDLE
 This function returns a handle to a global block of memory that
contains various information about the kinds of controls the library
is capable of supporting.  This data block can, for example, be used
by the dialog editor when determining the capabilities of a
particular control library.
 Note that this handle becomes the property of the caller once this
function returns.  This implies that the caller must call GlobalFree
once it is finished with the data.*/
HANDLE FAR PASCAL RainbowInfo()
{       HANDLE          hCtlInfo;
        LPCTLINFO       lpCtlInfo;

        /* allocate space for information structure */
        hCtlInfo = GlobalAlloc( GHND, (DWORD)sizeof(CTLINFO) );
        if ( hCtlInfo ) {
```

---

[1] In reality, all Window class names must be unique, not just control class names. Name space conflicts do seem to be more of a problem with controls, however, since there is an overwhelming temptation to name them something pithy and descriptive like **Gauge** rather than something more probably unique like **MEH_Gauge_147.**

```
                    /* attempt to lock it down */
                    lpCtlInfo = (LPCTLINFO)GlobalLock( hCtlInfo );
                    if ( lpCtlInfo ) {

                    /* define the fixed portion of the structure */
                            lpCtlInfo->wVersion = 100;
                            lpCtlInfo->wCtlTypes = 1;
                            lstrcpy( lpCtlInfo->szClass, RAINBOWCLASS );
                            lstrcpy( lpCtlInfo->szTitle,
                                    "Sample User Control" );

                    /* define the variable portion of the structure */
                            lpCtlInfo->Type[0].wWidth = 33;
                            lpCtlInfo->Type[0].wHeight = 20;
                            lpCtlInfo->Type[0].dwStyle = WS_CHILD;
                            lstrcpy( lpCtlInfo->Type[0].szDescr,
                                            "Rainbow" );

                    /* unlock it */
                            GlobalUnlock( hCtlInfo );

                    } else {
                            GlobalFree( hCtlInfo );
                            hCtlInfo = NULL;
                    }
            }
            /* return result */
            return( hCtlInfo );
}
/*
RainbowStyle(hWnd, CtlStyle,lpfnVeriyId,lpfnGetIdStr ): BOOL;
 hWnd          handle to parent window
 hCtlStyle     handle to control style
 lpfnVerifyId  pointer to the VerifyId function from Dialog
               editor
 lpfnGetIdStr  pointer to the GetIdStr function from Dialog
               editor
        This function enables the user to edit the style of a
particular control provided.  The current control style information
is passed in using a handle to a control style data structure.
        This function returns this same handle (referencing updated
information) if the dialog box is normally closed.  A value of NULL
is returned if the user cancelled the operation.
*/
BOOL FAR PASCAL RainbowStyle(
        HWND          hWnd,
        HANDLE        hCtlStyle,
        LPFNSTRTOID   pfnVerifyId,
        LPFNIDTOSTR   lpfnGetIdStr )
{
        FARPROC lpDlgFn;
        HANDLE hNewCtlStyle;
```

```
        /* initialization */
        hLibData = hCtlStyle;
        lpfnVerId = lpfnVerifyId;
        lpfnIdStr = lpfnGetIdStr;

        /* display dialog box */
        lpDlgFn = MakeProcInstance( (FARPROC)RainbowDlgFn,
                hLibInstance );
        hNewCtlStyle = ( DialogBox( hLibInstance, "RainbowStyle",
                hWnd,lpDlgFn) ) ? hLibData : NULL;
        FreeProcInstance( lpDlgFn );

        /* return updated data block */
        return( hNewCtlStyle );
}
/*
RainbowFlags( wFlags, lpszString, wMaxString ) : WORD;
    wFlags          class style flags
    lpszString      class style string
    wMaxString      maximum size of class style string

    This function translates the class style flags provided into
a corresponding text string for output to an RC file.  The general
windows flags (contained in the low byte) are not interpreted, only
those in the high byte.
    The value returned by this function is the library instance
handle when sucessful, and NULL otherwise.
    The Rainbow control doesn't support any class style flags, so
it always returns NULL. Other controls might need class style flags.
*/
WORD FAR PASCAL RainbowFlags(
        WORD        wFlags,
        LPSTR       lpszString,
        WORD        wMaxString )
{
        lpszString[0] = NULL;
        return( 0 );
}
```

Prior to Windows 3, it was not possible to make custom controls known to the dialog editor. What was normally done was to create a text block or rectangle for the control with the dialog editor, and then to change the dialog resource file with a text editor—for instance, you'd draw a text box in the dialog editor, and then change "text" to "mycontrol" in the .DLG file. You wouldn't normally bother making the control a DLL: you'd include the code in your own executable. It is still possible to put control code in your EXE under Windows 3: while you give up the flexibility of designing WYSISYG dialog boxes with the dialog editor if you do this, it ensures that your own version of the control—and not some other developer's control with the same name—is used by your code.

Multiple Local Heaps

New Windows developers usually have a lot of trouble understanding how to manage dynamic memory. The classic case is someone who needs to store strings for a text editor.

If you store each string with a **GlobalAlloc()**, you will eventually run out of global segment selectors; 8192 strings may not be enough! On the other hand, if you store each string with **LocalAlloc()**, you will quickly run out of space; 64KB is almost never enough RAM!

There are two "easy" solutions for in-RAM storage of strings: you can use the atom manager to store the strings globally, or you can suballocate global memory blocks in multiple local heaps. Using the atom manager is left as an exercise for the student, since it is only useful for strings, and can't be generalized to other kinds of data.

You know, of course, that you get one local heap for free when your application starts. In small and medium models, the default local heap shares your data segment with your stack and your static data. If you need a lot of stack space because your functions allocate big structures as automatic local variables, you won't have much room for a local heap. If you change those local variables to statics, you'll make things even worse, since your static and global variables use their space for the duration of your program.

We'll discuss later how to cut down on static variables by storing string constants as string resources, by using extra window bytes, and by allocating global structures for the duration of a dialog box. For now, let's look at how you'd implement suballocation. By the way, I originally learned this material from Mike Geary; it has since been published by Paul Yao in his book (see the reading list at the end of this chapter) and in an article in the January 1991 issue of *Microsoft Systems Journal* (*MSJ*). *MSJ* listings are available for downloading from many online services and bulletin boards.

The basic scheme for suballocation is this: start by initializing the suballocation package. This means globally allocating one segment (with **Global-Alloc**) and saving its handle. Lock the global block down (with **GlobalLock**), and initialize the local heap in the block (with **LocalInit**). The size you'll use for the local heap is the size of the global block (which you get with **Global-Size**) less the size of the local heap header (16). Release the global block twice: once for **GlobalLock**, and once for **LocalInit**. Of course you'll clean up and return false if anything fails.

For the rest of the functions to deal with multiple local heaps, you'll basically put a wrapper around the ordinary local memory functions that locks and unlocks the global block, and pushes, sets, and pops DS. This last is done most cleanly with some embedded assembly language. Each local block can then be identified with two handles: the handle of its local block, and the handle of its global block.

Essentially, we have:

```
LONG SubXXX( <argument list> ) {
     <automatic variables for pointers and so on>
     PointerToGlobalBlock=GlobalLock(HandleOfGlobalBlock)
     if(PointerToGlobalBlock==NULL)
          return LONG_FALSE;
     Selector=HIWORD(PointerToGlobalBlock);
     _asm {
          push ds
          mov ax, Selector
          mov ds, ax
          }

     <call the Local memory function here>

     _asm  pop ds
     GlobalUnlock(HandleOfGlobalBlock);
     if(ReturnFromLocalFunction==NULL)
          return LONG_FALSE
     else
          return MAKELONG(HandleOfLocalBlock,
                          HandleOfGlobalBlock);
     }
```

The code given above is quite general. When implementing all of these functions, some interesting issues arise—for instance, when it is necessary to create many local heaps (not just two). Yao's implementation (as given in the *MSJ* article) is set up for a single secondary local heap of size=(4096-16),[2] which isn't all that useful—although the choice of 4K heaps will make for efficient paging in enhanced mode. In a real program you'd have multiple secondary local heaps, perhaps of size=(64K-16), and you'd create and destroy heaps as necessary. Managing the heaps efficiently would require some control structures to track the memory usage by heap. When you have to make room for a really big local allocation you *might* want to move blocks from heap to heap— but then you'd have to update all the stored handles that reference the moved blocks, which would be difficult. In most cases, a simple array of handles plus an array of free memory sizes will suffice to control multiple heaps. You could get fancy and use a linked list of control structures, but that hardly seems necessary—memory available is more likely to be a limit than the number of 64K blocks you can track with an array of dimension 20.

If you have a C compiler that doesn't support in-line assembly statements, the code as given above won't work. As an alternative, you can write short C-

---

[2] The choice of 4096 for the global block size is less important than one might think, since Windows will automatically try a `GlobalRealloc` on the global block if a `LocalAlloc` with the block fails. Still, if you know you're going to need the space, there is no need to incur a lot of overhead with constant `GlobalRealloc` calls.

callable **PUSHDS** and **POPDS** functions in assembly language that will do the same thing.

For your convenience, I've included a suballocation library—one that's even more sophisticated than what I've described above—on the companion disks. The **smalloc** library was written by Howie Long; if you use it, let Howie know.

Exports and MakeProcInstance

Two of the most troublesome items in Windows programs are the need to **EXPORT** all callback functions, and the need to **MakeProcInstance** dialog procedures and other dynamic callback functions.

If you don't already know what I'm talking about, now is the time to reread Petzold on "thunks." But the good news is that you don't really have to worry about this stuff anymore if you restrict your program to protected mode and/or use Michael Geary's FIXDS program. Borland's "Smart Callback" linking option in TLINK and SLR's OPTLINK both implement Michael's FIXDS algorithm.

I'm a belt-and-suspenders kind of programmer: you'll find **MakeProc-Instance** calls in my programs even when I know I'll be using FIXDS on the final EXE file. You'll also find my callback functions prototyped with the **_export** keyword. But you don't have to do this yourself.

FIXDS basically changes the prologue of all FAR functions to copy **SS** into **DS**. For this reason FIXDS works only on EXE files; most DLLs use different **SS** and **DS** values—the caller's **SS** and their own **DS**. Some DLLs don't have their own data segment, and keep the caller's **DS**—this is flagged with a **DATA NONE** module definition.

If you want, you can have your any callback functions in an EXE file explicitly start by calling a function that copies **SS** into **DS** and returns the previous **DS**; they should end with a function that restores the previous **DS** value. If you do this, you won't have to worry about **MakeProcInstance** or **EXPORT**s. This trick (suggested by Lee Hasiuk of Lotus) is the equivalent of using FIXDS or Borland's "Smart Callbacks"; it's advantages are that you don't have to modify OBJ or EXE files, and that it is portable across compilers.

In DLLs, you can avoid the long prologue generated by **/Gw** by instead using the **/Au** compiler flag and/or the **_loadds** keyword in exported functions. David Weise of Microsoft has blessed this as a supported technique for protected mode, and it is used by Lotus in shipping Windows applications.

If this section confused you, don't worry too much about it. But if you run into a situation where strange things happen as soon as a dialog procedure is called, consider the possibility that you forgot an **EXPORT** or a **MakeProcInstance**; consider also that it may be time to start using one of the alternatives discussed above.

Efficient Structuring of Windows Programs

If you want your medium memory model Windows program to run well in all modes, you need to have good modularity and segmentation. There are some tradeoffs to be made, but my general rule of thumb is to make three classes of modules: "small" object modules about 4KB, "medium" object modules about 8KB, and (if necessary) "large" object modules about 16KB. Why should one module be "small" and another "large"? "Small" modules tend to have little utility functions in them; "medium" modules have a number of related functions, often including a dialog box function and a number of helper functions; "large" modules have truly complicated functions that can't easily be broken up without a significant loss of execution speed.

In real mode it helps if all your segments are small. For practical reasons, it is convenient to make segments and modules the same in most cases. Every once in a while (perhaps once a week during active development), make a directory sorted by size of all the .OBJ files in your project. If your program will be used primarily in real mode, flag all the files that are bigger than 8KB (measured *without* CodeView information). Edit the C files for all the flagged object modules, and try to split each in half logically. If there are multiple functions in the file, this is pretty easy: clone the **#include** lines to a new file, and move roughly half the functions to the new file. You'll have to update your **make** and **def** files to correspond to the new source code organization, but you'll quickly get the hang of making such changes efficiently.

If your program will run primarily in standard or enhanced mode, you can gain some runtime efficiency by allowing your object files to be bigger: about 16KB would be quite reasonable. One advantage of larger segments is that you can group like functions together, and make any functions called only from within the module **NEAR**, which simplifies the function call prologue and epilogue and makes the code run a tad faster.

By the way, you should make all code segments moveable and discardable unless it is absolutely, positively necessary to do otherwise. If you have a lot of nondiscardable code, your program won't run in low memory situations. If you have large fixed segments, they will cause fragmentation of memory in real mode, which will interfere with Windows's ability to manage the global heap efficiently.

Manually segmenting your Windows code can be tedious, but the gains in runtime performance can be more than noticeable. If you have more money than time, you can buy a software tool—The Segmentor, from MicroQuill—to automate the process of determining optimum segment layouts. The Segmentor relies heavily on MSC's **alloc_text** pragma.

DPMI, 32-Bit Memory, and All That

Programmers who port from DOS to Windows often have DOS device drivers and TSRs to deal with. While just about everything that can be done by DOS device drivers and TSRs can be done equally well (and sometimes better) by Windows device drivers and DLLs, it takes time to rewrite the code—and even more time to learn the intricacies of Windows device drivers.

If you're writing for Windows from scratch, you don't have to worry about any of this—unless you need to support some special hardware. If neither applies, you can safely skip over this rather technical stuff and pick up with the next section.

One way to deal with the transition from DOS to Windows is in stages. For instance, you can keep the DOS device driver or TSR, port the application to Windows, and communicate with the DOS portion via the DOS Protected Mode Interface (*DPMI*). Alternatively, you can write a virtual device driver to translate selectors to and from segments and reflect interrupts down to real mode.

The DPMI specification includes services for managing the *LDT* (Local Descriptor Table), DOS memory, extended memory, pages, interrupts, and real-to-protected mode translation. For the purposes of Windows programs, there are just a few major services that are needed to communicate with DOS. For DOS programs running in a Windows DOS session, the DPMI services are rather more interesting.

To begin with, you can get the real-to-protected mode switch address from a DOS box under Windows (or under OS/2 2.0) using **Int 2FH** service **1687H**. You can call the address returned to switch into protected mode if the call was successful. The address returned should point to an **ARPL** instruction, which will fault in V86 mode and cause a switch to protected mode.

Once you know that a DPMI host is available and have switched to protected mode, you can detect your current CPU mode using **Int 2FH** service **1686H**. If the interrupt returns with AX=0, you are in protected mode. If AX is left nonzero, you are in real or V86 mode. If your program runs only in protected mode, you dont need to bother with this.

The key DPMI services are listed in the table below. Starred services may be called by Windows DLLs; unstarred services should be called only by DOS programs that have used DPMI to switch to protected mode. According to Microsoft, Windows EXEs should not call DPMI at all.

Because the DPMI specification is still changing as I write, you should request the current specification from Intel if you want to do serious development using DPMI.

DPMI services are called through **Int 31H**, with the service number in AX.

Service	Description
0002H	Map Real-Mode Segment to Descriptor
000AH	Create Code Segment Alias Descriptor
0100H	Allocate DOS Memory Block
0101H	Free DOS Memory Block
0102H	Resize DOS Memory Block
0200H	Get Real-Mode Interrupt Vector[*]
0201H	Set Real-Mode Interrupt Vector[*]
0202H	Get Processor Exception Handler Vector
0203H	Set Processor Exception Handler Vector
0204H	Get Protected-Mode Interrupt Vector
0205H	Set Protected-Mode Interrupt Vector
0300H	Simulate Real-Mode Interrupt[*]
0301H	Call Real-Mode Procedure with Far Return Frame[*]
0302H	Call Real-Mode Procedure with Interrupt Return Frame[*]
0303H	Allocate Real-Mode Callback Address[*]
0304H	Free Real-Mode Callback Address[*]
0800H	Physical Address Mapping

[*]Service may be called by Windows programs, as long as the call resides in a DLL.

The following example of switching to and from protected mode using DPMI was kindly provided by Microsoft; I have added additional comments here for clarity. The original appears on the companion disks as **pmode.c**; similar code can be found in the DPMI 1.0 specification.

```
void main()
{
        unsigned long PMode_Entry_Addr = 0;
        _asm {
Get_Entry_Point:
        mov ax, 1687h  ;Get PMode Entry Point
        int 2Fh
        test ax, ax           ;AX != 0 is failure
        jnz Cant_Enter_PMode
;Note: at this point a number of flags are set in the registers:
; AX=0 means DPMI is present; if that is true, then also:
; BX holds Flags, with bit 0=1 if 32-bit programs are supported
```

```
; CL holds the processor type (2=80286, 3=80386, 4=80486)
; DH holds the DPMI major version number
; DL holds the DPMI minor version number
; SI holds the number of paragraphs required for DPMI private data
; ES:DI hold the DPMI mode switch entry point
        mov WORD PTR [PMode_Entry_Addr]+2, es          ;PMode Entry
        mov WORD PTR [PMode_Entry_Addr], di     ;Seg & Off
; Allocate memory for use by DOS extender if necessary
; NOTE: This code assumes that the program has already
; shrunk its memory block so that the DOS
; memory allocation call will work
        test si, si     ;SI == 0 is no memory needed
        jz Enter_PMode_Now
        mov bx, si      ;Allocate SI paragraphs of mem
        mov ah, 48h     ;DOS Allocate Memory
        int 21h
        jc Cant_Enter_PMode
        mov es, ax      ;segment of first paragraph
; Enter protected mode as a 16-bit program
 Enter_PMode_Now:
        xor ax, ax
        call DWORD PTR [PMode_Entry_Addr] ;PMode entry point
        jc Cant_Enter_PMode
; The program is running in protected mode now!
; Protected mode initialization code would go here.
; Mark program's real mode memory as pageable, etc.
        }
        printf( "\n\tNow in 16-bit Protected Mode.\n" );
 _asm {
        mov ax, 1686h
        int 2Fh
        test ax, ax
        jz Exit_Prog
        }
        printf( "*Not* in protected mode according to DPMI!\n" );
 _asm {
        jmp Exit_Prog
 Cant_Enter_PMode:
        }
        printf( "Couldn't enter Protect Mode." );
 Exit_Prog:
        printf( "Terminating. Now in REAL (or V86) mode." );
 _asm {
; Quit the program and return to real mode DOS
        mov ax, 4C00h
        int 21h
        }
 }
```

Windows has its own services for real-memory and segment management. For instance, **GlobalDosAlloc** and **GlobalDosFree** correspond to DPMI services 0100H and 0101H. **AllocDStoCSAlias** corresponds to DPMI service 000AH. **ChangeSelector** offers an alternative to **AllocDStoCSAlias**: it generates a temporary code selector from a data selector, or a temporary data selector from a code selector. You can lock down blocks with **GlobalFix** and lock down pages with **GlobalPageLock**; **GlobalUnfix** and **GlobalPageUnlock** unlock blocks and pages. Understand that applications *don't* normally need any of these functions, and *shouldn't* use them; device drivers and other programs dealing with hardware *do* need these functions, and *should* use them.

Another Windows component, WINMEM32.DLL, supplies a standard method for implementing a 32-bit flat memory model. It gives your application access to services for allocating, reallocating, and freeing 32-bit memory objects; for translating 32-bit pointers to 16-bit pointers that can be used by Windows and DOS functions; and for aliasing a data segment to a code segment so you can execute code loaded into a 32-bit segment.

Your application should load WINMEM32.DLL only when Windows is in 386 enhanced mode, since that is the only mode in which the 32-bit registers of the 80386/80486 processor are available. You can find out the current Windows mode with the **GetWinFlags** function.

Note that an application using 32-bit registers can't call Windows functions directly because its far pointers are in 16:32 segment:offset form rather than the 16:16 form that Windows expects. All calls to Windows functions must be made in a nondiscardable 16-bit helper segment, which contains code to convert the 16:32 pointers to 16:16 pointers, takes care of preserving 32-bit registers around 16-bit API calls, and sign-extends 16-bit return values to 32-bit return values.

WINMEM32.DLL contains eight functions that enable your application to access 32-bit memory:

Function	Description
Global32Alloc	Allocates a block of 32-bit memory.
Global32Realloc	Changes the size of a 32-bit memory object.
Global32Free	Frees a 32-bit memory object.
Global16PointerAlloc	Converts a 32-bit pointer to 16-bit pointer.
Global16PointerFree	Frees a pointer alias created by Global16PointerAlloc.
Global32CodeAlias	Creates a code alias for a 32-bit memory object, allowing code in the the object to be executed.
Global32CodeAliasFree	Frees a code alias created by Global32CodeAlias.
GetWinMem32Version	Returns the version number of the WINMEM32.DLL API.

Windows has another API for the use of DOS programs that need to be aware of multitasking, which operates through **Int 2FH**. There are **Int 2FH** call-in interfaces so that the application can influence multitasking, and **Int 2FH** call-out interfaces so that Enhanced Windows can notify TSRs and device drivers of various activities.

DOS programs that poll the keyboard should add a call to **Int 2FH** service **1680H**, Release Time Slice, to their keyboard loop. Ideally the program would call the Release Time Slice service any time the keyboard buffer was found to be empty and no other actions were pending.

The **Int 2FH** call-in services are:

Service	Description
1600H	Enhanced Windows Installation Check
1680H	Release Time Slice
1681H	Begin Critical Section
1682H	End Critical Section
1683H	Get Current Virtual Machine ID
1684H	Get Device API Entry Point
1685H	Switch VMs and Call Back
1686H	Get CPU Mode
1687H	Get Real-to-Protected Mode Switch Entry Point
168AH	Get Vendor-Specific API Entry Point

The **Int 2FH** call-outs are:

AX	Notification
1605H	Extender Initialization
1606H	Extender Exit
1607H	Device Call-out
1608H	Enhanced Windows Initialization Complete
1609H	Enhanced Windows Begin Exit

The Windows Virtual Device Services (VDS) supply even more control to device drivers running in Enhanced mode. Virtual device drivers (VxDs) all run in a single, protection ring 0, 32-bit segment with the Windows Virtual Machine Manager (VMM).

Windows applications can't use VDS directly; however, it is useful to know what can be accomplished by a VxD. By and large, VxDs take care of handling hardware correctly in a multitasking environment—things that in ordinary DOS would be done by device drivers, and gut-level programs that assume they are the only process running on the machine. Examples include virtualizing DMA channels, translating APIs, changing the timer tick interval, hooking and masking IRQs, sending keys to a windowed DOS virtual machine, hooking device services, and placing a specific virtual machine in the foreground.

Common Dialogs

One new feature of Windows 3.1 is *common dialog windows*; these are dialog windows that applications display by calling a single function rather than by creating a dialog template resource and a corresponding dialog procedure. Both the resource and procedure reside in COMMDLG.DLL.

There are three major advantages to common dialog windows. First, it's a lot less work for the programmer. Second, the common dialogs save RAM and disk space. Last, but not least, common dialogs give the user a standard, consistent set of controls used by many applications.

Currently, the common dialogs are:

- Color selection (RGB and HLS models)
- Font selection
- Filename selection (open and save file dialogs)
- Find and replace strings of text
- Print (configure printer and start print job)

Learning by Example

Anna Karenina starts, in one translation: *All happy families are alike, but each unhappy family is unhappy in its own way.* We could apply this sobering maxim (the novel ends with Anna throwing herself under a train) to Windows programs: *All working Windows programs are alike, but each broken Windows program fails in its own way.*

Windows code isn't simple. When you have to deal with hundreds of functions and hundreds of messages, things can get just a little confusing. The important thing for a blossoming Windows programmer is to get a feel for what services are provided by the system. Once you know what's out there, you can avoid reinventing basic services. You don't need to memorize all the Windows function calls and messages with their parameter lists, but you do need to know that list-box messages start with LB_, that various resources are accessed with Loadxxx functions, that GDI functions need a device context, and that only one window can have the input focus at a time.

The best Windows programming is done by copying and modifying working code. So: Steal this code. If there are fragments in this book that do what you want, use them freely in your own programs. If you can't find an example that does exactly what you want to do, start with something that works but does the wrong thing; by successive modification and testing you should end up with something that works and does the right thing.

Don't try to create Windows programs *ab initio*—there are just too many ways to go wrong. And don't try to learn Windows as you build a major, time-constrained project—learn the system first on little projects that won't bankrupt your company if they don't work out.

Play with Windows. Try things out. Do little experiments. Write a hundred variations on examples you find in the SDK and in books. Figure out how programs you like work and try the same techniques yourself. And most of all, have fun.

Recommended Reading

Microsoft Windows Software Development Kit *Guide to Programming*, Redmond, WA, Microsoft Corporation, 1990.

Microsoft Windows Software Development Kit *Reference—Volume 1*, Redmond, WA, Microsoft Corporation, 1990.

Microsoft Windows Software Development Kit *Reference—Volume 2*, Redmond, WA, Microsoft Corporation, 1990.

Microsoft Windows Software Development Kit *Tools*, Redmond, WA, Microsoft Corporation, 1990.

Charles Petzold, *Programming Windows, Second Edition*, Redmond, WA, Microsoft Press, 1990. *The best introduction available to Windows programming, with many small, clear, well-written examples. Covers about 90 percent of the basic material you need to write small Windows programs.*

Peter Norton and Paul Yao, *Peter Norton's Windows 3.0 Power Programming Techniques*, New York, NY, Bantam Computer Books, 1990. *Despite the title, this is even more of an elementary book than Petzold. Useful for the detailed explanations of how things work in the Windows system. Has examples of multiple local heaps.*

Alan Southerton, *Windows 3.0 Programming Primer*, Reading, MA, Addison-Wesley, 1990. *Short on explanation, but long on example code. Includes a toolkit disk with a number of short, useful functions for manipulating windows. Has examples of subclassing.*

Jeffrey M. Richter, *Windows 3: A Developer's Guide*, Redwood City, CA, M & T Books, 1991. *Includes chapters on subclassing and superclassing, dialog boxes, custom controls, printer setup, tasks, queues and hooks, MDI, and program installation. Somewhat uneven but still useful as a supplement to Petzold.*

Magazines and Journals: The *Microsoft Systems Journal* publishes Windows programming articles with source code in almost every issue. *Byte Magazine* publishes my column on Windows and OS/2 and stays on top of the technology, but rarely publishes listings. *Dr. Dobb's Journal* sometimes publishes Windows programming articles; when they're good, they're very, very good. And *Programmer's Journal* occasionally publishes Windows programming articles. Any of these periodicals can pay back a year's subscription with a single good idea, tip, or technique—but only if you take the time to look for and read interesting articles.

2

In which we deal with the basic stuff: setting up your development machine, building your program, and doing the simplest sorts of testing and debugging.

Some Fundamentals

· ·

If you're already developing Windows programs, you can safely skip this chapter. But if you haven't started, read on: everything you need to know to get started should be right here.

Setting up a Windows Development Machine

An ideal machine for developing Windows programs is as fast as possible—a fast (33Mhz) 80386 or 80486-based computer with lots of memory (8 MB is nice), a mouse, two monitors (either one VGA and one monochrome, or one 8514 and one VGA), and a terminal (connected to a serial port). You'll want at least 100MB of hard disk space, and the faster the hard disk, the better: a 14ms access-time ESDI disk with a smart caching controller would be great.

On the other hand, a "good enough" machine might have a 16 Mhz 386SX, 2 MB of memory, a mouse, one monitor (EGA or better), and a 40 MB hard disk. Considering that an ideal setup would cost at least $5,000,[1] it is of some interest

---

[1] The price of computers being volatile, you may need to reassess the market when costing out machines. In 1990 an "ideal" Windows development machine was $10,000+, since the 486 chip was relatively new and commanded a premium price. In late 1991, 486 machines had already become commodities.

that a "good enough" setup can be had for $2,000. But you'll pay for the slower machine eventually, in lost productivity.

If you want to use one of Microsoft's debuggers, you'll want to have one of three things: a second monitor for CodeView (CVW), a terminal for WDEB386 or SYMDEB, or software (for instance CV/1, from Nu-Mega Technologies) to make CodeView run on the Windows desktop. The requirement for a second monitor is specific to the version of CodeView for Windows that shipped with the Windows 3.0 SDK. An update to MSC 6.0a, shipped in March of 1991, contains a version of CVW that will flip screens on a single monitor—but screen flipping can be very annoying. Later CVW versions, for instance the version that shipped with the Windows 3.1 SDK, can also flip screens.

An alternative to debuggers is to track down bugs by adding code; this is workable, and we'll discuss how to do it, but you still might prefer to have debugging available to you: there's nothing more frustrating than having a bug without knowing where to look for the bug or having a way to isolate it.

If you choose to have a second monitor there will still be times you'll want a terminal (for instance, to run the debugging kernels); if you choose to have a terminal there may be times you'll want a second monitor (for instance, to run CodeView on two screens). Mike Geary's DOS device driver OX.SYS (available on BIX, CompuServe, and most Windows-oriented BBSs) can help you redirect things from the serial port to the second monitor; Anders Thun's WINRIP (included on the companion disks) can help you redirect RIPs and UAEs to your primary or secondary monitor. We'll explain RIPs and UAEs shortly: don't panic if the terminology is unfamiliar.

Using the Windows SDK Effectively

Before you start to work with the SDK you should understand the purpose of each of the SDK tools. As we just mentioned, there are three debuggers: CVW, SYMDEB, and WDEB386.

CVW is a protected-mode source-level debugger that runs as an application from the Windows desktop; the Windows 3.0 version of CVW requires you to have two monitors. CVW is by far the easiest of the three debuggers to use, and the tool of choice for identifying obscure errors in C source code. If you want to use CVW at the source level, you need to compile with full symbolic information (/**zi**) and link with CodeView information (/**co**).

SYMDEB is a real-mode symbolic debugger—not a source-level debugger. You'd only use it to debug in real mode; avoid doing so if you can. You run SYMDEB from the DOS command line, and load both Windows and your program under SYMDEB. You need a serial port and attached terminal (or terminal emulator) to run SYMDEB. To give SYMDEB symbolic information, you need to compile with symbolic information (/**zd**) and link with line numbers in the map (/**LI**). After linking you must run MAPSYM to generate a symbol table from your map file. You can prepare for SYMDEB and CVW at the same time if you wish by compiling with /**Zi**, linking with /**LI/CO**, and running MAPSYM.

WDEB386 is an advanced protected-mode symbolic debugger. If you think of it as SYMDEB for protected mode with a few extra commands (for examining descriptor tables and such), you won't be far wrong. You prepare files for WDEB386, run it from the DOS command line, and control it with a terminal in much the same way as you work with SYMDEB.

The SDK comes with a set of debugging kernels. You can swap these for the retail versions of KERNEL, USER, and GDI to detect runtime call errors, such as invalid handles. The debugging kernels will also give you a stack trace on the terminal (or to the debugger) when there is a fatal system error (RIP) or unrecoverable application error (UAE). The term RIP is Windows slang: it stands for Rest in Peace, and refers to the words "said" when Windows "dies."

By the way, the most advanced features of WDEB386—the dot commands for enhanced mode—are not supported unless you have the Windows Device Driver Kit (DDK). To activate these commands, save your retail WIN386.EXE and copy the big (900KB) debugging version of WIN386.EXE into your windows system directory.

HeapWalk (or, sometimes, Luke HeapWalker, after the "Star Wars" character Luke Skywalker) is a fairly versatile utility for examining Windows memory. HeapWalk shows you a snapshot of the global heap, and on demand can generate another snapshot, show you a selected memory object, allocate memory, or display a selected local heap. HeapWalk is useful for tracking down memory leakage problems and finding unreleased resources.

Spy (which has an icon reminiscent of *Mad Magazine*'s "Spy vs. Spy©" cartoon) is an easy way to peek at the Windows message stream. Remember, Windows is a message-passing system; pieces of code run in response to a particular message.

Many times, bugs in Windows programs turn out to stem from a misunderstanding of the message stream: you may, for instance, write code to unconditionally respond to a message not realizing that the message may occur in a context you can't handle. For instance, you may want to move a child window any time your main window is resized; however, your main window might get a WM_SIZE message before the child window has been created. The debugging kernels will complain of an invalid window handle in this case; Spy will show you the WM_SIZE message in the stream before the child Window's creation messages. You can also monitor the message stream from CVW using its **wwm** (Watch Windows Messages) command; in many cases Spy is more convenient.

Shaker is most useful in real mode: it moves memory around to help you find handles that haven't been properly locked and similar errors. If you test your program all by itself without anything else happening on the Windows desktop, you can easily miss errors that occur only when segment motion happens at a critical time. Shaker gives you a controlled amount of background segment motion so you can flush these critters out into the open.

Profiler is a set of utilities for analyzing your application's CPU usage. You can use it in real mode or enhanced mode (but not in standard mode) to identify the "hot spots" that need attention in your code.

Swap is another set of utilities to let you analyze far function calls through a code "thunk," far calls that cause swapping, and segments discarded. Swap complements Profiler: by minimizing the amount of swapping and the number of far calls you can make a big difference in the performance of your program, especially in low memory situations. These improvements are largely separate from improvements you can make in your CPU usage, although there are times when you will have to trade code size off against code speed to optimize your program for its target environment.

CL, LINK, RC, and NMAKE are the tools you use to build your program. CL is the C compiler, LINK the linker, RC the resource compiler, and NMAKE an automation utility.

SDKPaint can be used for designing bitmaps, cursors, and icons. Dialog Editor is a visual tool for layout of dialog boxes; it can also be used to manage the symbolic names of dialog controls. Note that you need to keep the symbols for each dialog box in a separate file; otherwise, the Dialog Editor will mash them together and possibly lose some of your definitions. It is good practice to back up all your .H and .DLG files before running the Dialog Editor.

The Windows Font Editor is a design tool for bitmapped fonts. After you build a set of fonts (.FNT files), you need to link them into a DLL (.FON file). If you want to build vector fonts, you'll have to write a program. An example of how to do this, VECTFONT.ARC, is available in the microsoft/listings area of BIX.

The Help compiler, HC, can turn marked-up RTF files (produced, for instance, using Word for Windows) into hypertext acceptable to the Windows Help engine. Developing good hypertext files is quite an art in itself, but you shouldn't neglect to write clear and comprehensive help files for your program: the savings in support time will more than repay your efforts.

There are a couple of new tools for preparing help files in Windows 3.1: MRBC and SHED. SHED is used to edit hyperlinks or "hot spots" in bitmaps for help files. MRBC is used to combine multiple resolutions of bitmap into a single resource so that the Windows 3.1 help engine can display a bitmap that looks correct for the current screen.

Windows development entails dealing with a lot of separate pieces. Automating your procedures is about the only way of maintaining your sanity. Use "make" files to put the pieces together; learn to use "grep" utilities to find variables and pieces of code; use "c-tags" or any other code browser you can make work for you to find function definitions; use QuickHelp and Windows HELP files; and, in general, make the computer do as much of the grunt work as possible. Don't try to keep everything in your head—keep it at your fingertips, instead.

If you are not familiar with the names, **make**, **grep**, and **ctags** are commonly available software tools that originated on Unix systems. **make** uses a script and production rules to rebuild any executables whose dependent files have changed. **grep** uses regular expressions to find text patterns in multiple files. **ctags** generates a cross-reference that helps a programmer's editor find function and variable definitions in multiple files.

If you want, you can use the Windows SDK as a fairly good prototyping tool. Start with GENERIC or one of the other examples; then edit the menu structure and definition file to list all the items you want in your application. Build the program and play with it: see if the menu structure makes sense. Show it to people and see what they think. Add accelerator key assignments. In a few hours, or at most a few days, you'll have the shell of an application running. Then all you'll have to do is fill in the guts. As you go you'll almost always have a working prototype to show people; one by one, you'll get the menu picks doing what they're supposed to do. It's a lot nicer working this way than putting together a bunch of pieces at the end of a long development effort, only to find that they don't fit.

Building Windows Programs with MSC and the SDK

If you installed Microsoft C, Windows, and the Windows SDK correctly, you'll have Windows, all your compilation tools, and all the Windows development tools on your path. You'll also have environment variables for **LIB**, **INCLUDE**, **TEMP**, and **TMP**.

To verify that you've done it all correctly, rebuild the Generic example. Go to your **WINDEV/SAMPLES/GENERIC** directory, delete any **.OBJ**, **.EXE**, and **.RES** files you find there, and run **NMAKE**. You should wind up with a **GENERIC.EXE** file you can run under Windows.

Note that **NMAKE** assumes that it is looking for a file named **makefile**. The Windows 3 SDK examples use the older **MAKE** convention for file naming: the make file for the Generic example is just plain **generic**. To make **NMAKE** work, invoke it with **NMAKE GENERIC**. Under DOS, you can save some memory by instead using **NMK**, that is, **NMK GENERIC**.

If you are using a compiler other than Microsoft C, see the Appendices of this book for some hints about setting up and testing your development environment.

Testing Windows Programs

First try running the Generic example in your default configuration: from the DOS command line (*not* a virtual machine under Windows) type **WIN GENERIC**. Pull down all the menu items and test each in turn. Save **Exit** from the system menu for last. You should be able to bring up the **About** box, minimize and maximize the window, move, and resize the window. The Generic example can't do much more.

Now exit Windows and hook up your debugging terminal. Type **N2D** to install the Windows debugging kernels.

Rerun the tests you did with the retail kernels. You should see all of the same things, except that everything will run a little slower because of the checking in the debugging kernels. You probably won't see any activity on your terminal at this point.

Check the Program Manager **About** box to see what memory mode you're running in. If it's Enhanced mode, exit Windows and restart with **WIN /2 GENERIC**; this will get you into standard mode. If you had a large swap file in enhanced mode, you'll have less memory available in standard mode. Testing in standard mode might, for instance, tell you if you need to implement your own virtual memory management scheme.

After you've tried standard mode, restart with **WIN /R GENERIC**. This will get you into real mode. If you have EMS, your default real mode will use large frame EMS memory, so also try **WIN /R /E:999 GENERIC**—which will force small frame EMS memory—and **WIN /R /N GENERIC**, which will disable all use of EMS memory. In each mode, make sure the whole program behaves as you expect. On a larger program than **GENERIC**, you might find that the program simply won't load in some modes; or you might get weird error messages that indirectly point to a lack of memory.

Introduction to Debugging Windows Programs

The Generic example doesn't have any bugs, does it? Lets see what happens when we do have a bug. Try *bebugging* (that's right: bebugging, not debugging) the Generic example : for starters, edit the file **GENERIC.C.** Copy the whole Generic example to a new directory for this exercise. Find the **WM_COMMAND** message case and add the **FatalExit()** call as shown below.

```
       case WM_COMMAND:/* message: command from application menu */
           if (wParam == IDM_ABOUT) {
               lpProcAbout = MakeProcInstance(About, hInst);


               DialogBox(hInst,      /* current instance            */
                   "AboutBox",       /* resource to use             */
```

```
        hWnd,                    /* parent handle          */
        lpProcAbout); /* About() instance address */

    FreeProcInstance(lpProcAbout);
    FatalExit(999); //TEST! Add this line to the example!
    break;
```

Now retest the "buggy" program. (It's not really buggy: you've just added a FatalExit.) After the **About** box is dismissed you should see some action on your debugging terminal: this is an RIP. The traceback and call stack aren't too meaningful; we'll fix this in a moment.

Understanding Unrecoverable Application Errors

This RIP was from our program, but it just as easily could have been a fatal exit from Windows or an unrecoverable application error. To see one of these, replace the **FatalExit()** call with an invalid call to a Windows routine. For example, let's clone the **DialogBox** call, but pass **NULL** for some of the parameters:

```
    DialogBox(NULL,          /* NULL current instance   */
        "AboutBox",          /* resource to use         */
        NULL,                /* NULL parent handle      */
        lpProcAbout);        /* invalid About() instance */
    //BUG— should generate UAE
```

Rebuild your copy of **Generic** and run it again. You should see a message that you've got an Unrecoverable Application Error, and you should see a traceback on your terminal. The last routine identified by name in the call stack will be **DialogBox**; the routines above **DialogBox** were called internal to Windows. If we didn't know where and what our bug actually was, the call stack would tell us only to look for a **DialogBox** call; our testing history would tell us to look for the second **DialogBox** call in the code, which handles **WM_COMMAND IDM_ABOUT**. That might well be enough information to find the bug; but, then again, it might not.

Adding Symbolic Information

We can improve the readability of the call stack by adding line numbers to the map. To do this we'll make a couple of small changes to the Generic make file.

Edit the file **GENERIC**. Find the line that starts with **cl** and then find the switch **Zpe**. Add an **i** so that the switch now reads **Zpei**. This tells the compiler to generate full debug information. Then find the line the starts with **link** and add **/MA/LI/CO** to the end of the line, which will tell the linker to generate a full map, include line number information in the map, and include CodeView information in the executable. Finally, add the line **mapsym generic** after the

link line; **mapsym** will generate a symbol file from the map. Delete the **generic.obj** file and rebuild the program; when you run generic again you should see a more readable call stack.

Localizing Errors

On my machine, running the bebugged Generic application rebuilt for debugging, as described in the previous paragraph, gives a symbolic call stack dump as follows:

```
KERNEL!_MISCTEXT:12E1
USER!_DLGBEGIN:CREATEDIALOGPARAM+0014
USER!_DLGCORE:DIALOGBOXPARAM+0093
USER!_DLGCORE:DIALOGBOX+001B
GENERIC!_TEXT:MainWndProc+007B
USER_FFFE:DISPATCHMESSAGE+004A
GENERIC!_TEXT:WINMAIN+003B
GENERIC!_TEXT:__astart+0060
```

Let's have a good look at this backtrace. On the top line, the **_MISCTEXT** segment in Windows' KERNEL.DLL is what is generating the messages. The **CreateDialogParam** function in segment **_DLGBEGIN** of Windows' USER.DLL detected the **NULL** parameter and called **MISCTEXT**. **CreateDialogParam** was called by function **DialogBoxParam** in segment **_DLGCORE** of USER, which was in turn called by **DialogBox** in the same segment.

As an interesting aside, we just found out that, in Windows 3.0, **DialogBox** (which creates a modal dialog) is a special case of **DialogBoxParam** with a **NULL** parameter pointer, and that **DialogBoxParam** in turn calls **Create-DialogParam**—the function that creates a modeless dialog box with a parameter block. No doubt **CreateDialog** also calls **CreateDialogParam**.

The next line is our payoff: **MainWndProc+007B** is the return address from the place in our code that called **DialogBox** with bad parameters. We can nail this down quickly. Looking in **generic.map** we find:

```
Address    Export            Alias

0001:01C1 About              About
0001:012A MainWndProc        MainWndProc
...


Line numbers for generic.obj(generic.c) segment _TEXT

    51 0001:0010    58 0001:0016    59 0001:001C    60 0001:0027
    64 0001:002B    72 0001:003A    74 0001:003C    75 0001:0046
    76 0001:0050    77 0001:0063    78 0001:0066   103 0001:006C

   111 0001:0072   114 0001:007C   115 0001:0084   116 0001:008A
   117 0001:009E   118 0001:00AF   119 0001:00BA   120 0001:00C2
```

```
124 0001:00CA    126 0001:00D4    147 0001:00D8    175 0001:00DE
180 0001:0112    181 0001:011B    182 0001:0123    184 0001:0126
208 0001:012A    215 0001:0137    238 0001:0143    217 0001:0159
218 0001:015F    223 0001:0176    225 0001:018B    230 0001:0196
235 0001:01AA    241 0001:01AC    247 0001:01B4    248 0001:01B7
272 0001:01C1    277 0001:01CB    283 0001:01D0    284 0001:01DC
279 0001:01E8    289 0001:01F5    290 0001:
```

Program entry point at 0001:0211

A little hex arithmetic (with the Windows calculator accessory) tells us that **MainWndProc+007B** is at **0001:01A5**, and the line number table puts that around line 235 of file generic.c. Looking at line 235, we see that it is the **break** statement immediately after our deliberately buggy **DialogBox** call. Knowing this, we can examine the parameters to **DialogBox** and see that **NULL** is invalid.

The UAE call stack, with a little work on our part, got us right to the error line. But sometimes things aren't so straightforward.

Sometimes we need to know if a specific piece of code has executed—code that is not right at the source of a trap. One way to handle this is to seed **MessageBox** calls through your source code; this can help you pinpoint the actual error without needing to do any hex arithmetic. As we'll discuss in a later chapter, **MessageBox** calls have a few side effects; they shouldn't be used, for instance, inside your paint procedure.

If your problem can't be found from the call stack or by a few quick **MessageBox** probes inserted into your source code, it may be time to resort to a debugger. If you built your executable as we just did for Generic—with both CodeView information and a symbol table—you can choose any Windows debugger and plow ahead. But be warned: unless you first develop a good feel for the message context in which your error occurs, you could be in for a lengthy session with the debugger.

We'll come back to the topic of debugging in Chapter 6; now it's time to roll up our sleeves and build an application.

3

In which we build a "real" program from components. We do some basic performance tuning and test the program in a multitasking environment.

Displaying and Printing DIBs

. . . .

Before we start to work with device-independent bitmaps (DIBs), we should know something about them. You'll find the current definitions in windows.h, from which the listing in the next section was extracted. The DIB data structures are documented in volume 2 of the Windows SDK *Reference.*

If you're not familiar with DIBs, some history is in order. When Windows 1 was first designed, a "hot" PC was an IBM XT with 640KB of RAM, a 10 MB hard disk, and either a CGA or Hercules card. Even with a color monitor, you could only see black and white at the CGA's best 640x200 pixel resolution. The memory representation of a CGA or Hercules screen image could conveniently be represented with 1 bit per pixel.

When the EGA and later the VGA came along, most Windows drivers for them were limited to 8 colors, organized in 3 planes. Late in the evolution of Windows 2 it finally became common to see 16-color EGA and VGA drivers, but most users found them too slow for regular use. Besides, they said, 8 colors is plenty for business graphics.

Each one of these adapters had its own mapping to RAM, and thus its own version of the bitmap format. Most software couldn't deal with color bitmaps very well, since the only format that was sure to be displayable was the old 1-bit-per-pixel black-and-white bitmap.

OS/2 had a better bitmap format: a single file could be displayed on any device. Each file had (and has) two parts: the header, and the image data. The OS/2 device-independent bitmap (DIB) descriptor was included in Windows 3 as the BITMAPCOREHEADER type; an enhancement that allowed for compression was also included, as the BITMAPINFO type. Compression is important: a full-screen 256-color DIB for a SuperVGA (640x480x8) is about 300KB uncompressed, and depending on content can be as small as 20KB compressed.

Bitmap and DIB Structures

The best way to understand the data structures is to look at them carefully; they are listed below. There are a few key points to notice when looking through the DIB data structures. First, since there are several types of bitmap (device-dependent and two types of device-independent), there are several different structures. The BITMAP type is the device-dependent bitmap (DDB), which dates from Windows 1; it represents a black and white or "chunky-planar" color image with no provision for a palette. DDBs don't allow for a palette; DIBs allow for a palette but don't require the palette to be filled in.

Color DDBs have a physical layout that corresponds to the memory architecture of their corresponding video adapter. Three-bit EGA DDBs have their color planes arranged scan-line by scan-line just like the EGA hardware. Four-bit VGA DDBs have their color planes arranged just like the 16-color mode of the VGA hardware.

The RGBTRIPLE palette color representation type is used, along with a BITMAPCOREHEADER, inside the BITMAPCOREINFO type, which—as we mentioned before—is considered the "old" device-independent bitmap structure and is compatible with OS/2 1.x bitmaps. The RGBQUAD color representation type is used inside the "new" BITMAPINFO type, along with a BITMAPINFOHEADER. The BITMAPINFOHEADER includes a field to tag compression types: the currently defined values for **biCompression** allow for uncompressed (**BI_RGB**), run-length encoded 16-color (**BI_RLE4**), and run-length encoded 256-color (**BI_RLE8**) images.

We'll need to talk about the different variations of bitmap many times in the course of this chapter. If we say "DDB," we mean a device-dependent bitmap, both the header and the image bits. If we say "DIB," we mean either a BITMAPCOREINFO or a BITMAPINFO structure, plus the image bits. If we say "bitmap," we may be speaking of any of the three variations, but are most likely to mean the device-dependent bitmap.

You'll notice that the BITMAP structure includes a pointer to its image bit array, and that neither of the DIB header structures has such a pointer. When dealing with DIBs, we have to keep track of two separate handles—one for the header-cum-palette, and one for the actual array of bytes that represents the pixels of the image.

```
/* Bitmap Header Definition */
typedef struct tagBITMAP
  {
    int        bmType;
    int        bmWidth;
    int        bmHeight;
    int        bmWidthBytes;
    BYTE       bmPlanes;
    BYTE       bmBitsPixel;
    LPSTR      bmBits;
  } BITMAP;
typedef BITMAP                  *PBITMAP;
typedef BITMAP NEAR      *NPBITMAP;
typedef BITMAP FAR       *LPBITMAP;

typedef struct tagRGBTRIPLE {
      BYTE    rgbtBlue;
      BYTE    rgbtGreen;
      BYTE    rgbtRed;
} RGBTRIPLE;

typedef struct tagRGBQUAD {
      BYTE    rgbBlue;
      BYTE    rgbGreen;
      BYTE    rgbRed;
      BYTE    rgbReserved;
} RGBQUAD;

/* structures for defining DIBs */
typedef struct tagBITMAPCOREHEADER {
      DWORD   bcSize;         /* used to get to color table */
      WORD    bcWidth;
      WORD    bcHeight;
      WORD    bcPlanes;
      WORD    bcBitCount;
} BITMAPCOREHEADER;
typedef BITMAPCOREHEADER FAR *LPBITMAPCOREHEADER;
typedef BITMAPCOREHEADER *PBITMAPCOREHEADER;

typedef struct tagBITMAPINFOHEADER{
      DWORD     biSize;
      DWORD     biWidth;
      DWORD     biHeight;
      WORD      biPlanes;
      WORD      biBitCount;
      DWORD     biCompression;
      DWORD     biSizeImage;
      DWORD     biXPelsPerMeter;
```

```
        DWORD       biYPelsPerMeter;
        DWORD       biClrUsed;
        DWORD       biClrImportant;
} BITMAPINFOHEADER;
typedef BITMAPINFOHEADER FAR *LPBITMAPINFOHEADER;
typedef BITMAPINFOHEADER *PBITMAPINFOHEADER;

/* constants for the biCompression field */
#define BI_RGB      0L
#define BI_RLE8     1L
#define BI_RLE4     2L

typedef struct tagBITMAPINFO {
    BITMAPINFOHEADER bmiHeader;
    RGBQUAD          bmiColors[1];
} BITMAPINFO;
typedef BITMAPINFO FAR *LPBITMAPINFO;
typedef BITMAPINFO *PBITMAPINFO;

typedef struct tagBITMAPCOREINFO {
    BITMAPCOREHEADER bmciHeader;
    RGBTRIPLE        bmciColors[1];
} BITMAPCOREINFO;
typedef BITMAPCOREINFO FAR *LPBITMAPCOREINFO;
typedef BITMAPCOREINFO *PBITMAPCOREINFO;

typedef struct tagBITMAPFILEHEADER {
    WORD    bfType;
    DWORD   bfSize;
     WORD     bfReserved1;
     WORD     bfReserved2;
    DWORD   bfOffBits;
} BITMAPFILEHEADER;
typedef BITMAPFILEHEADER FAR *LPBITMAPFILEHEADER;
typedef BITMAPFILEHEADER *PBITMAPFILEHEADER;
```

The final data type, BITMAPFILEHEADER, is used only in files. It is followed immediately in the file by a BITMAPINFO or BITMAPCOREINFO data structure. The initial **bfType** word must be the signature BM; the **bfSize** doubleword specifies the size of the file, also in doublewords; and the **bfOffBits** doubleword specifies the offset of the actual image bits in the file, in bytes. The discrepancy in length units is understandable when you realize that a byte offset can be used in an **_llseek** call to jump directly to the image.

Examining the SHOWDIB SDK Example Program

SHOWDIB (Figure 3.1) is a medium model program divided into six source files: showdib.c, print.c, dib.c, drawdib.c, dlgopen.c and dlgopena.asm. It also has

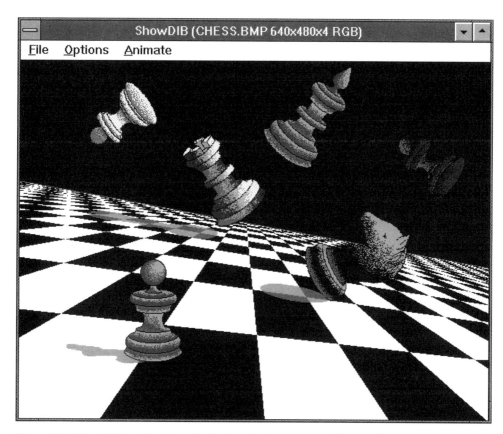

Figure 3.1. ShowDIB application, displaying CHESS.BMP Windows wallpaper

the usual assortment of definition, resource, and "make" files. It is worth spending a few minutes looking at the function descriptions: we'll be using a lot of these routines in the applications we build.

```
PROGRAM:            ShowDIB.c
PURPOSE:            Application to illustrate the use of the GDI
                    DIB (Device Independent Bitmap) and Palette
                    manager functions.
FUNCTIONS:
WinMain()           Creates the app.window and enters the
                    message loop.
WndProc()           Processes app. window messages.
MenuCommand()       Processes menu commands.
FreeDIB()           Frees currently active objects.
InitDIB()           Reads DIB from a file and loads it.
MODULE:             Print.c
DESCRIPTION:        Routines used for printing.
FUNCTIONS:
```

GetPrinterDC()	Gets default printer from WIN.INI and creates a DC for it.
InitPrinting()	Initializes print job.
TermPrinting()	Terminates print job.
PrintDlgProc()	Dialog function for the "Cancel Printing" dialog.
AbortProc()	Peeks at message queue for messages from the print dialog.
MODULE:	DIB.C
DESCRIPTION:	Routines for dealing with Device Independent Bitmaps.
FUNCTIONS:	
OpenDIB()	Opens DIB file and creates a memory DIB
WriteDIB()	Writes a global handle in CF_DIB format to a file.
DibInfo()	Retrieves the info. block associated with a CF_DIB format memory block.
CreateBIPalette()	Creates a GDI palette given a pointer to a BITMAPINFO structure.
CreateDibPalette()	Creates a GDI palette given a HANDLE to a BITMAPINFO structure.
ReadDibBitmapInfo()	Reads a file in DIB format and returns a global handle to it's BITMAPINFO
PaletteSize()	Calculates the palette size in bytes of given DIB
DibNumColors()	Determines the number of colors in DIB
BitmapFromDib()	Creates a DDB given a global handle to a block in CF_DIB format.
DibFromBitmap()	Creates a DIB repr. the DDB passed in.
DrawBitmap()	Draws a bitmap at specified position in the DC.
DibBlt()	Draws a bitmap in CIF_DIB format using SetDIBitsToDevice()
StretchDibBlt()	Draws a bitmap in CIF_DIB format using StretchDIBits()
lread()	Private routine to read more than 64k
lwrite()	Private routine to write more than 64k
MODULE:	DrawDIB.c
PURPOSE:	Handles most of the SHOWDIB's DIB drawing and clipboard operations.
FUNCTIONS:	
PrintDIB()	Sets the current DIB bits to the printer DC.
AppPaint()	Sets the DIB/bitmap bits on the screen or the given device.
DrawSelect()	Draws selected clip rectangle on the DC/screen.
NormalizeRect()	Swaps reversed rectangle coords.
TrackMouse()	Draws rubberbanding rectangle and displays its dimensions.
BandDIB()	Outputs DIB in bands to device.

```
SizeWindow()                         Sizes app. window based on client dimensions
                                     and style.
GetRealClientRect()                  Calculates client rectangle dimensions if
                                     scrollbars are present.
SetScrollRanges()                    Sets global scroll ranges.
CopyHandle()                         Makes a copy of memory block.
CopyPalette()                        Makes a copy of the GDI logical palette.
CopyBitmap()                         Copies given bitmap to another.
CropBitmap()                         Crops a bitmap to the given size.
RenderFormat()                       renders currently displayed DIB in CF_BITMAP
                                     or CF_DIB format.
RealizeDibFormat()                   Realizes the DIB in given format.
ErrMsg()                             Pops an error message to user.
fDialog()                            Displays a dialog box.
AppAbout()                           Shows the About.. dialog box.


MODULE:                              DLGOPEN.C
DESCRIPTION:                         Routines to display a standard File/Open and
                                     File/Save dialog boxes.
FUNCTIONS:
DlgOpenFile()                        Displays a dialog box for opening or saving
                                     a file.
DlgfnOpen()                          Dialog function for the above dialog.
AddExt()                             Adds an extension to a filename if not
                                     already present.
FSearchSpec()                        Checks if given string contains a wildcard
                                     character.
FillListBox()                        Fills listbox with files that match specs.
DlgCheckOkEnable()                   Enables <OK> button iff there's text in the
                                     edit control.
NOTE : These routines (in DLGOPEN.C) require that the app. be running
                                     SS = DS since they use near pointers into the
                                     stack. Don't try to use them in a DLL.
MODULE:                              DLGOPENA.ASM
DESCRIPTION:                         Assembly language helper routines for
                                     DLGOPEN.C
FUNCTIONS:
chdir()                              change to specified asciiz directory.
```

Let's examine the techniques used in SHOWDIB. How does it load a DIB? The function **InitDIB** in module SHOWDIB.C accomplishes this with the general structure of the following code, which has the error handling clauses and the palette conversion code removed for clarity:

```
FreeDib();
fh = OpenFile (achFileName, (LPOFSTRUCT)&of, OF_READ);
hbiCurrent = ReadDibBitmapInfo(fh);
dwOffset = _llseek(fh, 0L, SEEK_CUR);
_lclose (fh);
DibInfo(hbiCurrent,&bi);
```

```
hpalCurrent = CreateDibPalette(hbiCurrent);
//Convert the DIB color table to palette relative indexes
//      <code omitted for clarity>
hdibCurrent = OpenDIB(achFileName);
hbmCurrent = BitmapFromDib(hdibCurrent,hpalCurrent);
```

The code shown uses a number of helper functions that require further explanation. **FreeDib** (in SHOWDIB.C) does some cleanup—a few **DeleteObject** calls, a **GlobalFree**—and zeroes the global variables used by the DIB package. **OpenFile** is the standard Windows routine for opening a binary file by file handle. Note that **OpenFile** doesn't open a stream—you'd have to do that separately with the C library routine **fdopen**. **OpenFile** has many advantages over the standard C library file opening routines: the most compelling is that it automatically searches all the right directories (including the windows\system directory, which is not normally on the path) in the normal order (current directory first) to find the file.

ReadDibBitmapInfo (in DIB.C) does a lot of low-level grunt work (with Windows file services like **_llseek** and **_lread**) to read the DIB header from a file into a global memory block that it allocates. Along the way it converts old-format information (the BITMAPCOREINFO structure, and color in RGB triplets) to new-style color information (the BITMAPINFOHEADER structure, and color in RGB quads) if necessary and fills in some information that may have been omitted from the file. **ReadDibBitmapInfo** is a useful routine with plenty of error checking, which will return FALSE—a NULL bitmap handle—if the file handle it has been passed turns out not to point to a valid DIB. We'll probably want to use **ReadDibBitmapInfo** in our programs without any changes—it does everything right.

After calling **ReadDibBitmapInfo**, **InitDIB** gets the offset of the bitmap bits with **_llseek** and closes the file with **_lclose**. What **InitDIB** has done so far is to get the header information and the offset of the bits; it closes the file now, apparently because the palette processing it is about to do might take a while, and might also fail.

DibInfo (in DIB.C) fills in a BITMAPHEADER with the size and number of colors of an image, since some programs leave these fields at 0. **CreateDib-Palette**, which in turn calls **CreateBIPalette**, copies the color palette information from a BITMAPHEADER to a GDI logical palette. If the DIB uses 24-bit color, **CreateBIPalette** creates a bogus 256-color palette with stock colors. We may need to change **CreateBIPalette** to more intelligently reduce the palette of 24-bit DIBs, if we want to display 24-bit color files on 8-bit color devices using the palette manager.

OpenDIB opens the file and calls **ReadDibBitmapInfo** and **DibInfo** to get the DIB header for use within **OpenDIB**. Then it allocates a global memory block for the DIB bits, and reads the bits from the file to the global block using

lread, which basically grabs 32K of the file at a time to avoid violating segment boundaries.

A question arises here: why did **InitDIB** get the offset of the DIB bits and save them in a global variable, only to call **OpenDIB** later? The answer is that **OpenDIB** may well fail for lack of memory, in which case the DIB routines will read from the file directly to the screen or printer device context in bands. Banding is slow enough without the extra overhead of figuring out where to start in the file on each pass.

Assuming **OpenDIB** has been successful (and assuming this option has been enabled in the code), **InitDIB** calls **BitmapFromDIB** to create a device-dependent bitmap to match the screen display context. Why? To make drawing the image on the screen more efficient. There is no gain if the image is drawn only once, but if, as is often the case, window motion causes part of the DIB display to become invalid, having a device-dependent bitmap already prepared will minimize the amount of CPU time needed for a screen repaint. The choice of whether to create the bitmap for the screen (for speed) or to draw the DIB directly in the screen device context (for space) depends on whether you have enough memory available to maintain the extra bitmap. We may want to add some logic to the program later to make this decision in a rational way.

How to Display a DIB

Examining **InitDIB** and the routines it calls has told us how to load a DIB into memory, but it hasn't told us how to display a DIB on the screen or printer. The logical place to find that information is in a Windows program's paint procedure. Looking in SHOWDIB.C, we search for WM_PAINT and find that the work is done by **AppPaint**, which is in DRAWDIB.C:

```
void AppPaint (hWnd, hDC, x, y)
HWND hWnd;
HDC hDC;
int x, y;
{
      HPALETTE hpalT;
      BITMAPINFOHEADER bi;
      LPBITMAPINFOHEADER lpbi;

      SetWindowOrg (hDC, x, y);
      SetBkMode (hDC, wTransparent);
      if (bLegitDraw) {
            hpalT = SelectPalette (hDC, hpalCurrent, FALSE);
            RealizePalette (hDC);
            if (hbmCurrent && !bDIBToDevice) {
                  DrawBitmap (hDC, 0, 0, hbmCurrent, SRCCOPY);
                  }
```

```
        else if (hdibCurrent) {
                DibInfo (hdibCurrent, &bi);
                DibBlt (hDC,    0,0,
                        (int)bi.biWidth,
                        (int)bi.biHeight,
                        hdibCurrent,    0,0,
                        SRCCOPY);
                }
        else if (achFileName[0]) {
                BandDIB (hWnd, hDC, 0, 0);
                }
        SelectPalette(hDC,hpalT,FALSE);
        }
        DrawSelect(hDC, TRUE);
}
```

Examining **AppPaint** we find that it has not one method for painting the screen, but three! Under the control of flag **bDIBtoDevice**, **AppPaint** either uses the routine **DrawBitmap** to place the previously created screen-compatible bitmap on the screen, or the routine **DibBlt** to directly draw the DIB in the screen device context. If there is no current DIB in memory, but there is a valid filename saved, **AppPaint** calls **BandDIB** to draw the bitmap from the disk file to the screen device context band by band.

DrawBitmap creates a compatible memory device context, selects the bitmap into the memory device context, and then uses **DibBlt** to copy the bitmap from the memory device context to the display device context. **DibBlt** uses **SetDIBitsToDevice** to draw a DIB in the display device context.

BandDIB allocates the biggest memory bitmap it can for a band buffer. Then it plows through the DIB file band by band: for each band it copies the DIB bits into memory with lread, then draws the band image into the device context using one of two methods. If the flag **bDIBtoDevice** is set, **BandDIB** uses **SetDIBitsToDevice**; if not, **BandDIB** first does a **SetDIBits**, and then a **DibBlt**.

The palette management calls used by **AppPaint** deserve some comment. Before doing any painting, **AppPaint** selects and realizes the DIBs palette, saving the handle of the palette previously in the device context:

```
hpalT = SelectPalette (hDC, hpalCurrent, FALSE);
RealizePalette (hDC);
```

Then, after it has sent the bitmap to the screen (one way or another), it restores the saved palette:

```
SelectPalette(hDC,hpalT,FALSE);
```

What **SelectPalette** does in the first instance is to make **hpalCurrent** the palette that GDI will use to control colors for all its subsequent operations.

The value of **FALSE** in the third argument specifies that this palette will be the foreground palette when its window has the input focus. If the third argument were instead nonzero, the palette loaded would always be treated as a background palette.

RealizePalette, on the other hand, tells the Windows palette manager to actually change the system palette to match the logical palette in the device context, and map colors as necessary. For a foreground window **RealizePalette** tells Windows to display as many of the colors in the logical palette as possible (up to the total number available on the display less the reserved system colors), and map the rest of the logical palette to the nearest matching colors in the system palette. For a background window, RealizePalette requests that the logical palette be mapped as well as possible to the current system palette.

How to Print a DIB

At first glance, you'd think that printing a DIB was much the same as displaying the DIB on the screen. Unfortunately, it is not that simple.

Our three methods for displaying a DIB on a screen ultimately used either **SetDIBitsToDevice** or **BitBlt** as the final step of getting the bits to the device. We won't want to use either of these to go to a printer, because of the scaling problem.

Think about the resolution of a screen: a VGA typically runs 640x480 pixels. Now, what about a printer? A typical laser printer with 300 dpi resolution and a printable area of 8x10.5 inches measures 2400x3150 pixels. Our DIB is more than likely somewhere near screen resolution: it'll be tiny on a printed page.

Since we won't have to worry about repainting, the most efficient method would be a one-step function that starts with a DIB, automatically stretches the image and converts the colors to match the printer's capabilities, and writes the image to the printer. Does Windows have such a wonder? Yes, it does: **StretchDIBits**. In fact, if we look at the function **PrintDIB** in drawdib.c, we see that it calls **StretchDibBlt**, which in turn calls **StretchDIBits**. That'll take care of it, right?

Unfortunately, no. We can't depend on every printer driver supporting **StretchDIBits**: try printing from ShowDIB to a PostScript printer, and you'll most likely get a nice gray-scaled rendering of your image; but try printing to an HP LaserJet, and you'll probably get an ugly black-and-white rendering.

ShowDIB isn't sophisticated enough to adapt to the capabilities of the printer it is using: we'll have to add our own logic here. Basically what we need to do is query the raster capabilities of the printer, and choose the right printing method based on what the printer can handle. So much for device independence.

The appropriate call to find out which raster calls are supported is:

```
wRasterCaps=GetDeviceCaps(hPrinterDC,RASTERCAPS);
```

The results will be bit-encoded in **wRasterCaps**; we'll have to test the word against a series of bit masks, defined in windows.h:

RC_BITBLT	0x0001	Can do standard BLT
RC_BANDING	0x0002	Device requires banding support
RC_SCALING	0x0004	Device requires scaling support
RC_BITMAP64	0x0008	Device can support >64K bitmap
RC_GDI20_OUTPUT	0x0010	has 2.0 output calls
RC_DI_BITMAP	0x0080	supports DIB to memory
RC_PALETTE	0x0100	supports a palette
RC_DIBTODEV	0x0200	supports DIBitsToDevice
RC_BIGFONT	0x0400	supports >64K fonts
RC_STRETCHBLT	0x0800	supports StretchBlt
RC_FLOODFILL	0x1000	supports FloodFill
RC_STRETCHDIB	0x2000	supports StretchDIBits

If the printer asserts **RC_STRETCHDIB**, we'll be all set with the logic we have now. If it doesn't, we can test for **RC_DIBTODEV** to see if **DIBitsToDevice** is supported, **RC_STRETCHBLT** to see if **StretchBlt** is supported, **RC_BITMAP64** to see if the device can support big bitmaps, and **RC_BITBLT** to see if the device supports standard BLTs. We may also want to test **RC_PALETTE** to see if the printer is a palette-based color device; in that case we might be able to use some special calls (not the palette management calls we used for the video display) to set the printer's hardware palette to match our logical palette.

That's one strategy, anyway. But ShowDIB doesn't go through all that rigamarole; it only tests for **RC_DIBTODEV**. You'll find the following code in showdib.c, right after the **WM_CREATE** and **WM_WININICHANGE** cases:

```
if (hDC = GetPrinterDC()) {
    EnableMenuItem(hMenu,
     IDM_PRINT,
     (RC_DIBTODEV &
    GetDeviceCaps(hDC, RASTERCAPS)) ?
     MF_ENABLED : MF_GRAYED | MF_DISABLED);
    DeleteDC(hDC);
    }
```

This code turns out to be good enough for most purposes. If you are feeling ambitious, you can change the logic to test other flags as we discussed above, and use these flags to control the printing method actually used.

Handling Various Color Displays

We mentioned earlier that **RealizePalette** makes the Windows Palette Manager do its thing. If the Windows display handles 24-bit color, the Palette Manager has nothing to do, because as many colors are displayable (about 16 million) as can be represented in a DIB. If the display handles only 3-bit or 4-bit color (or 1-bit black and white), the Palette Manager has nothing to do, this time because there are 20 color slots reserved for the system—more than the device can display.

It is only when an 8-bit (256-color) display is present that the Palette Manager has work to do. But we must also consider the image.

If the DIB we're displaying uses a palette of 256 colors, we don't have a problem: we just set the system palette to the DIB palette, and we're off to the races. If you remember, this is done in **CreateBIPalette**. You may also remember that we didn't like the way **CreateBIPalette** handles 24-bit palettes.

Creating a "generic" system palette is probably not the best strategy for displaying 24-bit images on an 8-bit display. It'll work, and it's fast, but the images may look pretty lousy. The trouble is that the alternatives take some computation. A better but slow color mapping would make sense if you were converting the 24-bit image file to an 8-bit image file, but might not make sense for one-time display.

There are several alternatives to a uniform mapping for the *color quantization* problem. The "popularity algorithm" (Heckbert) chooses the most frequently occurring colors for the color table. The "median cut algorithm" (Heckbert) tries to select the colors in such a way that each represents approximately the same number of pixels. Finally, the "octree quantization algorithm" (Gervautz) iteratively merges nearby colors and replaces them with their mean. The octree is the data structure used to make it easy to recognize colors that are close together.

We might want to add an option to our program to choose the color quantization method used for display, so that the user can choose better speed or better color rendering. If Michael Gervautz (the author of the octree quantization method) is correct, we needn't bother with the popularity or median cut algorithms, as octree quantization gives better results in less time. This will be left as an exercise for the student.

Handling Compression and Other DIB Variations

You'll recall for the earlier section on DIB structures that a DIB can have RLL compression if it is either 4 bits-per-pixel or 8 bits-per-pixel. Given that disk space is always at a premium, we should preferentially store DIBs with compression. On the other hand, compression can also introduce some difficulties.

In a low-memory situation (such as in real mode), ShowDIB will resort to displaying a DIB by banding. The banding routine, **BandDIB** (in drawdib.c), implicitly assumes it can walk through the array of bits by calculating offsets in the DIB file. Unfortunately, RLL compression makes that assumption invalid— so, if we are low on memory, we'll have to use more disk space.

Another consideration is that OS/2 bitmaps cannot use compression: they use the older BITMAPCOREHEADER structure, which doesn't have a compression field. If we want to write DIB files readable by both OS/2 and Windows, we'll need to write the older format.

How do we convert between different DIB formats? The API we'll need to use is **GetDIBits**, which is pretty complicated: its action is controlled by the contents of structures passed via long pointers. In fact, we need to fill in part of the BITMAPINFOHEADER structure, call **GetDIBits** with a NULL pointer to the bitmap bits so that it will fill in the size information; then we need to allocate the global memory block for the bitmap bits and call **GetDIBits** again. The whole procedure is done in function **DibFromBitmap** (in dib.c):

```
HANDLE DibFromBitmap (hbm, biStyle, biBits, hpal)
HBITMAP        hbm;
DWORD          biStyle;
WORD           biBits;
HPALETTE       hpal;
{
      BITMAP  bm;
      BITMAPINFOHEADER        bi;
      BITMAPINFOHEADER FAR *lpbi;
      DWORD    dwLen;
      HANDLE hdib;
      HANDLE h;
      HDC hdc;

      if (!hbm)
            return NULL;
      if (hpal == NULL)
            hpal = GetStockObject(DEFAULT_PALETTE);
      GetObject(hbm,sizeof(bm),(LPSTR)&bm);
      if (biBits == 0)
            biBits =  bm.bmPlanes * bm.bmBitsPixel;
      bi.biSize                = sizeof(BITMAPINFOHEADER);
      bi.biWidth               = bm.bmWidth;
      bi.biHeight              = bm.bmHeight;
      bi.biPlanes              = 1;
      bi.biBitCount     = biBits;
      bi.biCompression         = biStyle;
      bi.biSizeImage     = 0;
      bi.biXPelsPerMeter       = 0;
```

```
       bi.biYPelsPerMeter            = 0;
       bi.biClrUsed                  = 0;
       bi.biClrImportant             = 0;
       dwLen = bi.biSize + PaletteSize(&bi);
       hdc = GetDC(NULL);
       hpal = SelectPalette(hdc,hpal,FALSE);
       RealizePalette(hdc);
       hdib = GlobalAlloc(GHND,dwLen);
       if (!hdib){
               SelectPalette(hdc,hpal,FALSE);
               ReleaseDC(NULL,hdc);
               return NULL;
               }
       lpbi = (VOID FAR *)GlobalLock(hdib);
       *lpbi = bi;
/* call GetDIBits with a NULL lpBits param, so it will   calculate
   the biSizeImage field for us       */
       GetDIBits(hdc, hbm, 0, (WORD)bi.biHeight,
               NULL, (LPBITMAPINFO)lpbi, DIB_RGB_COLORS);
       bi = *lpbi;
       GlobalUnlock(hdib);
/* If the driver did not fill in the biSizeImage field,
   make one up */
       if (bi.biSizeImage == 0){
               bi.biSizeImage = WIDTHBYTES((DWORD)bm.bmWidth *
               biBits) * bm.bmHeight;

               if (biStyle != BI_RGB)
                       bi.biSizeImage = (bi.biSizeImage * 3) / 2;
       }
/* realloc the buffer big enough to hold all the bits */
       dwLen = bi.biSize + PaletteSize(&bi) + bi.biSizeImage;
       if (h = GlobalReAlloc(hdib,dwLen,0))
               hdib = h;
       else {
               GlobalFree(hdib);
               hdib = NULL;
               SelectPalette(hdc,hpal,FALSE);
               ReleaseDC(NULL,hdc);
               return hdib;
               }
/* call GetDIBits with a NON-NULL lpBits param, and actually get
   the bits this time         */
       lpbi = (VOID FAR *)GlobalLock(hdib);
       if (GetDIBits( hdc,   hbm,    0,(WORD)bi.biHeight,
               (LPSTR)lpbi + (WORD)lpbi->biSize + PaletteSize(lpbi),
               (LPBITMAPINFO)lpbi, DIB_RGB_COLORS) == 0) {
               GlobalUnlock(hdib);
               hdib = NULL;
               SelectPalette(hdc,hpal,FALSE);
               ReleaseDC(NULL,hdc);
               return NULL;
               }
```

```
    bi = *lpbi;
    GlobalUnlock(hdib);
    SelectPalette(hdc,hpal,FALSE);
    ReleaseDC(NULL,hdc);
    return hdib;
}
```

The Frankenstein Method: Sewing Unmatched Pieces Together

ShowDIB is a start at what we want, but it doesn't have all the pieces we'll need. In the next few sections, what we'll be doing is rummaging through graveyards for the parts we need. We've got the body: we'll need a head, and limbs, and maybe a new heart and brain.

When we've assembled all the pieces, we'll have to rearrange them and then sew them together. Finally, when a thunderstorm passes overhead, we can expose the body to the lightning and see if it walks.

Unlike Dr. Frankenstein, we don't have to worry about this monster killing anyone—except that it might make Windows crash, or it might wipe out our hard disk. But before we can try the experiment, we have to learn how to do surgery. In this case, surgery means modular programming.

Aside: Windows Modular ProgrammingTechniques

Modularity is important in any programming project. As projects get bigger, modularity gets even more important—if you don't modularize, your number of errors will, in general, go as the square of the program size instead of increasing linearly with the program size.

Modularity has additional benefits for Windows programs. Because of the way Windows manages memory in real and standard modes—discarding unneeded code segments to make room for needed code segments—good segmentation can make an enormous difference in performance. Every time Windows needs to load a segment, it gets it from the original EXE file on disk. Remember that disks are much slower than RAM. If you segment your program badly, it will "thrash" on the disk in a low-memory situation—things that should happen in seconds will take minutes.

Divide and Conquer

SHOWDIB is already divided into modules, and the functions seem to be grouped fairly logically within each source file. Instead of adding to any of the existing source files, we'll be adding functionality in new source files.

There are a number of benefits to this practice. For one, it will help us keep new functions from interfering with existing functions: we won't have to worry about accidently stomping on static variables from another module, although we will still have to be careful of global variables.[1]

For another, it will help keep the compile time short for new functions. Actually, we not only want our source modules to be relatively short, we want the individual functions to be reasonably simple. Some authorities recommend restricting each function to a single screen, or a single page of listing; unfortunately, it is not always practical to keep Windows programs within these limits.

The general framework of the bulk of a Windows program is a giant **switch** statement based on the message identifier received, with smaller, nested **switch** statements based on the message parameters. Often the code to handle a message is very simple—two or three lines for something like the **WM_DESTROY** message. On the other hand, the code to handle **WM_COMMAND** has a nested switch that enumerates every menu item in the program. You can control the complexity of this kind of code by encapsulating each level of switch in a function. For instance:

```
    switch (iMessage) {
       case WM_DESTROY:
               /* Clean up and quit */
               FreeDib();
               PostQuitMessage(0);
               break ;
<intervening code here>
       case WM_COMMAND:
               /* Process menu commands */
               return MenuCommand (hWnd, wParam);
               break;
<intervening code here>
         } //end of switch (iMessage)

BOOL MenuCommand (hWnd, id)
HWND hWnd;
WORD id;
{
<declarations here>
    switch (id) {
       case IDM_ABOUT:
```

---

[1] We will also have to be careful about the naming of functions. The whole area of names tends to be a religious issue with many programmers. In this project we are building on ShowDIB, a sample program written at Microsoft. ShowDIB uses function and variable naming conventions that are consistent with those used in the Windows API, which in turn were based loosely on the Hungarian naming conventions developed by Charles Simonyi. I have left names used in ShowDIB alone, despite the fact that they could easily be confused with Windows API names. As I add functions later I will choose my own names for them that follow different conventions; some people will like my names because they are easily distinguishable from API calls, and some people will hate them because they are not consistent with the rest of the project.

```
                    /* Show About .. box */
                    fDialog (ABOUTBOX, hWnd,AppAbout);
                    break;

        case IDM_COPY:
                    if (!bLegitDraw)
                        return 0L;

                    /* Clean clipboard of contents */
                    if (OpenClipboard(hWnd)) {
                        EmptyClipboard ();
                        SetClipboardData (CF_DIB    ,NULL);
                        SetClipboardData (CF_BITMAP   ,NULL);
                        SetClipboardData (CF_PALETTE ,NULL);
                        CloseClipboard ();
<and so on>
```

There is a metric that measures the depth of a function's logic trees: *cyclomatic complexity*, defined by Tom McCabe as the number of decision-making statements in a function plus 1. If you run a code metrics program (such as PC-Metric from Set Laboratories, Inc.) against your source files, you can quickly get cyclomatic complexity numbers for each function; numbers above some cutoff indicate that the function needs to be made simpler. My own experiments show that Windows programs usually have higher average cyclomatic complexity per function than DOS programs—which means that Windows programs tend to be harder to understand and debug than DOS programs.

A variation on cyclomatic complexity invented by Glenford Myers, *extended cyclomatic complexity*, adds the number of decision-making predicates to the number of decision-making statements in a function. By this measure the logic to handle **WM_COMMAND** in a *real* Windows program is very high indeed. Both the plain and extended forms of cyclomatic complexity (as well as other metrics from software science) correlate experimentally with the difficulty of the code. The message from software science to programmers boils down to: "Simplify and encapsulate, or spend your life debugging."

Modular or structured programming was the programming panacea of the Seventies. Object-oriented programming was the software engineering panacea of the Eighties. In some ways, object-oriented programming is just structured programming plus an additional level of encapsulation that helps to keep the data with the code. But in other ways object-oriented programming, with its class hierarchies, virtual methods, and other abstractions, adds another level of sophistication: it takes a much better programmer to design and implement a good set of object classes than it does to design and implement a good set of functions.

The gigantic **switch** statements you find in the typical Windows program in C are the natural consequence of trying to write a message-handling program in a language designed for sequential programming. In an object-oriented language like C++, all those **switch** statements would be replaced by **methods**, which should (at least theoretically) be easier to understand and use.

Keeping your Edit-Compile-Link Cycles Short

Besides making your code more understandable, modularity helps to make your code compile more quickly. You can improve your turn-around time (by which I mean the time between when you finish editing a change in your code and when you can start testing the change) with Microsoft C by using the incremental linker (**ILINK**), using the quick compiler (**/qc**) and using the incremental compilation option (**/Gi**).

I set up my make files with a **DEBUG** variable. If **DEBUG** is defined (in the environment, in the make file, or in the **nmake** command line), Windows C programs are compiled with **CL /c /AM /qc /Gswi /Od /Zpi** and, if there are many object modules, linked with **ILINK**; otherwise, programs are compiled with **CL /c /AM /Gsw /Owls /Zp** and linked with **LINK**. Give priority to the amount of time *you* spend when you are developing and debugging; give priority to the amount of time the *user* will spend with the program when you build the production version. In other words, compile as quickly as possible in the development phase, and optimize the code as well as possible in the production phase.

Adding Other File Formats

SHOWDIB has some features we don't need, and is missing a lot of features we want. Examining the menu (kept in showdib.rc) we see that the editing commands, contrary to the guidelines of SAA/CUA, are on the **Options** menu; we want them to be on an **Edit** menu. We don't need the other controls on the **Options** menu—they are there for developers like us to play with, and will just confuse users. There is no need for us to keep the **Animate** menu, but we do need a **Help** menu—which is where the **About** item should go to conform to SAA/CUA and Windows 3 standards.

```
showdib MENU
    BEGIN
        POPUP "&File"
            BEGIN
                MENUITEM "&Open...",                        IDM_OPEN
                MENUITEM "&Save...",                        IDM_SAVE
                MENUITEM "&Print",                          IDM_PRINT
                MENUITEM SEPARATOR
                MENUITEM "E&xit",                IDM_EXIT
                MENUITEM SEPARATOR
```

```
                        MENUITEM "&About ShowDIB ...",IDM_ABOUT
            END
        POPUP "&Options"
            BEGIN
                MENUITEM "&Update Colors",              IDM_UPDATECOL
                MENUITEM "&Hide Changes",                  IDM_NOUGLY
                MENUITEM "&DIB to Screen",              IDM_DIBSCREEN
                MENUITEM "&Memory DIBs",               IDM_MEMORYDIB
                MENUITEM "&Transparent",              IDM_TRANSPARENT

                MENUITEM SEPARATOR
                MENUITEM "&Paste DIB",             IDM_PASTEDIB
                MENUITEM "&Paste DDB",             IDM_PASTEDDB
                MENUITEM "&Paste Palette",           IDM_PASTEPAL
                MENUITEM "&Copy",                  IDM_COPY
            END

        POPUP "&Animate"
            BEGIN
            MENUITEM "Steal Colors",IDM_STEALCOL
                MENUITEM "Off",             IDM_ANIMATE0
                MENUITEM "5",               IDM_ANIMATE5
                MENUITEM "50",              IDM_ANIMATE50
                MENUITEM "100",             IDM_ANIMATE100
                MENUITEM "200",             IDM_ANIMATE200
                MENUITEM "LongTime",        IDM_ANIMATE201
            END
    END
```

We'll call our new program SHOWIMG. It will have a simpler menu structure than SHOWDIB, but the file opening process will be more complicated, since we will support many more file formats, at least for input. We'll also make all the shortcut letters unique in the menus (unlike SHOWDIB, which uses P for several different items on the Options menu).

In keeping with our philosophy that the program should make its best guess about a file format and then let the user override the guess if necessary, we might want to look for signatures in the files, and then present a list box to the user with our guess already picked. The user could override the guess by picking another format, start the process by pressing OK, or end the process by picking Cancel.

On the other hand, it might be better to keep it simple. Generally the user expects to indicate the kind of file by its extension; we can then check that the signature matches the file type implied by the extension. To be nice in case the extension is incorrect, we might want to pop up a dialog; otherwise, we could read the file with no intervention from the user. We'll put the framework for popping up a dialog in the code, but leave the implementation to the student.

The process for generating SHOWIMG from SHOWDIB is simple, at least in concept. First, we create a new directory and copy all the files from the

SHOWDIB directory to the SHOWIMG directory. Then we rename all the files named SHOWDIB.* to SHOWIMG.*. Third, we edit all the files changing **showdib** to **showimg**. Finally, we start our specific editing: changing the menus, adding to the dialog boxes as necessary, stripping out definitions and code we don't need, and adding new code. As we make changes we recompile and link; we set the **DEBUG** variable in our make file (now renamed "makefile," the default for **nmake**) to tell it to compile quickly and generate debug information for CodeView, SYMDEB, and WDEB386.

GIF

The Graphics Interchange Format (GIF) was developed by CompuServe as a way to store graphics that can be viewed on just about any computer. Version 89a of the specification appears on the companion disks as GIF89A.DOC; the file is in plain ASCII text format. You can always find the most current version of the GIF specification, along with GIF viewers for a variety of hardware, in the PICS forum on CompuServe. GIF is copyright property of CompuServe Incorporated, but CompuServe has granted a blanket limited, nonexclusive, royalty-free license to all developers for the use of GIF in computer software. Of all the bitmapped image formats available, GIF is about the most prevalent on bulletin boards, online services, and image library disks and CD-ROMs.

The GIF format has several interesting features. It implements an effective compression scheme, variable-length LZW (so called after its developers, Lempel, Ziv, and Welch). The GIF file of an image is typically *much* smaller than the BMP file of the same image. GIF allows for interleaving of scan-lines, for multiple images in a single file, for global and local color tables of up to 256 colors, and for user-defined extension blocks.

The GIF89A specification tells us: "The Variable-Length-Code LZW Compression is a variation of the Lempel-Ziv Compression algorithm in which variable-length codes are used to replace patterns detected in the original data. The algorithm uses a code or translation table constructed from the patterns encountered in the original data; each new pattern is entered into the table and its index is used to replace it in the compressed stream."

The Stone Soup Group, an informal group of graphics developers who "hang out" on CompuServe, BIX, and other online services, and which is headed by Bert Tyler, produces and maintains FRACTINT, a program for calculating and displaying fractals of various sorts under DOS, and WINFRACT, a Windows version that shares the computation code with FRACTINT. Both programs are distributed free of charge, with source code, and can be downloaded from BIX, CompuServe, or almost any large bulletin board system. FRACTINT and WINFRACT use GIF (with an extension) to store fractal images. There are several other freely available GIF libraries, but the GIF section of WINFRACT is probably as good as any of them as long as you can live with the restrictions of one image per file and no interlacing; in addition, this code has already been proved to work under Windows.

As you might expect, GIF files contain the signature **GIF**; this is followed by the GIF version number. Known signature/versions as of July 1990 are **GIF87a** and **GIF89a**. The work of turning an array of pixels into the LZW-compressed GIF format is done by an *encoder*, and the work of reading the compressed GIF format and expanding it to pixels is done by a *decoder*. Not surprisingly, these tasks are done in modules encoder.c and decoder.c. The function **gifview** acts as a front end for the decoder: opening the file, checking the signature, and interpreting the various block types supported by the format. The plan is to adapt **gifview** to conform to the overall logic and interface of InitDIB, and put its call into the **IDM_OPEN** section of SHOWIMG.C.

The full GIF code (including code for writing GIF files that we don't use in the example programs) and a test image appear on the companion disks; code for converting GIF to DIB appears in GIF.C in the SHOWIMG listing. For the information of anyone doing a similar task, the entire job of extracting the GIF code from WINFRACT, cleaning it up, adapting it to SHOWIMG, installing it in SHOWIMG, and debugging it took me about three days. My first attempt trapped out whenever the program tried to read a 16-color GIF file; using a stack traceback, I found that I was allocating palette space for the number of colors in the DIB but always copying 256 colors.

Other mistakes didn't generate UAE or FatalExits, but caused the images not to display; I found them using CVW and by comparing the code for reading GIF files with the code for displaying DIB files. One error was forgetting to add the bitmap information and palette before the actual bits in the hdibCurrent buffer. Another error was setting the number of planes in the DIB description to the number of planes in the GIF description; the only legal value for the number of planes in a DIB is 1. My last problem had to do with 16-color images: the palettes weren't getting set properly. I had mistaken some code to handle 16-color displays for code to handle 16-color images; once I took out that logic, all noninterlaced GIF images displayed properly. We'll leave the support of interlaced GIF files as an exercise for the student.

The speed of the code to read and decode GIF images leaves something to be desired, at least before optimization. The code to read the images might be speeded up by using low-level I/O routines instead of stream I/O routines; the function that decodes the LZW compression scheme used in GIF files will probably benefit from some compiler optimization and possibly from some hand-tweaking. However, the important thing is to get the code working: we can always make it faster, later in the project.

PCX

The PCX specification is available free on request from ZSoft Corporation, 450 Franklin Rd. Suite 100, Marietta, Georgia, 30067. Their voice line is (404)428-0008; FAX is (404)427-1150, and their BBS is (404)427-1045 (9600 baud Telebit, 8 bits, No parity, 1 Stop bit). Ask for the *Technical Reference Manual.* You can also download information from their bulletin board system.

The ZSoft technical reference manual includes sample C code for reading and writing PCX files as well as documenting the file format. PCX files are used by the various versions of Paintbrush, including Windows Paintbrush. My code started with the ZSoft sample code. However, I quickly found that the ZSoft examples don't really deal with the complexities of the format or the device-dependencies.

PCX image files begin with a 128-byte header. Following the header, the image data is run-length encoded. Palette information can be in one of several formats: EGA/VGA 16-color, VGA 256-color, and CGA. The standard RGB format of the palette colors uses triples of values in the range [0,255].

Unlike DIB files, the PCX format is highly device dependent. I had no trouble writing code to convert black-and-white PCX images to DIBs, but the code to convert 16-color (four planes, one bit-per-pixel) VGA images gave me fits. The problem is that the PCX image is line-planar: within each row of pixels, there is a block of bits for the first plane, then a block of bits for the second plane, and so on.[2] Each plane corresponds to a bit in the index to the color map. The 4-bit DIB format uses a nibble per color index—it is one plane with four bits per pixel.

My first, naive cut at PCX-to-DIB code (based on the simple loop given the ZSoft documentation) showed me an upside-down image. When I corrected the line order, I saw 2-color images properly, but 16-color images had vertical bands. When I found that problem (a logic error having to do with the chunky-planar format), I still didn't see correct colors, and a lot of the image edges looked blurry.

I knew roughly where the problem was in my code—it had to be in the 16-bit section of PCX.C—but I couldn't find it. After about three days of spinning my wheels, I posted the code on BIX with a request for help. Several people responded with suggestions and useful information about the peccadilloes of the PCX format (they are all mentioned in the code); but it was Jay Slupesky of Fall Creek Systems who finally found the critical problem. (Thanks, Jay!)

The worst of the errors was that I computed a byte index based on a width

---

[2] It is no accident that 4-plane DDBs and 4-plane PCX files have almost the same layout: both largely correspond to the memory map of a VGA board in 16-color mode.

in bits; dividing by 8 fixed the problem. You'd think a Ph.D. physicist would remember to do dimensional analysis on all formulae. I didn't remember, and it cost me. Strict adherence to Hungarian conventions might possibly have helped me, as long as I remembered what prefix to use for a byte index and what to use for a value in bits.

I guess that one moral here is that you can't always find the bugs in your own code: after looking at the same stuff for a couple of days you can't see it or think about it anymore. If, like me, you normally work alone, you might want to hook up with one of the timesharing services that Windows programmers frequent, be it BIX, CompuServe, GEnie, or Online.

Even with the 4-plane PCX code correct, the routine still had problems that turned up in testing. Not all PCX files have correct palettes; I had to add logic that both checks the PCX version in the header, and checks that the palette is nonzero. I had also forgotten about 3-plane PCX files. Since there is no 3-bit-per-pixel DIB format, 3-plane 1-bit PCX files have to be converted to 1-plane 4-bit DIB images.

All in all, I spent the better part of two weeks trying to get PCX-to-DIB conversions right. It was frustrating that the process took so long, and that the PCX documentation turned out to be so sketchy.

Even after all that work, there are still two relatively minor known bugs in the PCX code: one has to do with odd row lengths, and the other has to do with 3-bit PCX files. These errors can be demonstrated using files problem1.pcx and problem2.pcx in the pcx subdirectory. You may want to try to find these problems yourself as a debugging exercise.

TIFF

TIFF, the Tagged Image File Format, looks as complicated as all the other formats put together—although, really, it is not that much worse than the DIB format. The full TIFF 5.0 specification appears on the companion disk as file TIFFSPEC.TXT, in plain ASCII. You can always get the most current TIFF specification from the Aldus forum on CompuServe, or by request from either Aldus or Microsoft:

Developers Desk   Windows Marketing Group
Aldus Corporation   Microsoft Corporation
411 First Ave. South   16011 NE 36th Way
Suite 200   Box 97017
Seattle, WA 98104   Redmond, WA 98073-9717
(206) 622-5500   (206) 882-8080

I based my code on the freely available Berkeley TIFF library by Sam Leffler. You can obtain a current version of the code by anonymous FTP from UCBVAX.

As Leffler's code was written for Unix, you can't expect it to run under DOS without some tweaking: it took me about two hours to get the code to compile without errors with MSC under DOS. I don't currently have FTP capability; I thank Craig Lindley, author of *Practical Image Processing in C*, for downloading version 2.2 of TIFFLIB for me.

TIFF images fall into one of five classes. Class B TIFF files contain black-and-white images, with one bit per pixel and three possible types of compression—none, CCITT Group 3, and PackBits. Class G TIFF files contain gray-scale images with four or eight bits per pixel and two possible types of compression—none, and LZW. Class P TIFF files contain palette-color images with one to eight bits per pixel, and either no compression or LZW compression. Class R TIFF files contain 24-bit RGB true-color images, which may or may not be LZW compressed. Class F TIFF files are used for FAX images.

Sometimes people talk about TIFF X. This is not actually a class, but a general way of referring to the five TIFF classes. Also, people often add their own extensions to TIFF without registering them: a case in point is PIXAR's use of the PICIO compression scheme for Class R files.

We'll convert class B TIFF images to 1-bit-per-pixel DIBs. Class F, G and P TIFF images should go to 4- or 8-bit-per-pixel DIBs; for class F and G TIFFs we will create a gray-scale palette, while for class P TIFFs we'll copy the palette. Class R TIFFs will translate to 24-bit DIBs.

The full Berkeley TIFF code and some test images reside on the companion disks. You'll find my code to read TIFFs and convert them to DIBs in the SHOWIMG listing; the support code derived from Leffler's TIFFLIB is not listed in this book, for reasons of space (we're talking about 7,000 lines of code—more than anyone would ever want to type from a listing), but is of course included on the companion disks.

In my first cut at converting Leffler's code for use under Windows, I proceeded by writing code to call the routines I needed (**TIFFOpen**, **TIFFGet-Field**, **TIFFScanlineSize**, **TIFFReadScanline**, and **TIFFClose**) and using the linker to tell me what other routines were required. I used **fgrep** to find the routines in their source modules, and added the appropriate source modules to SHOWIMG. The TIFF support quickly grew to half the modules in SHOWIMG, and not quite half the lines of source code.

I converted **TIFFError** and **TIFFWarning** to use message boxes instead of writing to **stderr**, and started debugging. I made no effort at first to convert TIFFLIB's memory management from its use of **malloc** and **free**. I found that the TIFF code seemed to work; but when the program went to convert the DIB built from the TIFF scan-lines to a screen-compatible bitmap, it hung—the program never came back from the call to **CreateDIBitmap**.

Since I knew I'd been somewhat cavalier in leaving malloc and free calls in the code—they map to **LocalAlloc(LMEM_FIXED,...)** and **LocalFree()**

calls in medium model Windows—I just assumed I'd clogged up the local heap without verifying the problem. I decided to convert to far heap allocations using **_fmalloc**, since Windows converts **_fmalloc** calls to **Global-Alloc(GMEM_FIXED...)** automatically.

It took me a long, boring day to convert the TIFF code to work with **FAR** pointers. The grossest changes were done in TIFFIO.H, at the preprocessor level:

```
#ifdef _WINDOWS
        #ifndef PASCAL
                #define NOCOMM
                #define NOKANJI
                #undef NULL
                #include <windows.h>
        #endif
        #include <assert.h>
        #define exit(X) assert(1)
        #define FAR far
        #undef malloc
        #undef free
        #undef strcpy
        #undef strlen
        #undef realloc
        #define malloc(a) _fmalloc(a)
        #define realloc(a,b) _frealloc(a,b)
        #define free(a) _ffree(a)
        #define strcpy(a,b) lstrcpy(a,b)
        #define strlen(a) lstrlen(a)
#else
        #define FAR
#endif
#define PTIFF TIFF FAR *
```

Within the code, I had to change all the **TIFF *** variables and parameters to my new **PTIFF**,[3] and add the **FAR** keyword to every pointer definition. When I was all done—after many iterations using MSC and Brief to find and fix errors—the code still crashed after reading through the TIFF file, except this time it not only hung up the program, it killed Windows and DOS and forced me to turn off my machine to reboot. My theory at this point was that something in my TIFF.C or something inside the TIFFLIB code was corrupting the Windows global heap or somehow getting a selector to a piece of memory outside the program. The latter is exactly the sort of problem protected mode is supposed to make impossible, so my bets were on global heap corruption. In the past, the most effective ways I have found to isolate heap problems have been to scatter

---

[3] Note that I declared the type **PTIFF**, where Hungarian purists might insist on **LPTIFF**. My rationale is that the length of the TIFF structure pointer is conditional—long if **_WINDOWS** is defined, and short otherwise.

`GlobalCompact` calls through my code, and to run HeapWalk before and after exercising suspect program sections. `GlobalCompact` has to walk the heap to compact it; if the heap is corrupt `GlobalCompact` usually notices.

However, I started by walking through tiffview with CodeView, just to see what I could see. Lo, and behold! This time the code generated a clean segment violation in **_fmemcopy**, called by **DumpModeDecode**, called by **TIFF-ReadScanline**, called by **tiffview**. Interestingly enough, the row argument to TIFFReadScanline was 0, and the fourth argument—set to a literal zero in the source code—appeared as 49072 in the stack trace.

This led me to suspect that **tiff.obj** had not been updated when **tiffio.h** was changed. Sure enough, **tiff.obj** was in the wrong section of **makefile**; when I moved it from the list of object modules not dependent on **tiffio.h** to one of the lists of modules dependent on **tiffio.h**, **nmake** recognized that it was out of date and recompiled it.

After recompilation, the same sequence showed up with a protection violation—but at least the arguments made sense, and I was able to debug the source code. Debugging was quite tedious; all the different variations of TIFF mean that there's a lot of code.

In fact, my debugging of the TIFF code was not complete at this stage. In particular, I was still suspicious of module **tif_dir.c** because of some compiler diagnostics and some data-dependent errors. I left some of the bugs in; you'll see them in Chapter 6.

Targa

The Targa file format specification is available free on request from Truevision, Inc., 7340 Shadeland Station, Indianapolis, IN 46256-3925. Request the TGA technical manual by voice at (317)841-0332, by FAX at (317)576-7700, or by modem at (317)577-8783. The specification from which I wrote code is for TGA version 2.0; the technical manual revision is 2.2, dated January 1991.

TGA image files come in several types. Unlike some other formats, the TGA signature (which is "TRUEVISION-XFILE") is at the end of the file, at bytes 8-23 of a 26-byte file footer. The original TGA format (prior to September 1989) had no footer, so it is possible that valid—but old—TGA files have no signature. Old-format TGA files should, however, have a valid image type: we'll accept types 1 (uncompressed color-mapped image), 2 (uncompressed true-color image), 3 (uncompressed black-and-white image), 9 (run-length encoded, color-mapped image), 10 (run-length encoded, true-color image), and 11 (run-length encoded, black-and-white image) as valid.

I based my code for reading TARGA files primarily on **read_tga**, written by Ian J. MacPhedran of the University of Saskatchewan for Michael Mauldin's Fuzzy BitMap library. Fltga.c contains the source for **read_tga** and **write_tga**, and resides in the tga directory of the companion disks. I found the Truevision technical manual useful in understanding the code. I had to change **fltga** to use **GlobalAlloc()** instead of **malloc()**; I also had to change the target image from Mauldin's FBM to a Windows DIB, and change all the error handling to conform with Windows practice.

Even though I started with **read_tga**, my initial **tgaview** routine did not work properly: the tops of the images did not display, and some files displayed in vertical bands of red, green, and blue. We'll track this error down in Chapter 6, as an example of how to use a debugger effectively.

VICAR and Other Government Formats

VICAR (Video Image Communication and Retrieval), FITS (Flexible Image Transport), and PDS (Planetary Data Sciences) ODL (Object Description Language) formats are labels used for astronomy image interchange. They are either used as ASCII headers for binary files containing image data, or as separate files. In the latter case they contain a pointer to the actual data file.

The capability to read VICAR and related formats is interesting because there is a great wealth of satellite images available quite cheaply on CD-ROM. All the Viking and Voyager pictures of the solar system are available in this format; so is a lot of Landsat, air reconnaissance, and side-looking radar data. I obtained the SIGCAT/GRIPS CD-ROM from Meridian Data (reachable at 703-620-4200) for about $10; it contains lots of planetary and earth images, as well as PC and Mac programs to read and display the images.

The PC imaging program, IMDISP, was the basis for my Windows code to convert VICAR and other labeled binary images to DIBs. IMDISP and the other source code supplied on this CD-ROM also have interesting examples of image-processing code. The test image of Saturn (SATURN.IMG in the VICAR subdirectory) is one of the smaller files on the CD-ROM, at 600KB (800x800 with 8 bits of gray-scale); the largest image, a satellite photo of the Washington, D.C. area from SPOT, is 85 MB. Needless to say, I haven't included the SPOT photo on the *Advanced Windows Programming* companion disks.

Planetary data is typically taken in 256 shades of gray. On rare occasions, the same image is scanned in three wavebands to make a color image. More often, the gray-scale is viewed with a variety of palettes: pseudocolor palettes to bring out geographical features, continuous-color palettes to approximate the actual colors. The Saturn image supplied is often displayed with a palette that ranges from dark red, through orange, to white. IMDISP has facilities for loading palettes independent of images, for histogramming the range of intensity values in the image, and for mapping data values to palette entries.

It took about two days to extract and adapt the relevant portions of IMDISP for use in **ShowIMG**. The memory allocation had to be changed from **malloc()** to **GlobalAlloc()** and **GlobalLock()**; buffers had to be passed with far or huge pointers; and error reporting had to be changed to use message boxes. All in all, the conversion was fairly smooth, with few surprises. As expected, the order of scan-lines had to be reversed for correct storage as a DIB.

RAW Image Formats

Not every image needs a fancy format. One way to handle 24-bit data is simply to write a file of the RGB values pixel by pixel and line by line. For instance, Kodak supplied sample images from the PhotoCD process with 8 bits per color, pixel interleaved, and no header information. Four pictures were contained on one CD-ROM disc, each at three resolutions: 768x512, 1536x1024, and 3072x2048. Kodak uses a file type of RGB to identify these images; I also allow the file type RAW in the ShowIMG program.

RAW to DIB conversion is simply a matter of getting the image size and reading the file. Because most raw images are stored top to bottom while DIBs keep their lines bottom to top, the code in raw.c reverses the order of the scan-lines. And because most raw images have pixel colors in red-green-blue order while DIBs store their colors blue-green-red, the code also exchanges the red and blue bytes of each triplet.

I have supported two 24-bit RAW formats (pixel interleaved, and planar) and allowed for a third (line interleaved) in Image2; the code in ShowImg allows for only pixel-interleaved format. Should you encounter other raw image file formats that you'd like to support, it should be a simple matter to add options to the code and appropriate controls to the dialog box.

The one problem I found with RAW files seems to be a driver or Windows kernel problem. Kodak's images are big and have a lot of colors; they display quickly using a "hi-color" mode capable of displaying 32,768 colors, but may seem to hang Windows if you try to display them in a 256-color mode. They aren't really hanging: if you wait long enough, Windows will come back from realizing the image against the current 256-color palette.

Some scanned images come in RAW format, as well. Files barefoot.bmp and motherhd.bmp (see plates) were scanned from my negatives, and saved in raw planar format; I converted them to BMP format using Image2.

ShowIMG: Highlights of the Program

The complete code and resources for ShowIMG can be found on the companion disks. In the printed listings below we include only functions of special interest.

showimg.rc

```
#include "windows.h"
#include "showimg.h"
#include "rawdlg.h"
#include "showimg.dlg"

SHOWICON ICON showimg.ico

showimg MENU
      BEGIN
      POPUP "&File"
            BEGIN
            MENUITEM "&Open...",          IDM_OPEN
            MENUITEM "&Save...",          IDM_SAVE
            MENUITEM "&Print",            IDM_PRINT
            MENUITEM SEPARATOR
            MENUITEM "E&xit",             IDM_EXIT
            END
      POPUP "&Edit"
            BEGIN
            MENUITEM "&Paste DIB",        IDM_PASTEDIB
            MENUITEM "&Paste DDB",        IDM_PASTEDDB
            MENUITEM "&Paste Palette",    IDM_PASTEPAL
            MENUITEM "&Copy",             IDM_COPY
            END
      POPUP  "&Help"
            BEGIN
            MENUITEM        "&Index",       IDM_HELP_INDEX
            MENUITEM        "&Keyboard",    IDM_HELP_KEYBOARD
            MENUITEM        "Using &Help",  IDM_HELP_HELP
            MENUITEM        SEPARATOR
            MENUITEM        "&About...",    IDM_ABOUT
            END
      END

rcinclude about.dlg
rcinclude rawdlg.dlg
```

showimg.h

```
#ifdef _MT
#define _FAR_ _far
#else
#define _FAR_
#endif
#ifndef _VA_LIST_DEFINED
typedef char _FAR_ *va_list;
#define _VA_LIST_DEFINED
#endif
/* Macro to restrict a given value to an upper or lower boundary
      value */
```

```
#define BOUND(x,min,max) ((x) < (min) ? (min) : ((x) > (max) ? (max) :
(x)))
/* Macro to swap two values */
#define SWAP(x,y)    ((x)^=(y)^=(x)^=(y))
/* Macro to find the minimum of two values */
#define MIN(x,y) (((x) <= (y)) : x ? y)
/* Macros to display/remove hourglass cursor */
#define StartWait() hcurSave =
SetCursor(hCursor=LoadCursor(NULL,IDC_WAIT));\
                    bAbortRequested=FALSE
#define EndWait()   SetCursor(hCursor=hcurSave)
#define MINBAND       50 /* Minimum band size used by the program */
#define BANDINCREMENT      20 /* Decrement for band size while
                            trying  to determine optimum band size. */
/* Bit values for the DIB attributes flag (fFileOptions). Also used as
control IDs for the radiobuttons for DIB bitcount in the File/Open
dialog */
#define F_1BPP         DLGOPEN_1BPP
#define F_4BPP         DLGOPEN_4BPP
#define F_8BPP         DLGOPEN_8BPP
#define F_24BPP        DLGOPEN_24BPP
/* Bit values for the DIB attributes flag (fFileOptions), also used as
control IDs for the radiobuttons for DIB compression type in the File/
Open dialog */
#define F_RLE4         DLGOPEN_RLE4
#define F_RLE8         DLGOPEN_RLE8
#define F_RGB  DLGOPEN_RGB
#ifndef SEEK_CUR
/* flags for _lseek */
#define     SEEK_CUR 1
#define     SEEK_END 2
#define     SEEK_SET 0
#endif
/* struct to be passed in for the SETDIBSCALING printer escape */
typedef struct {
     short ScaleMode;
     short dx, dy;
} DIBPARAMS;
/* Menu IDs */
#define IDM_OPEN               1002
#define IDM_EXIT               1003
#define IDM_ABOUT              1004
#define IDM_PRINT       1010
#define IDM_COPY               1012
#define IDM_MEMORYDIB          1014
#define IDM_SAVE               1015
#define IDM_PASTEDIB    1020
#define IDM_PASTEDDB    1021
#define IDM_PASTEPAL    1022
#define IDM_HELP_INDEX         1090
#define IDM_HELP_KEYBOARD      1091
#define IDM_HELP_HELP          1092
#define IDI_APP                2000
```

```
#define ABOUTBOX                        100
#define RAWDLG                          110
extern HWND hWndApp;  /* The handle to the app. window      */
#define MAXREAD  32768         /* Number of bytes to be read during */
                               /* each read operation.      */
/* Header signatures for various resources */
#define BFT_ICON        0x4349 /* 'IC' */
#define BFT_BITMAP 0x4d42       /* 'BM' */
#define BFT_CURSOR 0x5450       /* 'PT' */
/* macro to determine if resource is a DIB */
#define ISDIB(bft) ((bft) == BFT_BITMAP)
/* Macro to align given value to the closest DWORD (unsigned long) */
#define ALIGNULONG(i)         ((i+3)/4*4)
/* Macro to determine to round off the given value to the closest
byte */
#define WIDTHBYTES(i)         ((i+31)/32*4)
#define PALVERSION               0x300
#define MAXPALETTE    256        /* max. # supported palette entries */
/********** THE FOLLOWING ARE USED IN DLGOPEN.C ***************/
/* IDs for controls in the DlgOpen dialog */
#define DLGOPEN_EDIT            101
#define DLGOPEN_FILE_LISTBOX 102
#define DLGOPEN_DIR_LISTBOX 103
#define DLGOPEN_PATH           104
#define DLGOPEN_TEXT           105
#define DLGOPEN_FOLDOUT            106
#define DLGOPEN_BIG                107
#define DLGOPEN_SMALL              108
#define DLGOPEN_OPTION             0xF000
#define DLGOPEN_1BPP         0x0001
#define DLGOPEN_4BPP         0x0002
#define DLGOPEN_8BPP         0x0004
#define DLGOPEN_24BPP              0x0008
#define DLGOPEN_RLE4         0x0010
#define DLGOPEN_RLE8         0x0020
#define DLGOPEN_RGB                0x0040
#define DLGOPEN_OPTION8            0x0080
/*  flags:
 *      The LOWORD is the standard FileOpen() flags (OF_*)
 *      the HIWORD can be any of the following:
 */
#define OF_MUSTEXIST 0x00010000             /* file must exist if the
                                            user hits Ok   */
#define OF_NOSHOWSPEC       0x00020000      /* DO NOT Show search spec
                                            in the edit box*/
#define OF_SHOWSPEC  0x00000000             /* Show the search spec in
                                            the edit box   */
#define OF_SAVE      0x00040000  /* Ok button will say "Save" */
#define OF_OPEN      0x00080000  /* Ok button will say "Open" */
#define OF_NOOPTIONS 0x00100000  /* Disable the options fold out */
/* Attributes for DlgDirLst() */
#define ATTRFILELIST 0x0000 /* include files only */
#define ATTRDIRLIST  0xC010  /* directories and drives ONLY */
```

```
#define CBEXTMAX       6        /* Number of bytes in "\*.txt" */
#define IDF(id)          ((id) & ~DLGOPEN_OPTION)
                         /* extracts flag from control ID */
#define FID(f)           ((f)  |  DLGOPEN_OPTION)
                         /* extracts control ID from flag */
/**************** GLOBAL VARIABLES ************************/
extern char   achFileName[128]; /* File pathname    */
extern DWORD dwOffset; /* Current position if DIB file pointer  */
extern RECT   rcClip;/* Current clip rectangle */
extern BOOL   fPalColors; /* TRUE if the current DIB's color table
               contains palette indexes not rgb values */
extern BOOL   bDIBToDevice; /* Use SetDIBitsToDevice() to BLT data*/
extern BOOL   bLegitDraw;   /* We have a valid bitmap to draw   */
extern WORD   wTransparent; /* Mode of DC */
extern char   szAppName[];  /* App. name */
extern HPALETTE hpalCurrent; /* Handle to current palette      */
extern HANDLE hdibCurrent; /* Handle to current memory DIB      */
extern HBITMAP hbmCurrent;  /* Handle to current memory BITMAP*/
extern HANDLE hbiCurrent; /* Handle to current bitmap info struct*/
extern DWORD  dwStyle; /* Style bits of the App. window  */
extern int file_format; /* Identifies type of raster file */
#define FI_DIB 0
#define FI_GIF 1
#define FI_TIF 2
#define FI_TGA 3
#define FI_PCX 4
#define FI_VICAR 5
#define FI_RAW 6
extern BOOL bAbortRequested;
extern HCURSOR hCursor;
/**************** FUNCTION DECLARATIONS ******************/
DWORD PASCAL lread(int fh, VOID FAR *pv, DWORD ul);
DWORD PASCAL lwrite(int fh, VOID FAR *pv, DWORD ul);
/********************************************************/
/* Declarations of functions used in showimg.c module    */
/********************************************************/
long   FAR PASCAL WndProc  (HWND, unsigned, WORD, LONG) ;
BOOL   MenuCommand (HWND hWnd, WORD wParam);
int    InitDIB (HWND);
void   FreeDib (void);
int    identify_file_format(void);
BOOL   SpinTheMessageLoop(void);
/********************************************************/
/* Declarations of functions used in dib.c module         */
/********************************************************/
HANDLE        OpenDIB (LPSTR szFile);
BOOL          WriteDIB (LPSTR szFile,HANDLE hdib);
WORD          PaletteSize (VOID FAR * pv);
WORD          DibNumColors (VOID FAR * pv);
HPALETTE      CreateDibPalette (HANDLE hdib);
HPALETTE      CreateBIPalette (LPBITMAPINFOHEADER lpbi);
HANDLE        DibFromBitmap (HBITMAP hbm, DWORD biStyle,
                      WORD biBits, HPALETTE hpal);
```

```
HANDLE           BitmapFromDib (HANDLE hdib, HPALETTE hpal);
BOOL             DibBlt (HDC hdc, int x0, int y0, int dx, int dy,
                     HANDLE hdib, int x1, int y1, LONG rop);
BOOL             StretchDibBlt (HDC hdc, int x0, int y0, int dx,
                     int dy, HANDLE hdib, int x1, int y1, int dx1,
                  int dy1, LONG rop);
BOOL             DibInfo (HANDLE hdib,LPBITMAPINFOHEADER lpbi);
HANDLE           ReadDibBitmapInfo (int fh);
BOOL             DrawBitmap (HDC hdc, int x, int y, HBITMAP hbm,
                          DWORD rop);
/*************************************************************/
/* Declarations of functions used in drawdib. c module      */
/*************************************************************/
void             PrintDIB (HWND hWnd, HDC hDC, int x, int y, int
dx, int dy);
void             AppPaint (HWND hWnd, HDC hDC, int x, int y);
int              ErrMsg (PSTR sz,...);
BOOL             fDialog (int id, HWND hwnd, FARPROC fpfn);
void             BandDIB (HWND hWnd, HDC hDC, int x, int y);
BOOL     FAR PASCAL AppAbout (HWND, unsigned, WORD, LONG) ;
HANDLE           CopyHandle (HANDLE h);
void             SizeWindow (HWND hWnd);
void             GetRealClientRect (HWND hwnd, PRECT lprc);
void             SetScrollRanges (HWND hwnd);
void             DrawSelect (HDC hdc, BOOL fDraw);
void     PASCAL NormalizeRect (RECT *prc);
void             TrackMouse (HWND hwnd, POINT pt);
HBITMAP          CopyBitmap (HBITMAP hbm);
HPALETTE         CopyPalette (HPALETTE hpal);
HBITMAP          CropBitmap (HBITMAP hbm, PRECT prc);
HANDLE           RenderFormat (int cf);
HANDLE           RealizeDibFormat (DWORD biStyle, WORD biBits);
/*************************************************************/
/* Declarations of functions used in the print.c module    */
/*************************************************************/
BOOL    PASCAL InitPrinting (HDC hDC, HWND hWnd, HANDLE hInst,
                          LPSTR msg);
void    PASCAL TermPrinting (HDC hDC);
HDC     PASCAL GetPrinterDC (void);
/*************************************************************/
/* Declarations of functions used in the dlgopen.c module   */
/*************************************************************/
int FAR PASCAL DlgfnOpen();
int FAR PASCAL DlgOpenFile (
     HWND           hwndParent,
     char           *szTitle,
     DWORD          flags,
     char           *szExtIn,
     char           *szFileNameIn,
     WORD           *pfOpt
);
/* Global Declarations for GIF.C module */
int    get_byte(void);
```

```
void    putcolor(int x,int y,int  color);
int     put_line(int rownum,int leftpt,int rightpt,
               unsigned char *localvalues);
int     out_line(unsigned char *localvalues,int numberofdots);
void    spindac(int direction,int step);
int     gifview(HWND hWnd);
short decoder(short linewidth);
/* Debugging Stuff */
void OkMsgBox (char *szCaption, char *szFormat, ...);
/* PCX, TGA, TIFF, VICAR, and RAW stuff */
int   pcxview(HWND hWnd);
int   vicarview(unsigned int  hWnd);
int   rawview(unsigned int    hWnd);
int   tiffview(unsigned int   hWnd);
int   tgaview(unsigned int    hWnd);
/* used in TIFF modules and in standard includes: */
#define _WINDOWS 1
```

showimg.c

```
//ShowIMG
//From Advanced Windows Programming
//by Martin Heller
//Copyright (c) 1991 John Wiley & Sons, Inc. All rights reserved.

//Credits: built starting with Microsoft's ShowDIB example program
//      GIF code adapted from FRACTINT, by The Stone Soup Group
//      TGA code adapted from FLTGA by Ian J. MacPhedran
//      TIFF code adapted from Sam Leffler's TIFF library
#define NOCOMM
#define NOKANJI
#include <windows.h>
#include "showimg.h"
#include <io.h>
#include <stdio.h>
#include <string.h>
DIBPARAMS     DIBParams;      /* params for the SETSCALING escape */
char          achFileName[128] = "";
DWORD         dwOffset;
NPLOGPALETTE pLogPal;
HPALETTE      hpalSave = NULL;
HANDLE        hInst;
RECT          rcClip;
static HCURSOR hcurSave;
BOOL fPalColors = FALSE; /* TRUE if the current DIB's color table
      contains palette indexes not rgb values */
WORD    UpdateCount = 0;
BOOL    bMemoryDIB = FALSE; /* Load Entire DIB into memory in
                    CF_DIB format */
BOOL    bUpdateColors = TRUE;    /* Directly update screen colors */
BOOL    bDIBToDevice = FALSE; /* Use SetDIBitsToDevice() */
BOOL    bNoUgly = FALSE; /* Make window black on a
                    WM_PALETTEISCHANGING */
```

```
BOOL      bLegitDraw = FALSE; /* We have a valid bitmap */
char      szBitmapExt[]="*.BMP;*.DIB;*.RLE;*.GIF;*.TIF;*.TGA;"
                        "*.PCX;*.IMG;*.RAW;*.RGB";
WORD      wTransparent = TRANSPARENT;        /* Mode of DC */
char      szAppName[] = "ShowIMG" ;/* App. name     */
HPALETTE hpalCurrent = NULL;/* Handle to current palette  */
HANDLE hdibCurrent = NULL;    /* Handle to current memory DIB     */
HBITMAP hbmCurrent = NULL;   /* Handle to current memory BITMAP   */
HANDLE hbiCurrent = NULL;     /* Handle to curr. bitmap info struct*/
HWND         hWndApp;  /* Handle to app. window */
HCURSOR hCursor;
BOOL bCursorReset;
/* Styles of app. window */
DWORD  dwStyle = WS_OVERLAPPED | WS_CAPTION | WS_SYSMENU |
       WS_MAXIMIZEBOX | WS_MINIMIZEBOX | WS_THICKFRAME;
int file_format = FI_DIB; /* Identifies type of raster file */
BOOL bAbortRequested = FALSE;
/*
       FUNCTION      : WinMain(HANDLE, HANDLE, LPSTR, int)
       PURPOSE       : Creates the app. window and enters the message
                             loop.
 */
int PASCAL WinMain(hInstance, hPrevInstance, lpszCmdLine, nCmdShow)
HANDLE hInstance, hPrevInstance;
LPSTR   lpszCmdLine;
int    nCmdShow;
{
       HWND            hWnd;
       WNDCLASS        wndclass;
       MSG             msg;
       short           xScreen, yScreen;
       char            ach[40];

       hInst = hInstance;
         /* default to MEMORY DIB's if Protected Mode Windows */
       bMemoryDIB = GetWinFlags() & WF_PMODE;
         /* Initialize clip rectangle */
       SetRectEmpty(&rcClip);
       if (!hPrevInstance) {
              wndclass.style = CS_DBLCLKS;
              wndclass.lpfnWndProc = WndProc;
              wndclass.cbClsExtra = 0;
              wndclass.cbWndExtra = 0;
              wndclass.hInstance = hInstance;
              wndclass.hIcon = LoadIcon(hInst, "SHOWICON");
              wndclass.hCursor = NULL;
              wndclass.hbrBackground = GetStockObject(BLACK_BRUSH);
              wndclass.lpszMenuName = szAppName;
              wndclass.lpszClassName = szAppName;
              if (!RegisterClass(&wndclass))
                     return FALSE;
              }
```

```
if (!GetProfileString("extensions", "bmp", "",
            ach, sizeof (ach)))
    WriteProfileString("extensions", "bmp",
            "showimg.exe ^.bmp");
if (!GetProfileString("extensions", "dib", "",
            ach, sizeof (ach)))
    WriteProfileString("extensions", "dib",
            "showimg.exe ^.dib");
if (!GetProfileString("extensions", "rle", "",
            ach, sizeof (ach)))
    WriteProfileString("extensions", "rle",
            "showimg.exe ^.rle");
if (!GetProfileString("extensions", "gif", "",
            ach, sizeof (ach)))
    WriteProfileString("extensions", "gif",
            "showimg.exe ^.gif");
if (!GetProfileString("extensions", "tga", "",
            ach, sizeof (ach)))
    WriteProfileString("extensions", "tga",
            "showimg.exe ^.tga");
if (!GetProfileString("extensions", "pcx", "",
            ach, sizeof (ach)))
    WriteProfileString("extensions", "pcx",
            "showimg.exe ^.pcx");
if (!GetProfileString("extensions", "tif", "",
            ach, sizeof (ach)))
    WriteProfileString("extensions", "tif",
            "showimg.exe ^.tif");
if (!GetProfileString("extensions", "raw", "",
            ach, sizeof (ach)))
    WriteProfileString("extensions", "raw",
            "showimg.exe ^.raw");
if (!GetProfileString("extensions", "rgb", "",
            ach, sizeof (ach)))
    WriteProfileString("extensions", "rgb",
            "showimg.exe ^.rgb");
if (!GetProfileString("extensions", "img", "",
            ach, sizeof (ach)))
    WriteProfileString("extensions", "img",
            "showimg.exe ^.img");
hCursor=LoadCursor(NULL, IDC_ARROW);
bAbortRequested=FALSE;
  /* Save the pointer to the command line */
lstrcpy(achFileName, lpszCmdLine);
xScreen = GetSystemMetrics(SM_CXSCREEN);
yScreen = GetSystemMetrics(SM_CYSCREEN);
  /* Create the app. window */
hWnd = CreateWindow(szAppName,
        szAppName,
        dwStyle,
        CW_USEDEFAULT,
        0,
        xScreen / 2,
```

```
                    yScreen / 2,
                    NULL,
                    NULL,
                    hInstance,
                    NULL);
        ShowWindow(hWndApp = hWnd, nCmdShow);
            /* Enter message loop */
        while (GetMessage(&msg, NULL, 0, 0)) {
                TranslateMessage(&msg);
                DispatchMessage(&msg);
                }
        return msg.wParam;
}
/*

        FUNCTION      : WndProc (hWnd, iMessage, wParam, lParam)
        PURPOSE               : Processes window messages.
*/
long    FAR PASCAL WndProc(hWnd, iMessage, wParam, lParam)
HWND            hWnd;
unsigned iMessage;
WORD            wParam;
LONG            lParam;
{
        PAINTSTRUCT             ps;
        HDC                             hDC;
        HANDLE                  h;
        int                             i;
        int                             iMax;
        int                             iMin;
        int                             iPos;
        int                             dn;
        RECT                            rc, Rect;
        HPALETTE                        hOldPal;
        HMENU                           hMenu;

//This statement starts the "switch from Hell" that processes all
//messages to the main application Window
        switch (iMessage) {
  case WM_DESTROY:
                        /* Clean up and quit */
                FreeDib();
                PostQuitMessage(0);
                break;
  case WM_CREATE:
                        /* Allocate space for our logical palette */
                pLogPal = (NPLOGPALETTE) LocalAlloc(LMEM_FIXED,
                        (sizeof(LOGPALETTE) +
                        (sizeof(PALETTEENTRY) * (MAXPALETTE))));
                        /* fall through */
  case WM_WININICHANGE:
                hMenu = GetMenu(hWnd);
 /* If printer initialization succeeds, enable appropriate
 * menu item and clean up. */
```

```
                if (hDC = GetPrinterDC()) {
                        EnableMenuItem(hMenu,
                                IDM_PRINT,
                                (RC_DIBTODEV &
                                GetDeviceCaps(hDC, RASTERCAPS)) ?
                                MF_ENABLED :
                                MF_GRAYED | MF_DISABLED);
                        DeleteDC(hDC);
                        }
                break;
  case WM_PALETTEISCHANGING:
/* if ShowIMG was not responsible for palette change and if
 * ok to hide changes, paint app. window black. */
                if (wParam != hWnd && bNoUgly) {
                        GetClientRect(hWnd, &Rect);
                        hDC = GetDC(hWnd);
                        FillRect(hDC, (LPRECT) &Rect,
                                GetStockObject(BLACK_BRUSH));
                        ReleaseDC(hWnd, hDC);
                        }
                break;
  case WM_ACTIVATE:
                if (!wParam)            /* app. is being de-activated */
                        break;
/* If the app. is moving to the foreground, fall through and
 * redraw full client area with the newly realized palette,
 * if the palette has changed.          */
  case WM_QUERYNEWPALETTE:
/* If palette realization causes a palette change,
 * we need to do a full redraw.         */
                if (bLegitDraw) {
                        hDC = GetDC(hWnd);
                        hOldPal = SelectPalette(hDC, hpalCurrent, 0);
                        i = RealizePalette(hDC);
                        SelectPalette(hDC, hOldPal, 0);
                        ReleaseDC(hWnd, hDC);
                        if (i) {
                                InvalidateRect(hWnd, (LPRECT) (NULL), 1);
                                UpdateCount = 0;
                                return 1;
                                }
                        else
                                return FALSE;
                        }
                else
                        return FALSE;
                break;
  case WM_PALETTECHANGED:
/* if ShowIMG was not responsible for palette change and if
 * palette realization causes a palette change, do a redraw.*/
                if (wParam != hWnd) {
                        if (bLegitDraw) {
                                hDC = GetDC(hWnd);
```

```
                                        hOldPal = SelectPalette(hDC,
                                                        hpalCurrent, 0);
                                        i = RealizePalette(hDC);
                                        if (i) {
                                                if (bUpdateColors) {
                                                        UpdateColors(hDC);
                                                        UpdateCount++;
                                                        }
                                                else
                                                        InvalidateRect(hWnd,
                                                                (LPRECT) (NULL), 1);
                                                }
                                        SelectPalette(hDC, hOldPal, 0);
                                        ReleaseDC(hWnd, hDC);
                                        }
                                }
                        break;
                case WM_RENDERALLFORMATS:
                /* Ensure that clipboard data can be rendered even though
                 * app. is being destroyed. */
                        SendMessage(hWnd, WM_RENDERFORMAT, CF_DIB, 0L);
                        SendMessage(hWnd, WM_RENDERFORMAT, CF_BITMAP, 0L);
                        SendMessage(hWnd, WM_RENDERFORMAT, CF_PALETTE, 0L);
                        break;
                case WM_RENDERFORMAT:
                /* Format data in manner specified and pass the data
                 * handle to clipboard.  */
                        if (h = RenderFormat(wParam))
                                SetClipboardData(wParam, h);
                        break;
                case WM_COMMAND:
                /* Process menu commands */
                        return MenuCommand(hWnd, wParam);
        //Note that the above keeps the cyclomatic complexity reasonable.
                        break;
                case WM_TIMER:
                        break;
                case WM_PAINT:
                /* If we have updated more than once, the rest of our
                 * window is not in some level of degradation worse than
                 * our redraw...        we need to redraw the whole area */
                        if (UpdateCount > 1) {
                                BeginPaint(hWnd, &ps);
                                EndPaint(hWnd, &ps);
                                UpdateCount = 0;
                                InvalidateRect(hWnd, (LPRECT) (NULL), 1);
                                break;
                                }
                        hDC = BeginPaint(hWnd, &ps);
                        AppPaint(hWnd,
                                hDC,
                                GetScrollPos(hWnd, SB_HORZ),
                                GetScrollPos(hWnd, SB_VERT));
```

```
                    EndPaint(hWnd, &ps);
                    break;
  case WM_SIZE:
                    SetScrollRanges(hWnd);
                    break;
  case WM_KEYDOWN:
/* Translate keyboard messages to scroll commands */
                switch (wParam) {
        case VK_UP:
                        PostMessage(hWnd, WM_VSCROLL, SB_LINEUP, 0L);
                        break;
        case VK_DOWN:
                        PostMessage(hWnd, WM_VSCROLL, SB_LINEDOWN, 0L);
                        break;
        case VK_PRIOR:
                        PostMessage(hWnd, WM_VSCROLL, SB_PAGEUP, 0L);
                        break;
        case VK_NEXT:
                        PostMessage(hWnd, WM_VSCROLL, SB_PAGEDOWN, 0L);
                        break;
        case VK_HOME:
                        PostMessage(hWnd, WM_HSCROLL, SB_PAGEUP, 0L);
                        break;
        case VK_END:
                        PostMessage(hWnd, WM_HSCROLL, SB_PAGEDOWN, 0L);
                        break;
        case VK_LEFT:
                        PostMessage(hWnd, WM_HSCROLL, SB_LINEUP, 0L);
                        break;
        case VK_RIGHT:
                        PostMessage(hWnd, WM_HSCROLL, SB_LINEDOWN, 0L);
                        break;
                        }
                break;
  case WM_KEYUP:
                switch (wParam) {
        case VK_UP:
        case VK_DOWN:
        case VK_PRIOR:
        case VK_NEXT:
                        PostMessage(hWnd, WM_VSCROLL, SB_ENDSCROLL, 0L);
                        break;
        case VK_HOME:
        case VK_END:
        case VK_LEFT:
        case VK_RIGHT:
                        PostMessage(hWnd, WM_HSCROLL, SB_ENDSCROLL, 0L);
                        break;
                        }
                break;
     case WM_CHAR:
                switch(wParam) {
```

```
                    case VK_ESCAPE:
                        bAbortRequested=TRUE;
                        break;
                    }
                break;
case WM_VSCROLL:
                    /* Calculate new vertical scroll position */
                GetScrollRange(hWnd, SB_VERT, &iMin, &iMax);
                iPos = GetScrollPos(hWnd, SB_VERT);
                GetClientRect(hWnd, &rc);
                switch (wParam) {
        case SB_LINEDOWN:
                        dn = rc.bottom / 16 + 1;
                        break;
        case SB_LINEUP:
                        dn = -rc.bottom / 16 + 1;
                        break;
        case SB_PAGEDOWN:
                        dn = rc.bottom / 2 + 1;
                        break;
        case SB_PAGEUP:
                        dn = -rc.bottom / 2 + 1;
                        break;
        case SB_THUMBTRACK:
        case SB_THUMBPOSITION:
                        dn = LOWORD(lParam) - iPos;
                        break;
        default:
                        dn = 0;
                        }
                    /* Limit scrolling to current scroll range */
                if (dn = BOUND (iPos + dn, iMin, iMax) - iPos) {
                ScrollWindow(hWnd, 0, -dn, NULL, NULL);
                SetScrollPos(hWnd, SB_VERT, iPos + dn, TRUE);
                }
                break;
case WM_HSCROLL:
                    /* Calculate new horizontal scroll position */
                GetScrollRange(hWnd, SB_HORZ, &iMin, &iMax);
                iPos = GetScrollPos(hWnd, SB_HORZ);
                GetClientRect(hWnd, &rc);
                switch (wParam) {
        case SB_LINEDOWN:
                        dn = rc.right / 16 + 1;
                        break;
        case SB_LINEUP:
                        dn = -rc.right / 16 + 1;
                        break;
        case SB_PAGEDOWN:
                        dn = rc.right / 2 + 1;
                        break;
        case SB_PAGEUP:
                        dn = -rc.right / 2 + 1;
                        break;
```

```
            case SB_THUMBTRACK:
            case SB_THUMBPOSITION:
                        dn = LOWORD (lParam) - iPos;
                        break;
            default:
                        dn = 0;
                        }
                        /* Limit scrolling to current scroll range */
                if (dn = BOUND (iPos + dn, iMin, iMax) - iPos) {
                        ScrollWindow(hWnd, -dn, 0, NULL, NULL);
                        SetScrollPos(hWnd, SB_HORZ, iPos + dn, TRUE);
                        }
                break;
        case WM_NCMOUSEMOVE:
                break;
        case WM_MOUSEMOVE:
                SetCursor(hCursor);
                break;
    case WM_LBUTTONDOWN:
        /* Start rubberbanding a rect. and track it's dimensions.
         * set the clip rectangle to it's dimensions.       */
                TrackMouse(hWnd, MAKEPOINT (lParam));
                break;
    case WM_LBUTTONDBLCLK:
                break;
    case WM_INITMENU:
/* check/uncheck menu items depending on state of related flags */
                EnableMenuItem(wParam, IDM_PASTEDIB,
                        IsClipboardFormatAvailable(CF_DIB)
                            ? MF_ENABLED : MF_GRAYED);
                EnableMenuItem(wParam, IDM_PASTEDDB,
                        IsClipboardFormatAvailable(CF_BITMAP)
                            ? MF_ENABLED : MF_GRAYED);
                EnableMenuItem(wParam, IDM_PASTEPAL,
                        IsClipboardFormatAvailable(CF_PALETTE)
                            ? MF_ENABLED : MF_GRAYED);
                EnableMenuItem(wParam, IDM_PRINT,
                        bLegitDraw ? MF_ENABLED : MF_GRAYED);
                EnableMenuItem(wParam, IDM_SAVE,
                        bLegitDraw ? MF_ENABLED : MF_GRAYED);
                EnableMenuItem(wParam, IDM_COPY,
                        bLegitDraw ? MF_ENABLED : MF_GRAYED);
                break;
    default:
                return DefWindowProc(hWnd, iMessage, wParam, lParam);
                }
        return 0L;
}
/*
        FUNCTION    : MenuCommand ( HWND hWnd, WORD wParam)
        PURPOSE              : Processes menu commands.
        RETURNS                   : TRUE  - if command could be processed.
                    FALSE - otherwise
```

```
*/
BOOL MenuCommand(hWnd, id)
HWND hWnd;
WORD id;
{
        BITMAPINFOHEADER  bi;
        HDC                hDC;
        HANDLE             h;
        HBITMAP       hbm;
        HPALETTE           hpal;
        int                i;
        char               Name[40];
        BOOL               bSave;
        int                xSize, ySize, xRes, yRes, dx, dy;
        RECT               Rect;
        int                fh;
        WORD               fFileOptions;
        switch (id) {
  case IDM_ABOUT:
                                            /* Show About .. box */
                fDialog(ABOUTBOX, hWnd, AppAbout);
                break;
  case IDM_COPY:
                if (!bLegitDraw)
                        return 0L;
                                         /* Clean clipboard of contents */
                if (OpenClipboard(hWnd)) {
                        EmptyClipboard();
                        SetClipboardData(CF_DIB, NULL);
                        SetClipboardData(CF_BITMAP, NULL);
                        SetClipboardData(CF_PALETTE, NULL);
                        CloseClipboard();
                        }
                break;
  case IDM_PASTEPAL:
                if (OpenClipboard(hWnd)) {
                        if (h = GetClipboardData(CF_PALETTE)) {
/* Delete current palette and get the CF_PALETTE data
 * from the clipboard */
                                if (hpalCurrent)
                                        DeleteObject(hpalCurrent);
                                hpalCurrent = CopyPalette(h);
/* If we have a bitmap realized against the old palette
 * delete the bitmap and rebuild it using the new palette.      */
                                if (hbmCurrent) {
                                        DeleteObject(hbmCurrent);
                                        hbmCurrent = NULL;
                                        if (hdibCurrent)
                                                hbmCurrent =
                                                BitmapFromDib(hdibCurrent,
                                                        hpalCurrent);
```

```
                                                    }
                                                }
                                CloseClipboard();
                                            }
                        break;
    case IDM_PASTEDIB:
                    if (OpenClipboard(hWnd)) {
                                    if (h = GetClipboardData(CF_DIB)) {
/* Delete current DIB and get CF_DIB and CF_PALETTE format data
        from the clipboard      */
                                        hpal = GetClipboardData(CF_PALETTE);
                                        FreeDib();
                                        hdibCurrent = CopyHandle(h);
                                        if (hdibCurrent) {
                                          bLegitDraw = TRUE;
                                          lstrcpy(achFileName, <Clipboard>");
                                          hbiCurrent = hdibCurrent;
/* If there is a CF_PALETTE object in the
 * clipboard, this is the palette to assume
 * the DIB should be realized against, otherwise
 * create a palette for it.
 */
                                          if (hpal)
                                           hpalCurrent = CopyPalette(hpal);
                                          else
                                           hpalCurrent =
                                                CreateDibPalette(hdibCurrent);
                                          SizeWindow(hWnd);
                                          }
                                        else {
                                          bLegitDraw = FALSE;
                                          ErrMsg("No Memory Available!");
                                          }
                                        }
                                CloseClipboard();
                                }
                        break;
    case IDM_PASTEDDB:
                    if (OpenClipboard(hWnd)) {
                            if (hbm = GetClipboardData(CF_BITMAP)) {
                                    hpal = GetClipboardData(CF_PALETTE);
                                    FreeDib();
/* If there is a CF_PALETTE object in the
 * clipboard, this is the palette to assume
 * the bitmap is realized against. */
                                    if (hpal)
                                     hpalCurrent = CopyPalette(hpal);
                                    else
                                     hpalCurrent =
                                            GetStockObject(DEFAULT_PALETTE);
                                    hdibCurrent = DibFromBitmap(hbm, BI_RGB,
                                            0, hpalCurrent);
                                    if (hdibCurrent) {
                                            bLegitDraw = TRUE;
```

```
                                        lstrcpy(achFileName,"<Clipboard>");
                                        hbiCurrent = hdibCurrent;
                                        if (bMemoryDIB)
                                                hbmCurrent =
                                BitmapFromDib(hdibCurrent, hpalCurrent);
                                        SizeWindow(hWnd);
                                        }
                                else {
                                        bLegitDraw = FALSE;
                                        ErrMsg("No Memory Available!");
                                        }
                                }
                        CloseClipboard();
                        }
                break;
        case IDM_PRINT:
                GetWindowText(hWnd, Name, sizeof (Name));
                DibInfo(hbiCurrent, &bi);
                if (!IsRectEmpty(&rcClip)) {
                        bi.biWidth = rcClip.right - rcClip.left;
                        bi.biHeight = rcClip.bottom - rcClip.top;
                        }
                 /* Initialise printer stuff */
                if (!(hDC = GetPrinterDC()))
                        break;
                xSize = GetDeviceCaps(hDC, HORZRES);
                ySize = GetDeviceCaps(hDC, VERTRES);
                xRes = GetDeviceCaps(hDC, LOGPIXELSX);
                yRes = GetDeviceCaps(hDC, LOGPIXELSY);
/* Use half inch margins on left and right
 * and one inch on top. Maintain the same aspect ratio. */
                dx = xSize - xRes;
                dy = (int) ((long) dx * bi.biHeight / bi.biWidth);
/* Fix bounding rectangle for the picture .. */
                Rect.top = yRes;
                Rect.left = xRes / 2;
                Rect.bottom = yRes + dy;
                Rect.right = xRes / 2 + dx;
/* ... and inform the driver */
                Escape(hDC, SET_BOUNDS, sizeof(RECT),
                                (LPSTR) &Rect, NULL);
                bSave = TRUE;
                if (InitPrinting(hDC, hWnd, hInst, Name)) {
                        PrintDIB(hWnd, hDC, xRes / 2, yRes, dx, dy);
/* Signal to the driver to begin translating the drawing
 * commands to printer output...      */
                        Escape(hDC, NEWFRAME, NULL, NULL, NULL);
                        TermPrinting(hDC);
                        }
                DeleteDC(hDC);
                break;
        case IDM_OPEN:
                 /* Bring up File/Open ... dialog */
```

```
            fh = DlgOpenFile(hWnd,
                "Select an image to display",
                (LONG) OF_EXIST | OF_MUSTEXIST | OF_NOOPTIONS,
                szBitmapExt,
                achFileName,
                NULL
                );
/*  Load up the DIB or other format if the user did not cancel */
            if (fh > 0) {
                file_format = identify_file_format();
                StartWait();
                switch (file_format) {
          case FI_GIF:
                    if (gifview(hWnd))
                        InvalidateRect(hWnd, NULL, FALSE);
                    else
                        bLegitDraw = FALSE;
                    break;
          case FI_TIF:
                    if (tiffview(hWnd))
                        InvalidateRect(hWnd, NULL, FALSE);
                    else
                        bLegitDraw = FALSE;
                    break;
          case FI_TGA:
                    if (tgaview(hWnd))
                        InvalidateRect(hWnd, NULL, FALSE);
                    else
                        bLegitDraw = FALSE;
                    break;
          case FI_VICAR:
                    if (vicarview(hWnd))
                        InvalidateRect(hWnd, NULL, FALSE);
                    else
                        bLegitDraw = FALSE;
                    break;
          case FI_PCX:
                    if (pcxview(hWnd))
                        InvalidateRect(hWnd, NULL, FALSE);
                    else
                        bLegitDraw = FALSE;
                    break;
          case FI_RAW:
                    if (rawview(hWnd))
                        InvalidateRect(hWnd, NULL, FALSE);
                    else
                        bLegitDraw = FALSE;
                    break;
          case FI_DIB:
          default:
                    if (InitDIB(hWnd))
                        InvalidateRect(hWnd, NULL, FALSE);
                    else
                        bLegitDraw = FALSE;
```

```
                                        break;
                                    }
                             EndWait();
                           }
                    break;
   case IDM_SAVE:
                    DibInfo(hbiCurrent, &bi);
                    fFileOptions = 0;
/* Depending on compression type for current DIB,
 * set the appropriate bit in the fFileOptions flag        */
                    if (bi.biCompression == BI_RGB)
                            fFileOptions |= F_RGB;
                    else if (bi.biCompression == BI_RLE4)
                            fFileOptions |= F_RLE4;
                    else if (bi.biCompression == BI_RLE8)
                            fFileOptions |= F_RLE8;
/* Depending on bits/pixel type for current DIB,
 * set the appropriate bit in the fFileOptions flag        */
                    switch (bi.biBitCount) {
            case 1:
                            fFileOptions |= F_1BPP;
                            break;
            case 4:
                            fFileOptions |= F_4BPP;
                            break;
            case 8:
                            fFileOptions |= F_8BPP;
                            break;
            case 24:
                            fFileOptions |= F_24BPP;
                           }
/* Bring up File/Save... dialog and get info. about filename,
 * compression, and bits/pix. of DIB to be written. */
                    fh = DlgOpenFile(hWnd,
                            "Select File in which to save image",
                            (LONG) OF_EXIST | OF_SAVE | OF_NOSHOWSPEC,
                            szBitmapExt,
                            achFileName,
                            &fFileOptions);
/* Extract DIB specs. if the user did not press cancel */
                    if (fh != 0) {
                            if (fFileOptions & F_RGB)
                                    bi.biCompression = BI_RGB;
                            if (fFileOptions & F_RLE4)
                                    bi.biCompression = BI_RLE4;
                            if (fFileOptions & F_RLE8)
                                    bi.biCompression = BI_RLE8;
                            if (fFileOptions & F_1BPP)
                                    bi.biBitCount = 1;
                            if (fFileOptions & F_4BPP)
                                    bi.biBitCount = 4;
                            if (fFileOptions & F_8BPP)
                                    bi.biBitCount = 8;
```

```
                          if (fFileOptions & F_24BPP)
                                bi.biBitCount = 24;
/* Realize a DIB in the specified format and obtain a
 * handle to it. */
                          hdibCurrent = RealizeDibFormat(bi.biCompression,
                                                bi.biBitCount);
                          if (!hdibCurrent) {
                           ErrMsg("Unable to save the specified file");
                           return 0L;
                           }
                                        /* Write the DIB */
                          StartWait();
                          if (!WriteDIB(achFileName, hdibCurrent))
                           ErrMsg("Unable to save the specified file");
                          EndWait();
                          }
              break;
      case IDM_EXIT:
              PostMessage(hWnd, WM_SYSCOMMAND, SC_CLOSE, 0L);
              break;
      default:
              break;
              }
       return TRUE;
}
/*      FUNCTION     : InitDIB(hWnd)
        PURPOSE      : Reads a DIB from a file, obtains a handle to
               its BITMAPINFO struct, sets up the palette and loads
               the DIB. *
        RETURNS          : TRUE  - DIB loads ok
                          FALSE - otherwise

*/
int InitDIB(hWnd)
HWND hWnd;
{
      unsigned                  fh;
      LPBITMAPINFOHEADER        lpbi;
      WORD FAR *                pw;
      int                       i;
      BITMAPINFOHEADER          bi;
      OFSTRUCT                  of;
      FreeDib();
       /* Open the file and get a handle to its BITMAPINFO */
      fh = OpenFile(achFileName, (LPOFSTRUCT) &of, OF_READ);
      if (fh == -1) {
              ErrMsg("Can't open file '%ls'", (LPSTR) achFileName);
              return FALSE;
              }
      hbiCurrent = ReadDibBitmapInfo(fh);
      dwOffset = _llseek(fh, 0L, SEEK_CUR);
      _lclose(fh);
      if (hbiCurrent == NULL) {
```

```
                        ErrMsg("%ls is not a Legitimate DIB File!",
                                (LPSTR) achFileName);
                        return FALSE;
                        }
        DibInfo(hbiCurrent, &bi);
          /* Set up the palette */
        hpalCurrent = CreateDibPalette(hbiCurrent);
        if (hpalCurrent == NULL) {
                        ErrMsg("CreatePalette() Failed");
                        return FALSE;
                        }
/*  Convert the DIB color table to palette relative indexes, so
 *  SetDIBits() and SetDIBitsToDevice() can avoid color matching.
 *  We can do this because the palette we realize is identical
 *  to the color table of the bitmap, ie the indexes match 1 to 1
 *
 *  Now that the DIB color table is palette indexes not RGB values
 *  we must use DIB_PAL_COLORS as the wUsage parameter to
 *  SetDIBits()
 */
        lpbi = (VOID FAR *) GlobalLock(hbiCurrent);
        if (lpbi->biBitCount != 24) {
                fPalColors = TRUE;
                pw = (WORD FAR *) ((LPSTR) lpbi + lpbi->biSize);
                for (i = 0;  i < (int) lpbi->biClrUsed;  i++)
                        *pw++ = (WORD) i;
                }
        GlobalUnlock(hbiCurrent);
        bLegitDraw = TRUE;
/*  If the input bitmap is not in RGB FORMAT the banding code will
 *  not work! we need to load the DIB bits into memory.
 *  if memory DIB, load it all NOW!  This will avoid calling the
 *  banding code.
 */
        if (bMemoryDIB || bi.biCompression != BI_RGB)
                hdibCurrent = OpenDIB(achFileName);
/* If the RLE could not be loaded all at once, exit gracefully NOW,
 *  to avoid calling the banding code
 */
        if ((bi.biCompression != BI_RGB) && !hdibCurrent) {
                ErrMsg("Could not load RLE!");
                FreeDib();
                return FALSE;
                }
        if (hdibCurrent && !bDIBToDevice && bMemoryDIB) {
                hbmCurrent = BitmapFromDib(hdibCurrent, hpalCurrent);
                if (!hbmCurrent) {
                        ErrMsg("Could not create bitmap!");
                        bDIBToDevice = TRUE; //mh: adapt to conditions!
                        }
                }
        SizeWindow(hWnd);
        return TRUE;
```

```
}
/*      FUNCTION      : FreeDib(void)
        PURPOSE       : Frees all currently active bitmap, DIB and
                        palette objects and initializes their handles.
*/
void FreeDib(void){
        if (hpalCurrent)
                DeleteObject(hpalCurrent);
        if (hbmCurrent)
                DeleteObject(hbmCurrent);
        if (hdibCurrent)
                GlobalFree(hdibCurrent);
        if (hbiCurrent && hbiCurrent != hdibCurrent)
                GlobalFree(hbiCurrent);
        fPalColors = FALSE;
        bLegitDraw = FALSE;
        hpalCurrent = NULL;
        hdibCurrent = NULL;
        hbmCurrent = NULL;
        hbiCurrent = NULL;
        SetRectEmpty(&rcClip);
}
/*      FUNCTION       : identify_file_format(void)
        PURPOSE : identify file format (aren't these headers
                        superfluous when you write descriptive function
                        names?)
*/
int identify_file_format(){
        int ff = FI_DIB;                //default
                //look first at file extension
        if (strstr(achFileName, ".GIF")) {
                ff = FI_GIF;
                }
        else if (strstr(achFileName, ".PCX")) {
                ff = FI_PCX;
                }
        else if (strstr(achFileName, ".TGA")) {
                ff = FI_TGA;
                }
        else if (strstr(achFileName, ".TIF")) {
                ff = FI_TIF;
                }
        else if (strstr(achFileName, ".IMG")) {
                ff = FI_VICAR;
                }
        else if (strstr(achFileName, ".RAW")
                || strstr(achFileName, ".RGB")) {
                ff = FI_RAW;
                }
        else if (strstr(achFileName, ".DIB")
                || strstr(achFileName, ".BMP")
                || strstr(achFileName, ".RLE")) {
                ff = FI_DIB;
                }
```

```
            //if file signature matches type of extension we are all set
            //otherwise look at signature and make tentative ID (future)
            //let user approve ID if it doesn't match extension (future)
            switch (ff) {
  case FI_DIB:         //more to do here
                break;
  case FI_GIF:
                break;
  case FI_PCX:
                break;
  case FI_TGA:
                break;
  case FI_TIF:
                break;
  case FI_VICAR:
                break;
  case FI_RAW:
                break;
  default:
                OkMsgBox("ShowIMG", "Unknown file format %d", ff);
                break;
                }
        return ff;
}
//Credit: I got OkMsgBox from Charles Petzold's book,
//Programming Windows, and only changed the prototype
void OkMsgBox(char *szCaption, char *szFormat, ...){
        char szBuffer[256] ;
        char *pArguments;
        pArguments = (char *) &szFormat + sizeof (szFormat);
        vsprintf(szBuffer, szFormat, pArguments);
        MessageBox(GetActiveWindow(), szBuffer, szCaption, MB_OK);
}
// I think I'll let you take a wild guess about this function...
BOOL SpinTheMessageLoop(void)
{
        MSG msg;
        if(PeekMessage((LPMSG)&msg,NULL,0,0,PM_REMOVE)) {
                if(msg.message==WM_QUIT || msg.message==WM_PAINT)
                        return bAbortRequested;
                else
                    {
                        TranslateMessage((LPMSG)&msg);
                        DispatchMessage((LPMSG)&msg);
                        }
                }
        return bAbortRequested;
}
```

pcx.h

```
typedef struct pcxhdr {
        BYTE manu;      //10=ZSoft
```

```
        BYTE ver;       /* 0=PaintBrush 2.5
                           2= 2.8 w/palette,
                           3=  2.8 w/o palette
                           4= PC Paintbrush for Windows
                           5= Version 3.0 + of PC Paintbrush, PC
                                 Paintbrush +, and  Publisher's Paintbrush
              */
        BYTE encod;     // 1= PCX RLE
        BYTE bpp;       // Bits per pixel - 1, 2, 4, or 8
        int Xmin;       //Window dimensions
        int Ymin;
        int Xmax;
        int Ymax;
        int Hdpi;       //Horizontal resolution
        int Vdpi;       //Vertical resolution
        RGBTRIPLE pal1[16];     //palette
        BYTE junk;
        BYTE planes;            //number of color planes
        int BytesPerLine;       //number of bytes to allocate for a
                                //scanline plane
        int paltype;            //1=Color/BW, 2=Grayscale
                                //(ignored in PB IV, IV+)
        int Hscrsize;   //horizontal screen size (PB IV)
        int Vscrsize;   //vertical screen size (PB IV)
        BYTE filler[54];
        } PCXHDR;

/* Note: If ver=5 there may be a VGA 256 color palette at the end
of the file. Check for it at the end of file less 769 bytes: the
value will be 12 if there is a 256-color palette */

typedef struct pcxpal256 {
        BYTE flag;      //12= 256-color palette present
        RGBTRIPLE pal2[256];
        } PCXPAL256;
```

pcx.c

```
#define NOCOMM
#define NOKANJI
#include <windows.h>
#include "showimg.h"
#include <io.h>
#include <stdio.h>
#include <string.h>
#include "pcx.h"
static HCURSOR hcurSave;
extern BOOL bMemoryDIB;
RGBTRIPLE DefaultPalette[16]={
        { 0,            0,              0 },
        { 0,            0,            255 },
        { 0,          255,              0 },
        { 0,          255,            255 },
```

```
        { 255, 0,            0 },
        { 255, 0,            255 },
        { 255, 255,    0 },
        { 255, 255,    255 },
        { 85, 85,      255 },
        { 85, 85,      85 },
        { 0,           170,    0 },
        { 170, 0,            0 },
        { 85, 255,     255 },
        { 255, 85,     255 },
        { 255, 255,    85 },
        { 255, 255,    255 }
        };
int pcx_encget(BYTE *pbyt, int *pcnt, FILE *fid)
{
        int i;
        *pcnt=1;
        if(EOF==(i=getc(fid)))
                return(EOF);
        if(0xC0==(0xC0 & i)) {
                *pcnt=0x3F & i;
                if(EOF==(i=getc(fid)))
                        return(EOF);
                }
        *pbyt= (BYTE)i;
        return(0); //valid data stored
}
int pcxview(HWND hWnd)
{
LPBITMAPINFOHEADER lpbi;
RGBQUAD FAR *pRgb;
RGBTRIPLE *pRgbt;
int i,j,colors,cnt,row,col,maxrow,plane,padbytes;
BYTE chr,mask,bit,highbit;
DWORD dwBits,dwLen;
long off;
PCXHDR hdr;
PCXPAL256 pal;
int fh,valid;
FILE *fp;
OFSTRUCT        of;
long l,lsize,ltotal;
unsigned char huge *pixels;
unsigned char huge *pPix;

        FreeDib();
        /* Open the file */
    fh = OpenFile (achFileName, (LPOFSTRUCT)&of, OF_READ);
    if (fh == -1) {
                ErrMsg("Can't open file '%ls'", (LPSTR)achFileName);
                return FALSE;
        }
        /* Get the header info */
```

```
      off = _llseek(fh, 0L, SEEK_SET);
    if (sizeof (hdr) != _lread (fh, (LPSTR)&hdr, sizeof (hdr)))
       return FALSE;
     if(hdr.manu != 10) {
            _lclose (fh);
            ErrMsg("File '%ls' is not a valid PCX file",
                   (LPSTR)achFileName);
            return FALSE;
            }
     if(hdr.bpp * hdr.planes == 1)
            colors=2;
     else
            colors=16;
     pRgbt= hdr.pal1;
     if(hdr.ver==5) {
            off = _llseek(fh, -769L, SEEK_END);
        if (sizeof(pal) == _lread (fh, (LPSTR)&pal, sizeof (pal))
                   && pal.flag==12) {
                   colors=256;
                   pRgbt= pal.pal2;
                   }
            }
     /* Create the bitmap header */
   hbiCurrent=GlobalAlloc(GHND, (LONG)sizeof(BITMAPINFOHEADER) +
            colors * sizeof(RGBQUAD));
   if (!hbiCurrent)
      return NULL;
   lpbi = (VOID FAR *)GlobalLock (hbiCurrent);
   lpbi->biSize=sizeof(BITMAPINFOHEADER);
   lpbi->biWidth=1+hdr.Xmax-hdr.Xmin;
   lpbi->biHeight=1+hdr.Ymax-hdr.Ymin;
   lpbi->biPlanes=1; //nb: NOT equal to planes from PCX
   lpbi->biBitCount= hdr.bpp * hdr.planes;
   if(lpbi->biBitCount==3)
      lpbi->biBitCount=4;
   lpbi->biCompression= BI_RGB;
   dwBits=lpbi->biSizeImage=
      (DWORD)(8/lpbi->biBitCount)*(DWORD)lpbi->biWidth*
            (DWORD)lpbi->biHeight;
   lpbi->biXPelsPerMeter     = 0;
   lpbi->biYPelsPerMeter     = 0;
   lpbi->biClrUsed           = colors;
   lpbi->biClrImportant      = colors;

// fill in intensities for all palette entry colors
// note the order change between PCX and DIB
// Several people pointed the order change out to me, including
// Jay Slupesky, William van Ryper, and David Jones
   pRgb = (RGBQUAD FAR *)((LPSTR)lpbi + lpbi->biSize);
   for (i = 0; i < colors; i++) {
      pRgb[i].rgbRed   = pRgbt[i].rgbtBlue;      //NB: order reversed
      pRgb[i].rgbGreen = pRgbt[i].rgbtGreen;
      pRgb[i].rgbBlue  = pRgbt[i].rgbtRed;
      }
```

```
//Marc Adler of Magma Software points out that not all PCX files
//have valid palettes
   valid=0;
   if(hdr.ver==2 || hdr.ver>=4)                  //don't look at versions
                                                 //without palettes
     for (i = 0; i < colors && !valid; i++) {
               if(pRgb[i].rgbRed!=0
               || pRgb[i].rgbGreen!=0
               || pRgb[i].rgbBlue!=0)
                       valid=1;
               }
      if(!valid) {                   //set default palettes
               if(16>=colors) {       //16-color BIOS default palette
                   for(i=0; i<colors; i++) {
                     pRgb[i].rgbRed   = DefaultPalette[i].rgbtRed;
                     pRgb[i].rgbGreen = DefaultPalette[i].rgbtGreen;
                     pRgb[i].rgbBlue  = DefaultPalette[i].rgbtBlue;
                     }
                   }
               else if(256==colors) { //256-color spread palette
                       ErrMsg("Unimplemented: default palette 256");
                       }
               else {
                       ErrMsg("Unimplemented: default palette,"
                             " colors betweem 16 and 256");
                       }
               }
      hpalCurrent=CreateDibPalette(hbiCurrent);
      dwLen=lpbi->biSize + (DWORD)colors*sizeof(RGBQUAD) + dwBits;
      hdibCurrent=GlobalAlloc(GHND,dwLen);
                       //Note: GHND implies zeroed memory
      if(!hdibCurrent) {
               ErrMsg("Couldn't create DIB for PCX conversion");
               _lclose(fh);
               FreeDib();
               return(NULL);
               }
      pixels=(unsigned char huge *)GlobalLock(hdibCurrent);
      _fmemcpy(pixels,lpbi,(size_t)(dwLen-dwBits));
      GlobalUnlock(hbiCurrent);
      pixels += dwLen-dwBits;
//this does the grunt work of reading the PCX file into the DIB
      StartWait();
      fp=fdopen(fh,"rb");
      fseek(fp,(long)sizeof(hdr),SEEK_SET);
      ltotal=(long)hdr.BytesPerLine*hdr.planes;
      //NB: David Jones of Pilot Software points out that each
      //scan line in the DIB must end on a long boundary — pad it
      padbytes=ltotal%4;
      lsize=ltotal*(1+hdr.Ymax-hdr.Ymin);
      if(hdr.planes==3)
               ltotal=(long)hdr.BytesPerLine*4;
      row=0;
      col=0;
```

```
        maxrow=hdr.Ymax-hdr.Ymin;
        for(l=0;l<lsize;) {//get next byte and byte count
                if(EOF==pcx_encget(&chr,&cnt,fp))
                        break;
                for(i=0;i<cnt;i++) {//figure where this goes
                        col = (int) ((l+i) % ltotal);
                        //ignore unused bytes at end of scanline
            /*      if(col > (lpbi->biBitCount * (lpbi->biWidth  8)))
                                continue; */
                        row = (int) ((l+i) / ltotal);
                        if(row>maxrow || row<0) {
                        ErrMsg("PCX addressing error, row '%d'",row);
                        goto red_exit;
                        }
                        if(hdr.planes==3) {
                                plane  = col / (lpbi->biWidth / 8);
                                if(plane<0 || plane>=4) {
                                  ErrMsg("PCX plane error, row '%d',"
                                        " plane '%d'",row,plane);
                                  goto red_exit;
                                }
                                col    = col % (lpbi->biWidth / 8);
                                bit    = 0x0f & (0x01 <<  plane);
                                highbit= 0xf0 & (0x01 << (plane+4));
                                pPix= pixels + col*4L +
                                    (long)(maxrow-row)*(ltotal+padbytes);
                for (j=0; j<8; j += 2) {
                //distribute 8 bits over 8 nibbles
                        mask = 0x80 >> j;
                        *pPix |= (chr & mask) ? highbit : 0;
                        mask = 0x80 >> (j+1);
                        *pPix++ |= (chr & mask) ? bit : 0;
                        }
                        }
//Jay Slupesky pointed out the need to divide lpbi->biWidth by 8
                else if(hdr.planes==4) {

                        plane  = col / (lpbi->biWidth / 8);
                        if(plane<0 || plane>=4) {
                        ErrMsg("PCX plane error, row '%d', plane '%d'",
                                   row,plane);
                        goto red_exit;
                        }
                        col = col % (lpbi->biWidth / 8);
                        bit = 0x0f & (0x01 <<  plane);
                        highbit = 0xf0 & (0x01 << (plane+4));
                        pPix= pixels + col*4L + (long)(maxrow-
                                row)*(ltotal+padbytes);
                        for (j=0; j<8; j += 2) {
  //distribute 8 bits over 8 nibbles
                        mask = 0x80 >> j;
                        *pPix |= (chr & mask) ? highbit : 0;
                        mask = 0x80 >> (j+1);
```

```
                     *pPix++ |= (chr & mask) ? bit : 0;
             }
          }
        else {
         pPix= pixels + col + (maxrow-row)*(ltotal+padbytes);
         *pPix = chr;
         }
      }
 l += cnt;
 if(SpinTheMessageLoop())
      break;
 }
 red_exit:
  fclose(fp);
  _lclose(fh);
  EndWait();
 //now make the bitmap and clean up
  GlobalUnlock(hdibCurrent);
  bLegitDraw=bMemoryDIB=TRUE;
  if (hdibCurrent && !bDIBToDevice){
   hbmCurrent = BitmapFromDib(hdibCurrent,hpalCurrent);
   if (!hbmCurrent){
       ErrMsg ("Could not create bitmap!");
       bDIBToDevice=TRUE;     //mh: adapt to conditions!
       }
    }
   SizeWindow(hWnd);
   return(TRUE);
 }
```

raw.c

```
#define NOCOMM
#define NOKANJI
#include <windows.h>
#include "showimg.h"
#include <stdio.h>
#include <string.h>
#include "rawdlg.h"
extern BOOL   bMemoryDIB;
BOOL _export FAR PASCAL RawDlgProc(HWND hWndDlg, unsigned message,
                               WORD wParam, LONG lParam);
static int width=768, height=512, bitsperpix=24;
static HCURSOR hcurSave;
int rawview(HWND hWnd)
{
      int istatus = 0, fh = 0, i;
      int numcolors = 0;
      LPBITMAPINFOHEADER lpbi;
      DWORD dwBits, dwLen;
      unsigned char huge *pixels;
      unsigned char huge *buffer;
      unsigned char temp;
```

```
WORD linelen;
OFSTRUCT of;
long j;

FreeDib();

//Get RAW file description from user
if(!fDialog(RAWDLG, hWnd, RawDlgProc))
        return FALSE;
if(bitsperpix<=8)
        numcolors= 1 << bitsperpix;

//open file
fh = OpenFile(achFileName, (LPOFSTRUCT) &of, OF_READ);
if (fh == -1) {
        ErrMsg("Can't open file '%ls'", (LPSTR) achFileName);
        return FALSE;
        }

//Create the DIB structures

hbiCurrent = GlobalAlloc(GHND, (LONG) sizeof
        (BITMAPINFOHEADER) + numcolors * sizeof(RGBQUAD));
if (!hbiCurrent)
        goto red_exit;

lpbi = (VOID FAR *) GlobalLock(hbiCurrent);
lpbi->biSize = sizeof(BITMAPINFOHEADER);
lpbi->biWidth = width;
lpbi->biHeight = height;
lpbi->biPlanes = 1;
lpbi->biBitCount = bitsperpix;
lpbi->biCompression = BI_RGB;
dwBits =
        lpbi->biSizeImage =
        (DWORD) width * height * (bitsperpix / 8);
lpbi->biXPelsPerMeter = 0;
lpbi->biYPelsPerMeter = 0;
lpbi->biClrUsed = numcolors;
lpbi->biClrImportant = numcolors;

hpalCurrent = CreateDibPalette(hbiCurrent);
dwLen = lpbi->biSize + (DWORD) numcolors *
        sizeof(RGBQUAD) + dwBits;
hdibCurrent = GlobalAlloc(GHND, dwLen);
if (!hdibCurrent) {
        ErrMsg("Couldn't create DIB for RAW conversion");
        FreeDib();
        istatus = -1;
        goto red_exit;
        }
pixels = (unsigned char huge *) GlobalLock(hdibCurrent);
```

```
        _fmemcpy((void far *) pixels, lpbi,
                (size_t) (dwLen - dwBits));
        GlobalUnlock(hbiCurrent);
        pixels += dwLen - dwBits;

        StartWait();
        linelen=(WORD)((long)width*(long)bitsperpix/8L);
        for (i=1;i<=height;i++) {        //read, fixing direction
                buffer=pixels + (long)(height-i)*(long)linelen;
                if (_lread(fh, buffer, linelen) != linelen)
                        break;
                if(bitsperpix==24) {
                        for(j=0;j<(long)linelen;j+=3) {
        //fix color order
                                temp        = *(buffer+j);
                                *(buffer+j)   = *(buffer+j+2);
                                *(buffer+j+2) = temp;
                                }
                        }
                if(SpinTheMessageLoop())
                        break;
                }
        EndWait();

        GlobalUnlock(hdibCurrent);
        bLegitDraw = bMemoryDIB = TRUE;
        if (hdibCurrent && !bDIBToDevice) {
                hbmCurrent = BitmapFromDib(hdibCurrent, hpalCurrent);
                if (!hbmCurrent) {
                        ErrMsg("Could not create bitmap!");
                        bDIBToDevice=TRUE;//mh: adapt to conditions!
                        }
                }
        istatus=0;

red_exit:
        _lclose(fh);
        SizeWindow(hWnd);
        return (!istatus);
}

BOOL _export FAR PASCAL RawDlgProc(HWND hWndDlg, unsigned message,
                WORD wParam, LONG lParam)
{
        switch (message)
        {
        case WM_INITDIALOG:
                SetDlgItemInt(hWndDlg,idwidth,width,0);
                SetDlgItemInt(hWndDlg,idheight,height,0);
                SetDlgItemInt(hWndDlg,idbpp,bitsperpix,0);
                SetDlgItemText(hWndDlg,idfilename,achFileName);
                EnableWindow(GetDlgItem(hWndDlg,idbpp),FALSE);
                break;
```

```
        case WM_COMMAND:
                switch (wParam)
                {
                case idok:
                        width=GetDlgItemInt(hWndDlg,idwidth,NULL,0);
                        height=GetDlgItemInt(hWndDlg,idheight,NULL,0);
                        bitsperpix=GetDlgItemInt(hWndDlg,idbpp,NULL,0);
                        EndDialog(hWndDlg, TRUE);
                        break;
                case idcancel:
                        EndDialog(hWndDlg, FALSE);
                        break;
                default:
                        return FALSE;
                }
                break;
        default:
                return FALSE;
        }
        return TRUE;
}
```

gif.c

```
#define NOCOMM
#define NOKANJI
#include <windows.h>
#include "showimg.h"
#include <stdio.h>
#include <string.h>
static HCURSOR hcurSave;
//GIF input routines, adapted for SHOWIMG by Martin Heller
/*
 *
 * This GIF decoder is designed for use with Bert Tyler's FRACTINT
 * program. It should be noted that "FRACTINT" only decodes
 * GIF files it creates, so this decoder code lacks full generality
 * in these respects: supports single image, non-interlaced GIF
 * files with no local color maps and no extension blocks.
 *
 * GIF and 'Graphics Interchange Format' are trademarks (tm) of
 * CompuServe, Incorporated, an H&R Block Company.
 *
 *
        Tim Wegner
 */
static short  init_exp(short  size);
static short  get_next_code(void);
static void   inittable(void);
static void   raster(unsigned int  code);
static void   close_file(void);
int rowcount;          /* row counter for screen */
extern NPLOGPALETTE pLogPal;
```

```
extern BOOL    bMemoryDIB;
static FILE *fpin = NULL;     /* FILE pointer            */
unsigned int height;
int    mapset;
unsigned char dacbox[256][3];
static int paletteVGA[16];              /* VGA Palette-to-DAC registers */
static unsigned char decoderline[2049]; /* write-line routines use
                                                  this */
static unsigned char win_andmask[8];
static unsigned char win_notmask[8];
static unsigned char win_bitshift[8];
int xdots, ydots, colors, maxiter;
int xposition, yposition, win_xoffset, win_yoffset,
              xpagesize, ypagesize;
int win_xdots, win_ydots;
unsigned char huge *pixels; /* the DIB pixels */
int pixels_per_byte;            /* pixels/byte in the pixmap */
long pixels_per_bytem1;         /* pixels / byte - 1 (for ANDing) */
int pixelshift_per_byte;        /* 0, 1, 2, or 3 */
int bytes_per_pixelline;        /* pixels/line / pixels/byte */
long win_bitmapsize;            /* bitmap size, in bytes */
int bad_code_count = 0;             /* needed by decoder module */
extern int rowcount;

int get_byte(){
        return (getc(fpin)); /* EOF is -1, as desired */
}
void putcolor(int x, int y, int color){
        long i;

        i = win_ydots - 1 - y;
        i = (i * win_xdots) + x;
        if (x >= 0 && x < xdots && y >= 0 && y < ydots) {
                if (pixelshift_per_byte == 0) {
                        pixels[i] = color % colors;
                        }
                else {
                        unsigned int j;

                        j = i & pixels_per_bytem1;
                        i = i >> pixelshift_per_byte;
                        pixels[i] = (pixels[i] & win_notmask[j]) +
                                (((unsigned char) (color % colors)) <<
                                        win_bitshift[j]);
                        }
                }
}
int put_line(int rownum, int leftpt, int rightpt,
                unsigned char *localvalues)
{
        int i, len;
        long startloc;
```

```
        len = rightpt - leftpt;
        if (rightpt >= xdots)
                len = xdots - 1 - leftpt;
        startloc = win_ydots - 1 - rownum;
        startloc = (startloc * win_xdots) + leftpt;

        if (rownum < 0 || rownum >= ydots || leftpt < 0) {
                return (0);
                }

        if (pixelshift_per_byte == 0) {
                for (i = 0;  i <= len;  i++)
                        pixels[startloc + i] = localvalues[i];
                }
        else {
                unsigned int j;
                long k;
                for (i = 0;  i <= len;  i++) {
                        k = startloc + i;
                        j = k & pixels_per_bytem1;
                        k = k >> pixelshift_per_byte;
                        pixels[k] = (pixels[k] & win_notmask[j]) +
                                (((unsigned char) (localvalues[i] %
                                        colors)) << win_bitshift[j]);
                        }                                   //for
                }                                           //else
        putcolor(leftpt, rownum, localvalues[0]);
        return (1);
}
int out_line(unsigned char *localvalues, int numberofdots)
{
  return (put_line(rowcount++, 0, numberofdots, localvalues));
}

/* Main entry decoder */
int gifview(HWND hWnd){
        unsigned numcolors;
        unsigned char buffer[16];
        unsigned width, finished;
        char temp1[81];
        LPBITMAPINFOHEADER lpbi;
        RGBQUAD FAR          *pRgb;
        int status = 0;
        int i, j, k, planes;
        DWORD dwBits, dwLen;

        FreeDib();                                 //mh

  /* initialize the row count for write-lines */
        rowcount = 0;

  /* zero out the full write-line */
        for (width = 0;  width < 2049;  width++)
```

```
                decoderline[width] = 0;

/* Open the file */
    strcpy(temp1, achFileName);
    if ((fpin = fopen(temp1, "rb")) == NULL)
            return FALSE;


/* Get the screen description */
    for (i = 0;  i < 13;  i++) {
            if ((buffer[i] = (unsigned char) get_byte()) < 0) {
                    close_file();
                    return FALSE;
                    }
            }
            /* use updated GIF specs */
        if (strncmp(buffer, "GIF87a", 3) ||
                buffer[3] < '0' || buffer[3] > '9' ||
                buffer[4] < '0' || buffer[4] > '9' ||
                buffer[5] < 'A' || buffer[5] > 'z') {
            close_file();
            return FALSE;
            }
    planes = (buffer[10] & 0xF) + 1;
    if ((buffer[10] & 0x80) == 0)        /* color map (better be!) */
            {
            close_file();
            return FALSE;
            }
    numcolors = 1 << planes;
    for (i = 0;  i < numcolors;  i++) {
      for (j = 0;  j < 3;  j++) {
            if ((buffer[j] = (unsigned char) get_byte()) < 0) {
                    close_file();
                    return FALSE;
                    }
            if (dacbox[0][0] != 255)
                    dacbox[i][j] = buffer[j] >> 2;
            }
        }


/* Now display one or more GIF objects */
    finished = 0;
    while (!finished) {
            switch (get_byte()) {
      case ';':                       /* End of the GIF dataset */


                    finished = 1;
                    status = 0;
                    break;

      case '!':                       /* GIF Extension Block */
                    get_byte();     /* read (and ignore) the ID */
```

```
                            while ((i = get_byte()) > 0)
                                       /* get the data length */
                                for (j = 0;  j < i;  j++)
                                        get_byte();   /* flush the data */
                        break;

            case ',':
        /*
         * Start of an image object. Read the image description.
         */
          for (i = 0;  i < 9;  i++) {
              if ((buffer[i] = (unsigned char) get_byte()) < 0) {
                      status = -1;
                      break;
                      }
                  }
          if (status < 0) {
              finished = 1;
              break;
              }
          width = buffer[4] | buffer[5] << 8;
          height = buffer[6] | buffer[7] << 8;
// fill in DIB stuff
          xdots = width;
          ydots = height;
          colors = numcolors;
          if (colors > 16)
              colors = 256;
              if (colors > 2 && colors < 16)
                      colors = 16;
              win_xdots = (xdots + 3) & 0xFFFC;
              win_ydots = ydots;
              pixelshift_per_byte = 0;
              pixels_per_byte = 1;
              pixels_per_bytem1 = 0;
              if (colors == 16) {
                      win_xdots = (xdots + 7) & 0xFFF8;
                      pixelshift_per_byte = 1;
                      pixels_per_byte = 2;
                      pixels_per_bytem1 = 1;
                      win_andmask[0] = 0xF0;
                      win_notmask[0] = 0xF;
                      win_bitshift[0] = 4;
                      win_andmask[1] = 0xF;
                      win_notmask[1] = 0xF0;
                      win_bitshift[1] = 0;
                      }
              if (colors == 2) {
                      win_xdots = (xdots + 31) & 0xFFE0;
                      pixelshift_per_byte = 3;
                      pixels_per_byte = 8;
                      pixels_per_bytem1 = 7;
                      win_andmask[0] = 0x80;
```

```
                win_notmask[0] = 0x7F;
                win_bitshift[0] = 7;
                for (i = 1;  i < 8;  i++) {
                        win_andmask[i]=win_andmask[i - 1] >> 1;
                        win_notmask[i]=(win_notmask[i - 1] >> 1)
                                              + 0x80;
                        win_bitshift[i]=win_bitshift[i - 1] - 1;
                        }
                }
        bytes_per_pixelline=win_xdots >> pixelshift_per_byte;
        hbiCurrent = GlobalAlloc(GHND,
                    (LONG)sizeof(BITMAPINFOHEADER) +
                     colors * sizeof(RGBQUAD));
        if (!hbiCurrent)
                return 0;

        lpbi = (VOID FAR *) GlobalLock(hbiCurrent);
        lpbi->biSize = sizeof(BITMAPINFOHEADER);
        lpbi->biWidth = width;
        lpbi->biHeight = height;
        lpbi->biPlanes = 1;    //nb: NOT equal to planes from GIF
        lpbi->biBitCount = 8 / pixels_per_byte;
        lpbi->biCompression = BI_RGB;
        dwBits =
          lpbi->biSizeImage = (DWORD) bytes_per_pixelline *
                                  win_ydots;
        lpbi->biXPelsPerMeter = 0;
        lpbi->biYPelsPerMeter = 0;
        lpbi->biClrUsed = colors;
        lpbi->biClrImportant = colors;
        win_bitmapsize = (((long) win_xdots * (long)
                win_ydots) >> pixelshift_per_byte) + 1;
/* fill in intensities for all palette entry colors */
        pRgb = (RGBQUAD FAR *) ((LPSTR) lpbi + lpbi->biSize);
        for (i = 0;  i < colors;  i++) {
                pRgb[i].rgbRed = ((BYTE) dacbox[i][0]) << 2;
                pRgb[i].rgbGreen = ((BYTE) dacbox[i][1]) << 2;
                pRgb[i].rgbBlue = ((BYTE) dacbox[i][2]) << 2;
                }
        hpalCurrent = CreateDibPalette(hbiCurrent);
        dwLen = lpbi->biSize + (DWORD) colors *
                        sizeof(RGBQUAD) + dwBits;
        hdibCurrent = GlobalAlloc(GHND, dwLen);
        if (!hdibCurrent) {
         ErrMsg("Couldn't create DIB for GIF conversion");
         FreeDib();
         finished = 1;
         status = -1;
         break;
         }
        pixels = (unsigned char huge *)
                        GlobalLock(hdibCurrent);
```

```
                _fmemcpy(pixels, lpbi, (size_t) (dwLen - dwBits));
                GlobalUnlock(hbiCurrent);
                pixels += dwLen - dwBits;
                StartWait();
                decoder(width);          //this does the grunt work
                EndWait();
                GlobalUnlock(hdibCurrent);
                bLegitDraw = bMemoryDIB = TRUE;
                if (hdibCurrent && !bDIBToDevice) {
                        hbmCurrent = BitmapFromDib(hdibCurrent,
                        hpalCurrent);
                        if (!hbmCurrent) {
                                ErrMsg("Could not create bitmap!");
                                bDIBToDevice = TRUE;
                                }
                        }
                finished = 1;
                break;
            default:
                status = -1;
                finished = 1;
                break;
                }
        }
close_file();
SizeWindow(hWnd);
return (!status);
}

static void close_file(){
        fclose(fpin);
        fpin = NULL;
}


/* DECODE.C - An LZW decoder for GIF
 * Copyright (C) 1987, by Steven A. Bennett
 *
Permission is given by the author to freely redistribute and include
this code in any program as long as this credit is given where due.

In accordance with the above, I want to credit Steve Wilhite who
wrote the code which this is heavily inspired by...
 *
 * GIF and 'Graphics Interchange Format' are trademarks (tm) of
 * CompuServe, Incorporated, an H&R Block Company.
 *
Release Notes: This file contains a decoder routine for GIF images
which is similar, structurally, to the original routine by Steve
Wilhite.
It is, however, somewhat noticably faster in most cases.
This routine was modified for use in FRACTINT in two ways.
```

```
1) The original #includes were folded into the routine strictly to
hold down the number of files we were dealing with.
2) The 'stack', 'suffix', 'prefix', and 'buf' arrays were changed
from static and 'malloc()'ed to external only so that the assembler
program could use the same array space for several independent
chunks of code.        Also, 'stack' was renamed to 'dstack' for TASM
compatibility.
3) The 'out_line()' external function has been changed to reference
   '*outln()' for flexibility (in particular, 3D transformations)
4) A call to 'keypressed()' has been added after the 'outln()' calls
to check for the presence of a key-press as a bail-out signal
 == (Bert Tyler and Timothy Wegner)
 */
#define LOCAL static
#define IMPORT extern
#define FAST register
typedef unsigned short UWORD;
typedef char TEXT;
typedef unsigned char UTINY;
typedef unsigned long ULONG;
typedef int INT;
/* Various error codes used by decoder
 * and my own routines...   It's okay
 * for you to define whatever you want,
 * as long as it's negative... It will be
 * returned intact up the various subroutine
 * levels...
 */
#define OUT_OF_MEMORY -10
#define BAD_CODE_SIZE -20
#define READ_ERROR -1
#define WRITE_ERROR -2
#define OPEN_ERROR -3
#define CREATE_ERROR -4
/* IMPORT INT get_byte()
 *
 *This external (machine specific) function is expected to return
 * either the next byte from the GIF file, or a negative number, as
 * defined in ERRS.H.
 */
//IMPORT INT get_byte();

/* IMPORT INT out_line(pixels, linelen)
 *      UBYTE pixels[];
 *      INT linelen;
 *
 * This function takes a full line of pixels (one byte per pixel)
and displays them (or does whatever your program wants with
them...).  It should return zero, or negative if an error or some
other event occurs which would require aborting the decode pro-
cess...  Note that the length passed will almost always be equal to
the line length passed to the decoder function, with the sole excep-
tion occurring when an ending code occurs in an odd place in the
```

```
GIF file...  In any case, linelen will be equal to the number of
pixels passed...
 */
//IMPORT INT out_line();
INT (*outln)(UTINY *, INT) = out_line;
/* IMPORT INT bad_code_count;
 *
 * This value is the only other global required by the using program,
and is incremented each time an out of range code is read by the de-
coder. When this value is non-zero after a decode, your GIF file is
probably corrupt in some way...
 */
//IMPORT INT bad_code_count;
/* whups, here are more globals, added by PB: */
INT skipxdots; /* 0 to get every dot, 1 for every 2nd, ... */
INT skipydots; /* ditto for rows */
#undef NULL
#define NULL    0L
#define MAX_CODES   4095
/* Static variables */
LOCAL short curr_size;          /* The current code size */
LOCAL short clear;              /* Value for a clear code */
LOCAL short ending;            /* Value for a ending code */
LOCAL short newcodes;          /* First available code */
LOCAL short top_slot;          /* Highest code for current size */
LOCAL short slot;              /* Last read code */

/* The following static variables are used
 * for seperating out codes
 */
LOCAL short navail_bytes = 0;        /* # bytes left in block */
LOCAL short nbits_left = 0; /* # bits left in current byte */
LOCAL UTINY b1;                     /* Current byte */
LOCAL UTINY byte_buff[257];/* Current block, reuse shared mem */
LOCAL UTINY *pbytes;          /* Pointer to next byte in block */
LOCAL LONG code_mask[13] = {
    0,
    0x0001, 0x0003,
    0x0007, 0x000F,
    0x001F, 0x003F,
    0x007F, 0x00FF,
    0x01FF, 0x03FF,
    0x07FF, 0x0FFF
    };
/* This function initializes the decoder for reading a new image.
 */
LOCAL short init_exp(size)
short size;
{
    curr_size = size + 1;
    top_slot = 1 << curr_size;
    clear = 1 << size;
    ending = clear + 1;
```

```
        slot = newcodes = ending + 1;
        navail_bytes = nbits_left = 0;
        return (0);
}
/* get_next_code()
 gets the next code from the GIF file.  Returns the code, or else
 a negative number in case of file errors...
*/
LOCAL short get_next_code(){
        short i, x;
        ULONG ret;
        if (nbits_left == 0) {
                if (navail_bytes <= 0) {
          /* Out of bytes in current block, so read next block
           */
                        pbytes = byte_buff;
                        if ((navail_bytes = get_byte()) < 0)
                                return (navail_bytes);
                        else if (navail_bytes) {
                                for (i = 0;  i < navail_bytes;  ++i) {
                                        if ((x = get_byte()) < 0)
                                                return (x);
                                        byte_buff[i] = x;
                                        }
                                }
                        }
                b1 = *pbytes++;
                nbits_left = 8;
                —navail_bytes;
                }
        ret = b1 >> (8 - nbits_left);
        while (curr_size > nbits_left) {
                if (navail_bytes <= 0) {
          /* Out of bytes in current block, so read next block
           */
                        pbytes = byte_buff;
                        if ((navail_bytes = get_byte()) < 0)
                                return (navail_bytes);
                        else if (navail_bytes) {
                                for (i = 0;  i < navail_bytes;  ++i) {
                                        if ((x = get_byte()) < 0)
                                                return (x);
                                        byte_buff[i] = x;
                                        }
                                }
                        }
                b1 = *pbytes++;
                ret |= b1 << nbits_left;
                nbits_left += 8;
                —navail_bytes;
                }
        nbits_left -= curr_size;
        ret &= code_mask[curr_size];
```

```
        return ((short) (ret));
}
/* The reason we have these seperated like this instead of using
a structure like the original Wilhite code did, is because this
stuff generally produces significantly faster code when compiled...
This code is full of similar speedups...  (For a good book on writing
C for speed or for space optomisation, see Efficient C by Tom Plum,
published by Plum-Hall Associates...)
 */


/*
I removed the LOCAL identifiers in the arrays below and replaced them
with 'extern's so as to declare (and reuse) the space elsewhere. The
arrays are actually declared in the assembler source.
                                        Bert Tyler
I put them back — m heller
*/
UTINY dstack[MAX_CODES + 1];    /* Stack for storing pixels */
UTINY suffix[MAX_CODES + 1];    /* Suffix table */
UWORD prefix[MAX_CODES + 1];    /* Prefix linked list */
//extern UTINY decoderline[2];          /* decoded line goes here */
/* short decoder(linewidth)
 *      short linewidth;                * Pixels per line of image *
This function decodes an LZW image, according to the method used
in the GIF spec.  Every *linewidth* "characters" (ie. pixels) decoded
will generate a call to out_line(), which is a user specific function
to display a line of pixels.  The function gets its codes from
get_next_code() which is responsible for reading blocks of data and
seperating them into the proper size codes. Finally, get_byte() is the
global routine to read the next byte from the GIF file.
It is generally a good idea to have linewidth correspond to the actual
width of a line (as specified in the Image header) to make your own
code a bit simpler, but it isn't absolutely necessary.
Returns: 0 if successful, else negative.  (See ERRS.H)
*/
short decoder(short linewidth){
      FAST UTINY *sp, *bufptr;
      UTINY *buf;
      FAST short code, fc, oc, bufcnt;
      short c, size, ret;
      short xskip, yskip;
   /* Initialize for decoding a new image... */
      if ((size = get_byte()) < 0)
            return (size);
      if (size < 2 || 9 < size)
            return (BAD_CODE_SIZE);
      init_exp(size);
      xskip = yskip = 0;

   /* Initialize in case they forgot to put in a clear code. (This
shouldn't happen, but we'll try and decode it anyway...) */
      oc = fc = 0;
      buf = decoderline;
```

```
        /* Set up the stack pointer and decode buffer pointer */
        sp = dstack;
        bufptr = buf;
        bufcnt = linewidth;
/* This is the main loop.  For each code we get we pass through the
linked list of prefix codes, pushing the corresponding "character"
for each code onto the stack.  When the list reaches a single "char-
acter" we push that on the stack too, and then start unstacking each
character for output in the correct order.  Special handling is
included for the clear code, and the whole thing ends when we get an
ending code. */
        while ((c = get_next_code()) != ending
                && !SpinTheMessageLoop()) {          //mh
/* If we had a file error, return without completing the decode */
            if (c < 0)
                    return (0);
/* If the code is a clear code, reinitialize all necessary items.*/
            if (c == clear) {
                    curr_size = size + 1;
                    slot = newcodes;
                    top_slot = 1 << curr_size;
        /* Continue reading codes until we get a non-clear code
         * (Another unlikely, but possible case...)
         */
                    while ((c = get_next_code()) == clear)
                            ;
        /* If we get an ending code immediately after a clear code
         * (Yet another unlikely case), then break out of the loop.
         */
                    if (c == ending)
                            break;
/* Finally, if the code is beyond the range of already set codes,
(This one had better NOT happen...  I have no idea what will result
from this, but I doubt it will look good...) then set it to color
zero. */
                    if (c >= slot)
                            c = 0;
                    oc = fc = c;
    /* And let us not forget to put the char into the buffer... */
                    *sp++ = c;
/* let the common code outside the if else stuff it */
                    }
            else
                    {
/* In this case, it's not a clear code or an ending code, so it must
be a code code...  So we can now decode the code into a stack of
character codes. (Clear as mud, right?)  */
                    code = c;
/* Here we go again with one of those off chances...  If, on the off
chance, the code we got is beyond the range of those already set up
(Another thing which had better NOT happen...) we trick the decoder
into thinking it actually got the last code read. (Hmmn... I'm not
sure why this works...  But it does...) */
```

```
                        if (code >= slot) {
                                if (code > slot)
                                        ++bad_code_count;
                                code = oc;
                                *sp++ = fc;
                                }
/* Here we scan back along the linked list of prefixes, pushing
helpless characters (ie. suffixes) onto the stack as we do so. */
                        while (code >= newcodes) {
                                *sp++ = suffix[code];
                                code = prefix[code];
                                }
/* Push the last character on the stack, and set up the new prefix
and suffix, and if the required slot number is greater than that
allowed by the current bit size, increase the bit size. (NOTE - If
we are all full, we *don't* save the new suffix and prefix...  I'm
not certain if this is correct... it might be more proper to
overwrite the last code... */
                        *sp++ = code;
                        if (slot < top_slot) {
                                suffix[slot] = fc = code;
                                prefix[slot++] = oc;
                                oc = c;
                                }
                        if (slot >= top_slot)
                                if (curr_size < 12) {
                                        top_slot <<= 1;
                                        ++curr_size;
                                        }

                        }
/* Now that we've pushed the decoded string (in reverse order) onto
the stack, lets pop it off and put it into our decode buffer...  And
when the decode buffer is full, write another line... */
                while (sp > dstack) {
                        --sp;
                        if (--xskip < 0) {
                                xskip = skipxdots;
                                *bufptr++ = *sp;
                                }
                        if (--bufcnt == 0)   /* finished an input row? */
                                {
                                if (--yskip < 0) {
                                  if ((ret = (*outln)(buf, bufptr - buf))
                                                < 0)
                                                return (ret);
                                 yskip = skipydots;
                                 }
//      if (keypressed())
//          return(-1);
                                bufptr = buf;
                                bufcnt = linewidth;
                                xskip = 0;
```

```
                              }
                    }
              }
/* PB note that if last line is incomplete, we're not going to try
to emit it;  original code did, but did so via out_line and  there-
fore couldn't have worked well in all cases... */
      return (0);
}
```

tiff.c

```
#define NOCOMM
#define NOKANJI
#include <windows.h>
#include "showimg.h"
#include "tiffio.h"

static HCURSOR hcurSave;
extern NPLOGPALETTE pLogPal;
extern BOOL    bMemoryDIB;

int tiffview(HWND hWnd)
{
      int status=0;
      int numcolors=0,j;
      unsigned int width, bitsperpix, photometric;
      unsigned int scanlinesize;
      int height,row;
      LPBITMAPINFOHEADER lpbi;
      DWORD dwBits,dwLen;
      unsigned char huge *pixels;
      PTIFF tif;
      RGBQUAD FAR *pRgb=NULL;
      float factor;

      FreeDib();

      tif = TIFFOpen(achFileName, "r");
      if(tif==NULL)
      return FALSE;

      //get the dimensions out for use in creating the buffer

      TIFFGetField(tif,TIFFTAG_IMAGELENGTH,   &height);
      TIFFGetField(tif,TIFFTAG_IMAGEWIDTH,    &width);
      TIFFGetField(tif,TIFFTAG_BITSPERSAMPLE, &bitsperpix);
      TIFFGetField(tif,TIFFTAG_PHOTOMETRIC, &photometric);
      if(photometric==PHOTOMETRIC_RGB)
            bitsperpix *= 3;
      else
            numcolors = 1 << bitsperpix;
      if(bitsperpix!=1 && bitsperpix!=4 && bitsperpix!=8
            && bitsperpix!=24) {
```

```
                ErrMsg("TIFF: %d bits per pixel not handled",
                       bitsperpix);
                FreeDib();
                status=-1;
                goto red_exit;
                }

        //Create the DIB structures

hbiCurrent=GlobalAlloc(GHND, (LONG)sizeof(BITMAPINFOHEADER) +
           numcolors * sizeof(RGBQUAD));
if (!hbiCurrent)
    goto red_exit;

lpbi = (VOID FAR *)GlobalLock (hbiCurrent);
lpbi->biSize=sizeof(BITMAPINFOHEADER);
    lpbi->biWidth=width;
    lpbi->biHeight=height;
    lpbi->biPlanes=1;
    lpbi->biBitCount= bitsperpix;
    lpbi->biCompression= BI_RGB;
dwBits=
    lpbi->biSizeImage = (DWORD)width*height*(long)bitsperpix/8;
lpbi->biXPelsPerMeter     = 0;
lpbi->biYPelsPerMeter     = 0;
lpbi->biClrUsed           = numcolors;
lpbi->biClrImportant      = numcolors;

    /* fill in intensities for all palette entry colors */

    if(photometric==PHOTOMETRIC_PALETTE) {
            u_short FAR *redmap;
            u_short FAR *greenmap;
            u_short FAR *bluemap;
            TIFFGetField(tif, TIFFTAG_COLORMAP, &redmap,
                              &greenmap, &bluemap);
            pRgb = (RGBQUAD FAR *) ((LPSTR) lpbi + lpbi->biSize);
            for (j = 0;  j < numcolors;  j++) {
                    pRgb[j].rgbRed   = HIBYTE(redmap[j]);
                    pRgb[j].rgbGreen = HIBYTE(greenmap[j]);
                    pRgb[j].rgbBlue  = HIBYTE(bluemap[j]);
                    }
            }
    else if(photometric==PHOTOMETRIC_MINISBLACK) {
            pRgb = (RGBQUAD FAR *) ((LPSTR) lpbi + lpbi->biSize);
            factor = 256.0f / numcolors;
            for (j = 0;  j < numcolors;  j++) {
                    pRgb[j].rgbRed =
                            pRgb[j].rgbGreen =
                            pRgb[j].rgbBlue = (BYTE) (j * factor);
                    }
            }
    else if(photometric==PHOTOMETRIC_MINISWHITE) {
            pRgb = (RGBQUAD FAR *) ((LPSTR) lpbi + lpbi->biSize);
```

```
                    factor = 256.0f / numcolors;
                    for (j = 0;  j < numcolors;  j++) {
                            pRgb[j].rgbRed =
                            pRgb[j].rgbGreen =
                            pRgb[j].rgbBlue = (BYTE) ((numcolors-j) *
                                                        factor);
                            }

                }

//Note: CreateDibPalette will make a default 256-color palette for
//      24-bit DIB's.
        hpalCurrent=CreateDibPalette(hbiCurrent);
        dwLen  = lpbi->biSize + (DWORD)numcolors*sizeof(RGBQUAD) +
                    dwBits;
        hdibCurrent=GlobalAlloc(GHND,dwLen);
        if(!hdibCurrent) {
                ErrMsg("Couldn't create DIB for TIFF conversion");
                FreeDib();
                status=-1;
                goto red_exit;
                }
        pixels=(unsigned char huge *)GlobalLock(hdibCurrent);
        _fmemcpy((void far *)pixels,lpbi,(size_t)(dwLen-dwBits));
        GlobalUnlock(hbiCurrent);
        pixels += dwLen-dwBits;
        scanlinesize=TIFFScanlineSize(tif);

        StartWait();
        {
        HANDLE hBuf;
        char *buf;
        long offset;
        unsigned char far *pPix;

        hBuf=LocalAlloc(LHND,scanlinesize);
        buf=LocalLock(hBuf);
        for (row = 0; row < height; row++) {
                offset=(height-(row+1))*(long)scanlinesize;
                pPix = pixels + offset;
                TIFFReadScanline(tif,buf,row,0);
                _fmemcpy(pPix,buf,scanlinesize);
                if(SpinTheMessageLoop())
                        break;
                }
        LocalUnlock(hBuf);
        LocalFree(hBuf);
        }
        EndWait();

        GlobalUnlock(hdibCurrent);
        TIFFClose(tif);
        bLegitDraw=bMemoryDIB=TRUE;
        if (hdibCurrent && !bDIBToDevice){
```

```
                        hbmCurrent = BitmapFromDib(hdibCurrent,hpalCurrent);
                        if (!hbmCurrent){
                        ErrMsg ("Could not create bitmap!");
                                bDIBToDevice=TRUE;      //mh: adapt to conditions!
                                }
                        }
        SizeWindow(hWnd);
        return(TRUE);

red_exit:
        TIFFClose(tif);
        SizeWindow(hWnd);
        return(!status);
}
```

tga.c

```
/****************************************************************
 * flsun.c: FBM Library 0.96 (Beta test) 07-Sep-89  Ian MacPhedran
 *
 * Author Ian MacPhedran.
 * Permission is given to use any portion of this file, (including
 * its entirety) for whatever you wish. Howvever, please note that
 * it was written for Michael Mauldin's FBM Library, and conditions
 * therein are more restrictive.
 *
 * fltga.c:
 *
 * CONTENTS
 *    read_tga (image, rfile, mstr, mlen)
 *    write_tga (image, wfile) //removed from Showimg version mh
 *
 * HISTORY
 * 16-May-91  Martin Heller
 * Major revisions for use under Windows, for SHOWIMG
 *
 * 26-Aug-89  Michael Mauldin (mlm) at Carnegie Mellon University
 *    Fix rowlen bug for odd widths
 *
 * 13-Mar-89  Ian J. MacPhedran, University of Saskatchewan.
 *    Add write_tga
 *
 * 07-Mar-89  Ian J. MacPhedran, University of Saskatchewan.
 *    Created.
 ****************************************************************/
#define NOCOMM
#define NOKANJI
#include <windows.h>
#include "showimg.h"
#include <stdio.h>
#include <string.h>
static HCURSOR hcurSave;
/* For convenience, the TGA header file is included herein. */
```

```
/*
 * Header file for Targa file definitions.
 *
 * These definitions will allow a consistant interface to build
 * Targa (.TGA) image files.
 *
 * Created NOV-15-1988 IJMP
 */
/* File header definition */
struct TGA_ImageHeader
     {
     unsigned char IDLength;        /* Length of Identifier String */
     unsigned char CoMapType; /* 0 = NoMap */
     unsigned char ImgType;   /* Image Type (1,2,3,9,10,11) */
     unsigned char Index_lo, Index_hi;
     /* Index of first colour map entry */
     unsigned char Length_lo, Length_hi;
     /* Length of colour map (number of entries) */
     unsigned char CoSize;    /* Length of colour map entry */
     unsigned char X_org_lo, X_org_hi;   /* X Origin of Image */
     unsigned char Y_org_lo, Y_org_hi;   /* Y Origin of Image */
     unsigned char Width_lo, Width_hi;   /* Width of Image */
     unsigned char Height_lo, Height_hi;/* Height of Image */
     unsigned char PixelSize;           /* Pixel Size (8,16,24) */
     unsigned AttBits : 4; /*Number of Attribute Bits per pixel*/
     unsigned Rsrvd : 1;   /* Reserved bit */
     unsigned OrgBit : 1;
     /* Origin Bit (0=lower left, 1=upper left) */
     unsigned IntrLve : 2;   /* Interleaving Flag */
     };
char TGA_ImageIDField[256];
/* Definitions for Image Types */
#define TGA_MapRGBType 1
#define TGA_RawRGBType 2
#define TGA_RawMonoType 3
#define TGA_MapEnCodeType 9
#define TGA_RawEnCodeType 10
#define TGA_MonoEncodeType 11
/* Define flags for mode - these indicate special conditions */
#define GREYSC 0
#define COLOUR 1
#define MAPPED 2
#define RLENCD 4
#define INTERL 8
#define FOURWY 16
int RLE_count = 0, RLE_flag = 0;
extern NPLOGPALETTE pLogPal;
extern BOOL    bMemoryDIB;
int  read_tga(struct  _iobuf *rfile, unsigned char huge *pixels,
struct TGA_ImageHeader *tga, unsigned height, unsigned width);
int  get_map_entry(struct  _iobuf *rfile, unsigned char far *Red,
unsigned char far *Grn, unsigned char far *Blu, int Size,int mode);
int  get_pixel(struct  _iobuf *rfile, unsigned char *rRed, unsigned
char *rGrn, unsigned char *rBlu, int Size, int mode);
```

```
static RGBTRIPLE far *ColourMap=NULL;

int tgaview(HWND hWnd)
{
    unsigned numcolors=0;        //no DIB palette for 24-bit files
    unsigned width, height;
    char temp1[81];
    LPBITMAPINFOHEADER lpbi;
    int status=0, NewTga=0;
    int itemp1, itemp2;
    DWORD dwBits,dwLen;
    FILE *fpin;
    unsigned char huge *pixels;
    char footer[26];
    struct TGA_ImageHeader header;

    FreeDib();
    strcpy(temp1,achFileName);
    if ((fpin = fopen(temp1, "rb")) == NULL)
        return FALSE;

        //make sure file is a valid TGA
        status=1;
        fseek(fpin, -26L, SEEK_END); //read footer
        if(fread(footer,1,26,fpin)!=26)
                goto red_exit;
        if(lstrcmp(footer,"TRUEVISION-XFILE.")==0) //check signature
                NewTga=TRUE;
        else
                NewTga=FALSE;
        fseek(fpin,0,SEEK_SET);        //no signature, look at header
        if ((fread(&header, 1, 18, fpin)) != 18
                || header.ImgType<1
                || header.ImgType>11) {
                    ErrMsg("%s is not a valid TGA file",temp1);
                    goto red_exit;
                    }

        //get the dimensions out for use in creating the buffer
        itemp1 = header.Height_lo;
        itemp2 = header.Height_hi;
        height= itemp1 + itemp2 * 256;
        itemp1 = header.Width_lo;
        itemp2 = header.Width_hi;
        width = itemp1 + itemp2 * 256;

    /* If this is odd number of bytes, add one */
        if ((width & 1) != 0)
                width++;

        //Create the DIB structures

    hbiCurrent=GlobalAlloc(GHND, (LONG)sizeof(BITMAPINFOHEADER) +
                numcolors * sizeof(RGBQUAD));
```

```
   if (!hbiCurrent)
       goto red_exit;

   lpbi = (VOID FAR *)GlobalLock (hbiCurrent);
   lpbi->biSize=sizeof(BITMAPINFOHEADER);
   lpbi->biWidth=width;
   lpbi->biHeight=height;
   lpbi->biPlanes=1;
   lpbi->biBitCount= 24;
   lpbi->biCompression= BI_RGB;
   dwBits=
       lpbi->biSizeImage = (DWORD)width*height*3;   // 24/8 == 3
   lpbi->biXPelsPerMeter     = 0;
   lpbi->biYPelsPerMeter     = 0;
   lpbi->biClrUsed           = numcolors;
   lpbi->biClrImportant      = numcolors;

//Note: CreateDibPalette will make a default 256-color palette for
//      24-bit DIB's.
   hpalCurrent=CreateDibPalette(hbiCurrent);
   dwLen=lpbi->biSize + (DWORD)numcolors*sizeof(RGBQUAD) + dwBits;
   hdibCurrent=GlobalAlloc(GHND,dwLen);
   if(!hdibCurrent) {
       ErrMsg("Couldn't create DIB for TGA conversion");
       FreeDib();
       status=-1;
       goto red_exit;
       }
   pixels=(unsigned char huge *)GlobalLock(hdibCurrent);
   _fmemcpy(pixels,lpbi,(size_t)(dwLen-dwBits));
   GlobalUnlock(hbiCurrent);
   pixels += dwLen-dwBits;
   StartWait();
   status=read_tga(fpin,pixels,&header,height,width);
   EndWait();
   GlobalUnlock(hdibCurrent);
   bLegitDraw=bMemoryDIB=TRUE;
   if (hdibCurrent && !bDIBToDevice){
       hbmCurrent = BitmapFromDib(hdibCurrent,hpalCurrent);
       if (!hbmCurrent){
               ErrMsg ("Could not create bitmap!");
               bDIBToDevice=TRUE;     //mh: adapt to conditions!
               }
       }
red_exit:
   fclose(fpin);
   SizeWindow(hWnd);
   return(!status);
}

int read_tga(FILE *rfile, unsigned char huge *pixels, struct
TGA_ImageHeader *tga, unsigned int height, unsigned int width)
{
```

```
      int       status=1;
      unsigned int  i, j;
      unsigned int  temp1, temp2, mode, ncolors;
      unsigned char r, g, b;
      unsigned long k, linewidth;
      unsigned char huge *Red, huge *Grn, huge *Blu,
                       huge *Redk,huge *Grnk,huge *Bluk;
      HANDLE hMap;


      switch (tga->ImgType)
            {
      case TGA_MapRGBType:
      case TGA_RawRGBType:
      case TGA_RawMonoType:
      case TGA_MapEnCodeType:
      case TGA_RawEnCodeType:
      case TGA_MonoEncodeType:
            break;

      default:
            ErrMsg("Targa File Type %d not supported",
                   tga->ImgType);
            goto error_exit;
            }

      if (tga->ImgType == TGA_RawMonoType ||
          tga->ImgType == TGA_MonoEncodeType)
            {
            mode = GREYSC;
            }
      else
            {
            mode = COLOUR;
            }

/* Read ID String, if present */
      if (tga->IDLength != 0)
            fread(TGA_ImageIDField, 1, tga->IDLength, rfile);

/* If present, read the colour map information */
      if (tga->CoMapType != 0) {
            temp1 = tga->Index_lo + tga->Index_hi * 256;
            temp2 = tga->Length_lo + tga->Length_hi * 256;
            ncolors=temp1 + temp2 + 1;

            //create a color map array
            hMap=GlobalAlloc(GHND,ncolors*3);
            ColourMap=(RGBTRIPLE far *)GlobalLock(hMap);
            if(ColourMap==NULL) {
             ErrMsg("Could not create color map array for TGA");
             if(hMap)
                   GlobalFree(hMap);
```

```
                        return -1;
                    }

                for (i = temp1;  i < (temp1 + temp2);  i++)
                    get_map_entry(rfile, &ColourMap[i].rgbtRed,
                            &ColourMap[i].rgbtGreen,
                            &ColourMap[i].rgbtBlue,
                            tga->CoSize, mode);
                if ((tga->ImgType != TGA_RawRGBType) &&
                    (tga->ImgType != TGA_RawMonoType) &&
                    (tga->ImgType != TGA_MonoEncodeType) &&
                    (tga->ImgType != TGA_RawEnCodeType))
                    mode = mode | MAPPED;
                }

/* Check Run Length Encoding */
        if ((tga->ImgType == TGA_MapEnCodeType) ||
            (tga->ImgType == TGA_MonoEncodeType) ||
             (tga->ImgType == TGA_RawEnCodeType))
            mode = mode | RLENCD;

/* Check for interlacing of the Targa file */
        switch (tga->IntrLve) {
        case 2:                         /* Four way interlace */
            mode = mode | FOURWY;
        case 1:                         /* Two way interlace */
            mode = mode | INTERL;
        case 0:                         /* No interlace */
            break;
        default:                        /* Reserved - we'll let it pass */
            break;
            }

/* Set up byte map for writing */

        Red = pixels;
        Grn = Red + 1;
        Blu = Grn + 1;
/* Read the Targa file body and convert to DIB format */
        linewidth = tga->Width_lo + tga->Width_hi * 256;
        for (i = 0;  i < height;  i++) {
        /* No interlace */
                if ((mode & INTERL) == 0) {
                    j = i;
                    }
        /* Two way interlace */
                else if ((mode & FOURWY) != 0) {
                    if (2 * i < height)
                        j = 2 * i;
                    else {
                        j = i - height / 2;
                        j = 2 * j + 1;
                        }
                    }
```

```
        /* Four way interlace */
            else {
                if (4 * i < height)
                        j = 4 * i;
                else if (2 * i < height) {
                        j = i - height / 4;
                        j = 4 * j + 1;
                        }
                else if (4 * i < 3 * height) {
                        j = i - height / 2;
                        j = 4 * j + 2;
                        }
                else {
                        j = i - height / 2 - height / 4;
                        j = 4 * j + 3;
                        }
                }
            k = (height - 1 - j) * width;
            Redk = Red + k;
            Grnk = Grn + k;
            Bluk = Blu + k;
            for (j = 0;  j < (unsigned int)linewidth;  j++) {
                    get_pixel(rfile,&r, &g, &b,
                                    tga->PixelSize, mode);
                    *Redk = r;
                    *Grnk = g;
                    *Bluk = b;
                    Redk += 3;
                    Grnk += 3;
                    Bluk += 3;
                    }
            if(SpinTheMessageLoop())
                    break;
            }
        status=0;
error_exit:
        if(ColourMap) {
                GlobalUnlock(hMap);
                GlobalFree(hMap);
                ColourMap=NULL;
                }
        return status;
        }

int get_map_entry(rfile,Red, Grn, Blu, Size, mode)
FILE *rfile;
unsigned char far *Red,far *Grn,far *Blu;
int Size, mode;
{
        unsigned int j, k, l;
        unsigned char i, r, g, b;
```

```
/* read appropriate number of bytes, break into rgb & put in map */
    switch (Size) {
    case 8:/* Grey Scale already, read and triplicate */
            fread(&i, 1, 1, rfile);
            r = i;
            g = i;
            b = i;
            break;

    case 16:        /* 5 bits each of red green and blue */
    case 15:        /* Watch for byte order */
            fread(&j, 1, 1, rfile);
            fread(&k, 1, 1, rfile);
            l = j + k * 256;
            r = ((l >> 10) & 31) << 3;
            g = ((l >> 5) & 31) << 3;
            b = (l & 31) << 3;
            break;

    case 32:        /* Read alpha byte & throw away */
    case 24:        /* Eight bits each of red green and blue */
            fread(&i, 1, 1, rfile);
            b = i;
            fread(&i, 1, 1, rfile);
            g = i;
            fread(&i, 1, 1, rfile);
            r = i;
            if (Size == 32)
                    fread(&i, 1, 1, rfile);
            break;

    default:
            ErrMsg("Unknown Pixel Size\n");
            return(1);
            }
    *Red = r;
    *Grn = g;
    *Blu = b;
    return 0;
    }

int get_pixel(rfile,rRed, rGrn, rBlu, Size, mode)
FILE *rfile;
unsigned char *rRed, *rGrn, *rBlu;
int Size, mode;
    {
    static unsigned char Red, Grn, Blu;
    unsigned char i, j, k;
    static unsigned int l;

      /* Check if run length encoded. */
    if ((mode & RLENCD) != 0)
            {
```

```
            if (RLE_count == 0)    /* Have to restart run */
                    {
                    fread(&i, 1, 1, rfile);
                    RLE_flag = (i & 0x80) >> 7;
                    if (RLE_flag == 0) { /* unencoded pixels */
                            RLE_count = i + 1;
                            }
                    else {            /* Single pixel replicated */
                            RLE_count = i - 127;
                            }
                    RLE_count—;    /* Decrement count & get pixel */
                    }
            else {
/* Have already read count & (at least) first pixel */
                    RLE_count—;
                    if (RLE_flag != 0)
                            {                /* Replicated pixels */
                            goto PixEncode;
                            }
                    }
            }
      /* Read appropriate number of bytes, break into RGB */
      switch (Size)
              {
      case 8: /* Grey Scale - read a byte and triplicate */
            fread(&i, 1, 1, rfile);
            Red = i;
            Grn = i;
            Blu = i;
            l = i;
            break;

      case 16:      /* Five bits each of red green and blue */
      case 15:      /* Watch byte order */
            fread(&j, 1, 1, rfile);
            fread(&k, 1, 1, rfile);
            l = j + k * 256;
            Red = ((k & 0x7C) << 1);
            Grn = ((k & 0x3) << 6) + ((j & 0xE0) >> 2);
            Blu = ((j & 0x1F) << 3);
            break;

      case 32:      /* Read alpha byte & throw away */
      case 24:      /* Eight bits each of red green and blue */
            fread(&i, 1, 1, rfile);
            Blu = i;
            fread(&i, 1, 1, rfile);
            Grn = i;
            fread(&i, 1, 1, rfile);
            Red = i;
            if (Size == 32)
                    fread(&i, 1, 1, rfile);
            l = 0;
            break;
```

```
        default:
                ErrMsg("Unknown Pixel Size");
                return(1);
                }

PixEncode:
        if ((mode & MAPPED) == MAPPED)        {
                *rRed = ColourMap[1].rgbtRed;
                *rGrn = ColourMap[1].rgbtGreen;
                *rBlu = ColourMap[1].rgbtBlue;
                }
        else {
                *rRed = Red;
                *rGrn = Grn;
                *rBlu = Blu;
                }
        return 0;
        }
```

vicar.c

```
#define NOCOMM
#define NOKANJI
#include <windows.h>
#include "showimg.h"
#include <stdio.h>
#include <string.h>
#include "vicar.h"
extern NPLOGPALETTE pLogPal;
extern BOOL   bMemoryDIB;
int nl, ns, bitsperpix;
int DNlow, DNhigh;
int OpenFileFlag;
int ByteSwap = 1;
static HCURSOR hcurSave;

int BadStatus(char *status)
/* Prints out error message if there is one.
   Returns true if error. */
{
        if (strlen(status) > 0) {
                ErrMsg(status);
                return (1);
                }
        else
                return (0);
}
int vicarview(HWND hWnd){
        int istatus = 0, fh = 0, i;
        unsigned numcolors = 0;
        unsigned width, height;
        char temp1[81];
```

```
           LPBITMAPINFOHEADER lpbi;
           DWORD dwBits, dwLen;
           RGBQUAD FAR *pRgb;
           unsigned char huge *pixels;
           unsigned char far *buffer;
           char status[80];
           float factor;

           FreeDib();
           strcpy(temp1, achFileName);
           //make sure file is a valid VICAR or similar labeled image
           istatus = 1;
           status[0] = '\0';
           OpenImage(temp1, 0, "read", &nl, &ns, &bitsperpix, status);
           if (BadStatus(status))
                  return 0;
           OpenFileFlag = 1;
           if ((bitsperpix != 8) && (bitsperpix != 16) &&
                  (bitsperpix != 4) && (bitsperpix != 1)) {
                  ErrMsg("Invalid bits per sample in VICAR file");
                  goto red_exit;
                  }
           if(bitsperpix != 8) {
                  ErrMsg("ShowIMG only supports 8-bit gray scale VICAR"
                          " images");
                  goto red_exit;
                  }
           DNlow = 0;
           DNhigh = (1 << ((bitsperpix < 14) ? bitsperpix : 14)) - 1;
           //get the dimensions out for use in creating the DIB buffer
           width = ns;
           height = nl;
           if(bitsperpix<=8)
                  numcolors= 1 << bitsperpix;
           //Create the DIB structures
           hbiCurrent = GlobalAlloc(GHND,
                          (LONG) sizeof(BITMAPINFOHEADER) +
                          numcolors * sizeof(RGBQUAD));
           if (!hbiCurrent)
                  goto red_exit;
           lpbi = (VOID FAR *) GlobalLock(hbiCurrent);
           lpbi->biSize = sizeof(BITMAPINFOHEADER);
           lpbi->biWidth = width;
           lpbi->biHeight = height;
           lpbi->biPlanes = 1;
           lpbi->biBitCount = bitsperpix;
           lpbi->biCompression = BI_RGB;
           dwBits =
            lpbi->biSizeImage=(DWORD) width * height * (bitsperpix / 8);
           lpbi->biXPelsPerMeter = 0;
           lpbi->biYPelsPerMeter = 0;
           lpbi->biClrUsed = numcolors;
           lpbi->biClrImportant = numcolors;
           //make gray scale palette
```

```
        pRgb = (RGBQUAD FAR *) ((LPSTR) lpbi + lpbi->biSize);
        factor = 256.0f / numcolors;
        for (i = 0;  i < numcolors;  i++) {
                pRgb[i].rgbRed =
                        pRgb[i].rgbGreen =
                        pRgb[i].rgbBlue = (int) (i * factor);
                }
        hpalCurrent = CreateDibPalette(hbiCurrent);
        dwLen = lpbi->biSize + (DWORD) numcolors * sizeof(RGBQUAD)
                                + dwBits;
        hdibCurrent = GlobalAlloc(GHND, dwLen);
        if (!hdibCurrent) {
                ErrMsg("Couldn't create DIB for VICAR conversion");
                FreeDib();
                istatus = -1;
                goto red_exit;
                }
        pixels = (unsigned char huge *) GlobalLock(hdibCurrent);
        _fmemcpy((void far *) pixels, lpbi,
                                (size_t) (dwLen - dwBits));
        GlobalUnlock(hbiCurrent);
        pixels += dwLen - dwBits;
        StartWait();
        for (i=1;i<=nl;i++) {
                buffer=pixels + (nl-i)*(long)ns*bitsperpix/8L;
                ReadLine(0, buffer, i, 1, ns, status);
                if(BadStatus(status))
                        break;
                if(SpinTheMessageLoop())
                        break;
                }
        EndWait();
        GlobalUnlock(hdibCurrent);
        bLegitDraw = bMemoryDIB = TRUE;
        if (hdibCurrent && !bDIBToDevice) {
                hbmCurrent = BitmapFromDib(hdibCurrent, hpalCurrent);
                if (!hbmCurrent) {
                        ErrMsg("Could not create bitmap!");
                        bDIBToDevice = TRUE;//mh: adapt to conditions!
                        }
                }
        istatus=0;
red_exit:
        CloseImage(0, status);
        SizeWindow(hWnd);
        return (!istatus);
}
```

makefile

```
all: showimg.exe

DEBUG=1              #comment this out when you go into production
```

```
!IFDEF DEBUG
O=/Od /Gi /qc # disable optimisation and invoke quick compiler
Z=/Zip              # generate debugging info
C=/CO/LI            #just codeview etc.
!ELSE
O=/Olws             # optimization
Z=/Zp               # pack structures
C=/LI               # put line numbers in map even for production
!ENDIF
CFLAGS= /AM /Gsw /W2 $O $Z
AFLAGS= -v -ML -Mx
OBJS = showimg.obj print.obj dib.obj drawdib.obj dlgopen.obj \
gif.obj pcx.obj tga.obj vicar.obj raw.obj imageio.obj \  labutil.obj
fileio.obj

OBJ1 = tiff.obj tif_open.obj tif_read.obj tif_clos.obj \
tif_swab.obj tif_dir.obj tif_erro.obj tif_flus.obj \
tif_warn.obj tif_writ.obj

OBJ2 = tif_comr.obj tif_ccit.obj tif_dump.obj tif_lzw.obj \
tif_fax3.obj tif_fax4.obj tif_pack.obj tif_comp.obj

INCS = showimg.h

showimg.exe: $(OBJS) $(OBJ1) $(OBJ2) showimg.def showimg.res
dlgopena.obj
        link @<<showimg.lnk
$(OBJS) +
$(OBJ1) +
$(OBJ2) +
dlgopena
showimg.exe/align:16/map
showimg
mlibcew libw /NOD/SE:255
showimg.def $C
<<keep                  #save link file for manual use
        mapsym showimg
!IFDEF DEBUG
        cvpack -p showimg.exe
!ENDIF
        rc showimg.res

$(OBJS): $(INCS)

$(OBJ1): $(INCS) tiffio.h tiff.h tiffcomp.h

$(OBJ2): $(INCS) tiffio.h tiff.h tiffcomp.h

pcx.obj: pcx.h

dlgopena.obj: dlgopena.asm

showimg.res: showimg.rc showimg.dlg showimg.ico about.dlg rawdlg.dlg
        rc -r showimg.rc
```

Adding Image Processing Capabilities

ShowIMG is already a useful program for viewing various file formats from Windows, for converting those formats to DIBs, and for clipping images. We can make it even more useful by adding a few simple image processing capabilities. The first of these, gray-scale conversion, can help make color images more suitable for printing.

While some printer drivers for Windows include gray-scale conversion code in their DIB support, many still do not—so it would be nice if we could do this in our program. Another advantage of doing the gray-scale conversion in our program is that we can easily transform 24-bit true-color images that have been gray-scaled to 8-bit palettes. Finally, we can convert only one color component at a time if we wish, or weight one color component more than the others, or change the range of gray-scale values used in the image, in order to control the appearance of the printed image.

Figure 3.2. Cat converted by the printer driver

Figure 3.3. Cat converted with maximum-intensity algorithm

Figure 3.4. Cat converted with weighted-mean algorithm, R=0.7,G=0.33,B=0.9

Converting RGB to Gray-Scale

A simple model for converting color images to gray-scale, which tends to make bright images, sets the brightness equal to the maximum (Red, Green, Blue) color component. A slightly more complicated model, which tends to make subdued images, takes the average of the three components. We can build an infinite variety of conversions by allowing the user to specify floating point weights for the red, green, and blue components.

The actual conversions will be easy—and for images with palettes, it will be quite fast, since we will be handling at most 256 triplets. We'll want to give the user some controls: perhaps radio buttons for the algo-

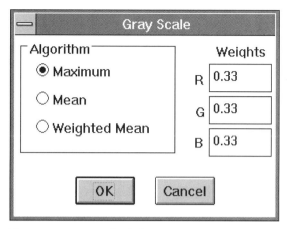

Figure 3.5. Gray-scale dialog

rithm, and edit boxes for the weighting of the red, green, and blue components in the "weighted average" model. We'll have the weights default to 0.33.

My first pass at a gray-scaling algorithm gave me weird images: random colors would turn into white or black. After a while I realized that the code to read a DIB (function InitDIB in Image1.C) converts RGB palettes to palette indices. Once I disabled that "optimization," the gray-scaling code worked correctly.

The gray-scaling code turned out to be even more useful than I had hoped. Using the weighted average method, I can customize the way colors are translated to gray to get a good print almost every time. For example, take the drawing of a cat in Figure 3.2 (redcat.bmp on the companion disks.) The cat's eyes are blue; the background is red; and the cat itself is black. Not too swift when you let the printer do the gray scaling.

In Figure 3.3, the cat has been converted with the maximum-color-intensity algorithm. I don't consider this an optimal picture—the background is too light. However, the image in Figure 3.4 looks a lot better: I've used the weighted-mean algorithm with a red weight of 0.7, green weight of 0.33, and blue weight of 0.9.

The code for RGB to gray-scale conversion resides in module process.c on your companion disks. The GrayScale function and dialog procedure (see Figure 3.5) follow:

```
static double _idd_blueweight, _idd_greenweight, _idd_redweight;
static WORD GrayMethod;
static HCURSOR hcurSave;

void GrayScale(HWND hWnd)
{
        LPBITMAPINFOHEADER lpbi;
        RGBQUAD FAR *pRgb;
```

```
LOGPALETTE   *pPal;
unsigned char huge *pixels;
char FAR *pb;
int colors,i;
DWORD l;
BYTE val;

if(!bLegitDraw || !hdibCurrent || !hbiCurrent) {
        OkMsgBox("GrayScale",szNothing);
        return;
        }
if(!fDialog(GRAYDLG, hWnd, GrayDlgProc))
        return;
lpbi=(VOID FAR *)GlobalLock(hbiCurrent);
if(lpbi==NULL) {
        MessageBeep(0);
        return;
        }
colors=DibNumColors(lpbi);
StartWait();

//If the DIB has a palette, just change the palette

if(colors) {
        pRgb = (RGBQUAD FAR *)((LPSTR)lpbi + lpbi->biSize);
        switch(GrayMethod) {
                case IDD_MAXIMUM:
                for (i=0;i<colors;i++) {
                 val=max(pRgb[i].rgbRed,
                         (max(pRgb[i].rgbGreen,pRgb[i].rgbBlue)));
                 pRgb[i].rgbRed   =
                        pRgb[i].rgbGreen =
                        pRgb[i].rgbBlue  = val;
                        }
                                break;
                case IDD_MEAN:
                for (i=0;i<colors;i++) {
                 val=min(255,pRgb[i].rgbRed/3
                                +pRgb[i].rgbGreen/3
                                 +pRgb[i].rgbBlue/3);
                 pRgb[i].rgbRed   =
                        pRgb[i].rgbGreen =
                        pRgb[i].rgbBlue  = val;
                        }
                        break;
                case IDD_WEIGHTED:
                for (i=0;i<colors;i++) {
                 val=min(255,(int)(
                   pRgb[i].rgbRed   * _idd_redweight
                  +pRgb[i].rgbGreen * _idd_greenweight
                  +pRgb[i].rgbBlue  * _idd_blueweight));
                 pRgb[i].rgbRed   =
                        pRgb[i].rgbGreen =
```

```
                                pRgb[i].rgbBlue  = val;
                                }
                        break;
                default:
                        MessageBeep(0);
                        break;
                }
        hpalCurrent=CreateDibPalette(hbiCurrent);
        pixels=(unsigned char huge *)GlobalLock(hdibCurrent);
        _fmemcpy(pixels,lpbi,
                (size_t)(lpbi->biSize +
                        (DWORD)colors*sizeof(RGBQUAD)));
        GlobalUnlock(hbiCurrent);
        GlobalUnlock(hdibCurrent);
        }


//Otherwise, change the colors

else {
        lpbi=(VOID far *)GlobalLock(hdibCurrent);
        pixels = (unsigned char huge *)(lpbi + lpbi->biSize);
        switch(GrayMethod) {
                case IDD_MAXIMUM:
                for(l=0;l<lpbi->biSizeImage;l+=3) {
                        pb=pixels+l;
                        val=max(*pb,(max(*(pb+1),*(pb+2))));
                        *pb = *(pb+1) = *(pb+2) = val;
                        }
                break;
                case IDD_MEAN:
                for(l=0;l<lpbi->biSizeImage;l+=3) {
                        pb=pixels+l;
                        val=min(255,
                                *(pb)/3 + *(pb+1)/3 + *(pb+2)/3);
                        *pb = *(pb+1) = *(pb+2) = val;
                        }
                        break;
                case IDD_WEIGHTED:
                for(l=0;l<lpbi->biSizeImage;l+=3) {
                        pb=pixels+l;
                        val=min(255,(int)
                         (*(pb)   * _idd_blueweight
                        + *(pb+1) * _idd_greenweight
                        + *(pb+2) * _idd_redweight));
                        *pb = *(pb+1) = *(pb+2) = val;
                        }
                        break;
                default:
                        MessageBeep(0);
                        break;
                }
        GlobalUnlock(hdibCurrent);
        colors = MAXPALETTE;
```

```
                pPal = (LOGPALETTE *) LocalAlloc(LPTR,
                 sizeof(LOGPALETTE) + colors * sizeof(PALETTEENTRY));
                if (!pPal) {
                        MessageBeep(0);
                        goto done;
                        }
                pPal->palNumEntries = colors;
                pPal->palVersion = PALVERSION;
                for (i = 0;  i < colors;  i++) {
                        pPal->palPalEntry[i].peRed=
                                pPal->palPalEntry[i].peGreen=
                                pPal->palPalEntry[i].peBlue = (BYTE) i;
                        pPal->palPalEntry[i].peFlags = (BYTE) 0;
                        }
                hpalCurrent = CreatePalette(pPal);
                LocalFree((HANDLE) pPal);
                }
done:
        EndWait();

        if (hdibCurrent && !bDIBToDevice) {
                if (hbmCurrent)
                        DeleteObject(hbmCurrent);
                hbmCurrent=NULL;
                hbmCurrent = BitmapFromDib(hdibCurrent, hpalCurrent);
                if (!hbmCurrent) {
                        ErrMsg("Could not create bitmap!");
                        bDIBToDevice = TRUE;//mh: adapt to conditions!
                        }
                }
        InvalidateRect(hWnd, NULL, TRUE);
}

BOOL _export FAR PASCAL GrayDlgProc(HWND hDlg, unsigned message,
                                        WORD wParam, LONG lParam)
{
  static char szString[132];

        switch (message)
        {
        case WM_INITDIALOG:
                GrayMethod=IDD_MAXIMUM;
                CheckRadioButton(hDlg,IDD_MAXIMUM,IDD_WEIGHTED,
                                 IDD_MAXIMUM );
                SetDlgItemText( hDlg, IDD_REDWEIGHT, "0.33" );
                SetDlgItemText( hDlg, IDD_GREENWEIGHT, "0.33" );
                SetDlgItemText( hDlg, IDD_BLUEWEIGHT, "0.33" );
                  break;
        case WM_COMMAND:
         switch (wParam)
         {
         case IDOK:
          GetDlgItemText( hDlg, IDD_REDWEIGHT, szString,
```

```
                       sizeof( szString ) );
          _idd_redweight = atof( szString );
          GetDlgItemText( hDlg, IDD_GREENWEIGHT, szString,
                     sizeof( szString ) );
          _idd_greenweight = atof( szString );
          GetDlgItemText( hDlg, IDD_BLUEWEIGHT, szString,
                     sizeof( szString ) );
          _idd_blueweight = atof( szString );
          EndDialog(hDlg, TRUE);
          break;
        case IDCANCEL:
             EndDialog(hDlg, FALSE);
             break;
        case IDD_MAXIMUM :
        case IDD_MEAN :
        case IDD_WEIGHTED :
             GrayMethod=wParam;
             CheckRadioButton(hDlg, IDD_MAXIMUM, IDD_WEIGHTED,
                                  wParam );
             break;
        default:
             return FALSE;
        }
        break;
  default:
        return FALSE;
  }
  return TRUE;
}
```

Adjusting Colors

We've seen how useful a nice collection of gray-scaling methods can be. Color adjustment should be another capability that is frequently needed (see Figure 3.6). Color scanning is notoriously difficult to do well: the scanner (with help from the operator) has to be in focus and calibrated for brightness, hue, and saturation.

Windows uses the RGB (Red, Green, Blue) color model internally, as it corresponds directly to the physics of a CRT with electron guns for Red, Green and Blue phosphors—the RGB primaries are additive, just like the light from the CRT. Other color models, however, may make it easier for the user to understand the controls. Typically, a photographer looks at a color print or slide and says "not enough contrast," "too dark," "too red," "not enough saturation," or something similar. How should we relate saturation or contrast to the RGB values for the current palette or pixels?

The HSV (hue, saturation, value) color model (where value is also called brightness), corresponds somewhat to the way artists and photographers think about color. The RGB color space forms a cube; the HSV color space forms a hexagonal cone, whose base corresponds to the RGB cube viewed along the principal diagonal. The tip of the cone corresponds to black.

The hue, H, in the HSV model is given as an angle, with red at 0°, green at 120°, and blue at 240°. The saturation, S, ranges from 0 on the center line (V axis) to one on the exterior of the hexagonal cone. Value ranges from 0 at the black tip of the cone to 1 at the base of the cone.

A variation on the HSV model, called HLS (hue, lightness/luminosity, saturation), pulls the white value out of the base of the HSV hex-cone, to form a double hex-cone. Full color values fall on the L=0.5 plane in the HLS; in the HSV model, they fall on the V=1.0 plane. The CYMK (cyan, yellow, magenta, black) model corresponds to the three subtractive primaries plus black, and matches the four-color printing process.

The Windows 3.1 common color dialog is set up to use both the HLS and RGB models to specify a color. However, we won't be picking individual colors in the IMAGE1 program—we'll be adjusting the overall color appearance of the image by specifying a color *transformation*. Bringing up the full color space would be confusing: all we'll need is three scroll bars and three radio buttons along with the usual push-buttons. The radio buttons will choose the color model (RGB, HSV, or HLS), and the scroll bars will control the three parameters of the current model. We'll update the image to show the effects of the controls.

If we are working with a palette-based screen driver, making temporary color changes could be a low-overhead operation: we would just change the Windows palette. We could do this on every scroll-bar message if we wanted. On the other hand, we'd only want to change the DIB palette or DIB pixel colors when OK was pressed in the color dialog box. For now, we'll keep it simple and make changes only when OK is pressed.

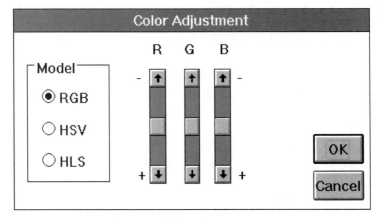

Figure 3.6. Color Adjustment dialog

You'll find code to convert among color models in most of the recommended readings for this chapter. I've followed Foley and van Dam, and translated their Pascal procedures to C functions. Transforming colors in RGB space is simple, of course—just add the color differences to the original colors and bound the results to the valid range [0–255]. In HSV or HLS space, each color is converted from RGB to the working color space, then each component added to the differences and bounded, and finally the result converted back to RGB.

The color conversion code took me a day or so. In practice, the RGB model is good for changing hues, and the HSV and HLS models are good for adjusting color saturation and brightness. Adjusting hues with the HSV and HLS models is a little strange, unless you want false color or posterization effects.

The code for color adjustment, like the gray-scale code, resides in process.c.

```c
void HSV_to_RGB(double h,double s,double v,double *r,
                double *g,double *b)
{
        double f, p, q, t;
        int i;

        if(s==0.0)
                *r=*g=*b=v;
        else {
                if(h==360.0)
                        h=0.0;
                h /= 60.0;
                i=(int)floor(h);
                f=h-i;
                p=v*(1.0-s);
                q=v*(1.0-(s*f));
                t=v*(1.0-(s*(1.0-f)));
                switch(i) {
                        case 0:
                                *r=v;
                                *g=t;
                                *b=p;
                                break;
                        case 1:
                                *r=q;
                                *g=v;
                                *b=p;
                                break;
                        case 2:
                                *r=p;
                                *g=v;
                                *b=t;
                                break;
                        case 3:
                                *r=p;
```

```
                                          *g=q;
                                          *b=v;
                                          break;
                            case 4:
                                          *r=t;
                                          *g=p;
                                          *b=v;
                                          break;
                            case 5:
                                          *r=v;
                                          *g=p;
                                          *b=q;
                                          break;
                      }
              }
}

void RGB_to_HSV(double r,double g,double b,double *h,
                      double *s,double *v)
{
      double mx,mn,delta;

      mx=max(r,max(g,b));
      mn=min(r,min(g,b));
      *v=mx;
      if(mx!=0.0)
              *s=(mx-mn)/mx;
      else
              *s=0.0;
      if(*s==0.0)
              *h=UNDEFINED;
      else {
              delta=mx-mn;
              if(r==mx)
                      *h=(g-b)/delta;
              else if(g==mx)
                      *h=2.0+(b-r)/delta;
              else if(b==mx)
                      *h=4.0+(r-g)/delta;
              *h *= 60.0;
              if(*h<0.0)
                      *h += 360.0;
              }
}

static double Value(double n1, double n2, double hue)
{
      if(hue>360.0)
              hue -= 360.0;
      else if(hue<0.0)
              hue += 360.0;
      if(hue<60.0)
              return(n1+(n2-n1)*hue/60.0);
```

```
        else if (hue<180.0)
             return n2;
        else if (hue<240.0)
             return(n1+(n2-n1)*(240.0-hue)/60.0);
        else
             return n1;
}

void HLS_to_RGB(double h,double l,double s,double *r,
                    double *g,double *b)
{
      double m2,m1;

      if(l<=0.5)
             m2=l*(1+s);
      else
             m2=l+s-l*s;
      m1=2.0*l-m2;
      if(s==0)
             *r = *g = *b = l;
      else {
             *r=Value(m1,m2,h+120.0);
             *g=Value(m1,m2,h);
             *b=Value(m1,m2,h-120.0);
             }
}

void RGB_to_HLS(double r,double g,double b,double *h,
                    double *l,double *s)
{
      double mx,mn,delta;

      mx=max(r,max(g,b));
      mn=min(r,min(g,b));
      *l=(mx+mn)/2.0;
      if(mx==mn) {
             *s=0.0;
             *h=UNDEFINED;
             }
      else {
             if(*l<=0.5)
                    *s=(mx-mn)/(mx+mn);
             else
                    *s=(mx-mn)/(2.0-mx-mn);
             delta=mx-mn;
             if(r==mx)
                    *h=(g-b)/delta;
             else if(g==mx)
                    *h=2.0+(b-r)/delta;
             else if(b==mx)
                    *h=4.0+(r-g)/delta;
             *h *= 60.0;
             if(*h<0.0)
```

```
                              *h += 360.0;
                }
}

void Color (HWND hWnd)
{
        int dr,dg,db;
        double r,g,b,dh,ds,dv,dl,h,s,v,l;
        LPBITMAPINFOHEADER lpbi;
        RGBQUAD FAR *pRgb;
        unsigned char huge *pixels;
        char FAR *pb;
        int colors,i;
        DWORD il;

        if(!bLegitDraw || !hdibCurrent) {
                OkMsgBox("Color",szNothing);
                return;
                }
        if(!fDialog(ADJCOLOR, hWnd, ColorDlgProc))
                return;
        switch(ColorModel) {
                case IDD_RGB:
                        dr=bar1;
                        dg=bar2;
                        db=bar3;
                        break;
                case IDD_HSV:
                        if(bar1<0)
                                bar1 =+ 360;
                        dh=bar1;
                        ds=bar2/100.0;
                        dv=bar3/100.0;
                        break;
                case IDD_HLS:
                        if(bar1<0)
                                bar1 =+ 360;
                        dh=bar1;
                        dl=bar2/100.0;
                        ds=bar3/100.0;
                        break;
                }
        lpbi=(VOID FAR *)GlobalLock(hbiCurrent);
        if(lpbi==NULL) {
                MessageBeep(0);
                return;
                }
        colors=DibNumColors(lpbi);
        StartWait();

        //If the DIB has a palette, just change the palette
```

```
if(colors) {
    pRgb = (RGBQUAD FAR *)((LPSTR)lpbi + lpbi->biSize);
    switch(ColorModel) {
    case IDD_RGB:
      for (i=0;i<colors;i++) {
       pRgb[i].rgbRed   =BOUND(pRgb[i].rgbRed  +dr,0,255);
       pRgb[i].rgbGreen=BOUND(pRgb[i].rgbGreen+dg,0,255);
       pRgb[i].rgbBlue =BOUND(pRgb[i].rgbBlue +db,0,255);
       }
      break;

    case IDD_HSV:
      for (i=0;i<colors;i++) {
          r=pRgb[i].rgbRed/255.0;
          g=pRgb[i].rgbGreen/255.0;
          b=pRgb[i].rgbBlue/255.0;
          RGB_to_HSV(r,g,b,&h,&s,&v);
          if(h!=UNDEFINED)
                 h = fmod(h+dh, 360.0);
          s = BOUND(s+ds,0.0,1.0);
          v = BOUND(v+dv,0.0,1.0);
          HSV_to_RGB(h,s,v,&r,&g,&b);
          pRgb[i].rgbRed   = r*255;
          pRgb[i].rgbGreen = g*255;
          pRgb[i].rgbBlue  = b*255;
          }
      break;

    case IDD_HLS:
      for (i=0;i<colors;i++) {
          r=pRgb[i].rgbRed/255.0;
          g=pRgb[i].rgbGreen/255.0;
          b=pRgb[i].rgbBlue/255.0;
          RGB_to_HLS(r,g,b,&h,&l,&s);
          if(h!=UNDEFINED)
                 h = fmod(h+dh, 360.0);
          l = BOUND(l+dl,0.0,1.0);
          s = BOUND(s+ds,0.0,1.0);
          HLS_to_RGB(h,l,s,&r,&g,&b);
          pRgb[i].rgbRed   = r*255;
          pRgb[i].rgbGreen = g*255;
          pRgb[i].rgbBlue  = b*255;
          }
      break;

    }
    hpalCurrent=CreateDibPalette(hbiCurrent);
    pixels=(unsigned char huge *)GlobalLock(hdibCurrent);
    _fmemcpy(pixels,lpbi,
          (size_t)(lpbi->biSize +
          (DWORD)colors*sizeof(RGBQUAD)));
    GlobalUnlock(hbiCurrent);
    GlobalUnlock(hdibCurrent);
    }
```

```
//Otherwise, change the colors

else {
        lpbi=(VOID far *)GlobalLock(hdibCurrent);
        pixels = (unsigned char huge *)(lpbi + lpbi->biSize);
        switch(ColorModel) {

        case IDD_RGB:
          for(il=0;il<lpbi->biSizeImage;il+=3) {
                pb=pixels+il;
                *pb     = BOUND(*pb    +db,0,255);
                *(pb+1) = BOUND(*(pb+1)+dg,0,255);
                *(pb+2) = BOUND(*(pb+2)+dr,0,255);
                }
          break;

        case IDD_HSV:
          for(il=0;il<lpbi->biSizeImage;il+=3) {
                pb=pixels+il;
                r= *(pb+2)/255.0;
                g= *(pb+1)/255.0;
                b= *(pb)  /255.0;
                RGB_to_HSV(r,g,b,&h,&s,&v);
                if(h!=UNDEFINED)
                        h = fmod(h+dh, 360.0);
                s = BOUND(s+ds,0.0,1.0);
                v = BOUND(v+dv,0.0,1.0);
                HSV_to_RGB(h,s,v,&r,&g,&b);
                *(pb+2) = r*255;
                *(pb+1) = g*255;
                *(pb)   = b*255;
                }
          break;

        case IDD_HLS:
          for(il=0;il<lpbi->biSizeImage;il+=3) {
                pb=pixels+il;
                r= *(pb+2)/255.0;
                g= *(pb+1)/255.0;
                b= *(pb)  /255.0;
                RGB_to_HLS(r,g,b,&h,&l,&s);
                if(h!=UNDEFINED)
                        h = fmod(h+dh, 360.0);
                l = BOUND(l+dl,0.0,1.0);
                s = BOUND(s+ds,0.0,1.0);
                HLS_to_RGB(h,l,s,&r,&g,&b);
                *(pb+2) = r*255;
                *(pb+1) = g*255;
                *(pb)   = b*255;
                }
          break;

        }
        GlobalUnlock(hdibCurrent);
```

```
                }
        EndWait();

        if (hdibCurrent && !bDIBToDevice) {
                if (hbmCurrent)
                        DeleteObject(hbmCurrent);
                hbmCurrent=NULL;
                hbmCurrent = BitmapFromDib(hdibCurrent, hpalCurrent);
                if (!hbmCurrent) {
                        ErrMsg("Could not create bitmap!");
                        bDIBToDevice = TRUE;  //mh: adapt to conditions!
                        }
                }
        InvalidateRect(hWnd, NULL, TRUE);

}
BOOL _export FAR PASCAL ColorDlgProc(HWND hDlg, unsigned message,
                        WORD wParam, LONG lParam)
{
        static HWND hSB1, hSB2, hSB3;
        switch (message)
        {
        case WM_INITDIALOG:
                ColorModel=IDD_RGB;
                CheckRadioButton( hDlg, IDD_RGB, IDD_HLS, ColorModel);
                SetDlgItemText( hDlg, IDD_TX1, "R" );
                SetDlgItemText( hDlg, IDD_TX2, "G" );
                SetDlgItemText( hDlg, IDD_TX3, "B" );
                hSB1=GetDlgItem(hDlg,IDD_SB1);
                hSB2=GetDlgItem(hDlg,IDD_SB2);
                hSB3=GetDlgItem(hDlg,IDD_SB3);
                SetScrollRange(hSB1,SB_CTL,-255,255,0);
                SetScrollRange(hSB2,SB_CTL,-255,255,0);
                SetScrollRange(hSB3,SB_CTL,-255,255,0);
                bar1=bar2=bar3=0;
                SetScrollPos(hSB1,SB_CTL,bar1,1);
                SetScrollPos(hSB2,SB_CTL,bar2,1);
                SetScrollPos(hSB3,SB_CTL,bar3,1);
                break;
        case WM_COMMAND:
                switch (wParam)
                {
                case IDOK:
                                EndDialog(hDlg, TRUE);
                                break;
                case IDCANCEL:
                                EndDialog(hDlg, FALSE);
                                break;
                case IDD_RGB :
                        ColorModel=wParam;
                        CheckRadioButton( hDlg, IDD_RGB, IDD_HLS,
                                ColorModel);
                        SetDlgItemText( hDlg, IDD_TX1, "R" );
```

```
                    SetDlgItemText( hDlg, IDD_TX2, "G" );
                    SetDlgItemText( hDlg, IDD_TX3, "B" );
                    SetScrollRange(hSB1,SB_CTL,-255,255,0);
                    SetScrollRange(hSB2,SB_CTL,-255,255,0);
                    SetScrollRange(hSB3,SB_CTL,-255,255,0);
                    bar1=bar2=bar3=0;
                    SetScrollPos(hSB1,SB_CTL,bar1,1);
                    SetScrollPos(hSB2,SB_CTL,bar2,1);
                    SetScrollPos(hSB3,SB_CTL,bar3,1);
                    break;
            case IDD_HSV :
                    ColorModel=wParam;
                    CheckRadioButton( hDlg, IDD_RGB, IDD_HLS,
                            ColorModel);
                    SetDlgItemText( hDlg, IDD_TX1, "H" );
                    SetDlgItemText( hDlg, IDD_TX2, "S" );
                    SetDlgItemText( hDlg, IDD_TX3, "V" );
                    SetScrollRange(hSB1,SB_CTL,-180,180,0);
                    SetScrollRange(hSB2,SB_CTL,-100,100,0);
                    SetScrollRange(hSB3,SB_CTL,-100,100,0);
                    bar1=bar2=bar3=0;
                    SetScrollPos(hSB1,SB_CTL,bar1,1);
                    SetScrollPos(hSB2,SB_CTL,bar2,1);
                    SetScrollPos(hSB3,SB_CTL,bar3,1);
                    break;
            case IDD_HLS :
                    ColorModel=wParam;
                    CheckRadioButton( hDlg, IDD_RGB, IDD_HLS,
                            ColorModel);
                    SetDlgItemText( hDlg, IDD_TX1, "H" );
                    SetDlgItemText( hDlg, IDD_TX2, "L" );
                    SetDlgItemText( hDlg, IDD_TX3, "S" );
                    SetScrollRange(hSB1,SB_CTL,-180,180,0);
                    SetScrollRange(hSB2,SB_CTL,-100,100,0);
                    SetScrollRange(hSB3,SB_CTL,-100,100,0);
                    bar1=bar2=bar3=0;
                    SetScrollPos(hSB1,SB_CTL,bar1,1);
                    SetScrollPos(hSB2,SB_CTL,bar2,1);
                    SetScrollPos(hSB3,SB_CTL,bar3,1);
                    break;
            default:
                    return FALSE;
            }
            break;

case WM_VSCROLL:
        {
        int *pBar, imin, imax;
        HWND hid=HIWORD(lParam);

        if(hid==hSB1)
                pBar=&bar1;
        else if(hid==hSB2)
```

```
                    pBar=&bar2;
            else if(hid==hSB3)
                    pBar=&bar3;
            else
                    return FALSE;
            GetScrollRange(hid,SB_CTL,&imin,&imax);
            switch(wParam) {
                    case SB_BOTTOM:
                            *pBar = imax;
                            break;
                    case SB_ENDSCROLL:
                            return TRUE;
                            break;
                    case SB_LINEDOWN:
                            *pBar += 1;
                            break;
                    case SB_LINEUP:
                            *pBar -= 1;
                            break;
                    case SB_PAGEDOWN:
                            *pBar += 20*imax/100;
                            break;
                    case SB_PAGEUP:
                            *pBar -= 20*imax/100;
                            break;
                    case SB_THUMBPOSITION:
                            *pBar = LOWORD(lParam);
                            break;
                    case SB_THUMBTRACK:
                            return TRUE;
                    case SB_TOP:
                            *pBar = imin;
                            break;
            }
            *pBar=BOUND(*pBar,imin,imax);
            SetScrollPos(hid,SB_CTL,*pBar,1);
            }
            break;

    default:
            return FALSE;
    }
    return TRUE;
}
```

From Image Display to Image Processing

We could go on forever adding image processing functions to IMAGE1. It is time to stop—at least for now—and concentrate on more general issues facing Windows developers.

If we *were* going to add image processing functions, we'd start by adding contrast enhancement, which we'd do by histogram equalization. Then we'd add beta correction to our collection of color adjustment algorithms. Both contrast enhancement and beta correction are *point processes*.

The next step would be to add *area processes*. This is often done using a *convolution filter*. Filters for blurring, sharpening, and edge enhancement are all straightforward matrices that operate using the same *convolution kernel*. Median filtering, an area process to clean up stray pixels, can't be done by convolution—but it is also fairly straightforward, involving only 9 pixels at a time.

Finally, we'd go on to *frame* and *geometric processes*. Examples include background subtraction, image combination, image rotation, image stretching, and image mirroring. All of these processes are covered in Craig Lindley's book *Practical Image Processing in C*, which I recommend. Lindley's software assumes a somewhat different data structure than the DIB we're dealing with, and is written for DOS rather than Windows. Nevertheless, the processes apply well to 24-bit RGB and 8-bit gray-scale DIBs. They could also be applied to arbitrary 8-bit color DIBs, with some extra overhead for color value lookup.

Tuning the Application

The IMAGE1 application is pretty far along, but there are still spots that seem slow or awkward. The difference between a good program and a great one is often a matter of user interface and performance tuning. Let's start first with performance, since it's easier to quantify.

Actual versus Perceived Speed

When a program slows down, users often wonder "Has the computer crashed?" The usual reaction at this point is to bang on keys or move the mouse—and finally to reboot the computer. However, if users see an indication that they're supposed to be waiting (the hourglass cursor) and see other processes continue to run (clocks ticking, and so on) they're less likely to panic.

To make this happen in Windows an application has to yield the CPU every few seconds. It also helps if the application indicates its progress in a positive way, such as updating a thermometer or other control.

Making Cooperative Multitasking Work

New Windows programmers often mistake the **Yield()** function for a way to make their applications multitask. They are often puzzled when it has no effect whatsoever. There is a somewhat cryptic note in the help for **Yield**:

> *Applications that contain windows should use a DispatchMessage, PeekMessage, or TranslateMessage loop rather than calling the Yield function directly. The PeekMessage loop handles message synchronization properly and yields at the appropriate times.*

I use a **PeekMessage()** loop by choice. Rather than have the same code sequence appear over and over again in every time-consuming part of my program, I generally build a **SpinTheMessageLoop()** function that is called wherever the application could hog the CPU for more than about 2 seconds. In its simplest form **SpinTheMessageLoop()** does a single **PeekMessage** call, and calls **TranslateMessage** and **DispatchMessage** if there is a message pending; but in practice I combine this with a test of a flag that indicates whether the user wants to stop the current process:

```
BOOL SpinTheMessageLoop(void)
{
        MSG msg;

        if(PeekMessage((LPMSG)&msg,NULL,0,0,PM_REMOVE)) {
                if(msg.message==WM_QUIT || msg.message==WM_PAINT)
                        return bAbortRequested;
                else if(TranslateAccelerator( hWndApp, hAccelTable,
                                                 (LPMSG)&msg)==0) {
                        TranslateMessage((LPMSG)&msg);
                        DispatchMessage((LPMSG)&msg);
                        }
                }
        return bAbortRequested;
}
```

If you wanted, you could change the **if** to a **while**; instead of processing one message each time through your loop, you'd process all pending messages. Which is preferable depends on how often **SpinTheMessageLoop** is called, and how heavy the other processing in the system happens to be. The choice of **if** is better in this case: the processing of a single line of pixels should take a lot less than two seconds. If we only called the routine every hundred scan-lines, a **while** would be more appropriate.

You might also want to remove the code that terminates the function on seeing a **WM_QUIT** or **WM_PAINT**. If you keep the code, then **SpinTheMessageLoop** will not allow a window to repaint; if you take it out, and the user starts moving windows around, you may not get the CPU back for a long time.

One problem you notice as soon as you add **SpinTheMessageLoop** calls to an application like ShowDIB is that hourglass cursors no longer "stick." What is happening is that **WM_MOUSEMOVE** messages start getting through, and Windows updates the cursor to the default arrow. The solution for this is to update the cursor at every **WM_MOUSEMOVE** message:

```
case WM_MOUSEMOVE:
        SetCursor(hCursor);
        break;
```

Here **hCursor** holds the current cursor handle. We have to set it to and from the hourglass somehow, as well:

```
#define StartWait()  hcurSave=SetCursor(hCursor=LoadCursor( \
                            NULL,IDC_WAIT)); bAbortRequested=FALSE
#define EndWait()    SetCursor(hCursor=hcurSave)
```

Two more changes are needed to make this work: instead of setting the application's window class to use the arrow cursor, we set it to **NULL**—which means that we will control the cursor ourselves. And we need to initialize **hCursor** when we initialize our instance:

```
  wndclass.hCursor = NULL;
...
  hCursor=LoadCursor(NULL, IDC_ARROW);
  bAbortRequested=FALSE;
```

Letting the User Stop the Process

We've seen that **SpinTheMessageLoop** checks **bAbortRequested**, but we haven't yet seen how that flag gets set. Actually, it's a piece of cake:

```
case WM_CHAR:
    switch(wParam) {
    case VK_ESCAPE:
       bAbortRequested=TRUE;
       break;
          }
    break;
```

Calling the **SpinTheMessageLoop** function allows the keystroke message to get through to our window procedure, which sets the **bAbortRequested** flag; when control returns the flag is set and can be passed back to the calling routine. So now the user can stop any long process loop with the Escape key if we bracket the loop with **StartWait** and **EndWait** macros, call **SpinTheMessageLoop** frequently during the process, and return from the loop if **SpinTheMessageLoop** returns **TRUE**.

Monitoring Performance

My principal monitoring tools are my eyes and, on rare occasions, a stopwatch. Of course, you can use profiling tools, and do swapping analyses; but the seat of the pants approach is often sufficient as a first step: it tells you where you need to put the probes to do the scientific measurements.

For instance, my observation is that reading GIF files in IMAGE1 feels slow compared with reading BMP files. Looking at the code, I see BMPs read in 32K gulps with a low-level routine, and I see very little processing going on in the process of reading BMPs. On the other hand, GIF files are read using the C stream library routines, which are about two levels removed from the _lread function; additionally, GIF files are LZW-encoded, and decoding them takes a fair bit of CPU time.

Experiment number one, then, is to see if turning on compiler optimization makes a difference in GIF read performance. As a control, I'll have the same file available as both GIF and BMP formats.

FLIGHT.GIF, a 52K 8-bit color image of the Fire Island lighthouse supplied by Dana Hudes, reads in 10 to 12 seconds without compiler optimizations using SHOWIMG.EXE or an early version of IMAGE1.EXE. The variation is due to disk caching. A BMP of the same image reads in about 2 seconds, even though the uncompressed DIB file takes up 308K on disk. The same file saved with RLE compression takes up 144K on disk, but reads in the same 2 seconds.

With compiler optimization turned on, the time to read the GIF goes down only to 9 seconds; the time to read the BMP stays constant at 2 seconds, and the time to read the RLE goes down to about 1 second. Whatever is chewing up the time, it isn't optimizing itself away.

Now let's try some science: add **ProfStart** and **ProfStop** calls around the call to **decoder** in gif.c, and **ProfStop** and **ProfStart** calls at the beginning and end of **SpinTheMessageLoop** in image1.c. The latter set of calls turn profiling off when we yield control, so that we don't wind up sampling another process. Finally, add DEVICE=VPROD.386 to the [386enh] section of SYSTEM.INI and restart Windows.

After running IMAGE1 and reading the GIF file, we exit Windows and run SHOWHITS, which generates the following output:

```
Here are the Hits for Unrecognized Segments

   0.1%       1   Hits on Segment 070E
   1.0%      10   Hits on Segment 0302
   0.1%       1   Hits on Segment B001
   0.1%       1   Hits on Segment 0594
   0.5%       5   Hits on Segment 0070
   1.9%      19   Hits on Segment FDC8
   2.7%      27   Hits on Segment 0039
   5.0%      50   Hits on Segment CB01
   0.5%       5   Hits on Segment FFFF

Here are the Hits for Known Segments

   0.1%       1   Hits on IMAGE1-0
   0.1%       1   Hits on IMAGE1-16
   1.2%      12   Hits on KRNL386-0
   0.2%       2   Hits on DISPLAY-0
   2.2%      22   Hits on SYSTEM-0
  84.2%     836   Hits on IMAGE1-6
```

```
   993  TOTAL HITS

IMAGE1!IMAGE1_TEXT

 0.1%          1  Hits between labels _SpinTheMessageLoop and end of
                     segment

IMAGE1!GIF_TEXT

11.2%        111  Hits between labels _get_byte and _putcolor
 0.4%          4  Hits between labels _putcolor and _put_line
59.9%        595  Hits between labels _put_line and _out_line
 8.8%         87  Hits between labels _gifview and _decoder
 3.9%         39  Hits between labels _decoder and end of segment

IMAGE1!_TEXT

 0.1%          1  Hits between labels PROFSTOP and ProfClear

Profiler Summary (Top 10 Hits):

59.9%        595  IMAGE1! GIF_TEXT! _put_line - _out_line
11.2%        111  IMAGE1! GIF_TEXT! _get_byte - _putcolor
 8.8%         87  IMAGE1! GIF_TEXT! _gifview - _decoder
 3.9%         39  IMAGE1! GIF_TEXT! _decoder - end of segment
 0.4%          4  IMAGE1! GIF_TEXT! _putcolor - _put_line
 0.1%          1  IMAGE1! _TEXT! PROFSTOP - ProfClear
 0.1%          1  IMAGE1! IMAGE1_TEXT! _SpinTheMessageLoop - end of
                     segment
```

Well! We need to look at **put_line** first, and then maybe at **get_byte**. That was certainly better than guessing where to put our efforts. The section of gif.c we need to look at is:

```c
int xdots, ydots, colors, maxiter;
int xposition, yposition, win_xoffset, win_yoffset, xpagesize,
     ypagesize;
int win_xdots, win_ydots;
unsigned char huge *pixels;   /* the device-independent bitmap
                                  pixels */
int pixels_per_byte;          /* pixels/byte in the pixmap */
long pixels_per_bytem1;       /* pixels / byte - 1 (for ANDing) */
int pixelshift_per_byte;      /* 0, 1, 2, or 3 */
int bytes_per_pixelline;      /* pixels/line / pixels/byte */
long win_bitmapsize;          /* bitmap size, in bytes */
int bad_code_count = 0;          /* needed by decoder module */
extern int rowcount;

int get_byte(){
     return (getc(fpin));  /* EOF is -1, as desired */
}
```

```
void putcolor(int x, int y, int color){
      long i;

      i = win_ydots - 1 - y;
      i = (i * win_xdots) + x;

      if (x >= 0 && x < xdots && y >= 0 && y < ydots) {
            if (pixelshift_per_byte == 0) {
                  pixels[i] = color % colors;
                  }
            else {
                  unsigned int j;

                  j = i & pixels_per_bytem1;
                  i = i >> pixelshift_per_byte;
                  pixels[i] = (pixels[i] & win_notmask[j]) +
                        (((unsigned char) (color % colors))
                              << win_bitshift[j]);
                  }
            }
}

int put_line(int rownum, int leftpt, int rightpt,
      unsigned char *localvalues)
{
      int i, len;
      long startloc;

      len = rightpt - leftpt;
      if (rightpt >= xdots)
            len = xdots - 1 - leftpt;
      startloc = win_ydots - 1 - rownum;
      startloc = (startloc * win_xdots) + leftpt;

      if (rownum < 0 || rownum >= ydots || leftpt < 0) {
            return (0);
            }

      if (pixelshift_per_byte == 0) {
            for (i = 0;  i <- len;  i++)
                  pixels[startloc + i] = localvalues[i];
            }
      else {
            unsigned int j;
            long k;
            for (i = 0;  i <= len;  i++) {
                  k = startloc + i;
                  j = k & pixels_per_bytem1;
                  k = k >> pixelshift_per_byte;
                  pixels[k] = (pixels[k] & win_notmask[j]) +
                        (((unsigned char) (localvalues[i] %
                              colors)) << win_bitshift[j]);
                  }                                           //for
            }                                                 //else
```

```
        putcolor(leftpt, rownum, localvalues[0]);
        return (1);
}

int out_line(unsigned char *localvalues, int numberofdots){
        return (put_line(rowcount++, 0, numberofdots, localvalues));
}
```

Hmm. For the 256-color GIF file we're testing, **pixel_shift_per_byte** is 0. So the inner loop of **put_line** that is executing is:

```
        for (i = 0;  i <= len;  i++)
                pixels[startloc + i] = localvalues[i];
```

Why should that be a problem? We certainly didn't expect a simple assignment to be the major bottleneck in the whole GIF reading process. Aha! The pointer **pixels** is **huge**, which means that each pass through the loop is doing segment/selector arithmetic—a big hit in protected mode. So let's rewrite the two lines as:

```
        _fmemcpy(pixels+startloc, localvalues,len);
```

The difference is pretty dramatic. The revised profile shows that we completely eliminated that particular loop as a bottleneck:

```
Profiler Summary (Top 10 Hits):

32.1%        115    IMAGE1! GIF_TEXT! _get_byte - _putcolor
22.1%         79    IMAGE1! GIF_TEXT! _gifview - _decoder
 9.5%         34    IMAGE1! GIF_TEXT! _decoder - end of segment
 0.8%          3    IMAGE1! _TEXT! __fmemcpy - __fmemset
```

Next on the list is **get_byte**. That's pretty odd for a one-line function—but then **getc** is pretty far removed from the guts of Windows. Let's rewrite **get_byte** to use a low-level function instead. For simplicity we'll read one byte at a time, just like **getc**. So instead of **getc(fpin)**, the function body will **_lread**. That also means we need to change from stream **fopen** and **fclose** calls to low-level **OpenFile** and **_lclose** calls.

After installing this set of changes, the time to read the GIF file went *up* to 30 seconds, and the profile showed all the time being spent in the Windows kernel. Obviously, calling **_lread** thousands of times is not very efficient. Suppose instead we buffer our own reads. With a global buffer of 20,000 bytes, the profile becomes:

```
38.0%        148    IMAGE1! GIF_TEXT! _get_byte - _putcolor
15.7%         61    IMAGE1! GIF_TEXT! _gifview - _decoder
 9.5%         37    IMAGE1! GIF_TEXT! _decoder - end of segment
 0.3%          1    IMAGE1! _TEXT! PROFSTART - PROFSTOP
 0.3%          1    IMAGE1! IMAGE1_TEXT! _SpinTheMessageLoop - end of
                        segment
```

The interesting question now, is "What about time we are not profiling?" Maybe we could call **SpinTheMessageLoop** a lot less. We take out the **SpinTheMessageLoop** call in **decode** and put one after the **_lread** call in **get_byte**. Now we have a new **get_byte** routine that should be more efficient:

```
static BYTE FAR *cbuf = NULL;
static HANDLE hcbuf = NULL;
#define cbufsize 16384        //note: buffer size is a multiple of the
                              //disk block size, for efficiency

int get_byte(){       //changed to use _lread by mh
        static int n=0,i=0;

        if(n==0) {
                n = _lread(hin,cbuf,cbufsize);
                i=0;
                if(SpinTheMessageLoop())
                        return (-1);
                }
        if(n) {
                --n;
                return (cbuf[i++]);
                }
        else
                return (-1);
}
```

The pointer **cbuf** is set with a **GlobalAlloc**/**GlobalLock** pair. This rewrite lowers the read time for this file to a few seconds, with a much improved profile:

```
Here are the Hits for Unrecognized Segments

  0.1%          1  Hits on Segment FDC8
  0.1%          1  Hits on Segment 0594
  0.1%          1  Hits on Segment 0070
  5.2%         90  Hits on Segment CB01
Here are the Hits for Known Segments

  0.8%         14  Hits on IMAGE1-16
  1.6%         27  Hits on KRNL386-0
  0.1%          1  Hits on GDI-20
  0.1%          1  Hits on IMAGE1-3
  1.8%         31  Hits on SYSTEM-0
 90.4%       1573  Hits on IMAGE1-6

   1740   TOTAL HITS

IMAGE1!DIB_TEXT

  0.1%          1  Hits between labels _CreateBIPalette and
                      _CreateDibPalette

IMAGE1!GIF_TEXT

 11.8%        206  Hits between labels _get_byte and _putcolor
  0.3%          6  Hits between labels _putcolor and _put_line
```

```
  0.2%        4   Hits between labels _put_line and _out_line
 19.9%      346   Hits between labels _gifview and _decoder
 58.1%     1011   Hits between labels _decoder and end of segment

IMAGE1!_TEXT

  0.8%       14   Hits between labels __fmemcpy and __fmemset

Profiler Summary (Top 10 Hits):

 58.1%     1011   IMAGE1! GIF_TEXT! _decoder - end of segment
 19.9%      346   IMAGE1! GIF_TEXT! _gifview - _decoder
 11.8%      206   IMAGE1! GIF_TEXT! _get_byte - _putcolor
  0.8%       14   IMAGE1! _TEXT! __fmemcpy - __fmemset
  0.3%        6   IMAGE1! GIF_TEXT! _putcolor - _put_line
  0.2%        4   IMAGE1! GIF_TEXT! _put_line - _out_line
  0.1%        1   IMAGE1! DIB_TEXT! _CreateBIPalette - _CreateDibPalette
```

Note that the time in **decoder** now dominates, as it should—where originally it was only 4 percent of the total. We did well optimizing GIF file reading; we could go through the same process for the other parts of the program as well. In the interest of brevity we'll leave this for an exercise.

Making the Human Interface Work for the User

In a reasonably simple program like IMAGE1, every function on the menus can also have an accelerator key assignment to make operating the program from the keyboard smoother. But in a very complex program, there will be hundreds of menu items—too many to assign to keys. (You know, of course, that Windows accelerator keys are typically Control-Key combinations.)

For such a complex program, you need to do some user testing and usability testing to decide what functions are most frequently used and most in need of accelerator keys. In any case you will want your assignments to conform to

- Windows standards
- Standards of programs similar to yours, and
- Mnemonics

To add accelerator key assignments you simply edit the application's RC file to define an accelerator, load the accelerator table in your program's initialization function, and modify your message loops to translate accelerators. This is adequately explained in the introductory Windows programming books. The changed sections of IMAGE1 look like this:

```
image1 MENU
       BEGIN
       POPUP "&File"
```

```
                        BEGIN
                          MENUITEM "&Open...   F3",   IDM_OPEN
                          MENUITEM "&Save...   F12",  IDM_SAVE
                          MENUITEM "&Print      ^P",  IDM_PRINT
                          MENUITEM SEPARATOR
                          MENUITEM "E&xit", IDM_EXIT
                        END
                POPUP "&Edit"
                        BEGIN
                          MENUITEM "&Paste DIB Shift-Ins", IDM_PASTEDIB
                          MENUITEM "&Paste DDB",          IDM_PASTEDDB
                          MENUITEM "&Paste Palette",     IDM_PASTEPAL
                          MENUITEM "&Copy       Ctrl-Ins",  IDM_COPY
                        END
                POPUP "&Process"
                        BEGIN
                          MENUITEM "&Grayscale ^G", IDM_GRAYSCALE
                          MENUITEM "&Color      ^C", IDM_COLOR
                        END
                POPUP   "&Help"
                        BEGIN
                           MENUITEM   "&Index          F1",IDM_HELP_INDEX
                           MENUITEM   "&Keyboard        F9",IDM_HELP_KEYBOARD
                           MENUITEM   "Using &Help   Shift-F10",IDM_HELP_HELP
                           MENUITEM   SEPARATOR
                           MENUITEM   "&About...",     IDM_ABOUT
                        END
                END
image1Acc ACCELERATORS
BEGIN
        VK_INSERT, IDM_COPY,  VIRTKEY, CONTROL
        VK_INSERT, IDM_PASTEDIB, VIRTKEY, SHIFT
        VK_HELP,      IDM_HELP_INDEX,  VIRTKEY
        VK_F1, IDM_HELP_INDEX,  VIRTKEY
        VK_F3, IDM_OPEN,  VIRTKEY
        VK_F9, IDM_HELP_KEYBOARD,  VIRTKEY
        VK_F10,       IDM_HELP_HELP,  VIRTKEY, SHIFT
        VK_F12,       IDM_SAVE,  VIRTKEY
        "^C", IDM_COLOR
        "^G", IDM_GRAYSCALE
        "^P", IDM_PRINT
END


static HANDLE hAccelTable;


...
        /* Enter message loop */
  while (GetMessage ( (LPMSG) & msg, NULL, 0, 0))
        {
        if (TranslateAccelerator (msg.hwnd, hAccelTable,
                              (LPMSG) & msg) == 0)
            {
            TranslateMessage ( (LPMSG) & msg);
```

```
                    DispatchMessage ( (LPMSG) & msg);
                    }
          }
...
  case WM_CREATE: /* Allocate space for our logical palette */
             pLogPal = (NPLOGPALETTE) LocalAlloc(LMEM_FIXED,
                    (sizeof(LOGPALETTE) +
                    (sizeof(PALETTEENTRY) * (MAXPALETTE))));
             hAccelTable = LoadAccelerators( hInst,
                                       (LPSTR)"image1Acc");
...
BOOL SpinTheMessageLoop(void)
{
        MSG msg;

        //ProfStop();
        if(PeekMessage((LPMSG)&msg,NULL,0,0,PM_REMOVE)) {
                if(msg.message==WM_QUIT || msg.message==WM_PAINT)
                        return bAbortRequested;
                else
                if(TranslateAccelerator( hWndApp, hAccelTable,
                                        (LPMSG)&msg)==0)
                    {
                        TranslateMessage((LPMSG)&msg);
                        DispatchMessage((LPMSG)&msg);
                        }
                }
        //ProfStart();
        return bAbortRequested;
}
```

Our menu structure for IMAGE1 is just fine. For a larger program, the rule of 7±2 would come into play. This rule says that 7 is an optimum number of choices from which to pick at any given time, with a tolerance of 2—so 5 choices are all right, and 9 are also OK.

By these design rules, the maximum allowable number of menu items in a Windows program done with one level of pop-up menus is 81. To handle more than 81 commands, you should organize them into, ideally, 49 groups. Then you would use two levels of pop-up to access the (ideally) 7x7x7=343 commands.

Another step in moving from a toy program to a commercial-grade program is to add help, preferably context-sensitive help. At this point, since IMAGE1 is so simple, we'll add only rudimentary help.

The basic process of adding help is easy, but sometimes tedious. First create a help file in Rich Text File (RTF) format. Then create a help project file that references your RTF files and any included bitmaps, and add the help files to your make script. Finally add WinHelp calls to your program.

For instance, the modifications to Image1 to access help, found in image1.c, are as follows:

```
char szHelpFileName[EXE_NAME_MAX_SIZE+1];  /* Help file name*/
void MakeHelpPathName(char *szFileName);
...
     ShowWindow(hWndApp = hWnd, nCmdShow);
     MakeHelpPathName(szHelpFileName);

        /* Enter message loop */
     while (GetMessage ( (LPMSG) & msg, NULL, 0, 0))
...
  case WM_DESTROY:
                                     /* Clean up and quit */
          FreeDib();
          WinHelp(hWnd,szHelpFileName,HELP_QUIT,0L);
          PostQuitMessage(0);
          break;
...
     case IDM_HELP_INDEX:
          WinHelp(hWnd,szHelpFileName,HELP_INDEX,0L);
          break;

     case IDM_HELP_KEYBOARD:
          WinHelp(hWnd,szHelpFileName,HELP_CONTEXT,100);
          break;

     case IDM_HELP_HELP:
          WinHelp(hWnd,szHelpFileName,HELP_HELPONHELP,0L);
          break;
```

The "make" file changes are:

```
all: image1.exe image1.hlp
...
image1.hlp: image1.rtf image1.hpj
     hc image1
```

And, finally, the help project file image1.hpj is at this point simply:

```
[FILES]
IMAGE1.RTF
KEYS.RTF

[OPTIONS]
TITLE=Image1

[BITMAPS]
HELPICON.BMP

[MAP]
Keyboard_topic        100
```

I built the rich text files using Word for Windows; any word processor capable of producing RTF will do. It's a tedious process, since hyperlinks are designated using underlining and hidden text. I've seen an early version of a

WYSIWYG help editor based on Word for Windows which should take a lot of the sting out of the process.

I started with the help files in the Windows SDK **helpex** example, took out the parts I didn't need, and added information specific to IMAGE1. It wasn't highly technical, but it did take some organization to get things right.

One word of caution: if you use Word for Windows to build help files, you should create the files at standard margin and paragraph settings. Attempting to alter the document size will confuse the Windows help engine so that it won't wrap text to fit inside the help window.

Another important step in tuning the application (albeit most important for real mode) is adjusting the segment sizes. Image1's object modules have a broad range of sizes:

dlgopena.obj	188	tif_comp.obj	347
tif_erro.obj	412	tif_warn.obj	418
tif_flus.obj	425	tif_fax4.obj	426
tif_clos.obj	496	tif_ccit.obj	654
tif_comr.obj	774	tif_swab.obj	1346
tif_dump.obj	1402	tif_pack.obj	1448
fileio.obj	1718	print.obj	1797
tif_open.obj	2004	raw.obj	2384
vicar.obj	2538	tiff.obj	2581
tif_read.obj	2888	dlgopen.obj	3388
pcx.obj	3850	tga.obj	3992
imageio.obj	4271	tif_writ.obj	4580
dib.obj	5135	gif.obj	5699
tif_lzw.obj	6187	drawdib.obj	7521
tif_fax3.obj	7563	labutil.obj	8312
image1.obj	10683	process.obj	12537
tif_dir.obj	18593		

What we should probably do is combine all the small (under 2K) tiff modules into one segment, and break up **tif_dir** into two or three segments. We can do both of these with **#pragma alloc_text** statements. We'll also have to modify our DEF file to reflect the new segments. You'll find the **alloc_text** pragmas scattered through the **tif_*.c** files in the image1 directory of the companion disks.

The Image1 **About** box (Figure 3.7) has our copyright, but it would be nice if it could also tell the current operating status of Windows, like the **About** boxes in the Program Manager, the File Manager, Word for Windows, and so on.

The information we need to display is the free memory, the free resources, the operating mode, EMS free if this is an EMS mode, and perhaps the presence of a numerical coprocessor. Information on modes is available in the Windows flags. Free memory can be obtained using the **GetFreeSpace** function. Free resources need a little more work.

Free resources are defined as the minimum available local heap in **USER** or

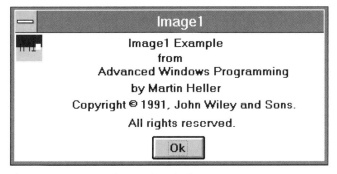

Figure 3.7. Image1 About... box before improvement

GDI. Local heap status can't be found using any documented functions in Windows 3.0, but the undocumented **GetHeapSpaces** function does what we want. I learned about this undocumented function from Dave Jewell— "fisherman" on BIX. In Windows 3.1, there are documented functions in **toolhelp. dll** to return the USER and GDI heap statuses. (There is also supposed to be a documented **GetFreeSystemResources** function in the kernel, but it hasn't been implemented as of this writing.) Our code looks like this:

```
#ifdef WIN31
#include <toolhelp.h>
WORD GetSystemResources(void)
{
        GDIHEAPINFO  gdi = {0};
        USERHEAPINFO user = {0};
        gdi.dwSize = sizeof (GDIHEAPINFO);
        GDIHeapInfo((GDIHEAPINFO  FAR *)&gdi);
        user.dwSize = sizeof (USERHEAPINFO);
        UserHeapInfo((USERHEAPINFO FAR *)&user);
        return(min(gdi.wPercentFree, user.wPercentFree));
}
#else
DWORD FAR PASCAL GetHeapSpaces(HANDLE);
WORD GetSystemResources(void)
{
 WORD wFree, wGDI, wSize, wUser ;
 DWORD dwInfo;

 // get the information on the GDI module
 dwInfo = GetHeapSpaces(GetModuleHandle("GDI"));
 wSize  = HIWORD(dwInfo);
 wFree  = LOWORD(dwInfo);
 wGDI   = LOWORD(((DWORD) wFree) * 100 / wSize);
 // get the information on the User module
 dwInfo = GetHeapSpaces(GetModuleHandle("User"));
 wSize  = HIWORD(dwInfo);
 wFree  = LOWORD(dwInfo);
 wUser  = LOWORD(((DWORD) wFree) * 100 / wSize);
```

```
 return(min(wGDI, wUser));
}
#endif

long BLD_WM_PAINTMsg(hWnd,message,wParam,lParam)
HWND hWnd;
unsigned message;
WORD wParam;
LONG lParam;
    {
        WORD  wPct;
        DWORD dwFree,dwFlags,dwFree2;
        HDC hDC;
        char szTemp[80];
        PAINTSTRUCT ps;

                wPct=GetSystemResources();
                dwFree=GetFreeSpace(GMEM_NOT_BANKED);
                dwFlags = GetWinFlags();
                hDC=BeginPaint(hWnd,&ps);
                if(dwFlags & (WF_LARGEFRAME | WF_SMALLFRAME)) {
                        dwFree2=GetFreeSpace(0);
                        sprintf(szTemp,"Memory free: %ld K below,"
                            " %ld K above",
                            dwFree/1024L,dwFree2/1024L);
                        }
                else
                        sprintf(szTemp,
                            "Memory free: %ld K",dwFree/1024L);
                TextOut(hDC,0,0,szTemp,lstrlen(szTemp));
                sprintf(szTemp,"Resources free: %d %%",wPct);
                TextOut(hDC,0,25,szTemp,lstrlen(szTemp));
                if(dwFlags & WF_STANDARD)
                        TextOut(hDC,0,50,"Standard Mode",13);
                else if(dwFlags & WF_ENHANCED)
                        TextOut(hDC,0,50,"Enhanced Mode",13);
                else if(!(dwFlags & WF_PMODE)) {
                        TextOut(hDC,0,50,"Real Mode",9);
                        if(dwFlags & WF_LARGEFRAME)
                                TextOut(hDC,0,75,"Large frame",11);
                        else if(dwFlags & WF_SMALLFRAME)
                                TextOut(hDC,0,75,"Small frame",11);
                        else
                                TextOut(hDC,0,75,"No EMS in use",13);
                        }
                if(dwFlags & WF_80x87)
                        TextOut(hDC,0,100,"80x87 Present",13);
                else
                        TextOut(hDC,0,100,"80x87 Absent",12);
                EndPaint(hWnd,&ps);

    return DefWindowProc(hWnd, message, wParam, lParam);
    }
```

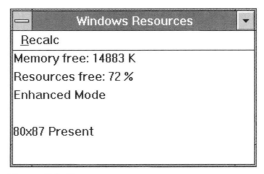

Figure 3.8. Resource test program

```
BOOL BLD_RecalcUDCFunc(hWnd,message,wParam,lParam)
HWND hWnd;
unsigned message;
WORD wParam;
LONG lParam;
    {
        InvalidateRect(hWnd,NULL,1);
        return TRUE;
    }
```

Before putting this code into Image1 I built a test program, **Resource** (Figure 3.8). For speed, I built the bulk of **Resource** with WindowsMaker Professional, a code generator. I had to put the specific code to do the work into the program myself. The full code for **Resource** is on the companion disks along with an executable file. Functions **BLD_WM_PAINTMsg** and **BLD_RecalcUDCFunc** are tied to the **WM_PAINT** message and the **Recalc** menu item, respectively.

Finally, I copied the working and tested code from Resource to Image1, in very slightly modified form (**SetDlgItemText** calls replace the **TextOut** calls), to activate an improved About box (Figure 3.9).

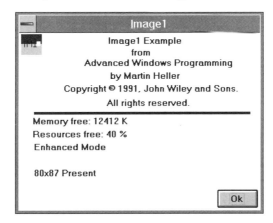

Figure 3.9. Improved About box

Recommended Reading

Beatty and Booth, *Tutorial: Computer Graphics*, Silver Spring, MD, IEEE Computer Society Press, 1982.

Burger and Gillies, *Interactive Computer Graphics*, Reading, MA, Addison-Wesley, 1989.

Foley, van Dam, Feiner, and Hughes, *Computer Graphics: Principles and Practice, Second Edition*, Reading, MA, Addison-Wesley, 1990.

Glassner, Andrew (ed.), *Graphics Gems*, San Diego, CA, Academic Press, 1990.

Lindley, Craig, *Practical Image Processing in C*, New York, NY, John Wiley & Sons, 1991.

Pavlidis, Theo, *Algorithms for Graphics and Image Processing*, Rockville, MD, Computer Science Press, 1982.

4

In which we learn to use the Windows clipboard for editing purposes. We add editing capabilities to our bitmap display program.

Exploiting the Clipboard

· ·

IMAGE1 already has some fairly straightforward editing capabilities: you can select a rectangle from the current DIB with the mouse, copy the current DIB or the current selection, paste a DIB from the clipboard, paste a DDB, and paste a palette. We can, however, improve the editing quite a bit.

It would be nice to be able to undo operations that turned out to be a mistake. We could implement a single-level undo by always posting the previous image to the clipboard. Or, we could maintain two DIBs within the program: the current DIB and the previous DIB. The latter would be more flexible as it wouldn't interfere with other uses of the Windows clipboard. The scheme amounts to maintaining a private clipboard, although with considerably less overhead than using the global clipboard, since it only involves copying a handle. In low memory situations, though, we'd have to abandon the old DIB to make room for the new one.

It would also be nice to be able to paste a clipping on top of a section of the current image; we'd want to preserve the current capability to replace the current image with the clipboard. To paste a small clipping in the right location, we'd have to be able to "float" the clipping and drag it to where it is going.

Suppose the current DIB is 8-bit and uses 256 colors. If the DIB to be pasted uses a different palette, we'll have to resolve the palette conflict. Most likely, the user will want to use the original palette, so the procedure to use would be to map each color in the new clipping to the nearest color in the current palette. Another interesting question is whether palette slots are actually unused (even though the DIB header may say that 256 colors out of 256 are important). We'll want to detect and eliminate duplicate palette entries, at the very least. Or, we could transform the images to 24-bit color and take care of palette reduction later.

Before we do any of that, let's go over the fundamentals of using the clipboard, and have a close look at how IMAGE1 already handles copying and pasting.

Posting Multiple Formats to the Clipboard

IMAGE1 posts information about the current image in three separate formats to the clipboard when the copy command is invoked: the DIB, the DDB, and the palette. Why multiple formats? The answer is that other programs may only understand some of them.

For instance, Word for Windows 1.1a can paste a DDB from the clipboard, but not a DIB or a palette. PhotoStyler can copy a DIB to the clipboard, but not a DDB or a palette. The most convenient way I have found to take images from PhotoStyler and put them in Word for Windows is to copy a DIB to the Windows clipboard from PhotoStyler; paste the DIB into IMAGE1; copy the DIB, DDB and palette back to the clipboard; and, finally, paste the DDB into Word. Of course, I could also save a file from PhotoStyler and import it into Word, but the clipboard turns out to be faster and more convenient, even with the extra steps required to change clipboard formats.

One important step in implementing clipboard handling is to enable the paste operations only when they are valid:

```
case WM_INITMENU:
/* check/uncheck menu items depending on state of related flags */
     EnableMenuItem(wParam, IDM_PASTEDIB,
      IsClipboardFormatAvailable(CF_DIB) ?
      MF_ENABLED : MF_GRAYED);
     EnableMenuItem(wParam, IDM_PASTEDDB,
      IsClipboardFormatAvailable(CF_BITMAP) ?
      MF_ENABLED : MF_GRAYED);
     EnableMenuItem(wParam, IDM_PASTEPAL,
      IsClipboardFormatAvailable(CF_PALETTE) ?
      MF_ENABLED : MF_GRAYED);
```

To copy material to the clipboard, we can either post valid handles with the information, or post **NULL** handles. **NULL** handles say that we will post the information on demand:

```
case IDM_COPY:
if (!bLegitDraw)
     return 0L;
                     /* Clean clipboard of contents */
if (OpenClipboard(hWnd)) {
     EmptyClipboard();
     SetClipboardData(CF_DIB, NULL);
     SetClipboardData(CF_BITMAP, NULL);
     SetClipboardData(CF_PALETTE, NULL);
     CloseClipboard();
     }
break;
```

To paste material, we open the clipboard and get the format we want. Sometimes we may want more than one format, for instance if we want to realize the posted DIB against the posted palette:

```
case IDM_PASTEPAL:
if (OpenClipboard(hWnd)) {
  if (h = GetClipboardData(CF_PALETTE)) {
/* Delete current palette and get the CF_PALETTE data
 * from the clipboard
 */
     if (hpalCurrent)
          DeleteObject(hpalCurrent);
     hpalCurrent = CopyPalette(h);
/*
 * If we have a bitmap realized against the old palette
 * delete the bitmap and rebuild it using the new palette.
 */
     if (hbmCurrent) {
          DeleteObject(hbmCurrent);
          hbmCurrent = NULL;
          if (hdibCurrent)
               hbmCurrent = BitmapFromDib(hdibCurrent,
                         hpalCurrent);
          }
     CloseClipboard();
     }
break;

case IDM_PASTEDIB:
if (OpenClipboard(hWnd)) {
     if (h = GetClipboardData(CF_DIB)) {
/* Delete current DIB and get CF_DIB and
 * CF_PALETTE format data from the clipboard
 */
          hpal = GetClipboardData(CF_PALETTE);
          FreeDib();
```

```
                hdibCurrent = CopyHandle(h);
                if (hdibCurrent) {
                        bLegitDraw = TRUE;
                        lstrcpy(achFileName, "<Clipboard>");
                        hbiCurrent = hdibCurrent;
 /* If there is a CF_PALETTE object in the
  * clipboard, this is the palette to assume
  * the DIB should be realized against, otherwise
  * create a palette for it.
  */
                        if (hpal)
                         hpalCurrent = CopyPalette(hpal);
                        else
                         hpalCurrent = CreateDibPalette(hdibCurrent);

                        SizeWindow(hWnd);
                        }
                else {
                        bLegitDraw = FALSE;
                        ErrMsg("No Memory Available!");
                        }
                }
        CloseClipboard();
        }
break;

case IDM_PASTEDDB:
if (OpenClipboard(hWnd)) {
        if (hbm = GetClipboardData(CF_BITMAP)) {
                hpal = GetClipboardData(CF_PALETTE);
                FreeDib();
/*
 * If there is a CF_PALETTE object in the
 * clipboard, this is the palette to assume
 * the bitmap is realized against.
 */
                if (hpal)
                        hpalCurrent = CopyPalette(hpal);
                else
                        hpalCurrent = GetStockObject(DEFAULT_PALETTE);
                hdibCurrent = DibFromBitmap(hbm, BI_RGB, 0,
                                            hpalCurrent);
                if (hdibCurrent) {
                        bLegitDraw = TRUE;
                        lstrcpy(achFileName, "<Clipboard>");
                        hbiCurrent = hdibCurrent;
                        if (bMemoryDIB)
                                hbmCurrent = BitmapFromDib(hdibCurrent,
                                                           hpalCurrent);
                        SizeWindow(hWnd);
                        }
                else {
                        bLegitDraw = FALSE;
                        ErrMsg("No Memory Available!");
```

```
                    }
                }
        CloseClipboard();
        }
break;
```

Suppose somebody wants us to provide one (or all) of the formats we promised? Render unto Caesar:

```
case WM_RENDERALLFORMATS:
/* Ensure that clipboard data can be rendered even tho'
 * app. is being destroyed.
 */
SendMessage(hWnd, WM_RENDERFORMAT, CF_DIB, 0L);
SendMessage(hWnd, WM_RENDERFORMAT, CF_BITMAP, 0L);
SendMessage(hWnd, WM_RENDERFORMAT, CF_PALETTE, 0L);
break;

case WM_RENDERFORMAT:
/* Format data in manner specified and pass the data
 * handle to clipboard.
 */
if (h = RenderFormat(wParam))
        SetClipboardData(wParam, h);
break;
```

The real work is done in function **RenderFormat**, in module DrawDIB.C:

```
HANDLE RenderFormat(cf)
int cf;
{
        HANDLE  h = NULL;
        HBITMAP hbm;

        if (!bLegitDraw)
                return NULL;

        switch (cf) {
  case CF_BITMAP:
                if (hbmCurrent && !IsRectEmpty(&rcClip))
                        h = CropBitmap(hbmCurrent, &rcClip);
                else {
                        if (hbmCurrent)
                                h = CopyBitmap(hbmCurrent);
                        else if (hdibCurrent)
                                h = BitmapFromDib(hdibCurrent,
                                            hpalCurrent);
                        else if (achFileName[0] &&
                                (hdibCurrent = OpenDIB(achFileName)))
                                h = BitmapFromDib(hdibCurrent,
                                        hpalCurrent);
                        else
                                h = NULL;
```

```
                            if (h && !IsRectEmpty(&rcClip)) {
                                    hbm = CropBitmap(h, &rcClip);
                                    DeleteObject(h);
                                    h = hbm;
                                    }
                            }
                    break;

        case CF_DIB:
                    if (!IsRectEmpty(&rcClip)) {
                            if (hbm = RenderFormat(CF_BITMAP)) {
                                    h = DibFromBitmap(hbm, BI_RGB, 0,
                                                    hpalCurrent);
                                    DeleteObject(hbm);
                                    }
                            }
                    else {
                            if (!hdibCurrent && hbmCurrent)
                                    h = DibFromBitmap(hbmCurrent, BI_RGB, 0,
                                                    hpalCurrent);
                            else if (hdibCurrent)
                                    h = CopyHandle(hdibCurrent);
                            else if (achFileName[0])
                                    h = OpenDIB(achFileName);
                            else
                                    h = NULL;
                            }
                    break;

        case CF_PALETTE:
                    if (hpalCurrent)
                            h = CopyPalette(hpalCurrent);
                    break;
                    }
            return h;
}
```

Note that we have some potential bugs here. Suppose the user copies the whole image, then draws a clipping rectangle, and finally pastes into another program. The user will expect the whole image to paste—but only the clipped region will actually paste. This is a real bug we need to fix.

Or suppose the sequence goes: copy image one, load image two, and then paste. What keeps image two from pasting where image one was expected? Nothing—that's exactly what happens in IMAGE1.

We should set a flag when an image has been copied but not rendered. Then if we do anything to change the image, we should first render the old image. But we can't render it blindly: somebody else might have already put something on the clipboard. We have to ask the clipboard for the current DIB, bitmap, and palette, if they exist. If one doesn't exist, then we're off the hook—somebody else has taken over the clipboard. If they all exist, we go through the motions of pasting them—only we throw them away when we get them. Once we've gone through this fire drill, we can clear the pending copy flag and go on about our business. The code that follows implements this idea; you can find it in IMAGE2.C.

```
BOOL bCopyPending = FALSE;
void RenderCurrentStuff(HWND hWnd);
...
  case WM_LBUTTONDOWN:
/* Start rubberbanding a rect. and track its dimensions.
 * set the clip rectangle to its dimensions.
 */
            if(bCopyPending)
                    RenderCurrentStuff(hWnd);
            TrackMouse(hWnd, MAKEPOINT (lParam));
            break;
...
  case IDM_COPY:
            if (!bLegitDraw)
                    return 0L;
                                    /* Clean clipboard of contents */
            if (OpenClipboard(hWnd)) {
                    EmptyClipboard();
                    SetClipboardData(CF_DIB, NULL);
                    SetClipboardData(CF_BITMAP, NULL);
                    SetClipboardData(CF_PALETTE, NULL);
                    CloseClipboard();
                    }
            bCopyPending=TRUE;
            break;
...
  case IDM_OPEN:
                /* Bring up File/Open ... dialog */
            fh = DlgOpenFile(hWnd,
                    "Select an image to display",
                    (LONG) OF_EXIST | OF_MUSTEXIST | OF_NOOPTIONS,
                    szBitmapExt,   achFileName,   NULL );
/*Load up the DIB or other format if the user did not press cancel*/
            if (fh > 0) {
                    file_format = identify_file_format();
                    if(bCopyPending)
                            RenderCurrentStuff(hWnd);
                    StartWait();
...
void RenderCurrentStuff(HWND hWnd)
{
      HANDLE h;
      if(IsClipboardFormatAvailable(CF_DIB) &&
            IsClipboardFormatAvailable(CF_BITMAP) &&
            IsClipboardFormatAvailable(CF_PALETTE) &&
            OpenClipboard(hWnd)) {
            h = GetClipboardData(CF_BITMAP);
            h = GetClipboardData(CF_DIB);
```

```
      h = GetClipboardData(CF_PALETTE);
      CloseClipboard();
      bCopyPending=FALSE;
      }
}
```

Picking Formats from the Clipboard

In the example above, we knew what format we wanted from the clipboard because the user chose the specific menu item for that format. In a more general case, we'd have to wade through the clipboard and see what formats were available, then choose the best one for our purposes.

It is important for applications to post formats in order of "richness"—that is, with the format of highest information content first. Then the application looking at the clipboard can call **EnumClipboardFormats** and accept the first format that it can handle. As the Windows SDK *Reference* puts it:

Syntax   *WORD EnumClipboardFormats(wFormat)*

This function enumerates the formats found in a list of available formats that belong to the clipboard. On each call to this function, the wFormat parameter specifies a known available format, and the function returns the format that appears next in the list. The first format in the list can be retrieved by setting wFormat to zero.

Parameter   Type/Description
wFormat   *WORD Specifies a known format.*

Return Value   *The return value specifies the next known clipboard data format. It is zero if wFormat specifies the last format in the list of available formats. It is zero if the clipboard is not open.*

Comments   *Before it enumerates the formats by using the EnumClipboardFormats function, an application must open the clipboard by using the OpenClipboard function. The order that an application uses for putting alternative formats for the same data into the clipboard is the same order that the enumerator uses when returning them to the pasting application. The pasting application should use the first format enumerated that it can handle. This gives the donor a chance to recommend formats that involve the least loss of data.*

Cutting a Region

IMAGE1 already knows how to copy a region to the clipboard, and paste a new image from the clipboard. Suppose we want to cut a region out of an image, manipulate the image, and then put it back. Or suppose we want to cut a region and then paste back multiple copies in different positions.

It's not going to be much harder to cut a region than it was to copy the region. We just saw the code to copy the region. The code to define the region is in function **TrackMouse**, module DrawDIB, which uses function **DrawSelect** to take care of the rubberband rectangle. Note that **DrawSelect** uses **PatBlt** calls with ROP code **DSTINVERT** to draw the bounding rectangle of the selected region; it uses **ExtTextOut** to write a formatted string denoting the size of the selection into a bitmap; and it uses **BitBlt** with the **SRCINVERT** parameter to transfer the written bitmap to the screen device context. The **fDraw** parameter to **DrawSelect** does not seem to be used.

```
void TrackMouse(hwnd, pt)
HWND hwnd;
POINT pt;
{
        POINT ptBase;
        HDC   hdc;
        MSG   msg;
        POINT ptOrigin;
        RECT  rcClient;

        hdc = GetDC(hwnd);
        SetCapture(hwnd);

        GetClientRect(hwnd, &rcClient);

    /* Get mouse coordinates relative to origin of DIB */
        ptOrigin.x = GetScrollPos(hwnd, SB_HORZ);
        ptOrigin.y = GetScrollPos(hwnd, SB_VERT);

        pt.x += ptOrigin.x;
        pt.y += ptOrigin.y;

    /* Display the coordinates */
        SetWindowOrg(hdc, ptOrigin.x, ptOrigin.y);
        DrawSelect(hdc, FALSE);

    /* Initialize clip rectangle to the point */
        rcClip.left = pt.x;
        rcClip.top = pt.y;
        rcClip.right = pt.x;
        rcClip.bottom = pt.y;

    /* Eat mouse messages until a WM_LBUTTONUP is encountered.
Meanwhile continue to draw a rubberbanding rectangle and display
its dimensions */
        for (;;) {
                WaitMessage();
                if (PeekMessage(&msg, NULL, WM_MOUSEFIRST,
                                WM_MOUSELAST, PM_REMOVE)) {
                        DrawSelect(hdc, FALSE);

                        rcClip.left = pt.x;
                        rcClip.top = pt.y;
                        rcClip.right = LOWORD(msg.lParam) + ptOrigin.x;
```

```
                              rcClip.bottom = HIWORD(msg.lParam) + ptOrigin.y;

                              NormalizeRect(&rcClip);
                              DrawSelect(hdc, TRUE);

                              if (msg.message == WM_LBUTTONUP)
                                    break;
                        }
                  else
                        continue;
                  }

      ReleaseCapture();
      ReleaseDC(hwnd, hdc);
}

void DrawSelect(hdc, fDraw)
HDC hdc;
BOOL fDraw;
{
      char  sz[80];
      DWORD dw;
      int   x, y, len, dx, dy;
      HDC   hdcBits;
      HBITMAP hbm;

      if (!IsRectEmpty(&rcClip)) {

      /* If a rectangular clip region has been selected, draw it */
            PatBlt(hdc, rcClip.left, rcClip.top,
                  rcClip.right - rcClip.left, 1, DSTINVERT);
            PatBlt(hdc, rcClip.left, rcClip.bottom, 1,
                  -(rcClip.bottom - rcClip.top), DSTINVERT);
            PatBlt(hdc, rcClip.right - 1, rcClip.top, 1,
                  rcClip.bottom - rcClip.top, DSTINVERT);
            PatBlt(hdc, rcClip.right, rcClip.bottom - 1,
                  -(rcClip.right - rcClip.left), 1, DSTINVERT);

      /* Format the dimensions string ...*/
            wsprintf(sz,
                  "%dx%d",
                  rcClip.right - rcClip.left,
                  rcClip.bottom - rcClip.top);
            len = lstrlen(sz);

      /* ... and center it in the rectangle */
            dw = GetTextExtent(hdc, sz, len);
            dx = LOWORD (dw);
            dy = HIWORD (dw);
            x = (rcClip.right + rcClip.left - dx) / 2;
            y = (rcClip.bottom + rcClip.top - dy) / 2;

            hdcBits = CreateCompatibleDC(hdc);
```

```
                SetTextColor(hdcBits, 0xFFFFFFL);
                SetBkColor(hdcBits, 0x0L);

        /* Output the text to the DC */
                if (hbm = CreateBitmap(dx, dy, 1, 1, NULL)) {
                        hbm = SelectObject(hdcBits, hbm);
                        ExtTextOut(hdcBits, 0, 0, 0, NULL, sz, len,
                                        NULL);
                        BitBlt(hdc, x, y, dx, dy, hdcBits, 0, 0,
                                        SRCINVERT);
                        hbm = SelectObject(hdcBits, hbm);
                        DeleteObject(hbm);
                        }
                DeleteDC(hdcBits);
                }
}

void PASCAL NormalizeRect(prc)
RECT *prc;
{
        if (prc->right < prc->left)
                SWAP(prc->right, prc->left);
        if (prc->bottom < prc->top)
                SWAP(prc->bottom, prc->top);
}
```

To cut a region, we'll basically copy the region and then turn it black. To delete a region, we'll just turn it black. To cut the whole image, we'll copy it to the clipboard and free it. To delete the whole image, we'll just free it.

from IMAGE2.C:

```
 case WM_INITMENU:
...
                EnableMenuItem(wParam, IDM_CUT,
                        bLegitDraw ? MF_ENABLED : MF_GRAYED);
                EnableMenuItem(wParam, IDM_DEL,
                        bLegitDraw ? MF_ENABLED : MF_GRAYED);
```

from MenuComm.C:

```
...
  case IDM_DEL:
      if (!bLegitDraw)
            return 0L;
      if(!IsRectEmpty(&rcClip)) {
            ClearRectToBackground(&rcClip);
            }
      else {
            FreeDib();
            SetWindowText(hWnd, szAppName);
            }
```

```
                InvalidateRect(hWnd,NULL,1);
        break;

  case IDM_CUT:
        if (!bLegitDraw)
                return 0L;
        SendMessage(hWnd,WM_COMMAND,IDM_COPY,0L);
        RenderCurrentStuff(hWnd);
        SendMessage(hWnd,WM_COMMAND,IDM_DEL,0L);
        break;
...
```

from DrawDIB.C:

```
void ClearRectToBackground(LPRECT lpRect)
{
        HDC     hMemDC;
        HDC     hdc;
        int     dx,dy;

        if(IsRectEmpty(lpRect) || !hbmCurrent)
                return;

        dx = lpRect->right - lpRect->left;
        dy = lpRect->bottom - lpRect->top;

        hdc = GetDC(NULL);
        hMemDC = CreateCompatibleDC(hdc);
        SelectObject(hMemDC, hbmCurrent);
        PatBlt(hMemDC,lpRect->left,lpRect->top,dx,dy,BLACKNESS);
        ReleaseDC(NULL, hdc);
        DeleteDC(hMemDC);
        if(hdibCurrent)
                GlobalFree(hdibCurrent);
        hdibCurrent=DibFromBitmap(hbmCurrent,BI_RGB, 0, hpalCurrent);
}
```

Pasting a Clipping

We want to be able to combine what's on the clipboard with our current image. The issues we have to address are:

1. Where should the clipping go by default?
2. What do we do if the clipping palette is different from the current image's palette?
3. How do we drag the clipping to another position?
4. How do we know when the clipping is in its final position?
5. How do we indicate that the clipping is still floating?
6. What do we do if the clipping is larger than the current image?

Plate 1 RedCat.BMP: See figures 3.2, 3.3, and 3.4 for gray-scaled versions of this.

Plate 3 Anchor_U.TIF as it should display.

Plate 2 BIRD.TIF as it should display. This is a 24-bit true-color TIFF image.

Plate 4 Barefoot.BMP: 24-bit color image converted from RAW scanned format. Photo: M. Heller

Plate 5 Motherhd.BMP converted from a RAW format scanned image and clipped using Image2; reduced from 24-bit color to 256 colors using the Microsoft BitEdit tool. Photo: M. Heller

Plate 6 Window.TGA as converted to BMP format by Image2. This is a ray-traced 24-bit image.

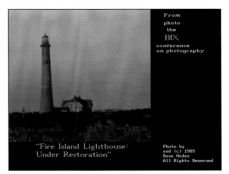

Plate 7 FILight.GIF as converted to BMP by Image2. Striations in the sky are an artifact of the color reduction process. Photo: Dana Hudes

Plate 8 Zoe.tga as converted to BMP format by Image2. At one point the Targa file displayed upside down; obviously that has been fixed. Photo: Dana Hudes

Plates 9-14 Sample files from the companion disks. Left to right : psgamma.tif, all256_u.tif, all16_u.tif, pal4_u.tif, photog_l.tif, and dsdrive2.pcx.

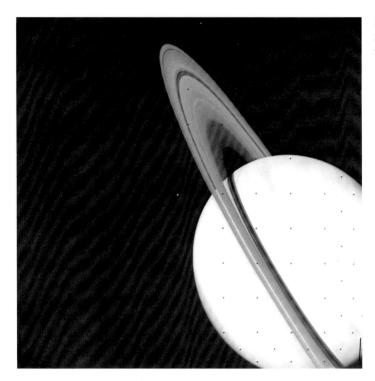

Plate 15 Saturn as imaged by the Voyager probe. Converted from VICAR format to BMP format by Image2.

Plate 16 Jupiter as imaged by the Voyager probe. Converted from VICAR format to BMP format by Image2.

Let's consider these one a time. If there is a current clipping rectangle, we assume that the user wants to use it, and the clipping being pasted should go into it. If we have to stretch or compress the clipping to fit the rectangle, we should do so automatically.

If there isn't a current clipping rectangle or the current clipping rectangle is smaller than two pixels in either direction, let's assume that the user wants the clipping to go in the upper left-hand corner of the image. If the clipping is smaller than the current image, let it cover only its own footprint. If it is larger than the current image, crop it to fit the size of the current image. After all, if the user wanted to import the clipboard image whole, she would choose **Paste DIB** or **Paste DDB** instead of **Paste Clipping**.

If the clipping and image both have palettes, any occupied slots in the image's palette have priority. We can fill unoccupied slots in the new palette with colors from the clipping's palette that do not already exist in the image's palette, until we run out of slots. If the clipping does not have a palette and the image has a palette, we will realize the clipping against the original image palette. Finally, if neither the clipping nor the image has a palette, we can skip all the palette-handling logic.

We can implement dragging several ways. We can **BitBlt** the clipping onto the screen device context with a **SRCCOPY** ROP code, and repaint the original image bitmap in preparation for each new clipping position. Or we could display the clipping in its own window: then we could let Windows do the work of moving the window around. Normally you drag a window using its title bar; we can accomplish the same thing in a frameless window by returning **HTCAPTION** to a **WM_NCHITTEST** message. The overall framework for the **Paste Clipping** function is found in MenuComm.C:

```
case IDM_PASTECLIP:
    if (OpenClipboard(hWnd)) {
            if (    h   =  GetClipboardData(CF_DIB)) {
                    hpal= GetClipboardData(CF_PALETTE);
                    hbm = GetClipboardData(CF_BITMAP);
// If there is a valid clipping rectangle in the
// current image, stretch the      clipping to fit.
                    if(!IsRectEmpty(&rcClip) &&
                            (rcClip.bottom-rcClip.top  > 2) &&
                            (rcClip.right -rcClip.left > 2))
                            fStretchClipping=TRUE;
// Otherwise put the clipping in the upper left corner
// of the image, and clip to size if necessary
                    else
                            fStretchClipping=FALSE;
//Now let the user drag the clipping
                    DragTheClipping(hWnd, h, hbm, hpal,
```

```
                                         fStretchClipping);
//Done dragging: combine the images
// If both image and clipping have palettes, merge the palettes
                    if(hpal && hpalCurrent)
                            hpalCurrent = MergePalettes(hpalCurrent,
                                                         hpal);
                            hdibCurrent = MergeImages(hdibCurrent, h,
                                                        hbm);
                            if (hdibCurrent) {
                                    bLegitDraw = TRUE;
                                    lstrcpy(achFileName, "<Merged>");
                                    hbiCurrent = hdibCurrent;
                                    SizeWindow(hWnd);
                                    }
                            else {
                                    bLegitDraw = FALSE;
                                    ErrMsg("Image Merge Failed");
                                    }
                            }
                    CloseClipboard();
                    }
            break;
```

We've left the work of dragging the clipping, merging the palettes, and merging the bitmaps for separate functions, called **DragTheClipping**, **MergePalettes**, and **MergeImages**.

Dragging the Paste Region

There are several points of interest in the code for dragging the paste region. One is the use of a window for the clipping. We could have just as easily drawn the bitmap directly on the screen, invalidated the rectangle underneath, and drawn the bitmap again at a new position. Using a window puts the burden of watching the mouse and moving the rectangle on Windows—so we take advantage of the careful optimization of window dragging already built into the environment.

Notice that we use a simpler **PeekMessage** loop than is implemented in **SpinTheMessageLoop**. The child window doesn't have any accelerators, so there was no need to translate accelerators. More important, the child window does need its **WM_PAINT** messages, and **SpinTheMessageLoop** filters paint requests to keep screen repaints from interfering with long processes. I am ashamed to admit that I wasted a day wondering why my window didn't paint before I realized that I had written **SpinTheMessageLoop** so that it wouldn't process **WM_PAINT**.

You may also find the mouse-handling logic in **FloatPicWndProc** interesting. The **WM_NCHITTEST** message is generated prior to any client or nonclient mouse messages; returning **HTCAPTION** means that Windows should act like the mouse is in the caption area. Since the caption is a nonclient area, nonclient mouse messages are generated for mouse button clicks and mouse motion. But clicking on the caption means you want to move the window, and so our borderless bitmap window tricks the system into moving it around. You might find it interesting to monitor mouse and nonclient messages going to the **FloatPic** window with Spy or a debugger.

To drag the clipping, the user moves the mouse over the bitmap. The cursor will change to a move/size double arrow. Then the user drags the window to its new location, as many times as needed. On each drag, Windows takes care of moving a frame with the mouse, and updating the old and new areas afterward. The user can accept the current bitmap position by double-clicking or pressing a key, and revert to the original bitmap position by clicking the right mouse button.

```
void DragTheClipping(HWND hWnd,HANDLE h,HBITMAP hbm,HPALETTE hpal,
                                           BOOL fStretchClipping)
{
     static HWND hWndFloatPic;
     LPBITMAPINFOHEADER lpbi;
     MSG msg;

     lpbi = (VOID FAR *) GlobalLock(h);
     width = (int)lpbi->biWidth;
     height = (int)lpbi->biHeight;
     GlobalUnlock(h);
     lpbi = NULL;

     if(fStretchClipping) {
           x=rcClip.left;
           y=rcClip.top;
           dx=rcClip.right - x;
           dy=rcClip.bottom - y;
           }
     else {
           x=0;
           y=0;
           dx=width;
           dy=height;
           }

     //create a window for the clipping and show it
     hWndFloatPic = CreateWindow("FloatPic", "Drag Me",
           WS_CHILD | WS_CLIPSIBLINGS,
           x, y, dx, dy, hWnd, 2, hInst, NULL);
     if(!hWndFloatPic) {
           MessageBeep(0);
           return;
           }
     bDragging=TRUE;
```

```
        hbmFloat=hbm;
        hdibFloat=h;
        hpalFloat=hpal;
        SetFocus(hWndFloatPic);
        InvalidateRect(hWndFloatPic,NULL,TRUE);
        ShowWindow(hWndFloatPic,SW_SHOWNORMAL);
        UpdateWindow(hWndFloatPic);

        //process messages until the user is done moving the window
        //Window will take care of its own destruction and updating
        // the rectangle
        while(bDragging) {
          if(PeekMessage((LPMSG)&msg,NULL,0,0,PM_REMOVE)) {
                if(msg.message==WM_QUIT)
                        break;
                TranslateMessage((LPMSG)&msg);
                DispatchMessage((LPMSG)&msg);
                }
        }
}
long _export FAR PASCAL FloatPicWndProc(HWND hWnd,
                unsigned iMessage, WORD wParam, LONG lParam)
{       PAINTSTRUCT    ps;
        HDC            hdc;
        HPALETTE hpalT;
        static RECT rc;
        int i,j;

        switch (iMessage) {
        case WM_DESTROY:
                break;

        case WM_CREATE:
                GetWindowRect(hWnd,&rc);
                break;

        case WM_PAINT:
                hdc = BeginPaint(hWnd, &ps);
                SetWindowOrg(hdc, 0, 0);
                SetBkMode(hdc, wTransparent);
                hpalT = SelectPalette(hdc, hpalFloat, FALSE);
                RealizePalette(hdc);
                if(hbmFloat) {   //use bitmap
                        HDC hdcBits;

                        hdcBits = CreateCompatibleDC(hdc);
                        SelectObject(hdcBits, hbmFloat);
                        StretchBlt(hdc, 0, 0, dx, dy, hdcBits, 0, 0,
                                width, height, SRCCOPY);
                        DeleteDC(hdcBits);
                        }
                else {      //use DIB
                        StretchDibBlt(hdc, 0, 0, dx,dy, hdibFloat, 0, 0,
                                width, height, SRCCOPY);
```

```
                          }
                SelectPalette(hdc, hpalT, FALSE);
                EndPaint(hWnd, &ps);
                break;

        case WM_MOUSEMOVE:
                SetCursor(hCursor);
                break;

        case WM_NCMOUSEMOVE:
                SetCursor(LoadCursor(NULL,IDC_SIZE));
                break;

        case WM_LBUTTONDOWN:
                break;

        case WM_RBUTTONDOWN:
        case WM_NCRBUTTONDOWN:
                bDragging=FALSE;
                DestroyWindow(hWnd);
                break;

        case WM_CHAR:
        case WM_LBUTTONUP:
        case WM_NCLBUTTONUP:
        case WM_LBUTTONDBLCLK:
        case WM_NCLBUTTONDBLCLK:
                GetWindowRect(hWnd,&rcClip);
                i=rcClip.left-rc.left;
                j=rcClip.top -rc.top;
                rcClip.left  =x + i;
                rcClip.top   =y + j;
                rcClip.right =x + i + dx;
                rcClip.bottom=y + j + dy;
                bDragging=FALSE;
                DestroyWindow(hWnd);
                break;

        case WM_NCHITTEST:
                return HTCAPTION;

        default:
                return DefWindowProc(hWnd, iMessage, wParam, lParam);

                }
        return 0L;
}
```

Merging Palettes

Our first cut at merging palettes works fine, as far as it goes. When the total of
the two palettes is less than 256 entries, it simply concatenates the palette
entries. When the total exceeds 256 entries, it removes duplicates and gives the

original picture priority. To do the best possible job of merging palettes, we'd need a separate function that removed unused palette entries from each DIB. We might also like to have a function that reduced the number of palette entries in a DIB to some specified number.

```
HPALETTE MergePalettes(HPALETTE hpalCurrent,HPALETTE hpal)
{
        PLOGPALETTE ppal;
        int nEntries1,nEntries2,ntotal,nRemoved,i,j,k;
        BOOL fDup;

        if(!hpal)
                return hpalCurrent;
        if(!hpalCurrent)
                return hpal;
        GetObject(hpalCurrent, sizeof(int), (LPSTR) &nEntries1);
        GetObject(hpal,        sizeof(int), (LPSTR) &nEntries2);
        ntotal=nEntries1+nEntries2;
        if(ntotal <= 256) {             //Plenty of palette entries
                ppal = (PLOGPALETTE) LocalAlloc(LPTR,
                        sizeof(LOGPALETTE) +
                        ntotal * sizeof(PALETTEENTRY));
                if (!ppal)
                        return hpalCurrent;
                ppal->palVersion = PALVERSION;
                ppal->palNumEntries = ntotal;
                GetPaletteEntries(hpalCurrent, 0, nEntries1,
                        ppal->palPalEntry);
                GetPaletteEntries(hpal, 0, nEntries2,
                        &ppal->palPalEntry[nEntries1]);
                }
        else {                          //Try to combine palettes
                ntotal=256;
                ppal = (PLOGPALETTE) LocalAlloc(LPTR,
                        sizeof(LOGPALETTE) +
                        ntotal * sizeof(PALETTEENTRY));
                if (!ppal)
                        return hpalCurrent;
                ppal->palVersion = PALVERSION;
                ppal->palNumEntries = ntotal;
                GetPaletteEntries(hpalCurrent, 0, nEntries1,
                        ppal->palPalEntry);
                nRemoved=0;
                for(i=0;i<nEntries1-1;i++) {
//eliminate duplicates in original
                        for(j=i+1;j<nEntries1;j++) {
                                if(IsDupPalEntry(ppal,i,j)) {
                                        RemovePalEntry(ppal,j,nEntries1);
                                        nRemoved++;
                                        break;
                                        }
                                }
                        }
```

```
                    i=nEntries1-nRemoved;
                    for(j;j<nEntries2 && i<ntotal;j++) {
//add new colors as possible
                        GetPaletteEntries(hpal,j,1,
                                &ppal->palPalEntry[i]);
                        fDup=FALSE;
                        for(k=0;k<i-1;k++) {
                                if(IsDupPalEntry(ppal,k,i)) {
                                        fDup=TRUE;
                                        break;
                                }
                        }
                        if(!fDup)
                                i++;
                    }
            }
        DeleteObject(hpalCurrent);
        hpalCurrent = CreatePalette(ppal);
        LocalFree((HANDLE) ppal);
        return hpalCurrent;
}
```

Merging Bitmaps

One major design choice for the image merging function was the ROP code. I've set the ROP code to **SRCCOPY** in all the StrechDibBlt calls; **SRCCOPY** has the effect of ignoring the original underneath the clipping. My second choice, **SRCPAINT**, has the effect of **or**-ing the bits of the source and destination, which looks pretty good if the background is black in both images, but somewhat strange if you put one colored image on top of another colored image.

```
HANDLE MergeImages(HANDLE hdibCurrent,HANDLE h,HPALETTE hpal,
                              RECT rcClip,BOOL fStretchClipping)
{
        HDC hdc,hdc1;
        int dx,dy;
        LPBITMAPINFOHEADER lpbi;
        HBITMAP hbmOld;
        HPALETTE hpalT;

        if(!hdibCurrent)
                return NULL;
        if(!h)
                return hdibCurrent;

        lpbi = (VOID FAR *) GlobalLock(h);
        dx = (int)lpbi->biWidth;
        dy = (int)lpbi->biHeight;
        GlobalUnlock(h);
        lpbi = NULL;
```

```
        //Regenerate current bitmap with new palette

    if(hbmCurrent)
            DeleteObject(hbmCurrent);
    if (hpal == NULL)
            hpal = GetStockObject(DEFAULT_PALETTE);
    hbmCurrent=BitmapFromDib(hdibCurrent,hpal);

        //put bitmap in a memory device context and overlay clipping

    hdc1 = GetDC(NULL);
    hdc  = CreateCompatibleDC(hdc1);
    ReleaseDC(NULL, hdc1);
    hpalT = SelectPalette(hdc, hpal, FALSE);
    hbmOld=SelectObject(hdc,hbmCurrent);

    if(fStretchClipping)
            StretchDibBlt(hdc,rcClip.left,rcClip.top,
                    rcClip.right-rcClip.left,
                    rcClip.bottom-rcClip.top,
                    h,0,0,dx,dy,SRCCOPY);
    else
      if(IsRectEmpty(&rcClip))
            StretchDibBlt(hdc,0,0,dx,dy,h,0,0,dx,dy,SRCCOPY);
      else
            StretchDibBlt(hdc,rcClip.left,rcClip.top,
                    rcClip.right-rcClip.left,
                    rcClip.bottom-rcClip.top,
                    h,0,0,dx,dy,SRCCOPY);
    SelectObject(hdc,hbmOld);
    SelectPalette(hdc, hpalT, FALSE);
    DeleteDC(hdc);

        //Convert revised bitmap to DIB

    GlobalFree(hdibCurrent);
    hdibCurrent=DibFromBitmap(hbmCurrent, BI_RGB, 0, hpal);
    return hdibCurrent;
}
```

Adding UNDO

As nice as all these editing operations are, it would be even nicer if we could try one, decide it was a mistake, and revert to the previous image. All this really requires is that we retain the previous DIB when we do an editing operation, and revert to it when **UNDO** is selected. We can always reconstruct the bitmap and palette from the DIB, so we don't need to retain them. To begin with, we need to modify **FreeDib** to keep the previous DIB around anytime we release the current memory blocks:

```
void FreeDib(void){z
     if (hpalCurrent)
          DeleteObject(hpalCurrent);
     if (hbmCurrent)
          DeleteObject(hbmCurrent);
     if(hdibPrior)                          //revised for UNDO
               GlobalFree(hdibPrior);
     if (hdibCurrent)                       //revised for UNDO
          hdibPrior=hdibCurrent;
     else
          hdibPrior=NULL;
     bCanUndo = (hdibPrior != NULL);
     if (hbiCurrent && hbiCurrent != hdibCurrent)
          GlobalFree(hbiCurrent);
     fPalColors = FALSE;
     bLegitDraw = FALSE;
     hpalCurrent = NULL;
     hdibCurrent = NULL;
     hbmCurrent = NULL;
     hbiCurrent = NULL;
     SetRectEmpty(&rcClip);
}
```

Since **FreeDib** doesn't release the prior DIB, we'll have to do that explicitly at window destruction time:

```
case WM_DESTROY:              /* Clean up and quit */
          FreeDib();
          if(hdibPrior)
               GlobalFree(hdibPrior);
          WinHelp(hWnd,szHelpFileName,HELP_QUIT,0L);
          PostQuitMessage(0);
          break;
```

Now we have to write an UNDO procedure:

```
     case IDM_UNDO:
          if(!hdibPrior || !bCanUndo)
               break;
          if (hpalCurrent)
               DeleteObject(hpalCurrent);
          if (hbmCurrent)
               DeleteObject(hbmCurrent);
          if (hbiCurrent && hbiCurrent != hdibCurrent)
               GlobalFree(hbiCurrent);
          fPalColors = FALSE;
          bLegitDraw = FALSE;
          hpalCurrent = NULL;
          hbmCurrent = NULL;
          hbiCurrent = NULL;
          SetRectEmpty(&rcClip);
```

```
            h = hdibCurrent;
            hdibCurrent = hdibPrior;
            hdibPrior = h;
            h=NULL;
            bLegitDraw = TRUE;
            lstrcpy(achFileName, "<Undone>");
            hbiCurrent = hdibCurrent;
            hpalCurrent = CreateDibPalette(hdibCurrent);
            SizeWindow(hWnd);
            break;
```

You'll note that we don't try to build a bitmap from the "undone" DIB. You could, of course, add a **BitmapFromDIB** call to the **UNDO** handler code; but my assumption is that once the user uses **UNDO**, he is in an editing mode—it is likely that the DIB will change before a repaint is needed, so that there is little to be gained from building a bitmap.

We've handled the bulk editing changes in **FreeDib**. But what about other changes, such as pasting a clipping, gray scaling the image, or changing the image colors? Let's make a little function that will back up the current DIB, using the **CopyHandle** function found in drawdib.c:

```
void BackupCurrentDIB(void)
{
        StartWait();
        if(!hdibCurrent)
                return;
        if(hdibPrior)
                GlobalFree(hdibPrior);
        hdibPrior=CopyHandle(hdibCurrent);
        bCanUndo = (hdibPrior != NULL);
        EndWait();
}
```

Finally, we can sprinkle **BackupCurrentDIB** calls in strategic places:

```
  case IDM_DEL:
if (!bLegitDraw)
        return 0L;
if(!IsRectEmpty(&rcClip)) {
        BackupCurrentDIB();
        ClearRectToBackground(&rcClip);
        }
else {
        FreeDib();
        SetWindowText(hWnd, szAppName);
        }
        InvalidateRect(hWnd,NULL,1);
break;
...
  case IDM_PASTECLIP:
```

```
        if (OpenClipboard(hWnd)) {
            if (h =  GetClipboardData(CF_DIB)) {
                hpal= GetClipboardData(CF_PALETTE);
                hbm = GetClipboardData(CF_BITMAP);
            // If there is a valid clipping rectangle in the
            // current image, stretch the clipping to fit.
                if(!IsRectEmpty(&rcClip) &&
                        (rcClip.bottom-rcClip.top  > 2) &&
                        (rcClip.right -rcClip.left > 2))
                        fStretchClipping=TRUE;
            // Otherwise put the clipping in the upper left corner
            // of the image, and clip to size if necessary
                else
                        fStretchClipping=FALSE;
                BackupCurrentDIB();
            //Now let the user drag the clipping
...
  case IDM_GRAYSCALE:
      BackupCurrentDIB();
      GrayScale(hWnd);
      break;
  case IDM_COLOR   :
      BackupCurrentDIB();
      Color(hWnd);
      break;
```

In this case, a full **UNDO** was quite easy—but then, keeping the old DIB around amounts to a brute force solution. In a more elegant implementation, we might keep only changed regions—in which case we could implement a multilevel **UNDO** rather than a single-level **UNDO**.

You'll note that **UNDO** doesn't use the Windows clipboard at all. For this particular task, there was much less overhead involved using a local copy of a handle than there would have been generating a global copy of a large memory block. You can't always assume that using a system facility will be easier than implementing a program facility; in this case the program facility was almost trivial. On the other hand, you won't want reinvent nontrivial system facilities, like DDE, as we'll see in the next chapter.

Exploiting DDE and OLE

. . . .

We introduced the concepts of DDE (Dynamic Data Exchange) and OLE
(Object Linking and Embedding) briefly in Chapter 1, but now it's time to
understand how to implement DDE and OLE in your own programs. You can
choose any of three levels at which to write DDE code: DDE messsages, DDEML
functions, or the OLE functions. If you need OLE you pretty much have to use
OLE functions.

Some people are surprised to hear that you can implement DDE using the
OLE functions, but it's true. Microsoft recommends using OLE functions rather
than DDEML functions or DDE messages for most programs; the exceptions are
programs that need to conduct multiple conversations with multiple topics
(which should use DDEML), and programs that need to run in real mode (which
have to use DDE messages).

DDE Fundamentals: Servers and Clients

Of the three levels—DDE messages, DDEML functions, and OLE functions—
DDE messages are the lowest/simplest. Of course, in software development,
using the lowest level or simplest services usually means you have to do the
most work to manage the service from your program. Nevertheless, it is crucial
for you to understand DDE messages no matter which of the three levels you

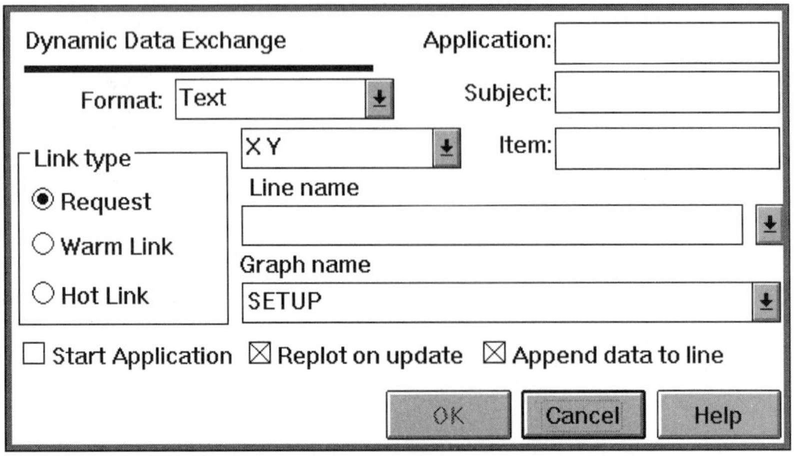

Figure 5.1. DDE setup dialog from EnPlot

plan to implement: the debugging tools you'll have to use will mostly operate at the message level.

In general, a DDE client asks for information that a DDE server provides. Server and client *applications* have *conversations* with *topics* and *items*. The server application is usually called initially from the client application. Often the user is responsible for specifying the details of the conversation, as illustrated in Figure 5.1.

There are only nine DDE messages. You'd think that would be pretty simple, but the DDE protocol is not at all simple.

WM_DDE_INITIATE takes atomic arguments that reference an application and topic. An application uses **SendMessage** to issue **WM_DDE_INITIATE**. A typical call would look like:

```
SendMessage(-1,                       //broadcast to all windows
            WM_DDE_INITIATE,          //Initiate DDE conversation
            hWndSender,               //Window of client issuing request
            MAKELONG(aApplication, aTopic));    //atoms
```

You will have to create the atoms for **aApplication** and **aTopic** with **GlobalAddAtom**. When **SendMessage** returns, you'll need to delete the **aApplication** and **aTopic** atoms.

You may wonder why we we're talking about physics and chemistry. We're not. In Windows, an *atom* is a special kind of string reference. Each atom is a hashed integer handle to a string; the lookup table and the string itself are kept in an *atom table*. Windows maintains a global atom table specifically for DDE and related uses; additionally, applications can create and use local atom tables. Managing global atoms is part of the drudgery you need to go through to implement DDE.

More drudgery: you'll notice that the third argument to the **SendMessage** call shown above is **hWndSender**. You might think that refers to the main window of the client application, but it doesn't. Because the window handle is used for uniquely identifying each application, your program should create an *object window* for each DDE conversation in which it participates. The object window is an ordinary but invisible window; the term *object* in this case means that the window is there to hold some information rather than to be displayed.

WM_DDE_ACK is used to reply to other messages. In response to **WM_DDE-_INITIATE**, **WM_DDE_ACK** is issued via **SendMessage**. All other DDE messages are issued and acknowledged via **PostMessage**.

As in many communications protocols, the DDE ACK is an acknowledgment of the receipt and processing of another message. Unlike other protocols, there is no DDE NAK (negative acknowledgment): instead, there is a bitmapped **wStatus** word in the acknowledgments to some messages that includes **fAck** and **fBusy** fields. If we slip and talk about a NAK later on, it is shorthand for **WM_DDE_ACK** with **fAck** set false.

The **WM_DDE_INITIATE** message is treated a little differently from other DDE requests. Because it's usually a broadcast, applications that know something about the topic and recognize their own name "raise their hands" by returning a **WM_DDE_ACK** with the supplied **aApplication** and **aTopic**. There is no need to NAK to say you don't know—just keep quiet. This keeps the message traffic to a minimum after the broadcast, but leads to an uncomfortable delay in the client application if nobody answers. The client will eventually have to time out, stop waiting for an ACK, and clean up its atoms and object windows.

Murphy says that the timeout setting will always be one second too short. The usual way of managing this problem is the let the user set the timeout in a profile (.INI) file. Alas and alack, most end users have trouble understanding why they need to adjust this kind of parameter, and instead call tech support to say that DDE doesn't work in your application. They also have trouble remembering to start the server application before the client application, and difficulty typing in the correct application name and topic for each conversation.

Both the client and server applications are responsible for keeping track of the two window handles that specify each conversation. Both must create object windows to guarantee that each conversation has unique identifiers. None of this is any fun.

Once you have a conversation started, you can ask for a specific data item in a specific format using the **WM_DDE_REQUEST** message. Here another complication enters: both client and server must agree on a data format. Excel asks for formats in order of "richness of information," with BIFF as the richest format. But because BIFF is so rich (that is, complicated) most other applications don't support it.

What happens is something of a comedy. Excel asks for BIFF. The server acknowledges the request with the **fAck** bit set false. Excel asks for its next richest format. The server denies this as well. After four or five tries, Excel asks for TEXT—and everybody supports text, so the server says OK.

Once the server sends an ACK with **fAck** true, the client waits for data. The server sends a **WM_DDE_DATA** message, which contains a handle to a global memory object, which is a **struct DDEDATA**. The server allocates the data structure using **GlobalAlloc** with the **GMEM_DDESHARE** option, and sets a bunch of bit fields to control what happens next.

If the **fAckReq** field is set, the client is expected to ACK the data message and reuse the atom; otherwise, it should not ACK, but should delete the atom. If the **fRelease** field is set and the client doesn't plan to NAK, the client should free the data object; otherwise, it should not free it. If the client NAKs the data message, the server has to free the data object. (Are you getting this? There will be a short quiz at the end of class.)

Once the client has a data handle, the procedure is very much like dealing with a handle from the clipboard: it needs to lock it down and copy or use the information out of it. But suppose the data handle is **NULL**? In this case, the client has to issue a **WM_DDE_REQUEST** to get the real information. That shouldn't happen in the context of an original REQUEST message, but there are other ways of asking for data.

WM_DDE_REQUEST asks for a data item once. **WM_DDE_ADVISE** asks for a data item to be updated whenever it changes. Like other DDE messages, **WM_DDE_ADVISE** has several options: a data format, a bit field for **fAckReq**, and a bit field for **fDeferUpd**. Setting **fAckReq** lets the two applications control the flow of information to avoid message queue overruns. If **fDeferUpd** is true, a *warm link* is requested—which means that the **WM_DDE_DATA** messages should be sent with **NULL** data handles. If **fDeferUpd** is false, the client wants a *hot link*—meaning that the real data is sent every time it changes.

Both the client and server have to track all the ADVISEs for each conversation. Both have to remember the data item and options for each link. The client is responsible for scanning its active conversations and links every time its data changes, and sending out the appropriate updates. As you might imagine, this can take a lot of code. When the data is coming from a communications link, and several conversations with active hot links are going on, the computer can easily bog down with message traffic and screen updates.

To end a warm or hot link, issue a **WM_DDE_UNADVISE** message. To end a conversation, issue a **WM_DDE_TERMINATE** message.

We have two DDE messages left: **WM_DDE_POKE** and **WM_DDE_EXECUTE**. **WM_DDE_POKE** is a back-channel data transfer mechanism: the client posts it to request the server to accept an unsolicited data item value. The server is expected to reply with a **WM_DDE_ACK** message, with the **fAck** bit field indicating acceptance or rejection of the data item. The **DDEPOKE** data structure referenced by the handle passed in the POKE message has fields **fRelease**, **cfFormat**, and **Value**.

As you can surely guess by now, **fRelease** specifies whether the server should free the passed memory object, and **cfFormat** specifies the standard or registered clipboard data format that is being passed. **Value** of course holds the actual data.

WM_DDE_EXECUTE is a remote-control mechanism: the client sends a string to the server to be processed as a series of commands. The server is expected to parse and execute the commands, and to reply with **WM_DDE_ACK** indicating success or failure. The Windows DDE specification suggests using the syntax:

```
[opcode string] [optional second opcode string] ...
```

where each opcode string consists of:

```
opcode (optional first parameter, optional second paramater, ...)
```

For instance, a communcations server might accept:

```
[connect][download(query1,results.txt)][disconnect]
```

and a spreadsheet might accept:

```
[open("sample.xlm")][run("r1c1")]
```

If we were going to enhance IMAGE2 to make it a DDE execute server, we'd have to write a little parser for such commands. We'd probably want to support one DDE command per menu item, so that remote control could do exactly the same things as an interactive user. It's not clear, yet, whether making IMAGE2 a DDE server of any kind makes sense: let's defer that sort of design decision until we understand DDEML and OLE.

The Windows SDK comes with a sample DDE client and a sample DDE server. Each supports only TEXT data transfer. Several function names are duplicated between the two without having the same content, so that if you try to build a combined client and server using these sources you will run into name clashes. The effort required to incorporate these samples in your own program is substantial: it took me three weeks to add DDE support at the message level to one of my application programs (EnPlot).

DDEML

After seeing how complicated it is to implement DDE in your application at the message level, you're probably hoping and praying that another implementation method will be easier. I've got good news and bad news about DDEML, the Dynamic Data Exchange Management Library: it implements a lot of the functionality needed (in fact more functionality that many DDE applications ever need), but you're going to have to learn yet another set of terms and concepts and function names.

Microsoft's introduction to DDEML:

> *The DDEML provides a set of API elements that simplifies the task of adding DDE capability to a Windows application. Instead of sending, posting, and processing DDE messages directly, an application uses the functions provided by the DDEML to manage DDE conversations. The DDEML also provides a facility for managing the strings and data that are passed among DDE applications. Applications create and exchange string handles and data handles instead of atoms and pointers to shared memory objects. A server-name service allows a server application to register the service names that it supports. The names are broadcast to other applications in the system which can then use the names to connect to the server. The DDEML also ensures compatibility among DDE applications by forcing them to implement the DDE protocol in a consistent manner.*

DDEML treats each message and acknowledgment in the DDE protocol as a *transaction*. You initiate a transaction by calling one of the DDEML functions; you are notified of a transaction through a callback function that you supply. The callback function may seem like a new concept, but it's not really: a window procedure is a callback function; a dialog procedure is a callback function. Think of the DDE callback function as your DDE procedure.

The transaction isn't really a new concept, either. If you're familiar with multiuser databases or networking protocols, you'll understand the transaction as the indivisible (but perhaps abortable) unit of communication. While the DDEML transaction has some specific additional meanings (just as the Windows message has additional meanings beyond the general term "message"), the concept of a "transaction" you may know from other contexts will be largely correct.

In DDEML's newspeak, the application name of a server is its *service name*. Servers can register their names, and tell the DDEML library to filter out unregistered names. You'll recall that when a client wants to start a conversation, it broadcasts the requested application name and topic to all Windows; name filtering keeps the application from seeing broadcasts that are really for other servers.

Server applications are supposed to support a "System" topic. Standard items within the system topic are:

Item	Description
SZDDESYS_ITEM_FORMATS	A list of DDE format numbers that the server can render. At a minimum, a server should support the CF_TEXT clipboard format for item names associated with the System topic.
SZDDESYS_ITEM_HELP	General help information.
SZDDESYS_ITEM_ITEMLIST	A list of the items that are common to all non-System topics (these may vary from moment to moment).
SZDDESYS_ITEM_STATUS	An indication of the current status of the server.
SZDDESYS_ITEM_SYSITEMS	A list of the items supported under the System topic by this server.
SZDDESYS_ITEM_TOPICS	A list of the topics supported by the server at the current time (this may vary from moment to moment).

DDEML spares your application from having to manage object windows, conversation lists, advise lists, and atoms. In dealing with DDEML you don't even have to think about atoms—but you do have to use *string handles*. The DDEML string handle functions are based on the Windows atom manager, just as you'd expect. Is there an advantage to string handle functions versus atom management functions? Only that there is less busy-work code for you to write.

Initializing DDEML

Because DDEML is a library, you need to initialize it before you use it. Part of the initialization process is defining your callback function:

```
DWORD idInst = 0L;    /* instance identifier      */
HANDLE hInst;         /* instance handle          */
FARPROC lpDdeProc;    /* procedure instance address */

lpDdeProc = MakeProcInstance((FARPROC) DdeCallback, hInst);
if (DdeInitialize(&idInst,    /* receives instance identifier   */
   (PFNCALLBACK) lpDdeProc,   /* points to callback function    */
    CBF_FAIL_EXECUTES |       /* filter XTYP_EXECUTE transactions */
    CBF_FAIL_POKES, 0L);      /* filter XTYP_POKE transactions   */
    return FALSE;
```

This particular example also tells DDEML not to send the application **XTYP_EXECUTE** or **XTYP_POKE** transactions—the equivalent of **WM_DDE_EXECUTE** and **WM_DDE_POKE** messages. When the application is done with DDEML, it has to free any application-owned data handles with **DdeFreeDataHandle**; and, it has to unlink its DDE callback function, terminate any open conversations, and free system resources with **DdeUninitialize**. In the SDK examples, this is done after the **GetMessage** loop in **WinMain**.

The DdeCallback Function

How does a DDE callback function look? Let's examine **DdeCallback** as implemented in \windev\samples\ddeml\client\dde.c:

```
HDDEDATA EXPENTRY DdeCallback(
WORD wType,             //transaction type
WORD wFmt,              //clipboard data format
HCONV hConv,           //handle of the conversation
HSZ hsz1,              //handle of a string
HSZ hsz2,              //handle of another string
HDDEDATA hData,        //handle of a global memory object
DWORD lData1,          //transaction-specific data
DWORD lData2)          //more transaction-specific data
{
    HWND hwnd;
    CONVINFO ci;
    XACT *pxact;
```

```
    if (hConv) {
        /*
         * update conversation status if it changed.
         */
        MYCONVINFO *pmci;

        ci.cb = sizeof(CONVINFO);
        if (!DdeQueryConvInfo(hConv, QID_SYNC, &ci)
        || (!IsWindow((HWND)ci.hUser))) {
/* This conversation does not yet have a corresponding MDI window or is
disconnected. */
            return 0;
        }
        if (pmci = (MYCONVINFO *)GetWindowWord((HWND)ci.hUser, 0)) {
            if (pmci->ci.wStatus != ci.wStatus ||
                    pmci->ci.wConvst != ci.wConvst ||
                    pmci->ci.wLastError != ci.wLastError) {
/* Things have changed, update the conversation window. */
                InvalidateRect((HWND)ci.hUser, NULL, TRUE);
            }
            if (ci.wConvst & ST_INLIST) {
/* update the associated list window (if any) as well. */
                if (hwnd = FindListWindow(ci.hConvList))
                    InvalidateRect(hwnd, NULL, TRUE);
            }
        }
    }
/* handle special block on next callback option here.  This demon-
strates the CBR_BLOCK feature. */
    if (fBlockNextCB && !(wType & XTYPF_NOBLOCK)) {
        fBlockNextCB = FALSE;
        return(CBR_BLOCK);
    }
/* handle special termination here.  This demonstrates that at any time
a client can drop a conversation. */
    if (fTermNextCB && hConv && wType != XTYP_DISCONNECT) {
        fTermNextCB = FALSE;
        MyDisconnect(hConv);
        return(0);
    }
    /*
     * Now we begin to sort out what to do.
     */
    switch (wType) {
    case XTYP_REGISTER:
    case XTYP_UNREGISTER:
/* This is where the client would insert code to keep track of what
servers are available.  This could cause the initiation of some conver-
sations. */
        break;

    case XTYP_DISCONNECT:
        if (fAutoReconnect) {
```

```
        /*
         * attempt a reconnection
         */
        if (hConv = DdeReconnect(hConv)) {
            AddConv(ci.hszServiceReq, ci.hszTopic, hConv,
                              FALSE);
            return 0;
        }
    }
    /*
     * update conv window to show its new state.
     */
    SendMessage((HWND)ci.hUser, UM_DISCONNECTED, 0, 0);
    return 0;
    break;

case XTYP_ADVDATA:
    /*
     * data from an active advise loop (from a server)
     */
    Delay(wDelay);
    hwnd = FindAdviseChild((HWND)ci.hUser, hsz2, wFmt);
    if (!IsWindow(hwnd)) {
        PSTR pszItem, pszFmt;
        /*
         * AdviseStart window is gone, make a new one.
         */
        pxact = (XACT *)MyAlloc(sizeof(XACT));
        pxact->wType = wType;
        pxact->hConv = hConv;
        pxact->wFmt = wFmt;
        pxact->hszItem = hsz2;
        DdeKeepStringHandle(idInst, hsz2);

        pszItem = GetHSZName(hsz2);
        pszFmt = GetFormatName(wFmt);

        hwnd = CreateInfoCtrl(NULL,
                (int)SendMessage((HWND)ci.hUser,
                              UM_GETNEXTCHILDX, 0, 0L),
                (int)SendMessage((HWND)ci.hUser,
                              UM_GETNEXTCHILDY, 0, 0L),
                200, 100,
                (HWND)ci.hUser, hInst,
                Type2String(wType, 0), (LPSTR)pszItem, NULL,
                NULL, (LPSTR)pszFmt, NULL,
                ICSTY_SHOWFOCUS, 0, (DWORD)(LPSTR)pxact);

        MyFree(pszFmt);
        MyFree(pszItem);

        if (!IsWindow(hwnd))
            return(DDE_FNOTPROCESSED);
```

```
            }
            if (!hData) {
/* XTYPF_NODATA case - request the info. (we do this synchronously for
simplicity) */
                hData = DdeClientTransaction(NULL, 0L, hConv, hsz2,
                        wFmt, XTYP_REQUEST, DefTimeout, NULL);
            }
            if (hData) {
                PSTR pData;
/* Show incoming data on corresponding transaction window.  */
                pData = GetTextData(hData);
                SendMessage(hwnd, ICM_SETSTRING, ICSID_CENTER,
                            (DWORD)(LPSTR)pData);
                MyFree(pData);
                DdeFreeDataHandle(hData);
            }
            SendMessage(hwnd, ICM_SETSTRING, ICSID_LL,
                (DWORD)(LPSTR)"Advised");
            return(DDE_FACK);
            break;

        case XTYP_XACT_COMPLETE:
/* An asynchronous transaction has completed.  Show the results. ...un-
less the XOPT_BLOCKRESULT is chosen. */
            ci.cb = sizeof(CONVINFO);
            if (DdeQueryConvInfo(hConv, lData1, &ci) &&
                    IsWindow((HWND)ci.hUser) &&
                    (pxact = (XACT *)GetWindowWord((HWND)ci.hUser,
                                    GWW_WUSER))) {
                if (pxact->fsOptions & XOPT_BLOCKRESULT) {
                    pxact->fsOptions &= ~XOPT_BLOCKRESULT;
                    return(CBR_BLOCK);
                }
                pxact->Result = lData2;
                pxact->ret = hData;
                CompleteTransaction((HWND)ci.hUser, pxact);
            }
            break;
    }
}
```

If you were hoping the **DdeCallback** function would be simple, I'm sure you're disappointed. Nevertheless, the code is at least readable. To understand the **switch** statements in the code, we'll need to understand the various transaction types, shown in the table on the following page.

The DDEML divides transactions into four classes by the type of return value expected. Each class is identified by a constant defined in the DDEML header file that begins with the **XCLASS_** prefix. The class constant is combined with the transaction type constant and is passed to the callback function of the receiving application.

Transaction	Receiver	Cause
XTYP_ADVDATA	Client	A server responded to an XTYP_ADVREQ transaction by returning a data handle.
XTYP_ADVREQ	Server	A server called the DdePostAdvise function, indicating that the value of a data item in an advise loop has changed.
XTYP_ADVSTART	Server	A client specified the XTYP_ADVSTART transaction in a call to the DdeClient-Transaction function.
XTYP_ADVSTOP	Server	A client specified the XTYP_ADVSTOP transaction in a call to the DdeClient-Transaction function.
XTYP_CONNECT	Server	A client called the DdeConnect function, specifying a service name and topic name supported by the server.
XTYP_CONNECT_CONFIRM	Server	The server returned TRUE in response to an XTYP_CONNECT or XTYP_WILD-CONNECT transaction.
XTYP_DISCONNECT	Client/Server	A partner in a conversation called the DdeDisconnect function causing both partners to receive this transaction.
XTYP_EXECUTE	Server	A client specified the XTYP_EXECUTE transaction in a call to the DdeClient-Transaction.
XTYP_MONITOR	DDE Monitor	A DDE event occurred in the system.
XTYP_XACT_COMPLETE	Client	An asynchronous transaction, issued when the client specified the TIME-OUT_ASYNC flag in a call to the DdeClientTransaction function, has completed.
XTYP_POKE	Server	A client specified the XTYP_POKE transaction in a call to the DdeClient-Transaction.
XTYP REGISTER	Client/Server	A server application used the DdeName-Service function to register a service name.
XTYP_REQUEST	Server	A client specified the XTYP_REQUEST transaction in a call to the DdeClient-Transaction.
XTYP_UNREGISTER	Client/Server	A server application used the DdeName-Service function to unregister a service name.
XTYP_WILDCONNECT	Server	A client called the DdeConnect or Dde-ConnectList function, specifying either a NULL service name, topic name, or both.

A transaction's class determines the return value that a callback function is expected to return if it processes the transaction. There are four transaction classes: XCLASS_BOOL, XCLASS_DATA, XCLASS_NOTIFICATION, and XCLASS_FLAGS.

Class	Return Value	Transactions
XCLASS_BOOL	TRUE or FALSE.	XTYP_ADVSTART, XTYP_CONNECT
XCLASS_DATA	A data handle, CBR_BLOCK, or NULL	XTYP_ADVREQ, XTYP_REQUEST, XTYP_WILDCONNECT
XCLASS_FLAGS	A transaction flag: DDE_FACK, DDE_FBUSY, or DDE_FNOTPROCESSED.	XTYP_ADVDATA, XTYP_EXECUTE, XTYP_POKE
XCLASS_NOTIFICATION	None.	XTYP_ADVSTOP, XTYP_CONNECT_CONFIRM, XTYP_XACT_COMPLETE, XTYP_DISCONNECT, XTYP_REGISTER, XTYP_UNREGISTER

String and Data Handles

Your application will have to create both data and string handles for DDEML. It can obtain a string handle for a particular string by calling the **DdeCreate-StringHandle** function, which registers the string with the system and returns a string handle to the application. For instance:

```
DWORD idInst;
HSZ hszServName;
HSZ hszSysTopic;

hszServName = DdeCreateStringHandle(
    idInst,          /* instance identifier (from DdeInitialize) */
    "MyServer",      /* string to register   */
    CP_WINANSI);     /* code page            */

hszSysTopic = DdeCreateStringHandle(
    idInst,             /* instance identifier */
    SZDDESYS_TOPIC,     /* system topic        */
    CP_WINANSI);        /* code page           */
```

To obtain a data handle, create a local buffer containing the data, then call the **DdeCreateDataHandle** function. This function allocates a global memory object, copies the data from the buffer to the memory object, and returns a data handle. For instance:

```
DdeCreateDataHandle(idInst,                  /* instance identifier  */
                    (LPBYTE) szBuf,          /* source buffer        */
                    strlen(szBuf) + 1,       /* size of global object */
                    0L,                      /* offset from beginning */
                    hszItemName,             /* item-name string     */
                    CF_TEXT,                 /* clipboard format     */
                    0);                      /* no creation flags    */
```

When accessing strings and data passed as handles, you typically need to determine the size of the data, allocate a buffer, and then copy the data. You do this by calling the appropriate DDEML function twice: once with a null output pointer to get the size, and once with a real output pointer to get the data. The **DdeQueryString** and **DdeGetData** functions are quite similar in this respect. Of course, if you already know the size of the data, you can dispense with the preliminaries:

```
cchServ = DdeQueryString(idInst,            //instance id
        ci.hszAppPartner,                   //string handle
        (LPSTR) &szAppPartner,              //output pointer
        sizeof(szAppPartner),           //buffer size
        CP_WINANSI);                        //code page of string
...
DdeGetData(hData,                           //data handle
        (LPBYTE) szBuf,                     //output pointer
        32L,                                //buffer size
        0L);                                //source offset
```

More DDEML Functions and Types

There are a few more DDEML functions to explain before you'll be anywhere near understanding the **DdeCallback** example: **DdeQueryConvInfo**, **Dde-Reconnect**, **DdeKeepStringHandle**, and **DdeClientTransaction**. We'll also need to look at the **CONVINFO** and **XACT** structures. Let's take them in order, and then mention some of the other important DDEML functions.

DdeQueryConvInfo retrieves information about a DDE transaction and about the conversation in which the transaction takes place. It takes three arguments: a handle to the conversation, a transaction identifier, and a pointer to a **CONVINFO** structure. Note that the **cb** element of the structure has to be initialized to the length of the buffer allocated for the structure, usually **sizeof(CONVINFO)**, prior to calling the function. A common bug when using this kind of Windows function is to initialize the whole structure to zero; when the function sees the zero buffer size, it simply returns, and the programmer will see only that the function failed.

The **CONVINFO** structure holds all the necessary information about a conversation and the current transaction. The manual page tells the whole story; the following page here is a summary.

```
#include <ddeml.h>     //required for all functions that use DDEML
typedef struct _CONVINFO {  /* ci */
 DWORD cb;             //length of structure in bytes
 DWORD hUser;          //handle to application-defined data
 HCONV hConvPartner;   //handle to partner if registered for DDEML
 HSZ   hszSvcPartner;  //handle to service name of partner
 HSZ   hszServiceReq;  //handle to service name of requested server
 HSZ   hszTopic;       //handle to topic name for conversation
 HSZ   hszItem;        //handle to item name for this transaction
 WORD  wFmt;           //format of data for this transaction
 WORD  wType;          //type of this transaction (XTYP_, see table)
 WORD  wStatus;        //bit-encoded status of this conversation (ST_)
 WORD  wConvst;        //state of this conversation (XST_)
 WORD  wLastError;     //error value of last transaction
 HCONV hConvList;      //handle to conversation list or NULL
 CONVCONTEXT ConvCtxt;       //conversation context structure
} CONVINFO;
```

The **wStatus** structure element, which represents independent elements of the conversation status, can be a *combination* of the following values:

```
ST_ADVISE, ST_BLOCKED, ST_BLOCKNEXT, ST_CLIENT, ST_CONNECTED,
ST_INLIST, ST_ISLOCAL, ST_ISSELF. ST_TERMINATED
```

The **wConvst** structure element, which specifies the current unique conversation state, can be *one* of the following values:

```
XST_ADVACKRCVD, XST_ADVDATAACKRCVD, XST_ADVDATASENT, XST_ADVSENT,
XST_CONNECTED, XST_DATARCVD, XST_EXECACKRCVD, XST_EXECSENT,
XST_INCOMPLETE, XST_INIT1, XST_INIT2, XST_NULL, XST_POKEACKRCVD,
XST_POKESENT, XST_REQSENT, XST_UNADVACKRCVD, XST_UNADVSENT
```

The **CONVINFO** structure includes another structure, **CONVCONTEXT**, as its last element. **CONVCONTEXT**, which specifies national language information that might affect the topic and item name strings, has its own **cb** item that should be set if you want the structure to actually be filled by a DDEML call.

```
typedef struct _CONVCONTEXT {   /* cc */
    WORD    cb;           //size of structure
    WORD    wFlags;       //conversation context flags (future)
    WORD    wCountryID;   //country-code id for topic and item
    int     iCodePage;    //code page for topic and item
    DWORD   dwLangID;     //language identifier for topic and item
    DWORD   dwSecurity;   //application-defined security code
} CONVCONTEXT;
```

DdeReconnect is used to reestablish a conversation when it has been disconnected. **DdeKeepStringHandle** increments the usage count of a string handle; this guarantees that a string handle received in a transaction will remain valid after the transaction. **DdeClientTransaction** begins a data transaction between a client and a server application. Only a DDE client application can call this function, and only after establishing a conversation with the server. In summary:

```
HDDEDATA DdeClientTransaction(lpbData, cbDataLen, hConv, hszItem, wFmt,
wType, dwTimeout, lpdwResult)
LPBYTE lpbData;        /* pointer to data to pass to server      */
DWORD cbDataLen;       /* length of the data */
IICONV hConv;          /* handle of the conversation      */
HSZ hszItem;           /* handle of the item-name string   */
WORD wFmt;             /* clipboard data format      */
WORD wType;            /* transaction type    */
DWORD dwTimeout;       /* timeout duration    */
LPDWORD lpdwResult;    /* points to transaction result      */
```

The **XACT** structure isn't a standard DDEML type. It's defined in client.h in the sample program and used to hold information for DDE transaction display windows. You might want to look at it if you need to implement DDE using DDEML, along with the rest of the DDEML client and server samples.

DDEML Protocol Walkthrough

We've seen enough of the details of DDEML. Now let's walk through the protocol to understand the flow of transactions.

To start, the client and server both **DdeInitialize**. The server also registers via **DdeNameService**. The client requests one or more conversations, with one or more servers.

To start a single conversation, the client issues **DdeConnect** for a service name and topic. DDEML then sends **XTYP_CONNECT** transactions to the callback functions of all servers with matching service names and all servers without service-name filtering.

If some server returns **TRUE** from the **XTYP_CONNECT** transaction (meaning it can converse on the stated topic), a conversation is established and the client receives a conversation handle; otherwise, the client receives **NULL** from the **DdeConnect** function. If a conversation is established, the server receives an **XTYP_CONNECT_CONFIRM** transaction with the conversation handle (unless it has filtered with **CBF_FAIL_CONFIRMS**). Note that DDEML takes care of managing the conversation handle, and that neither server nor client had to create an object window.

A client can use **NULL** service-name or topic-name string handles in **DdeConnect** to establish a "wildcard" conversation. In this case, DDEML sends an **XTYP_WILDCONNECT** transaction to *all* DDE applications except those that filter **XTYP_WILDCONNECT**. Server applications then return a list of matching service-name/topic-name pairs, from which DDEML picks *one* pair to start a conversation.

Anybody can end a conversation at any time by calling **DdeDisconnect**; the other partner is notified with the **XTYP_DISCONNECT** transaction.

A client can establish multiple conversations by calling **DdeConnectList**. DDEML then issues **XTYP_WILDCONNECT** transactions, and starts a conversation for *each* matching service-name/topic-name pair returned by a server. With NULL service- and topic-name string handles, a client can establish conversations with every DDE server on the system for every recognized topic with a single function call. Of course, that might turn out to be a lot of activity for very little benefit, so that it is best to avoid massive wildcard connections.

A client carrying on multiple conversations started with **DdeConnectList** can traverse the conversation list with **DdeQueryNextServer** and **DdeQueryConvInfo**. It can terminate individual conversations in the list with **DdeDisconnect**, or all of them with **DdeDisconnectList**.

Global data blocks are managed with **DdeCreateDataHandle**, **DdeAccessData**, **DdeGetData**, **DdeUnaccessData**, **DdeAddData**, and **DdeFreeDataHandle**. String handles for service, topic, and item names can be manipulated with **DdeCreateStringHandle**, **DdeCmpStringHandles**, **DdeKeepStringHandle**, and **DdeFreeStringHandle**.

The DDE client calls **DdeClientTransaction** with transaction type **XTYP_REQUEST** to ask for a data item—the equivalent of sending a **WM_DDE_REQUEST** message. DDEML passes the **XTYP_REQUEST** to the server's callback function, and returns the server's data handle (or **NULL**) to the caller.

In the same fashion, **DdeClientTransaction** with transaction type **XTYP_POKE** offers a data item to the server, **DdeClientTransaction** with **XTYP_ADVISE** asks for a warm or hot link, and **DdeClientTransaction** with **XTYP_EXECUTE** asks the server to execute a command or series of commands.

Synchronous and Asynchronous Transactions

DDEML transactions can be either synchronous or asynchronous. Synchronous transactions will not return until the server processes the transaction, the transaction fails, or the transaction times out. Client applications can process user input during a synchronous transaction, but cannot start another transaction.

Asynchronous transactions, specified by setting **TIMEOUT_ASYNC** in the **DdeClientTransaction** call, return as soon as the transaction has begun with a unique transaction identifier. When the transaction finishes, the client's callback function gets an **XTYP_XACT_COMPLETE** transaction bearing the transaction identifier of the original asynchronous transaction. If the client is no longer interested in the results of an open transaction, it can throw it away with **DdeAbandonTransaction**.

Applications can control incoming DDE transactions by returning **CBR_BLOCK** to a transaction and by using the **DdeEnableCallback** function. DDEML saves transactions for suspended conversations in a transaction queue (which is of "significant" but not infinite size). As long as your program doesn't wait too long to reenable callbacks, it can safely suspend conversations—for instance, to allow lengthy computations to proceed without interruption.

Microsoft claims that DDEML can reduce the work involved in implementing DDE by a factor of ten compared with using DDE messages. If that is the case, my three-week experience implementing DDE in EnPlot would have taken closer to two days had I been able to use DDEML. However, it took me more than two days to understand DDEML well enough to write this section—so take that estimate with a large grain of salt.

OLE

Microsoft's Object Linking and Embedding Specification (OLE) adds functionality to Dynamic Data Exchange. In addition to supporting all the features of DDE, it handles embedded compound documents, linked compound documents, and permanent registration of service names.

Like DDEML, OLE is built with seperate client and server dynamic link libraries that run only in protected mode. OLE clients call OLE API functions in the OLE client library, and OLE servers have callback functions that can be accessed by the OLE server library. OLE client and server libraries communicate using DDE, but OLE applications don't have to deal with the nitty-gritty of DDE.

OLE versus DDEML

Microsoft claims many advantages for the OLE libraries as compared with DDEML. First, the OLE libraries may be enhanced in the future to support new data formats, link tracking, in situ editing, and perhaps other things as yet undreamed of. Second, the OLE libraries make links more robust than DDE: the OLE libraries take care of reestablishing conversations, for instance when an embedded document is reopened. Users don't have to open the server before asking for an OLE link, and don't have to know about service names.

The OLE libraries already know how to display common data formats—text, bitmap, DIB, and metafile—in a display context. An OLE client that got a DIB from our Image program wouldn't have to know how to render the DIB—it could rely on the OLE library to display the DIB properly in the device context.

OLE also supports server rendering. For instance, we could define a data format of our own that specifies a number of DIBs, where they are placed in the device context, and what ROP to use for each DIB; it might even go on to specify a sequence of such compound images and timing for displaying them. That might be the beginning of a nice animation package—but it wouldn't be much use to other applications that didn't know the format. With OLE, the other applications know they are holding a foreign format, and know to call our rendering library to display it.

The static display of an animation might just show the first frame. OLE supports activating a server for editing, and also activating a server for playing the object. Playing an animation would cycle through all the frames; editing would bring up an application for controlling the sequence of frames. The architecture might even allow the sequence editor to bring up an image overlay editor, which could in turn bring up a palette editor or paint program. Levels within levels of a document can sound pretty confusing, but a good implementation makes it all seem easy to the user.

The OLE libraries take care of copying and pasting links to and from the clipboard, and exchanging objects via the clipboard. We've already built clipboard access into Image2, so that isn't all that important in our particular case; on the other hand, it might simplify the implementation of a new program if we used OLE for all interprocess communication.

OLE also directly supports exchanging data via files; DDE doesn't do this. Given the large size of some DIB images, especially 24-bit color images, file transfer makes a lot of sense, and some sort of protocol would simplify the process.

There are two disadvantages of OLE compared to DDEML. First, OLE conversations support only one item (object); DDEML conversations support multiple hot and/or warm links concerning multiple items. Second, OLE supports only standard DDE system topic items; DDEML can support additional application-defined topic items.

OLE Concepts

OLE implements services in support of *compound documents*. An example of a compound document is the front page of your local newspaper, which probably combines a big, fancy title and logo, one or two photographs, a small line drawing or two, and a lot of type.

Old-fashioned newspapers did page makeup by putting blocks of cast lead type and images together in a metal frame. Offset printing changed the process to paste-up, done with hot wax. Computerization of the newspaper industry initially streamlined the process of producing columns of type, and only later affected the page makeup process.

Desktop publishing programs like Aldus PageMaker and Ventura Publisher can help to transform page makeup into an all-electronic process. However, when building a compound document with such a program, you have to make some difficult choices.

If you are producing a document that will be printed once and then filed, it is easy to use the Windows clipboard or file transfer methods to place text and illustrations. If, however, you wish to produce a variation of the same document periodically—for instance, a weekly sales report that includes some graphs and tables—it would be time-consuming to redo the placement each time the information changes.

Hot links via DDE are only a partial solution. Yes, you can make a table in PageMaker or Word for Windows update every time the original Excel spreadsheet changes—but only as long as you remember to start Excel first, and don't ever move the original documents around. Send the document to somebody else and the hot link references are likely to suddenly have the wrong disk and pathnames—which means that the receiver will have to do a lot of fixup work.

OLE supports two new mechanisms for building compound documents: *embedded* objects, and *linked* objects. Embedded objects are an enhancement from placement of files or clipboard objects; the major new feature is that the user can double-click the embedded object to edit it, and OLE will automatically start a registered server for that type of object. In addition, the *container* or *client* application doesn't have to know anything about the object to display it—it can rely on OLE and registered OLE servers to render the object on demand.

Embedded objects are inherently reliable, but won't be automatically updated if their underlying data changes. Linked objects, on the other hand, are more like DDE hot links—they *are* automatically updated. One advantage of OLE links over DDE hot links is that OLE takes responsibility for starting the server application—the user doesn't have to worry about doing things in the right order.

OLE links can still be broken by moving a file around. That problem is solved in HP New Wave by implementing a second name space. New Wave keeps a database that relates DOS filenames to New Wave object names; in a New Wave document the links refer to New Wave names, which are resolved by the object manager from the name database. When a file moves within New Wave, the name database is updated, and all links to the file are redirected automatically. New Wave has only one kind of link, but it combines the best features of OLE embedding and OLE linking.

Without New Wave, the current generation of Windows and DOS don't preserve links across file movements. Future versions of DOS (possibly 6.0) and Windows (possibly 3.2 or 4.0) from Microsoft are supposed to implement an object-oriented file system that does solve the broken link problem without requiring a second filename space.

Embedded or linked OLE objects can display in their native format, or as an icon or bitmap. And OLE object that encapsulates another object and displays an icon or bitmap is called a *package*. Windows 3.1 ships with a Packager application, which can associate a file or data selection with an icon or graphic.

For instance, you might have a MIDI or waveform sound file embedded in a wordprocessing document. You wouldn't really want the music or piano roll notation for a MIDI file to display in a Word document, nor would you want the waveform shape for a sampled sound to display. What you might want to see on the screen is an icon—perhaps an eighth note or G clef for the MIDI object, perhaps a small sine wave or loadspeaker icon for the sampled sound—on which the user would double-click to play or single-click to edit the sound.

Play and *edit* are two possible actions for the sound. Both are *verbs*—both grammatically, and in OLE-speak. For a sound, the most typical use would be to play the sound—so its primary verb would be "Play." The next most typical use would be to edit the sound—so its secondary verb would be "Edit." The client application designates the primary and secondary verb for an object; the server application determines what the verb actually means. Text is never played, but often edited, so that the primary verb for text objects is usually "Edit." The secondary verb for text is usually "Print."

The user can invoke the primary verb for an object by double-clicking, and the secondary verb by single-clicking. The user can also invoke an object's subsidiary verbs by using the standard OLE Class Name Object menu or Links dialog box.

Clicking on a package is a little different from clicking on an ordinary embedded object. Double-clicking on either a regular object or a package invokes the primary verb—of the regular object, or of the object inside the package. Single-clicking on an object invokes its secondary verb. However, the secondary verb of a package is always "Edit Package," which starts the Packager application. If you want to invoke the secondary verb of an object in a package, you can do so from the Packager.

Let's think out loud for a minute. Image2 reads a lot of different file formats and converts them into the standard Windows DIB format. It also manipulates DIBs by changing their colors, cropping them, and pasting clippings into them.

At the same time, Windows PaintBrush (PBrush) also manipulates DIBs—by letting the user add text to them or paint on them. Paintbrush is normally registered as the "Edit" server for "Paintbrush" objects; BMP, MSP, and PCX objects are associated with PBrush both in win.ini and in the OLE registration database. Double-click on a BMP file in File Manager and it will come up in PBrush because of the win.ini association. Double-click on an embedded BMP and it will come up in PBrush because of the registration database association.

How could we make Image2 fit into the picture? We don't want to keep users from getting into PBrush via OLE, but might want them also to be able to get into Image2 via OLE. Maybe we can make Image2 a server for the "Process" verb, and somehow register it so that "Process" is a "Paintbrush" object's secondary verb. Let's think about that a little as we delve further into OLE.

There are actually three types of OLE processes: clients, servers, and object handlers. Clients can accept, display, and store OLE objects. Servers can activate an object on demand. The object typically has been selected in a client application; the activation request is passed from client to server by the OLE libraries. If the selected object is linked, the server loads the whole linked file and selects the linked portion of the file. If the selected object is embedded, it is passed from client to server by the libraries. When the user wants to save an embedded object, he chooses the Update menu item (which replaces the usual Save menu item); when he is done editing, he chooses Exit in the server, and is returned to the client application.

Object handlers are DLLs that act as intermediaries between client and server. For instance, rendering engines can be supplied as object handlers. Usually, object handler DLLs are supplied as adjuncts to server applications.

OLE is currently implemented using DDE. Client applications call OLECLI.DLL, the OLE client library; server applications are called by OLESVR.DLL, the OLE server library; and OLECLI talks to OLESVR via DDE messages. The server library starts and stops the server application as well as calling the server's callback functions and maintaining a DDE conversation with the client library.

OLE and the Clipboard

The Windows clipboard is often used for the first step in embedding or linking an OLE object, just as it is often used for the first step in creating a DDE hot link. The Paste Link command is familiar to Excel users; link pasting for OLE is a little more formal and structured than link pasting for DDE.

A simplified example: To create an embedded object, a server first posts a Native format object to the clipboard, and then posts an OwnerLink object. To create a linked object, a server first posts an OwnerLink object to the clipboard, and then may post a Native format object if used for presentation. If you are confused, finish and reread this section a couple of times: clipboard order is semantically important for OLE applications.

In addition to Native and OwnerLink formats, OLE servers also post a presentation format and ObjectLink data. Perhaps we should explain each format.

Native format completely specifies the object, but is meaningful only to the server. OwnerLink format is a text string that holds the class name, document name, and item name; nulls separate the three fields, and two nulls terminate the record. ObjectLink format is identical to OwnerLink format; however, it is used in a different way.

An OwnerLink describes the *owner* of a linked or embedded object. An ObjectLink describes the *source* of a linked object. The owner need not be the same as the source. The source is important for linked objects since the server will have to reopen the source to edit the object.

A presentation format is something the client can use to display the object in a document. Standard formats like CF_DIB make good presentation formats, but native data can be used for presentation if an object handler is defined for the class.

There are some subtleties here. You can't step into the same river twice, and you can't use the same native format twice for a single object. This is why order is so critical. If you supply Native format, then OwnerLink, you are specifying an embedded object. If you supply OwnerLink, then Native format, you are specifying a linked object that uses Native format for presentation.

We mentioned that the first field in the OwnerLink and ObjectLink formats is the class name; we should make it clear that the class name is the key for the registration database. Class names have to be unique, and have to be registered. Looking in the Registration database supplied with the Windows 3.1 SDK, we find "Pbrush" registered for Windows Paintbrush and BMP, PCX, and MSP files; "ExcelWorksheet" registered for Excel and XLS files; "ExcelChart" registered for Excel and XLC files; "wrifile" registered for Windows Write and WRI files; "Graph" registered for PowerPoint Graph; "txtfile" registered for Notepad and TXT files; and so on.

Servers put formats on the clipboard in order of fidelity. If there are formats with better fidelity than Native, they precede the Native format. Clients take the first acceptable format they find by going through the clipboard in order.

If the user chooses Paste in a client application, it will look through the clipboard formats and choose the first acceptable format. If the client is Word and the first acceptable format is RTF, Word will paste the RTF information just as it would without OLE. On the other hand, if the first acceptable format were Native, Word would create an embedded object. If the first acceptable format were OwnerLink, Word would create a linked object.

If the user chooses Paste Link in a client application, it will skip to the ObjectLink format. If it finds the ObjectLink format and a usable presentation format, it will create a linked OLE object. Other formats on the clipboard would be ignored. If there is no ObjectLink format, most OLE applications would look for a Link format; if found, they would create an ordinary DDE link.

Applications that don't support OLE can still use the clipboard information posted by an OLE server. However, they won't recognize Native, ObjectLink, or OwnerLink formats—instead they'll look for something familiar, and they'll paste the familiar format in their usual fashion.

It's beginning to look like OLE is more trouble than it's worth for an application like Image2. But let's continue to keep an open mind. Becoming an OLE server would let Image2 process bitmaps for other applications. Adding an OLE object handler would let OLE clients display a new format should we care to define one. Becoming an OLE client would let Image2 manage multiple bitmaps and other types of data (such as rich text) as well as letting it farm out bit-level editing to PaintBrush and text editing to Write. Whether any of these makes sense remains to be seen.

The System Registration Database

The OLE system registration database, supported by SHELL.DLL, enables the OLE libraries to recognize the correct server for a given object, the correct action for a given verb, and whether an object-handler exists for a given object. Servers register themselves when they are installed, and indicate which OLE protocols they support: "StdFileEditing," "Static," and/or "StdExecute." "StdFileEditing" is the protocol for linked and embedded objects. "Static" describes a picture that cannot be edited using standard OLE techniques. And "StdExecute" is the protocol for OLE remote execution, called via the **OleExecute** function. We spoke earlier about possibly supporting the **WM_DDE_EXECUTE** message; **OleExecute** support would be another alternative.

The command line for each server is kept in the system registration database. The OLE libraries use that stored command line, with "**-Embedding**" or "**-Embedding** *filename*" appended, to start the server when a client actives a linked or embedded object; the server, in turn, is supposed to recognize the "**-Embedding**" switch and start in a special way. For instance, it has to change its **File/Save** menu item to **File/Update**, and it doesn't show its window until the OLE libraries call its **Show** or **DoVerb** callback functions.

A server's callback functions are kept in an **OLEOBJECTVTBL** structure, which is a table of about 40 function pointers (a **VTBL**) for a specific OLE object. Servers need to implement the first ten functions in the table; object handlers can use any of the functions to modify default server behavior. Functions implemented via a function pointer table are called virtual functions or methods in the language of objects.

The OLE User Interface

An OLE client needs more editing commands than a normal application, and needs to do more with many of the commands. For example, Figure 5.2 shows the Windows 3.1 version of Windows Write with its edit menu pulled down. At the moment this snapshot was taken, there was an Excel spreadsheet on the clipboard, and another Excel spreadsheet (a linked object) was the currently selected object in Write.

We'll go down this menu quickly to understand what's behind each item. The highlighted "Undo Editing" menu item is enhanced from the sort of Undo we have in Image2: it knows how to undo all the changes made in a server session on an embedded object. The "Cut" and "Copy" commands are enhanced to use the **OleCopyToClipboard** function rather than ordinary clipboard functions when the current selection is an OLE object. They behave as normal when an ordinary region is selected.

The "Paste" command is enhanced to be able to embed an object at the current position in the current document, should the clipboard contain an OLE

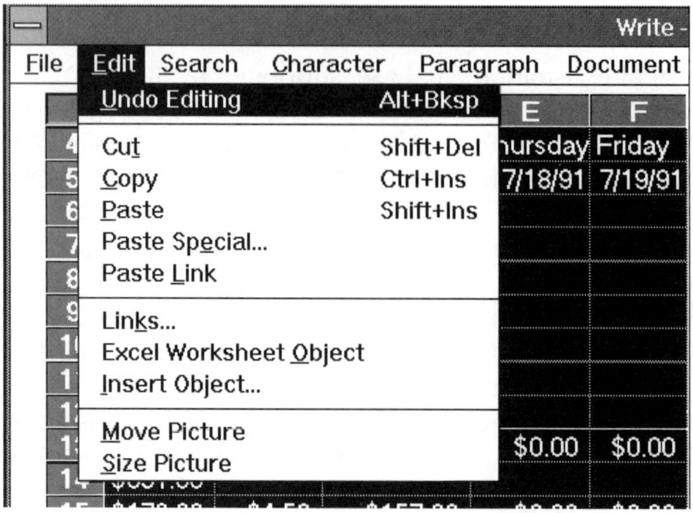

Figure 5.2. Windows Write edit menu showing OLE options

object. "Paste Special," an optional item, lets the user pick from the available clipboard formats as well as knowing how to embed and link objects. "Paste Link" inserts the current clipboard item as a link: it first tries to paste an OLE link; if that fails, it tries to paste a DDE link.

The "Links" menu item brings up a dialog that allows the user to change link updating options, update linked objects, cancel links, repair broken links, and invoke the verbs associated with linked objects. The "Excel Worksheet Object" item is a context-dependent "<Class Name> Object" menu entry that appears when an OLE object is selected; it allows the user to invoke the verbs for a linked or embedded object. "Insert Object" brings up a dialog box that lists the registered server classes, starts the selected server on a blank embedded object, and embeds the edited object produced by the server in the current document.

The "Move Picture" and "Size Picture" menu items are specific to Write: they allow the user to manipulate the appearance of the OLE object's bitmap display format. More capable desktop publishing applications would also be able to clip the viewed area of the picture.

While the OLE client interface adds a number of new menu items, the OLE server interface does not. The only changes that are immediately apparent to the user are that the title bar can say "Embedded Object" and the "Save" menu item changes to "Update." These are both illustrated in Figure 5.3.

OLE Client Application Structure

To add OLE client support to an application, you need to add initialization code for the OLE libraries as well as code to handle embedded objects. At startup, the

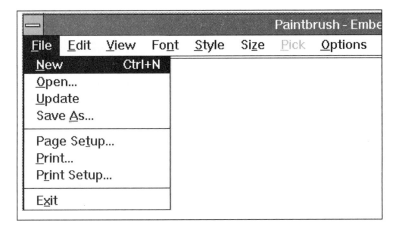

Figure 5.3. Ole Server Interface as illustrated by Windows Paintbrush

application needs to call **RegisterClipboardFormat** for "Native," "Owner-Link," "ObjectLink," and any other necessary clipboard formats. OLE, like DDE, uses clipboard format names.

In addition, the program has to allocate and initialize one **OLESTREAM** structure, plus one **OLECLIENT** structure for each object in the current document. These two structures are used to receive information from the OLE client library. The structures are fairly complex, and in turn point to **VTBL** structures, which as we mentioned before are tables of function pointers. The listings below are from the Microsoft Windows 3.1 SDK OLEDEMO sample.

```
if (!InitInstance(hInst, nCmdShow) || !InitClient(hInst))
        return FALSE;
...
/* InitClient() - Initialize the OLE client structures. */
BOOL FAR InitClient(HANDLE hInstance) {
    vcfLink      = RegisterClipboardFormat("ObjectLink");
    vcfNative    = RegisterClipboardFormat("Native");
    vcfOwnerLink = RegisterClipboardFormat("OwnerLink");

    if (!(hobjClient = GlobalAlloc(GMEM_FIXED | GMEM_ZEROINIT,
        sizeof(OLECLIENT)))
      || !(lpclient = (LPOLECLIENT)GlobalLock(hobjClient)))
          goto Error;

    lpclient->lpvtbl = (LPOLECLIENTVTBL)&clientTbl;

    if (!(hobjStream = GlobalAlloc(GMEM_FIXED | GMEM_ZEROINIT,
        sizeof(APPSTREAM)))
      || !(lpStream = (LPAPPSTREAM)GlobalLock(hobjStream)))
      goto Error;
```

```
        lpclient->lpvtbl->CallBack  =
                MakeProcInstance(CallBack, hInstance);

    lpStream->lpstbl = (LPOLESTREAMVTBL)&streamTbl;
    streamTbl.Get = (DWORD (FAR PASCAL *)
                (LPOLESTREAM, LPSTR, DWORD))
                MakeProcInstance((FARPROC)ReadStream, hInst);
        streamTbl.Put = (DWORD (FAR PASCAL *)
                (LPOLESTREAM, LPSTR, DWORD))
                MakeProcInstance((FARPROC)WriteStream, hInst);
    lpfnInsertNew    = MakeProcInstance(fnInsertNew, hInst);
    lpfnInvalidLink  = MakeProcInstance(fnInvalidLink, hInst);
    lpfnProperties   = MakeProcInstance(fnProperties, hInst);
    return TRUE;

Error:
    if (hobjStream)
        GlobalFree(hobjStream);

    if (lpclient) {
        GlobalUnlock(hobjClient);
        lpclient = NULL;
    }

    if (hobjClient)
        GlobalFree(hobjClient);

    return FALSE;
}
```

When opening a compound document, an OLE-aware program has to register the document before opening it. Once the document is open, the application has to call **OleLoadFromStream** and **OleQueryOutOfDate** for each object; then it should list out-of-date objects and let the user update them.

```
/* ReadFromFile() - Reads OLE objects from a file.Reads as many objects
as it can, in upwards order (better error recovery). Returns: TRUE iff
successful. */
BOOL ReadFromFile(void) {
    BOOL            fSuccess = FALSE;
    unsigned int    cFileObjects;

    Hourglass(TRUE);
    /* Go to the top of the file */
    _llseek(fh, 0L, 0);
    /* Read the number of items in the file */
    if (_lread(fh, (LPSTR)&cFileObjects, sizeof(int)) < sizeof(int)
      || cFileObjects > COBJECTSMAX) /* Invalid number of objects! */
        goto Error;
    /* Read in each object and get them in the right order */
    for (cManual = 0; cFileObjects; —cFileObjects) {
        if (!ObjRead(fh)) {
```

```
                ErrorMessage(E_FAILED_TO_READ_OBJECT);
                goto Error;
                   }
        }
    if (cManual)
        UpdateManualLinks();
    fSuccess = TRUE;
Error:
    _lclose(fh);
    fDirty = FALSE;
    Hourglass(FALSE);
    return fSuccess;
}
/* ObjRead() - Reads an object from the file handle fh.
 * SIDE EFFECT:  Advances the file pointer past the object.
 */
HWND FAR ObjRead(int fh) {
    BOOL              fIsWindow;
    LPOLEOBJECT       lpObject;
    OBJECTTYPE      otObject;
    RECT              rcObject;
    unsigned long   fhLoc;
    char        szTmp[CBOBJNAMEMAX];

    SetFile(SOP_FILE, fh, NULL);
    /* Is the item extant? */
    if (_lread(fh, (LPSTR)&fIsWindow, sizeof(BOOL)) < sizeof(BOOL))
        return NULL;
    if (!fIsWindow)
        return TRUE;
    if (_lread(fh, szTmp, CBOBJNAMEMAX) < CBOBJNAMEMAX )
        return NULL;
    ValidateName( szTmp );
    /* Save current position of file pointer */
    fhLoc = _llseek(fh, 0L, 1);
    /* Load the new object */
    if (Error(OleLoadFromStream((LPOLESTREAM)lpStream, PROTOCOL,
                lpclient, lhcdoc, szTmp, &lpObject))) {
        /* Reset file pointer, and try again */
        _llseek(fh, fhLoc, 0);
        /* Read it with the "Static" protocol */
        if (Error(OleLoadFromStream((LPOLESTREAM)lpStream,
            SPROTOCOL, lpclient, lhcdoc, szTmp, &lpObject)))
            return NULL;
    }
    /* Read its position and type */
    if (_lread(fh, (LPSTR)&rcObject, sizeof(RECT)) < sizeof(RECT)
     || _lread(fh, (LPSTR)&otObject, sizeof(OBJECTTYPE)) <
                    sizeof(OBJECTTYPE))
      return NULL;
    /* Create a window at the right place, and display the object */
    return CreateItemWindow(lpObject, (LPRECT)&rcObject, otObject,
                    TRUE);
```

```
}
/* UpdateManualLinks() -
        Update all manual links if the user so desires. */
void FAR UpdateManualLinks(void) {
   HWND    hwnd;
   char    szUpdate[CBMESSAGEMAX];
   /* Ask the user if they want to update the links */
   LoadString(hInst, IDS_UPDATELINKS, szUpdate, CBMESSAGEMAX);
   if (MessageBox(hwndFrame, szUpdate, szAppName,
                 MB_YESNO | MB_ICONQUESTION) == IDYES) {
   /* Yes?  Tell those manually link objects to update themselves */
      for (hwnd = GetTopWindow(hwndFrame);
            hwnd; hwnd = GetNextWindow(hwnd, GW_HWNDNEXT)) {
         if (ObjType(hwnd, FALSE) == LINK
          && ObjGetUpdateOptions(hwnd) == oleupdate_oncall)
            PostMessage(hwnd, WM_COMMAND, IDD_UPDATE, 0L);
      }
   }
}
```

An OLE client is reponsible for letting the OLE library know when a document has changed content or status. **OleRegisterClientDoc** tells the library that the document exists. **OleRenameClientDoc** tells the library that you've changed the document name. **OleRevertClientDoc** says that the document has reverted to a previously saved state. **OleRevokeClientDoc** notifies the library that the document should be closed or no longer exists. And **OleSavedClientDoc** lets that library know that you've saved the document.

To save a document with embedded objects, first save the data; then save each object with **OleSaveToStream**; and finally let the library know what you've done with **OleSavedClientDoc**. To close a document, first call **OleRelease** for each object; then call **OleRevertClientDoc** or **OleSaved-ClientDoc**, depending on whether the document was closed without changes or closed after a save; finally, when the OLE client library confirms that all the objects have been closed, call **OleRevokeClientDoc**.

Many OLE calls—those client calls that invoke server processes—begin asynchronous operations. When the operation begins, the client library returns **OLE_WAIT_FOR_RELEASE**; when the operation ends, the client receives **OLE_RELEASE**. If the client attempts to call a function for an object during another asynchronous operation on the same object, the function will return **OLE_BUSY** instead of **OLE_WAIT_FOR_RELEASE**.

The rules for handling **OLE_WAIT_FOR_RELEASE** are somewhat complicated; you should refer to Microsoft's documentation for the details. The safest strategy is to go into a message-dispatch loop and wait for **OLE_RELEASE**, but it may be more efficient to do other tasks while waiting for notification. You can handle **OLE_BUSY** by going into a message-dispatch loop that checks the release status and waits for **OLE_OK**:

```
while(OleQueryReleaseStatus(lpObject) != OLE_OK) {
      if(GetMessage(&msg,NULL,NULL,NULL)){
            TranslateMessage(&msg);
            DispatchMessage(&msg);
            }
      }
```

To display or print an object, set up the DC and bounding rectangle; then call **OleDraw**. **OLE_QUERY_PAINT** messages may be sent during the draw operation; the client should return **TRUE** to allow the drawing to continue or **FALSE** to stop the drawing process. Set the target device for the drawing with **OleSetTargetDevice** and the bounding rectangle with **OleQueryBounds**. If the user resizes the object, call **OleSetBounds**, **OleUpdate**, and **OleDraw**.

To open an object, first call **OleQueryReleaseStatus** to see if the object is busy. Once the object is not busy, call **OleActivate** to start the server. To tell if an object is already open, call **OleQueryOpen**. To close an open object, call **OleClose**. To reestablish a terminated connection with an open server, call **OleReconnect**. To delete an object, call **OleDelete**. **OleDelete** automatically closes the object before deleting it.

To copy an object to the clipboard with immediate rendering, open the clipboard as usual and call **OleCopyToClipboard**. To copy an object to the clipboard with delayed rendering, open the clipboard; empty the clipboard; put your preferred data formats on the clipboard; call **OleEnumFormats** to determine the formats for the object; call **SetClipboardData** with a **NULL** data handle for each format; put your presentation data formats on the clipboard; and close the clipboard. To cut an object, call **OleCopyToClipboard** and **OleDelete**.

Note that **OleCopyToClipboard** always copies **OwnerLink** format, not **ObjectLink** format. However, using **OleGetData** to retrieve data from a linked object requires **ObjectLink** format. They are the same thing: specify **ObjectLink** even though **OwnerLink** was found on the clipboard. (Why the awkwardness? Don't ask me: I don't know.)

An application, like OLEDEMO, which acts both as an OLE client and OLE server, has to do a little more work to put information on the clipboard. It has to allocate memory for the selection (determining the amount with **OleQuerySize**); register a "Clipboard" document with **OleRegisterClientDoc**; copy each object in the selection with **OleClone**, **OleSaveToStream**, and **OleRelease**; put the new document on the clipboard with **SetClipboardData**; and clean up with **OleSavedClientDoc**, followed by **OleRevokeClientDoc**.

There are a number of ways for an OLE client to create an object. **OleClone** makes an exact copy of an object. **OleCopyFromLink** creates an embedded object that is a copy of a linked object. **OleCreate** makes an embedded object of a specified class. **OleCreateFromClip** creates an embedded object from the clipboard. **OleCreateFromFile** creates an embedded object using the contents of a file. **OleCreateFromTemplate** creates one embedded object with the properties of another object. **OleCreateLinkFromClip** usually makes a linked object using information on the clipboard. **OleCreate-LinkFromFile** usually makes a linked object using data from a file.

To find out whether to enable the Paste command, first call **OleQuery-CreateFromClip** with "StdFileEditing" as the protocol; if it fails, try again with "Static" as the protocol. Call **OleQueryLinkFromClip** to determine whether to enable the Paste Link command. If there is usable data on the clipboard, enable the Paste command even if all three OLE clipboard queries fail.

To "Paste," open the clipboard and call **OleCreateFromClip**. To "Paste Link," open the clipboard and call **OleCreateLinkFromClip**. After you've pasted the object, close the clipboard and use **OleQueryType** to determine the kind of object created: the order of objects on the clipboard can sometimes cause **OleCreateFromClip** to make a link or **OleCreateLinkFromClip** to build an embedded object.

You can use **OleClone** for UNDO support: a client can make a copy of each object when it is opened. When the server is closed and the object is updated, if the user wants to undo all the changes made by the server, the client can revert to the cloned copy of the original object. Clients can implement the <Class Name> Object menu item using **OleActivate**, since **OleActivate** has the selected verb as a parameter.

The Links command is supposed to bring up a dialog box listing all the linked objects in the current document and their options. Use **OleActivate** to invoke verbs for the selected object, **OleGetLinkUpdateOptions** to determine the how often an object should be updated (automatically, when saved, or manually), and **OleSetLinkUpdateOptions** to change the update strategy for an object. Use **OleUpdate** to implement manual updating of an object, and use **OleObjectConvert** to replace a linked object with a static picture.

When closing an OLE client application, use **OleRelease** to delete all objects from memory—and wait for **OLE_OK** before terminating. Also, if the client owns the clipboard when it terminates, it should make sure that all data on the clipboard are complete and in the correct order. If the client used delayed rendering, it should render all formats before terminating.

OLE Server Application Structure

An OLE server application is implemented mainly as call-back functions for the OLE server library. It also has a small number of OLE server API functions it can call.

OleRegisterServer tells the library about the server; **OleRevokeServer** ends access to the specified server, closes all active OLE documents in that server, and ends communications with all clients. **OleBlockServer** asks the OLE libraries to queue up requests to the server; **OleUnblockServer** processes the queued requests.

OleRegisterServerDoc tells the library about a document currently active in the server. **OleRenameServerDoc** changes the registered name of a a document; **OleSavedServerDoc** lets the library know that a document has been saved; **OleRevertServerDoc** reverts the document to a previously saved state. **OleRevokeServerDoc** ends access to the specified document; **OleRevokeObject** ends access to a single object within a document.

To start up a server application, you need to register your main window class and window procedure and also window classes and procedures for your documents and objects. Then you must initialize the function tables for your **OLESERVERVTBL, OLESERVERDOCVTBL,** and **OLEOBJECTVTBL** structures.

Next, register your clipboard formats, allocate memory for your **OLESERVER** structure, register using **OleRegisterServer**, and check your command line for the "**-Embedding**" switch. The code below (extracted from the Microsoft OLEDEMO sample) illustrates server startup:

```
    if (!(vfServer = InitServer(hInst)))
        return FALSE;
    ProcessCmdLine(lpCmdLine);
    if (!fInvisible) {         // or  " !fServer "
        ShowWindow(hwndFrame, nCmdShow);
        UpdateWindow(hwndFrame);
    } else {
        switch (nCmdShow) {
        case SW_MINIMIZE:
        case SW_SHOWMINIMIZED:
        case SW_SHOWMINNOACTIVE:
            ShowWindow(hwndFrame, nCmdShow);
            break;

        default:
            ShowWindow(hwndFrame, SW_HIDE);
        }
    }
...
/* Fix the menus for the embedded instance */
#define ChangeMenuItem(id, idnew, sz) \
    ModifyMenu(hMenu, id, MF_BYCOMMAND | MF_STRING, idnew, sz)
/* InitServer() - Initializes the OLE server */
BOOL FAR InitServer(HANDLE hInst) {
    /* Allocate the server block */
    if (!(hServer = LocalAlloc(LMEM_MOVEABLE | LMEM_ZEROINIT,
      sizeof(PBSRVR))) ||
      !(vlpsrvr = (LPSAMPSRVR)LocalLock(hServer)))
        goto errRtn;
    /* Initialize the server, document, and item virtual tables */
    vsrvrvtbl.Create = MakeProcInstance(SrvrCreate, hInst);
```

```
    vsrvrvtbl.CreateFromTemplate =
       MakeProcInstance(SrvrCreateFromTemplate, hInst);
    vsrvrvtbl.Edit     = MakeProcInstance(SrvrEdit, hInst);
    vsrvrvtbl.Exit     = MakeProcInstance(SrvrExit, hInst);
    vsrvrvtbl.Open     = MakeProcInstance(SrvrOpen, hInst);
    vsrvrvtbl.Release  = MakeProcInstance(SrvrRelease, hInst);
    vdocvtbl.Close     = MakeProcInstance(DocClose, hInst);
    vdocvtbl.GetObject = MakeProcInstance(DocGetObject, hInst);
    vdocvtbl.Release   = MakeProcInstance(DocRelease, hInst);
    vdocvtbl.Save      = MakeProcInstance(DocSave, hInst);
    vdocvtbl.SetColorScheme =
       MakeProcInstance(DocSetColorScheme, hInst);
    vdocvtbl.SetDocDimensions =
       MakeProcInstance(DocSetDocDimensions, hInst);
    vdocvtbl.SetHostNames =
       MakeProcInstance(DocSetHostNames, hInst);
    vitemvtbl.DoVerb   = MakeProcInstance(ItemDoVerb, hInst);
    vitemvtbl.EnumFormats = MakeProcInstance(ItemEnumFormats,hInst);
    vitemvtbl.GetData     = MakeProcInstance(ItemGetData, hInst);
    vitemvtbl.QueryProtocol = (LPVOID (FAR PASCAL *)
       (LPOLEOBJECT, LPSTR))
       MakeProcInstance((FARPROC)ItemQueryProtocol, hInst);
    vitemvtbl.Release    = MakeProcInstance(ItemDelete, hInst);
    vitemvtbl.SetBounds  = MakeProcInstance(ItemSetBounds, hInst);
    vitemvtbl.SetColorScheme =
       MakeProcInstance(ItemSetColorScheme, hInst);
    vitemvtbl.SetData    = MakeProcInstance(ItemSetData, hInst);
    vitemvtbl.SetTargetDevice =
       MakeProcInstance(ItemSetTargetDevice, hInst);
    vitemvtbl.Show       = MakeProcInstance(ItemShow, hInst);
    /* Try to register the server */
    vlpsrvr->olesrvr.lpvtbl = &vsrvrvtbl;
    if (Error(OleRegisterServer((LPSTR)szAppName,
       (LPOLESERVER)vlpsrvr, (LONG FAR *)&vlpsrvr->lhsrvr, hInst,
       OLE_SERVER_MULTI)))
         goto errRtn;
    /* Initialize the client name */
    lstrcpy(szClientName, "");
    return TRUE;
errRtn:
    ErrorMessage(E_FAILED_TO_REGISTER_SERVER);
    /* If we failed, clean up */
    if (vlpsrvr) {
       LocalUnlock(hServer);
       vlpsrvr = NULL;
    }
    if (hServer)
       LocalFree(hServer);
    hServer = NULL;
    return FALSE;
}
/* ProcessCmdLine() - Processes the command line options.
 *
```

```
 * This routine can be extended to handle command line
 * file loading; if this is done, be sure to construct
 * a fully qualified pathname in szFileName[].
 */
void ProcessCmdLine(LPSTR lpCmdLine) {
    LPSTR lpTemp;

    lpTemp = lpCmdLine;
    /* Does the command line contain "/Embedding"? */
    if (Contains(lpCmdLine, (LPSTR)szEmbedding)
     || Contains(lpCmdLine, (LPSTR)szEmbedding2)) {
    fServer = fInvisible = TRUE;

    /* If so, set lpTemp to string following "/Embedding" */
    while (*lpTemp != 'g')
        lpTemp++;
    lpTemp++;

    // skip blanks
    while ( *lpTemp && *lpTemp == ' ')
        lpTemp++;
        *lpCmdLine = 0;
    }
    /* look for a file name */
    if (*lpTemp) {
        LPSTR       lpstrExt = szFileName;
        OFSTRUCT    ofs;

        /* Get a fully qualified pathname */
        ofs.cBytes = sizeof(OFSTRUCT);
        OpenFile(lpTemp, &ofs, OF_PARSE);
    lstrcpy(szFileName, ofs.szPathName);

    if (fInvisible)
        vlpdoc = InitDoc(vlpsrvr, NULL, szFileName);

        /* See if it has an extension */
        while (*lpstrExt && *lpstrExt != '.')
            lpstrExt = AnsiNext(lpstrExt);

        /* If not, append the default extension */
        if (!(*lpstrExt))
            lstrcpy(lpstrExt, szDefExtension);

        /* Load the specified file */
        SendMessage(hwndFrame, WM_COMMAND, IDM_LOAD, 0L);
    } else
        SendMessage(hwndFrame, WM_COMMAND, IDM_NEW, 0L);
}
```

Browsing through the **MakeProcInstance** lines above will quickly give you a feel for the many server callback functions that need to be implemented. Fortunately, you can make stub callback functions that simply return

`OLE_ERROR_GENERIC` for things you don't really need; fortunately as well, Microsoft has provided a reasonably good skeleton you can build from.

I urge you to investigate the OLEDEMO example thoroughly: it combines OLE client and server functionality and divides up the support code in a rational way. You should be able to reuse much of the code in this sample, although by the time you've turned the sample into a working part of a "real" program you'll probably have added another 1,000 lines of code to the 5,000 lines of sample provided.

Image2 Plus OLE or DDE: What Makes Sense?

Image2 deals primarily with three types of objects: DIB, BITMAP, and PALETTE. All are standard Windows clipboard objects. The BITMAP object is supported almost universally by Windows applications that deal with graphics; the DIB and PALETTE objects are often supported by applications that have been written for or updated to Windows 3.

Clipboard or file transfer probably make more sense than DDE or OLE transfer for these objects; so we'll pass up the opportunity to give Image2 DDE or OLE support.

When would we want or need OLE support for such a program? Several examples come to mind. First, if we wanted to change the data format to add features—to get other programs to recognize our new format and use it effectively we'd have to provide OLE server support for the new format as an OLE object. On the other hand, the Windows metafile format might well accommodate most of the features we'd want to add without having to invent a new format. Certainly metafiles can handle multiple DIBs; they can also handle text, lines, curves, and so on.

A second case for OLE would arise if we wanted to include other types of data in an image—we'd want to become an OLE client. It would be nearly trivial to overlay text edited in Write on a DIB if the text were held as an object and displayed in our device context by a server or DLL that knew about Rich Text Format. But again, selecting fonts and writing text aren't all that hard to do, and it might be easier just to implement that functionality internally. The OLE approach would still be more extensible, but hardly necessary in this case.

Is OLE useless? Not at all. For more sophisticated programs than ours, it makes eminent good sense. Take a desktop publishing program: it has to integrate text, images, and data from all the programs anyone can think up into one compound document. A week after the desktop publishing program comes out, somebody will have a new file format they want to integrate: with OLE support on both sides, it is an automatic process. Without OLE support, the vendors have to agree on a file format and the integration won't happen for six months.

From the user's point of view, the additional convenience, leverage and integration provided by OLE will be very important: eventually, few people will want to bother with a major Windows program that doesn't support OLE, because they want all their programs to work together. But in the case of our little image-processing program, simple clipboard exchange is more than adequate.

6

Debugging Windows Programs

. . . .

In Chapter 2 we tried our hand at debugging a trivial Windows program. In this chapter, we'll run through the arsenal of debugging tools available to the Windows programmer, and use them to find many of the bugs in Image2. We'll concentrate on tools included in the Windows SDK; but we'll also try out third-party debuggers and debuggers shipped with other compilers.

Using Message Boxes

One of the great innovations of our time is the "K.I.S.S. System." For those not already in the know, K.I.S.S. stands for "Keep it simple, stupid." The system is widely applicable.

Windows programming is hard enough without making things complicated. Sometimes all you need to know is whether or not a specific piece of code has executed. "Here I Am" messages will do fine.

It is as close to trivial as Windows programming gets to put up a message box or make the computer beep. You can scatter **MessageBox** and/or **Message-Beep** calls through your code and often get an idea what's happening rather quickly. For example, we know we have a bug in the code that converts TGA files to DIB format. So we could instrument the code a bit with **MessageBox** calls and see what sections run.

229

The simplest probe would be a fixed message, that is:

```
MessageBox(NULL, "This is the message", "This is the title", MB_OK);
```

Note that the **MessageBox** function also requires a Window handle; we have used **NULL** to save the trouble of passing handles around—which means that the message box will be a child of the Windows desktop. The next step up is to pass some information into the message. We have a function to do so already, in DrawDIB.C:

```
int ErrMsg(PSTR sz, ...){
    char ach[128];

    wvsprintf(ach, sz, (LPSTR) (&sz + 1));/* Format the string */
    MessageBox(NULL, ach, NULL,
            MB_OK | MB_ICONEXCLAMATION | MB_APPLMODAL);
    return FALSE;
}
```

The **ErrMsg** function is derived from Petzold's **OkMsgBox** function; the difference is that Petzold was writing originally for Windows 2, which didn't have a **wvsprintf** function. Petzold also made the choice to pass a caption:

```
void OkMsgBox (char *szCaption, char *szFormat, ...)
        {
        char szBuffer [256] ;
        char *pArguments ;

        pArguments = (char *) &szFormat + sizeof (szFormat) ;
        vsprintf (szBuffer, szFormat, pArguments) ;
        MessageBox (NULL, szBuffer, szCaption, MB_OK) ;
        }
```

If you wanted the message box to be a child of the current window instead of the desktop, you could replace the leading **NULL** parameter in the **Message-Box** calls above with **GetActiveWindow()**. Note that **ErrMsg**, which calls only Windows API functions, can be used from a DLL; **OkMsgBox**, which uses the C library routine **vsprintf**, cannot. **OkMsgBox** cannot be used with **FAR** parameters because of **vsprintf**, but it supports all standard C language format descriptors. On the other hand, **ErrMsg** uses **FAR** parameters but does not support floating point, because of **wvsprintf**.

A message box is not without side effects, nor is a call to the **vsprintf** or **wvsprintf** functions guaranteed not to interfere with the program you are trying to debug. Putting up a message box involves creating a window, sizing the window to the text, showing the window, painting the window's nonclient area, painting the background in the window's client area, drawing the caption text, and drawing the message text. The message window will likely obscure your application's window, and generate a **WM_PAINT** to your application after you dismiss the message.

For this reason, a message box in a paint procedure is a no-no: do it and you're likely to hang your program (and possibly Windows itself) quite thoroughly. It's also a bad idea to put up a message box in the context of a window creation or destruction message: you can imagine what happens inside Windows when a window's create procedure tries to create another window before it has itself been fully created.

The **sprintf** family of functions is notorious for using a lot of stack. It is possible to cause a serious stack overrun by adding an **OkMsgBox** or **ErrMsg** call at a point when your program is low on stack. You won't always know what happened—sometimes your program will wind up in outer space. Just be aware of the problem and try to recognize it if it starts happening to you. The cures, of course, are either to increase the program's stack, or to remove the diagnostic in favor of something less intrusive.

Intrusive diagnostics are a big problem in Windows programming. Sometimes **OkMsgBox** changes things less than turning on CodeView information; sometimes it changes them more. I have yet to find a Windows diagnostic that gave me all the information I needed without it *sometimes* affecting the problem I was trying to solve: Heisenberg's Uncertainty Principle applies quite well to debugging.

The least intrusive diagnostic of all is a **MessageBeep** call. Alas, the information content of a beep sound is somewhat limited. With the multimedia extensions to Windows, however, it is relatively easy to assign different sounds to different conditions.

Conditional Messages

As we saw earlier, paranoia can sometimes be useful to programmers. Inserting checks for highly unlikely conditions in your programs can sometimes save you from highly embarrassing program hangs. In standard C, the traditional method for detecting such conditions is the **assert** macro, defined in assert.h.

Under DOS, the assert macro prints to the error output stream. In Windows, the **assert** macro brings up a message box (Figure 6.1) and ends the program. You can suppress all **assert** macros while leaving them in the code by defining the symbol **NDEBUG** when you compile.

You can define your own variation on the assert macro, or use Petzold's **WinAssert** macro, if you want to flag unlikely but harmful situations without causing the program to abort. For instance, we could define **MyAssert** to call **OkMsgBox** if the assertion failed:

```
#define MyAssert(expression) {if(!expression) \
    OkMsgBox("Assertion Failed", \
    "Expression %s, File %s, Line %s", \
    #expression,__FILE__,__LINE__);
```

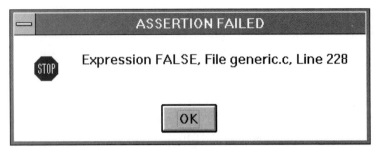

Figure 6.1. In Windows, the **assert** macro brings up a message box

Alternatively, we could have **MyAssert** send a message to the debugging terminal, ring the bell, and/or log the error in a file. Let's look at some of these other strategies in more detail.

Using the Debugging Terminal or Second Monitor

When you set up your Windows development environment, you'll want to consider having a second monitor or a debugging terminal. I use a debugging terminal on occasion. It's cheap, it gives you a second keyboard as well as a second screen, and you can also use it to call BIX while your computer is busy. However, it hogs space on your desk, forces you to move between two keyboards, and hogs a serial port on your computer.

You can use a second computer running communications software as a smart terminal: I find this works even better than a real terminal, since you can scroll back through the debugging session and save it to disk. Another advantage of a second computer used as a terminal is that you can drop out of the communications session to browse or edit your source code.

I've used a second monitor, too, when I could make it work. It's also cheap, but doesn't give you a second keyboard. It hogs just as much space on your desk as a terminal, but it doesn't use a serial port—instead, it uses a slot in your computer's backplane. The data rate to a second monitor is higher than the data rate to a terminal; with CVW and two monitors you can debug quite nicely.

I don't currently use a second monitor. Monochrome adapater cards are all 8-bit, and good VGA cards are 16-bit. On a 16-bit bus, most computers will insert a large number of wait states before *any* screen I/O if there is an 8-bit card in the system—so that just putting the mono card in your computer can slow down your VGA card noticeably. On my computer, that slowdown was horrendous—it made Windows too slow to use. I also never seem to have a free slot on my computer. Other people have had better luck with a dual-monitor setup than I have.

There are some one-screen solutions, too. They are good enough that I rarely hook up my second computer as a terminal these days. Anders Thun's WINRIP lets me send UAE and RIP messages to my VGA screen, and respond to the prompts. The new version of CVW flips screens on a single monitor—it works, but I find the mode flipping on my monitor pretty annoying. Nu-Mega's CV/1 lets me run CodeView for Windows on top of the Windows desktop—I like that a lot better. MultiScope runs nicely on the Windows desktop, and so does the Quick C for Windows integrated debugger.

Using the Debugging Kernels

We introduced the Windows debugging kernels in Chapter 2. Many of the debugging functions discussed below do nothing at all in the retail kernels, but are useful when the debugging kernels are active. The debugging kernels check the parameters of most Windows API calls as well as enabling the debugging function API group.

It is not necessary to do all your development work using the debugging kernels: you wouldn't be terribly happy about the slowdown if you tried it. However it *is* necessary to test your applications under the debugging kernels before shipping them to customers: certain kinds of errors can slip by unnoticed under the retail kernels that will cause the program to abort under the debugging kernels. You may consider such bugs harmless, but I can assure you that other developers who want to run your program while using the debugging kernels will not be pleased when they find them.

For your own self-respect, test with the debugging kernels. For your own convenience, use the debugging functions described below.

void DebugBreak(void)

The **DebugBreak** function is useful for stopping a program before it reaches a path that is under construction, or for making the debugger come up when a specific place in your code has been reached. In practice, it is slightly more convenient than setting a breakpoint with the debugger—you can't inadvertently forget to set the breakpoint, or accidently lose it.

The **DebugBreak** routine has nothing in it but an **Int 3** instruction and a return.

void FatalAppExit(WORD wAction, LPSTR lpszMessageText)

The **FatalAppExit** function displays a message box and terminates the application when the message box is closed. If Windows is running with a kernel debugger, the message box gives the user the opportunity to terminate the application or to cancel the message box and return to the caller.

The **wAction** parameter must be 0. The **lpszMessageText** parameter will be displayed in the message box, and is limited to 35 characters.

FatalAppExit is a last resort. In most cases you should not use it: if you have any control of your program, you should probably send yourself a **WM_QUIT** message. But if you think your stack or heap have been hosed, **FatalAppExit** might be a more reliable way to quit.

void FatalExit(int iCode)

The **FatalExit** function sends the current state of Windows to the debugger and prompts for instructions on how to proceed. Use this function only for debugging purposes; don't call the function in a retail application. Calling this function in the retail version of Windows will terminate the application.

The **FatalExit** display includes an error code (the **iCode** parameter) followed by a symbolic stack trace, showing the flow of execution up to the point of call. The **FatalExit** function prompts the user to respond to an Abort, Break or Ignore message. Responding **A** (Abort) causes a return to DOS. Responding **B** (Break) enters the debugger. Responding **I** (Ignore) returns to the caller.

void OutputDebugString(LPSTR lpszOutputString)

The **OutputDebugString** function displays a character string on the debugging terminal if a debugger is running. **OutputDebugString** preserves all registers.

I've found **OutputDebugString** to be one of the least intrusive debugging probes I can use. I sometimes use **OutputDebugString** rather than **MessageBox** in variations on the **ErrMsg** and **MyAssert** themes.

In some retail versions of Windows, **OutputDebugString** will send a message to AUX (usually COM1, sometimes COM2) or a second monitor, even though you would expect the message to be suppressed since neither a debugging kernel nor a debugger is running. If you want to be absolutely sure that users don't see your debugging messages, comment out your **OutputDebugString** calls or place them inside conditional code blocks.

You can try this trivial **DebugOut** macro to suppress **OutputDebugString** messages when not debugging:

```
#ifdef NDEBUG
#define DebugOut(message) ((void)0)
#else
#define DebugOut(message)    OutputDebugString(message)
#endif
```

void ValidateCodeSegments(void)

You'll use **ValidateCodeSegments** only in Windows 3.0, in real mode. It checks code segments for random memory overwrites in the real mode debugging kernels. Windows 3.1 doesn't support real mode, and Windows 2.1 didn't support this function.

void ValidateFreeSpaces(void)

`ValidateFreeSpaces` is a holdover from Windows 2. In the debugging version of Windows, with **`EnableFreeChecking=1`** and **`EnableHeapChecking=1`** set in the **`[kernel]`** section of win.ini, this function will make sure all free spaces are set to **`0CCH`**.

Don't use this function in enhanced mode—you're not going to be happy when Windows tries to initialize your swap file. **`ValidateFreeSpaces`** is of marginal utility in standard mode—the sorts of errors it is designed to find are likely to be detected much more quickly by the memory protection hardware.

Using Tool Help

An innovation of Windows 3.1 is the ToolHelp API group, implemented in TOOLHELP.DLL. These functions make it possible to give an application program the sorts of diagnostics previously available only to a debugger. We list the functions as a table; further information can be found in the Windows 3.1 manuals and online help.

Function / Structure	Description
ClassFirst	Retrieves information about first class in class list.
ClassNext	Retrieves information about next class in class list.
DirectedYield	Forces execution to continue at a specified task.
GDIHeapInfo function	Retrieves information about the GDI heap.
GetSystemDebugState	Returns system-state information to a debugger.
GlobalEntryHandle	Retrieves information about global memory block.
GlobalEntryModule	Retrieves information about specific memory block.
GlobalFirst	Retrieves information about first global memory block.
GlobalInfo function	Retrieves information about the global heap.
GlobalNext	Retrieves information about next global memory block.
InterruptRegister	Installs function to handle system interrupts.
InterruptUnRegister	Removes function that processed system interrupts.
LocalFirst	Retrieves information about first local memory block.
LocalInfo function	Fills structure with information about local heap.
LocalNext	Retrieves information about next local memory block.
LockInput	Locks input to all tasks except the current one.
MemManInfo function	Retrieves information about the memory manager.
MemoryRead	Reads memory from an arbitrary global heap segment.
MemoryWrite	Writes memory to an arbitrary global heap segment.
ModuleFindHandle	Retrieves information about a module.

ModuleFindName	Retrieves information about a module.
ModuleFirst	Retrieves information about first module.
ModuleNext	Retrieves information about next module.
NotifyRegister	Installs a notification callback function.
NotifyUnRegister	Removes a notification callback function.
QuerySendMessage	Determines if a message originated within a task.
StackTraceCSIPFirst	Retrieves information about a stack frame.
StackTraceFirst	Retrieves information about the first stack frame.
StackTraceNext	Retrieves information about the next stack frame.
TaskFindHandle	Retrieves information about a task.
TaskFirst	Retrieves information about first task in task queue.
TaskGetCSIP	Returns the next CS:IP value of a task.
TaskNext	Retrieves information about next task in the task queue.
TaskSetCSIP	Sets the CS:IP of a sleeping task.
TaskSwitch	Switches to a specific address within a new task.
TerminateApp	Terminates an application.
TimerCount	Fills in the TIMERINFO structure.
UserHeapInfo function	Retrieves information about the USER heap.
CLASSENTRY	Contains the name of a Windows class.
GDIHEAPINFO structure	Describes the GDI module.
GLOBALENTRY	Describes a block of memory on the global heap.
GLOBALINFO structure	Describes the global heap.
LOCALENTRY	Describes a block of memory on the local heap.
LOCALINFO structure	Describes the local heap.
MEMMANINFO structure	Describes the status of the virtual memory manager.
MODULEENTRY	Describes a module in the module list.
NFYLOADDLL	Describes the dynamic link library being loaded.
NFYLOADSEG	Describes the segment being loaded.
NFYRIP	Contains the RIP exit code and faulting CS:IP.
NFYSTARTTASK	Describes the task being started.
STACKTRACEENTRY	Describes one stack frame.
TASKENTRY	Describes a task.
TIMERINFO	Contains elapsed execution times of a task and VM.
USERHEAPINFO structure	Describes the USER module.

Using the Stress Library

In Chapter 1 I discussed stress-testing your application using different memory models. If you are building applications for Windows 3.1, running in real mode is no longer an option.

However, Windows 3.1 adds a library of stress-testing functions that let you easily use up system resources so that you can see how your application will react. You can build calls to these functions into a debugging menu in your application, build your own stress-testing diagnostic separate from your program, or use the slightly more limited resource-allocation functions built into HeapWalk.

The stress testing functions do pretty much what you'd guess from their names, so I'll just list their prototypes. GDIMem refers, of course, to the local heap used by the Graphical Device Interface portion of Windows to hold pens, brushes, fonts, and so on. UserMem refers to the local heap used by the User Interface portion of Windows to hold window structures and icons.

```
int AllocDiskSpace(LONG lLeft, WORD wDrive);
int AllocFileHandles(int nLeft);
BOOL AllocGDIMem(WORD wContig);
BOOL AllocMem(DWORD dwContig);
BOOL AllocUserMem(WORD wContig);
void FreeAllGDIMem(void);
void FreeAllMem(void);
void FreeAllUserMem(void);
void UnAllocDiskSpace(WORD wDrive);
void UnAllocFileHandles(void);
```

Using WDEB386

WDEB386 is Microsoft's "advanced" symbolic debugger for protected mode Windows. The term "advanced" is code for powerful but hard to use; symbolic means that you'll see global symbol names and assembly language, not source language, when you debug. WDEB386 works with a terminal attached to COM1 or COM2.

If you are writing applications, you probably will never need WDEB386: CodeView or another source-level debugger will be much easier for you to use. However, if you need to debug Windows device drivers and virtual device drivers, WDEB386 will let you get at the gut-level stuff you need to see.

I normally build a batch file to start my WDEB386 session. A typical command to start such a session might read:

```
wdeb386 /C:1 /S:rp.sym /S:\windows\system\user.sym
        /S:\windows\system\krnl386.sym /S:\windows\system\gdi.sym
        \windows\win.com /3 rp
```

This particular command line (continued on three lines here only for readability) says to start WDEB386 with control on COM1; to load symbol files for RP, USER, KRNL386, and GDI; to start Windows in enhanced mode; and to start the RP application. You might not need symbols for Windows internals, in which case you can leave out the second through fourth /S clauses.

Make sure you have your terminal set up before you start. Otherwise your machine will lock up quite thoroughly and you'll need the big red switch.

The first thing you should do when you get keyboard control in a WDEB386 session is to set breakpoints with the **bp** command. Then let Windows start using the **g** command. As you may have noticed, the basic WDEB386 commands are the same as in DEBUG—for instance, **d** displays data and **u** displays code. You can get a basic command list with **?** and an external command list with **.?**.

Run your program and exercise it so that it will encounter whatever breakpoints you have set. If you set a breakpoint on the window procedure you can disable it with **bc**. Use the **p** or **t** command to trace through the program. Use the **k** or **kv** command to backtrace the stack from within a function.

If you're doing device driver work, you may need to use **dg** to display the GDT, **di** to display the IDT, **dl** to display the LDT, and **dt** to display the TSS. Use **.df** to display the global free list, **.dg** to display the global heap, **.dh** to display the local heap, **.dm** to display the module list, **.dq** to display the task queues, and **.du** to display the least-recently-used global memory objects list. If things get badly munged, try **.reboot** before reaching for the red switch— a soft reboot doesn't stress your disk drives as badly as a power-off/power-on sequence.

Using SYMDEB

SYMDEB is in many ways the real-mode equivalent of WDEB386. Because of the special needs of real mode, SYMDEB reports on segment motion, segment loading, and segment discarding as well as acting as a not-so-advanced symbolic debugger.

Since real mode is going away in Windows 3.1, we'll leave documentation of SYMDEB to the history books.

Using Debugging Log Streams

Sometimes a program can generate so much data or go through loops so many times that it is tedious to trace with a debugger. In these cases you can sometimes resort to brute force: dump out all the information and plow through it afterward. The four places you are likely to put the information are the debugging terminal, your printer, a file, and a window.

Debugging to the Terminal

Putting information on the debugging terminal is simple with **Output-DebugString**; combine this with **wvsprintf** and you'll be able to put any non-floating-point variable out to the terminal. Combine it with **vsprintf** or **sprintf** and you'll be able to write out any local variable. Use WINRIP, and you can redirect the debugging terminal output to your Windows screen or debugging monitor.

Let's put together a simple function to send output to the debugging terminal. To save ourselves from forgetting the terminating "\r\n" (carriage return and line feed) in our format string, we'll output a set explicitly.

```
int DebugToTerm(PSTR sz, ...){
    char ach[128];

    wvsprintf(ach, sz, (LPSTR) (&sz + 1));/* Format the string */
    OutputDebugString(ach);
    OutputDebugString("\r\n");
    return FALSE;
}
```

To put information on the debugging terminal, all we have to do is insert some calls like this:

```
DebugToTerm("wParam in WinProc is %u",wParam);
```

We could of course put out more information, for instance:

```
DebugToTerm("Myfunc called with i=%d,lParam=%ld",i,lParam);
```

That wasn't too hard, was it? Now let's do the same for the other three output streams.

Debugging to a File

In debugging to a file we'll want to open the file, append the string to the end of the file, and close the file. This may involve a bit of overhead, but it guarantees that we can see what was in the file if our program aborts—or even if Windows aborts.

For simplicity, we'll fix the filename to "debug.log". It would of course be trivial to add a parameter for the filename—but the point here is to make getting the information out into the file as simple and reliable as possible. The **DebugToFile** call has exactly the same parameters as **DebugToTerm**.

```
int DebugToFile(PSTR sz, ...){
    char ach[128];
    char debugfile[]="debug.log";
    FILE *fh;

    wvsprintf(ach, sz, (LPSTR) (&sz + 1)); //Format the string
    fh=fopen(debugfile,"at");    //open for append, text mode
    if(NULL==fh)
            return TRUE;
    fputs(ach,fh);
    fputs("\n",fh);
    fclose(fh);
    return FALSE;
}
```

Debugging to a Printer

Actually, the printer is just a special case of a file, with name **PRN**. This makes the **DebugToPrinter** function a nearly trivial variation on **DebugToFile**. We open the device for writing, since appending is meaningless for the printer.

```
int DebugToPrinter(PSTR sz, ...){
      char ach[128];
      char debugfile[]="PRN";
      FILE *fh;

      wvsprintf(ach, sz, (LPSTR) (&sz + 1)); //Format the string
      fh=fopen(debugfile,"wt");  //open for write, text mode
      if(NULL==fh)
            return TRUE;
      fputs(ach,fh);
      fputs("\n",fh);
      return FALSE;
}
```

Debugging to a Window

As you might expect, writing to a window is a little more work than writing to streams. However, it isn't very hard. If we were more ambitious, we might want the window to buffer its previous contents, support scrollback, and allow additional logging to streams to be controlled by a dialog.[1] While I've built such smart systems in the past, I've found them more trouble than dumb functions that do what they are told without a lot of overhead.

All we really need is someplace to put a one-line message. If there's room for more messages, fine. But what we're going after here is just a way to let our program tell us what it is doing without messing up its own display or requiring us to press the OK button after every message. We need a way to create the debugging window; a debug window procedure; and a way to write into the debugging window.

We have some design decisions to make. Do we want the debugging Window to be a child of the application window, or independent? Should it be in a fixed position? Have a fixed size? Do we want a status bar at the bottom of the application window? Perhaps a column down the right side of the screen? Any of this is possible; it is easy to change the window's behavior by changing its window class parameters and its window procedure.

One good time to create a debugging window is when your main window is being created. The code below calls the debugging window a status window,

---

[1] Just such an ambitious debugging utility, written by Kevin Welch, can be found in the May 1988 issue of *Microsoft Systems Journal*.

and places it in the lower-right corner of the main window. I use this status window in Room Planner as a regular feature of the user interface, but it is just as useful for debugging.

```
case WM_CREATE: /* message: window being created */
     hDC=GetDC(hWnd);
     GetTextMetrics (hDC, &tm);
     xChar = tm.tmAveCharWidth;
     xChar0= (tm.tmMaxCharWidth+3*xChar)/4;
     yChar0= yChar = tm.tmHeight + tm.tmExternalLeading;
     ReleaseDC(hWnd,hDC);
     xClient=LOWORD(lParam);
     yClient=HIWORD(lParam);
     StatusWindowHeight=(int)(5.5*yChar0);
     StatusWindowWidth =20*xChar;
     hWndStatus =
           CreateWindow (szStatusClass,/* window class name */
           "Status",                   /* window caption    */
           WS_CHILD | WS_CAPTION |  /* window style */
           WS_CLIPSIBLINGS,
           CW_USEDEFAULT,         /* initial x position */
           CW_USEDEFAULT,         /* initial y position */
           StatusWindowWidth,     /* initial x size    */
           StatusWindowHeight,/* initial y size        */
           hWnd,                  /* parent window handle */
           2,                     /* window menu handle */
           hInst,          /* program instance handle */
           NULL) ;              /* create parameters         */
     ShowWindow (hWndStatus, SW_SHOWNORMAL) ;
     UpdateWindow (hWndStatus) ;
     break;
```

Of course, the **szStatusClass** window class has to be registered. I do this in my initialization procedure, right after registering the main window:

```
   pWndClass->style = CS_VREDRAW | CS_HREDRAW | CS_DBLCLKS;
   pWndClass->lpfnWndProc = rpWndProc;
   pWndClass->hInstance = hInstance;
   pWndClass->hIcon = LoadIcon(hInstance, (LPSTR)szAppName);
   pWndClass->hCursor = NULL;
   pWndClass->hbrBackground = hbrWhite;
   pWndClass->lpszMenuName = "rpMenu";
   pWndClass->lpszClassName = (LPSTR) "rp";
   bSuccess = RegisterClass(pWndClass);
//Register a class for the Status Window
   pWndClass->lpfnWndProc = ChildWndProc;
   pWndClass->lpszClassName = (LPSTR)szStatusClass;
   pWndClass->hIcon = NULL;
   pWndClass->lpszMenuName = NULL;
   pWndClass->hbrBackground = GetStockObject(LTGRAY_BRUSH);
   RegisterClass(pWndClass);
```

When the main window is resized, it would be nice if the status window snapped back into place. The user can move the status window around at will to see behind it, since its window class includes a caption; but the status window could disappear if the user made the main window smaller without first moving the status window. The code below to handle the main window's **WM_SIZE** message takes care of repositioning the status window:

```
case WM_SIZE:
     xClient=LOWORD(lParam);
     yClient=HIWORD(lParam);
     if(hWndStatus)
            SetWindowPos(hWndStatus,NULL,
                   xClient-StatusWindowWidth,
                   yClient-StatusWindowHeight,
                   0,0,SWP_NOSIZE | SWP_NOZORDER);
     break;
```

Writing to the debugging window is just a matter of doing some **TextOut** calls. If you have fixed information to display, you can have the windows paint procedure do all the work for you:

```
long _export FAR PASCAL ChildWndProc (hWnd, iMessage, wParam, lParam)
  HWND   hWnd ;
  unsigned iMessage ;
  WORD   wParam ;
  LONG   lParam ;
{
 char szTemp[30];
 PAINTSTRUCT ps;
 HDC hDC ;
 switch(iMessage) {
  case WM_PAINT:
      hDC = BeginPaint (hWnd, (LPPAINTSTRUCT)&ps) ;
      wsprintf(szTemp,"%4d Chairs  ",ChairCount);
      TextOut(hDC,0,2*yChar0,szTemp,lstrlen(szTemp));
      lstrcpy(szTemp,bDuplicate?"Copy / ":"Move / ");
      lstrcat(szTemp,GridSnap ?"Snap   ":"No Snap");
      TextOut(hDC,0,3*yChar0,szTemp,lstrlen(szTemp));
      EndPaint (hWnd, (LPPAINTSTRUCT)&ps) ;
      break;
default:
      return DefWindowProc (hWnd, iMessage, wParam, lParam);
      }
 return(NULL);
}
```

If you want to make a simple function to write to the first line of the window, try something like this:

```
DebugToStatusWindow(PSTR sz, ... ) {
     char ach[128];
```

```
    HDC hDC_Status;

    hDC_Status=GetDC(hWndStatus);
    wvsprintf(ach, sz, (LPSTR) (&sz + 1)); //Format the string
    TextOut(hDC,0,0,ach,lstrlen(ach));
    ReleaseDC(hWndStatus,hDC_Status);
    return FALSE;
}
```

In the above code, **hWndStatus** is of course a global variable of type **HWND**. **DebugToStatusWindow** is called with the same parameters as our other three debug functions.

Unless I'm going to use a status window or message bar in my application as part of the user interface, I don't usually bother creating one for debugging: the **DebugToTerm** function, coupled with WINRIP, is more than adequate to put a one-line message at the bottom of the screen. For more copious output, I send the debug output to the printer or a file, with **DebugToPrinter** or **Debug-ToFile**.

By the way, if you don't mind messing up your client area display, you can always put debug information right in your main window. The code would look a lot like **DebugToStatusWindow**, but you'd use your main window handle instead of **hWndStatus**.

Using CodeView for Windows

Source code debugging might be one of the most useful ways to understand what your program is doing; it is also one of the most abused items in a programmer's toolbox. An allegedly true story told to me by a highly experienced technical manager will illustrate my point.

It seems that a critical process module suddenly started failing at a customer's site. The customer had made some adjustments to the process, which might in turn have changed the timing requirements, at any rate it was an emergency.

The manager called in all his programmers to fix this problem over a weekend. One hotshot—a graduate of MIT—decided he could solve the problem alone with his debugging hardware and software, so he spent all day Saturday setting up an in-circuit emulator and other instrumentation. The other three programmers thought they could get farther by trying to understand and characterize the problem, so they printed a listing of the project source code and retired to a conference room.

Sunday morning rolled around, and Sunday evening. The brilliant hacker was surrounded by instruments in his lab and had finally gotten to the point where he could sometimes see the problem happen. Meanwhile the others had gone through the source and, by Sunday morning, had rewritten every module that they couldn't absolutely prove would meet the timing specifications. Then they'd installed their revised program at the customer's site Sunday afternoon, and watched it for several hours.

About the time the MIT graduate called in to say he'd isolated one problem and thought there might be another, the other team reported that they'd rewritten 17 doubtful sections of the program, and that the revised program had run for several hours without any problems whatsoever. The team also reported that they had proved mathematically that the critical timing specification would always be met by their new code.

With that in mind, let's talk about what CVW can do. If you build your program for debugging as described in Chapter 2 (specifically using **-Zi** and **-Od** for compilation, and **/CO** for linking), you can run it under CodeView and see source statements. You can trace the flow of execution, trap particular messages, set breakpoints at specific functions, examine local and global variables, set watchpoints on specific variables, and step through interesting program sections line by line.

To start CVW on a specific application, use a program manager item. For instance, my icon for "**CVW Image2**" has the command line:

```
cvw /V c:\advwin\image2\image2.exe
```

CodeView should come up showing some startup code. In this specific session, I want to debug problems in the TGA- and TIFF-reading code, so I set breakpoints at **tgaview** and **tiffview**. I normally set my initial breakpoints by typing in the **bp** command; if you are hesitant about this, by all means use CodeView's menus and the mouse to find and highlight each source code line where you want to set breakpoints, and then double-click or press **F9** to actually set the breakpoints. You can qualify breakpoints using CodeView's **Edit Breakpoints** dialog. I normally find unqualified breakpoints more than adequate at the beginning of a debug session; later on I may qualify specific breakpoints to isolate the ninth pass through a function, or to break if and only if a line of code is executed with some expression true.

Single-stepping through suspect code with F10 is often useful in helping you understand the flow of execution and how the variables change. Setting temporary breakpoints with the right mouse button lets you get past long **for** loops. Looking at the call stack when a deeply nested function is executed can help you understand how the program got there in the first place.

Breaking on a message sometimes turns out to be more convenient than breaking on a function. For instance, if we set a breakpoint at the beginning of our main window procedure, we'll generate constant interruptions—most of which will be for uninteresting messages. On the other hand, breaking only on a **WM_PAINT** message will let us debug our paint procedures quite nicely—even if the painting functions we expect to be called aren't reached for some reason. The command to break on a message in CodeView is **wbm**, for Windows Breakpoint Message. You can specify whole classes of messages, or specific messages for breakpoints. For example: **wbm WndProc WM_PAINT** says to break at WndProc on a paint message; **wbm MyDialogProc wni** says to break at MyDialogProc on a window management, input, or initialization message. You'll find full documentation for CVW's command syntax in the Microsoft SDK Tools manual.

You can grab control of a runaway program under CodeView by generating a **SysReq**. On most keyboards, **SysReq** shares the **Print Screen** key, and is accessed with the **Ctrl-Alt-SysReq** key combination. You can kill the current task with the **wka** command once you get into CodeView; it helps if you make sure that your application is actually the current task before pulling the trigger. The **wdg** (Windows Dump Global) command can help you determine if the current code segment belongs to your program.

The output from **wdg** is usually overwhelming—it shows you the entire global heap, segment by segment, including fonts and system segments that you'd probably not want to look at. And **wka** can leave Windows in an unstable state. So I usually avoid both: when I'm done debugging I quit CodeView (with the **q** command) and let my application run to completion. **Alt-F4** usually gets me out of the application quicker than I could recover from a **wka**.

I also tend to avoid using variable or expression watchpoints. In CVW local watchpoints are not reliable, and global watchpoints slow down execution so much that they make debugging a chore. I find I can do much better by setting strategic function or message breakpoints, walking through the suspect code, and examining variables as needed. But that's just my debugging style: you'll develop your own favorite debugging strategies with experience.

Neither CodeView nor any other debugger discussed here can browse Windows class hierarchies or examine Window words in a structured way. You can do a little of this with Spy, but if you need to debug object windows, extra window words, extra class words, subclassing, and superclassing, you're pretty much on your own.

Using MultiScope for Windows

The MultiScope Debuggers for Windows offer a variety of debugging options: debugging in any Windows mode; debugging right on the Windows desktop or in a flipped character-mode screen; debugging from a second computer over a serial port; debugging from a second computer over a network via NETBIOS; real-time debugging and postmortem debugging (Figure 6.2).

The MultiScope postmortem debugging option is fairly convenient. You can add **medwp** (MultiScope Execution Dump for Windows in Protected Mode) to your **load=** line in win.ini (or start it from the program manager), build your application as if for debugging with CodeView, and automatically get a postmortem dump on a protection violation. If you link with the appropriate

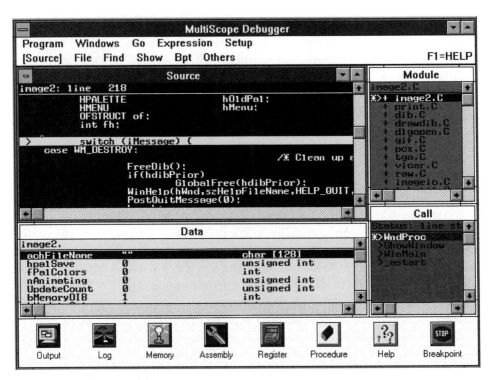

Figure 6.2. MultiScope debugging session

MED support library (lmedcw.lib is the correct one for Image2) and add a single call to **MEDInit** in your **WinMain** function, you can get postmortem dumps on other conditions, such as C runtime errors. If you want to add a few more lines of code to your application calling **MEDDump** or **MEDQueryDump**, you can also force postmortem dumps at specific places in your code. Running with **medwp** active doesn't slow down your execution speed .

Once you've generated a postmortem dump, you can figure out what happened using **wpmd**, MultiScope's Windows Postmortem Debugger. You'll normally find the **.PMD** file in the same directory as your application. **wpmd** shows you the full state of your program at the time the error was generated and relates it to source code— it lets you make short work of understanding UAEs, and lets you find problems that happen only in the field.

wrtdp, MultiScope's Windows Real-Time Debugger for Protected mode, gives you a lot of insight into your program and data with something like 11 Windows showing you different things, and it has a nice assortment of execution control commands; however, the versions I've used aren't totally reliable and are somewhat slow and unresponsive. I expect MultiScope to fix these problems.

Many of the same strategies I discussed for CodeView apply to the Multi-Scope debuggers, although there are usually more ways to reach your goals with MultiScope than there are with CodeView. MultiScope's graphic data window is one big distinguishing factor: you can actually see the structure of complex data and find the piece you want. Unfortunately it doesn't consider a window handle a structured type. Another distinguishing factor is that **wrtdp** sits on the Windows desktop and doesn't require screen flipping—a big plus in my book.

Using the Quick C for Windows Integrated Debugger

Yet another debugger that works on the Windows desktop comes built into Quick C for Windows (QCWin). This one is less ambitious than MultiScope, but it is very easy to use. It shares a lot of key assignments and commands with CodeView, but seems to make them more accessible through menus and dialog boxes; it also has an icon bar that includes buttons for "trace into" and "step over."

It's easy to set a breakpoint on a message using the QCWin debugger. Go into the debug menu and bring up the breakpoint dialog. From the "break" combo box choose "at WndProc when message received"; then you'll be able to choose message classes or individual messages. You'll find most of the other possible variations on breakpoint right on the same screen.

The QCWin debugger works at runtime—for postmortem debugging you'd have to use MultiScope or Dr. Watson (discussed below). But the QCWin debugger is so tightly integrated with QCWin's editing and compilation functions that it gives you the feeling that developing Windows programs is one continuous process—not separate editing, compiling, linking, and debugging tasks. I especially like QCWin's syntax-coloring feature: you can immediately pick out comments, strings, variables, and keywords in your code on the screen by their color (Figure 6.3).

To use the QCWin debugger, you must link from QCWin. If you've compiled with Microsoft C 6.0 rather than QCWin, you can resolve the dangling references by adding OLDNAMES.LIB to your QCWin project file. It is entirely possible to develop Windows programs without ever leaving the QCWin environment, but QCWin doesn't optimize object code. For this reason, it makes some sense to develop and debug under QCWin, while using MSC to compile and optimize modules for production.

Using the Borland, Zortech, and Watcom Debuggers

Borland's Turbo Debugger for Windows (TDW) is a variation on their fine Turbo Debugger for DOS. Like CodeView for Windows, TDW 2.5 requires you to flip screens between the character-mode debugger and the Windows desktop, or use a second (monochrome) screen for debugging. Although the

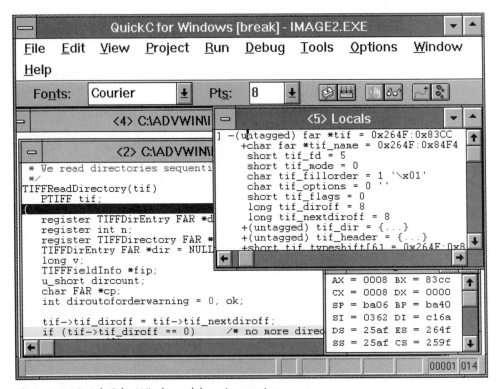

Figure 6.3. Quick C for Windows debugging session

DOS versions of Turbo Debugger can also work using a remote computer, TDW cannot. This is an observation, not a criticism: Turbo Debugger for DOS supports remote debugging over a serial link primarily because of the 640KB memory limit in DOS; there isn't nearly as much motivation to do this in Windows.

In version 2.5, TDW's screen-flipping logic doesn't really understand super-VGA screen modes; if you want to use this version of TDW effectively, you'll have to switch to a standard VGA driver. This problem is fixed in TDW 3.0.

Even the earlier version of TDW is smarter about swapping screens than CodeView—it'll switch to the Windows desktop only when you need to be there. Overall, TDW is a snappy debugging tool. Some distinguishing features are TDW's support for C++ and Turbo Pascal; its keyboard macros; its assortment of tracing, backtracing, stepping, and viewing functions; and its data inspection and data changing capability.

At first glance, it doesn't look like TDW knows how to set a breakpoint on a message. However, if you choose View Windows Messages you'll bring up a three-pane window. The upper-left pane is used for selecting windows to monitor by window procedure or window handle. The top-right pane lets you filter messages by class, or by a single message, as well as letting you decide whether to break on the messages or simply log them. The lower pane displays messages received. You can direct the log to a file if you wish.

TDW knows about the global and local heaps, and the module list. It can debug DLLs—including DLL startup code—as well as EXEs. It shows you the numeric processor or emulator register stack as 80-bit floating point numbers, and shows you all the numeric processor control bits. TDW even knows how to convert handles to pointers and vice versa.

To use TDW as a source-level debugger, you must compile with one of the Borland compilers, or postprocess Microsoft-compiled code with TDCNVRT. Borland C++ is such a fast compiler (even faster than Quick C for Windows because it can precompile headers) that having to use it for development is no hardship at all.

Zortech's Windows debugger ZDBW 3.0 can flip screens on a standard 640x480 VGA display (no doubt for the same reason as Borland's TDW 2.5), and also supports dual-monitor debugging. It does certain things better than CodeView. For instance, it does a better job of killing a program: if you quit from CodeView, your program will run to completion even though it may be corrupt; if you quit ZDBW and your program hasn't completed, ZDBW will kill the process safely. ZDBW of course knows about C++ as well as C.

You can use Windows messages in ZDBW in any debugging expression: specifically, to trigger breakpoints, watchpoints, and tracepoints. ZDBW also supports the use of the **OutputDebugString** and **DebugBreak** functions.

Watcom C 8.5 and Fortran 8.5 come with a windows version of Watcom's VIDEO debugger that works with a dual-monitor or dual-computer setup. In a two-computer setup, the link can be over a serial line, through the parallel ports, or over a NETBIOS network. VIDEO is a command-oriented debugger that supports invoking command files and logging output to a file, assigning macros to keys, and a number of other rather powerful but somewhat difficult features.

Other Debugging Tools

Debuggers aren't the only way to find problems in programs. We discussed basic strategies for isolating fatal errors using the information in a stack trace in Chapter 2. Dr. Watson, a utility shipped with Windows 3.1, uses the toolhelp API to save a copious amount of information when a program generates an Unrecoverable Application Error.

Memory allocation errors can often be found by examining the heap. The HeapWalk utility that ships with the Windows SDK makes quick work of examining the Windows global heap, local heaps, and resources.

You can find several kinds of errors most easily by watching the message stream. The Spy utility monitors and displays selected messages for selected Windows. A somewhat more specialized DdeSpy utility monitors DDE conversations.

Some problems go away when you build a program for debugging, either because of changed memory requirements or because of changed code optimization options. Isolating problems with an external utility can sometimes help you find such problems. At other times the presence of the utility will change the memory situation enough to cause a different problem to occur, or to prevent the original problem from manifesting. In these pathological cases the debug logging functions we discussed earlier in this chapter become indispensable.

Postmortem Dumps from Dr. Watson

MultiScope's MED utility generates a postmortem dump that includes the full state of a program that aborted and allows you to use their source-level postmortem debugger to isolate the problem. Dr. Watson doesn't do quite as much, but it does save most of the state of a program that aborts, and of the system running at the time, in an ASCII file. Dr. Watson ships with Windows 3.1; it is also widely available electronically for those still using Windows 3.0.

Dr. Watson doesn't require symbolic information to be present, but uses any SYM files it finds to make its output, which goes into **drwatson.log** in the **\windows** directory, more readable. The output that follows is the result of running the same bebugged **generic** sample as we did in Chapter 2, which as you remember called **DialogBox** with two **NULL** handles. Compare the information produced by Dr. Watson with the stack dump you saw in Chapter 2:

```
System Info (info)
Windows version 3.10
Retail build
Windows Build 3.1.043e
Username Martin Heller
Organization Martin Heller and Co.
System Free Space 14942464
Stack base 1898, top 6868, lowest 4980, size 4970
User heap free 56156, max 62607, 88% free, seg 0797
GDI heap free 55778, max 63199, 88% free, seg 05ef
LargestFree 26406912, MaxPagesAvail 6447, MaxPagesLockable 1694
TotalLinear 6911, TotalUnlockedPages 1701, FreePages 1340
TotalPages 1900, FreeLinearSpace 6448, SwapFilePages 2047
Page Size 4096
4 tasks executing.
WinFlags -
   Math coprocessor
   80386 or 80386 SX
   Enhanced mode
   Protect mode
```

```
Dr. Watson 0.79 Failure Report - Mon Sep 30 17:46:56 1991
GENERIC had a 'Invalid Parameter (700b)' fault at USER DIALOGBOX+000c
$tag$GENERIC$Invalid Parameter (700b)$USER DIALOGBOX+000c$param is
5c0000$Mon Sep 30 17:46:56 1991
$param$,  Invalid handle passed to USER DIALOGBOX+000c: 0x0000

Stack Dump (stack)
Stack Frame 0 is USER DIALOGBOX+000c          ss:bp 12b7:16c8
Stack Frame 1 is GENERIC MainWndProc+0080     ss:bp 12b7:16e2
Stack Frame 2 is USER GLOBALGETATOMNAME+0539  ss:bp 12b7:16f4
Stack Frame 3 is GENERIC WINMAIN+0040         ss:bp 12b7:1710
Stack Frame 4 is GENERIC __astart+0063        ss:bp 12b7:1742
***********************************************************************
```

To get this report, I had to set **showinfo=paramlog** in the **[Dr. Watson]** section of **win.ini**; invalid parameter reports were disabled by default in version 0.79 of Dr. Watson since so many programs generate them. (I got reports from **WinWord** and **Microman** in the same session as my deliberate problem in **generic**.) I could have gotten more information blocks had I enabled them in **win.ini**. As you see, the default output is good enough for our purposes.

Examining the Heap

HeapWalk is useful for finding a number of memory-related problems. For example, some Windows programs create and select fonts into their device context but never delete them. Fonts generated using **CreateFont** or **CreateFontIndirect** reside in GDI's heap. By examining the GDI heap with HeapWalk you can easily see how many fonts are currently active, and use this as a diagnostic to isolate the section of your code that's forgetting to put away its toys (Figure 6.4).

Window structures reside in the USER heap, and you can use HeapWalk to view that, too. You'll find DIBs and bitmaps in the global heap, along with code and data segments, font resource files, and other resources. You'll find device contexts, regions, palettes, pens, brushes, and small bitmaps in the GDI heap along with fonts.

Note the difference between a font realized with **CreateFont**—a single font, size, style and weight kept in the GDI heap—and a font resource file, which contains a number of different sizes of a given font and resides in the global heap. Also note the difference between full-fledged bitmaps, kept in the global heap, and little bitmaps (such as the maximize and minimize arrow bitmaps used in every window), kept in the GDI heap.

Watching the Message Stream

The flow of execution of a Windows program happens message by message. Spy's purpose in life is to watch messages. You'll also find it a handy tool for understanding Window hierarchies.

```
─                      HeapWalker-(Main Heap)                  ▼ ▲
 File   Walk   Sort   Object   Alloc   Add!
ADDRESS   HANDLE   SIZE LCK FLG HEAP OWNER      TYPE
80A34000  14A6    37696               HEAPWALK  Private        ↑
000250C0  21E6
00035760  13A6    ─              GDI Heap (Local Walk)
00013880  119E
00025060  1176    Heap   Sort   Add!
00024DC0  1386    OFFSET HANDLE   SIZE FLAGS      LCK TYPE
000356C0  1DCE     3602  0ABA      26 Moveable        Brush    ↑
00013280  1FAF     691A  0B5E      26 Moveable        Brush
806763A0  201E     35E2  0ABE      26 Moveable        Brush
80676140  1436     20AE  0A7E     210 Moveable     1  DC
806A9140  142E     58DE  341E     210 Moveable     1  DC
806A7840  14AE     34DE  0B0A      22 Moveable        DC
806A6D40  13CE     3E82  0D9A      22 Moveable        DC
806A1880  160E   2 3DD2  0D82      22 Moveable        DC
806A09A0  11D6     3D04  0D66      22 Moveable        DC
80A8B140  20EE    51968      Y      IMAGE2   DGroup
0003A300  1376     2592               IMAGE2   Module Database
00077E60  13FE    34144               IMAGE2   Private
80A75000  13BE    52864               IMAGE2   Private
00035660  2066       96               IMAGE2   Resource Accelerator
00024AC0  1FF6      416     D         IMAGE2   Resource Dialog
00025780  1186       32     D         IMAGE2   Resource Group_Icon
00039F60  205E      448     D         IMAGE2   Resource Menu
000355E0  118E      128     D         IMAGE2   Resource NameTable
000247A0  1D27      512               IMAGE2   Task
00000720  010E    21649               KERNEL   Code LCROUP (1)         ↓
←                                                               →
```

Figure 6.4. HeapWalk display: Global and GDI heaps

To use Spy as a Window browser, choose the **Window...** menu item from the Spy **Window** menu. You'll see a dialog for picking a window to monitor. The displayed information will change as you move the mouse around on the screen, showing you the class name, number, and parent of each window.

Click on a Window and then click on OK in the Spy dialog box, and you'll start to see Window messages displayed (Figure 6.5). Use Spy's **Options!** dialog box to filter out unwanted classes of Windows messages. Then watch the Spy display as you operate the program whose window you selected—you'll be surprised at how much you learn about the Windows message stream.

I've found lots of cases where monitoring the message stream on my own program isolated a bug to the point where I could immediately zero in on a few lines of source code. Then I'd fix the code without ever having to resort to a debugger. You can save yourself a lot of time with such an approach: start with the big things (in this case, the message context of the error) and work down to the details (the code called in the context of a specific message).

Recap: Debuggers are Not a Substitute for Analysis

We've looked at a number of ways to isolate and kill program errors. All of them require you to *visualize* what your program *should* be doing, to *look* at what it is *actually* doing, and to *analyze* how to make the two match.

Spy - WINWORD!OpusWwd			
Spy Window Options!			
3830	WM_MOUSEMOVE	0000	0087028C
3830	WM_NCHITTEST	0000	01A4033C
3830	WM_SETCURSOR	3830	02000001
3830	WM_MOUSEMOVE	0000	00CE02FC
3830	WM_NCHITTEST	0000	01C70355
3830	WM_SETCURSOR	3830	02000001
3830	WM_MOUSEMOVE	0000	00F10315
3830	WM_NCHITTEST	0000	01DE0355
3830	WM_SETCURSOR	3830	02000001
3830	WM_MOUSEMOVE	0000	01080315
3830	WM_NCHITTEST	0000	01E50355
3830	WM_SETCURSOR	3830	02000001
3830	WM_MOUSEMOVE	0000	010F0315
3830	WM_NCHITTEST	0000	01E60355
3830	WM_SETCURSOR	3830	02000001
3830	WM_MOUSEMOVE	0000	01100315

Figure 6.5. Spy monitoring Word for Windows messages

Debugging should be your last refuge. Before you fire up CodeView, play with the program. Find a procedure that will *always* reproduce the problem you are having: that way you'll know when you've fixed the problem. Look in your source code and make a list of code sequences that might have something to do with the problem you see.

Try to avoid jumping to conclusions. It is easy to grasp at the first possibility you see: "*That's* the problem!" Chances are that the first possibility won't have anything to do with the behavior you're seeing. Prove logically whether the code you are looking at is causing the error you are trying to correct. If the bug is not where you are looking, you are looking in the wrong place.

If you find yourself trying to reconcile two dearly held but incompatible facts, it's time to take a walk. Go out running, have a swim; anything to release the tension inherent in looking for bugs. Empty your mind: a solution will come to you.

Before slogging through your code with a debugger, slog through your source with a set of colored pens. If you have a pretty-printing program, use it: it's amazing how many mistakes look obvious in a neatly formatted listing. Look where you expect to find a problem, and look elsewhere as well.

Use your compiler for all it's worth: turn the error-checking up to its highest level and investigate every warning. If you have a LINT utility, run it on your whole project and go over the output.

Treat finding an error as a challenge to your abilities; don't feel that making the error in the first place was anything to be ashamed of. Everybody makes mistakes: it takes a good programmer to find and fix them.

Ask colleagues to look at your code: a fresh pair of eyes can see more than a tired pair. Explain the problem to someone: chances are you'll realize what's wrong as you speak.

If all else fails, by all means fire up the debugger, or salt your code with debugging statements. Just remember what it is you're trying to do. Keep your wits about you, keep focused, keep centered, keep your sense of humor, and you may possibly keep your sanity.

Debugging Image2

In Chapter 3 I mentioned some of the errors that I made and corrected in the course of turning ShowDIB into an image processing program. In this section I'd like to give you a blow-by-blow description as I try to find several bugs still lurking in Image2.

Figure 6.6. Bug in Image2 triples Targa image

First, let's look at the bug in Targa file display. Figure 6.6 illustrates the problem, using file window.tga. Clearly we are seeing the red, blue, and green components separated horizontally.

To fix this problem, first we need to find the block of code that converts this particular Targa format to DIB. We know perfectly well that all the code relevant to Targa format is in file TGA.C, and that the main Targa-reading function is **tgaview**. So we'll start by setting a break point at the beginning of **tgaview**. And we know the bulk of the work of reading the format is done in **read_tga**, so we'll also set a breakpoint there.

Tracing through **tgaview** and examining the local variables, we quickly find that window.tga is an old format 320x200 pixel Targa file with image type 2, meaning that it is an uncompressed true-color image. It has no ID field and no color map, it is not interleaved, and it uses 24 bits per pixel. The code we need to examine is the noninterlaced case in the following listing:

```
/* Set up byte map for writing */
      Red = pixels;
      Grn = Red + 1;
      Blu = Grn + 1;
/* Read the Targa file body and convert to DIB format */
      linewidth = tga->Width_lo + tga->Width_hi * 256;
      for (i = 0;  i < height;  i++) {
      /* No interlace */
```

```
                    if ((mode & INTERL) == 0) {
                          j = i;
                          }
/* Two way interlace */
                    else if ((mode & FOURWY) != 0) {
                          if (2 * i < height)
                                j = 2 * i;
                          else {
                                j = i - height / 2;
                                j - 2 * j + 1;
                                }
                          }
/* Four way interlace */
                    else {
                          if (4 * i < height)
                                j = 4 * i;
                          else if (2 * i < height) {
                                j = i - height / 4;
                                j = 4 * j + 1;
                                }
                          else if (4 * i < 3 * height) {
                                j = i - height / 2;
                                j = 4 * j + 2;
                                }
                          else {
                                j = i - height / 2 - height / 4;
                                j = 4 * j + 3;
                                }
                          }
              k = (height - 1 - j) * width;
              Redk = Red + k;
              Grnk = Grn + k;
              Bluk = Blu + k;
              for (j = 0;  j < (unsigned int)linewidth;  j++) {
                    get_pixel(rfile,&r, &g, &b,
                          tga->PixelSize, mode);
                    *Redk = r;
                    *Grnk = g;
                    *Bluk = b;
                    Redk += 3;
                    Grnk += 3;
                    Bluk += 3;
                    }
              if(SpinTheMessageLoop())
                    break;
        }
```

One thing that could be wrong here is the indexing scheme that sets the pointers **Red**, **Grn**, **Blu**, **Redk**, **Grnk**, and **Bluk**. Another possibility is that function **get_pixel** is not returning the correct bytes, either because the variable **mode** is set wrong or because of an incorrect assumption in the code.

The **mode** variable is set to 1. The code executed in **get_pixel** simply retrieves successive bytes in the file for the red, green, and blue values:

```
     case 24:        /* Eight bits each of red green and blue */
             fread(&i, 1, 1, rfile);
             Blu = i;
             fread(&i, 1, 1, rfile);
             Grn = i;
             fread(&i, 1, 1, rfile);
             Red = i;
...
             *rRed = Red;
             *rGrn = Grn;
             *rBlu = Blu;
...
     return 0;
```

There really isn't anything there that could be going wrong as long as the file is formatted as we think, in RGB triples. (The code is probably horribly inefficient because of the one-byte reads, but it should be correct.) On return from **get_pixel**, the local variable stack is:

```
[BP+0006] +_iobuf near *rfile = 0x1CB7:0x1578
[BP+0008] +uchar huge *pixels = 0x2627:0x0028
[BP+000C] -TGA_ImageHeader near *tga = 0x1CB7:0xB9EA
             uchar IDLength = 0 ''
             uchar CoMapType = 0 ''
             uchar ImgType = 2 '\x02'
             uchar Index_lo = 0 ''
             uchar Index_hi = 0 ''
             uchar Length_lo = 0 ''
             uchar Length_hi = 0 ''
             uchar CoSize = 0 ''
             uchar X_org_lo = 0 ''
             uchar X_org_hi = 0 ''
             uchar Y_org_lo = 0 ''
             uchar Y_org_hi = 0 ''
             uchar Width_lo = 64 '@'
             uchar Width_hi = 1 '\x01'
             uchar Height_lo = 200 'è'
             uchar Height_hi = 0 ''
             uchar PixelSize = 24 '\x18'
             AttBits = 0
             Rsrvd = 0
             OrgBit = 1
             IntrLve = 0
[BP+000E]  ushort height = 200
[BP+0010]  ushort width = 320
[BP-0010]  ushort ncolors = 47571
[BP-0032] +uchar huge *Grnk = 0x2627:0xF8E9
[BP-0016]  uchar b = 0 ''
[BP-0012]  uchar r = 0 ''
[BP-002A] +uchar huge *Blu = 0x2627:0x002A
[BP-0004]  short status = 1
[BP-000E]  ushort mode = 1
```

```
[BP-0038]   ushort hMap = 47554
[BP-002E]   +uchar huge *Redk = 0x2627:0xF8E8
[BP-0026]   +uchar huge *Grn = 0x2627:0x0029
[BP-0014]   uchar g = 0 ''
[BP-000A]   ushort temp1 = 47570
[BP-001E]   ulong linewidth = 320
[BP-000C]   ushort temp2 = 32770
[BP-0006]   ushort i = 0
[BP-0008]   ushort j = 0
[BP-0022]   +uchar huge *Red = 0x2627:0x0020
[BP-001A]   ulong k = 63680
[BP-0036]   +uchar huge *Bluk = 0x2627:0xF8EA
```

Note that within segment **0x2627**, pointers **Red**, **Grn**, and **Blu** are set to **0x0028**, **0x0029**, and **0x002A**, while pointers **Redk**, **Grnk**, and **BluK** are set to **0xF8E8**, **0xF8E9**, and **0xF8EA**. This doesn't quite appear correct: our experience converting raw data files indicates that the red and blue values should be swapped. However, that wouldn't cause us to split the image three ways horizontally—that would just distort the colors. Perhaps the index **k** is not being calculated correctly. The formula for **k** is:

```
k = (height - 1 - j) * width;
```

Superficially, that looks correct: it reverses top and bottom as we know must be done. But variables **height** and **width** have the dimensions of pixels, not bytes. **k** must be in bytes. We need to multiply **k** by **tga->PixelSize/8** to get it into bytes, and we need to exchange the blue and red bytes. When we try this, we get an image that still isn't correct (Figure 6.7).

At least there is no more tripling of the image. But why do we have nothing but a band of color at the bottom of the image? Time to look at the source code again, and perhaps break out the debugger once more.

Figure 6.7. Revised Image2 display: Still not right

Figure 6.8. Correct ray-traced image displayed by Image2

Two possible problems jump out at me this time through the code. The first is that the variable **j** is used both as a intermediate register for the computation of **k**, and as a loop variable. I add a new variable, **iloop**, which makes no difference whatsoever. So much for grasping at *that* straw.

The second problem is that variable **k** is an **unsigned long**, whereas the variables **width** and **height** used for computing **k** are typed **unsigned int**—this might cause integer overflow, which would display all the image in the first few lines. Bingo! The correct image displays now (Figure 6.8 and window.tga, plate 6). The revised formula for **k** is:

```
k = (height - 1 - j) * (unsigned long)width * tga->PixelSize/8;
```

One image isn't sufficient to test all our code, however. When I tried this version of Image2 on a scanned image of a girl (zoe.tga, plate 8, photograph by Dana Hudes), I saw that she was upside-down. Our current formula for **k** is correct only if **tga->OrgBit** is set true, as it is for window.tga: this means the origin is at the top of the image. For the case where **tga->OrgBit** is false, meaning the origin is at the bottom of the image just like a DIB, we *don't* want to reverse the line order. The formula for index **k** now reads:

```
if(!tga->OrgBit)
 k = j * (unsigned long)width * tga->PixelSize/8;
else
 k = (height - 1 - j) * (unsigned long)width * tga->PixelSize/8;
```

We aren't out of the woods yet. Yet another image shows us a problem with certain line widths: each line starts to the left of the line below it. The Targa code now pads odd pixel widths to even pixel widths, but what we really need is to pad each scan-line out to a long boundary. The existing code is:

```
/* If this is odd number of bytes, add one */
    if ((width & 1) != 0)
            width++;
```

It should really read:

```
/* Pad width to a long boundary */
   padbytes=width%4;
   width += padbytes;
```

That, finally, seems to get the Targa conversion code working: at least on all the images I have for testing. I haven't tested 16-bit Targa files, or interlaced files, or all sorts of other possible variations. But what I have works well, as you can see from the color plates.

The next bugs to find have to do with TIFF images. Only one kind of TIFF file seems to display properly in Image2 as originally listed in Chapter 3: a 256-color palette-based image, TIFF Class P. Other TIFF classes don't display—there is a message box complaining about the tags or the scan-line width, instead. On some images there is a GP fault.

I am suspicious of the code in tif_dir.c because of the large number of compiler diagnostics (73 from Quick C for Windows with level 3 reporting):

```
qcw /AM /W3 /Ze /G2w /Zp  /Zi /Od  -f C:\ADVWIN\IMAGE2\TIF_DIR.C
C:\ADVWIN\IMAGE2\TIF_DIR.C(296) : warning C4018: '!=' : signed/unsigned
    mismatch
C:\ADVWIN\IMAGE2\TIF_DIR.C(398) : warning C4135: conversion between
    different integral types
C:\ADVWIN\IMAGE2\TIF_DIR.C(413) : warning C4135: conversion between
    different integral types
C:\ADVWIN\IMAGE2\TIF_DIR.C(413) : warning C4061: long/short mismatch in
    argument : conversion supplied
C:\ADVWIN\IMAGE2\TIF_DIR.C(477) : warning C4135: conversion between
    different integral types
C:\ADVWIN\IMAGE2\TIF_DIR.C(477) : warning C4061: long/short mismatch in
    argument : conversion supplied
C:\ADVWIN\IMAGE2\TIF_DIR.C(534) : warning C4135: conversion between
    different integral types
C:\ADVWIN\IMAGE2\TIF_DIR.C(572) : warning C4035: 'MissingRequired' : no
    return value
C:\ADVWIN\IMAGE2\TIF_DIR.C(586) : warning C4135: conversion between
    different integral types
C:\ADVWIN\IMAGE2\TIF_DIR.C(588) : warning C4018: '==' : signed/unsigned
    mismatch
C:\ADVWIN\IMAGE2\TIF_DIR.C(592) : warning C4049: 'argument' : indirection
    to different types
C:\ADVWIN\IMAGE2\TIF_DIR.C(592) : warning C4024: 'TIFFSwabArrayOfShort' :
    different types : parameter 1
C:\ADVWIN\IMAGE2\TIF_DIR.C(592) : warning C4135: conversion between
    different integral types
C:\ADVWIN\IMAGE2\TIF_DIR.C(592) : warning C4061: long/short mismatch in
    argument : conversion supplied
C:\ADVWIN\IMAGE2\TIF_DIR.C(595) : warning C4049: 'argument' : indirection
    to different types
C:\ADVWIN\IMAGE2\TIF_DIR.C(595) : warning C4024: 'TIFFSwabArrayOfLong' :
    different types : parameter 1
```

```
C:\ADVWIN\IMAGE2\TIF_DIR.C(595) : warning C4135: conversion between
    different integral types
C:\ADVWIN\IMAGE2\TIF_DIR.C(595) : warning C4061: long/short mismatch in
    argument : conversion supplied
C:\ADVWIN\IMAGE2\TIF_DIR.C(598) : warning C4049: 'argument' : indirection
    to different types
C:\ADVWIN\IMAGE2\TIF_DIR.C(598) : warning C4024: 'TIFFSwabArrayOfLong' :
    different types : parameter 1
C:\ADVWIN\IMAGE2\TIF_DIR.C(598) : warning C4135: conversion between
    different integral types
C:\ADVWIN\IMAGE2\TIF_DIR.C(598) : warning C4061: long/short mismatch in
    argument : conversion supplied
C:\ADVWIN\IMAGE2\TIF_DIR.C(622) : warning C4135: conversion between
    different integral types
C:\ADVWIN\IMAGE2\TIF_DIR.C(622) : warning C4061: long/short mismatch in
    argument : conversion supplied
C:\ADVWIN\IMAGE2\TIF_DIR.C(657) : warning C4135: conversion between
    different integral types
C:\ADVWIN\IMAGE2\TIF_DIR.C(658) : warning C4135: conversion between
    different integral types
C:\ADVWIN\IMAGE2\TIF_DIR.C(660) : warning C4135: conversion between
    different integral types
C:\ADVWIN\IMAGE2\TIF_DIR.C(661) : warning C4135: conversion between
    different integral types
C:\ADVWIN\IMAGE2\TIF_DIR.C(663) : warning C4035: 'TIFFUnpackShorts' : no
    return value
C:\ADVWIN\IMAGE2\TIF_DIR.C(686) : warning C4135: conversion between
    different integral types
C:\ADVWIN\IMAGE2\TIF_DIR.C(691) : warning C4018: '<' : signed/unsigned
    mismatch
C:\ADVWIN\IMAGE2\TIF_DIR.C(691) : warning C4135: conversion between
    different integral types
C:\ADVWIN\IMAGE2\TIF_DIR.C(712) : warning C4018: '!=' : signed/unsigned
    mismatch
C:\ADVWIN\IMAGE2\TIF_DIR.C(723) : warning C4135: conversion between
    different integral types
C:\ADVWIN\IMAGE2\TIF_DIR.C(723) : warning C4061: long/short mismatch in
    argument : conversion supplied
C:\ADVWIN\IMAGE2\TIF_DIR.C(736) : warning C4135: conversion between
    different integral types
C:\ADVWIN\IMAGE2\TIF_DIR.C(736) : warning C4061: long/short mismatch in
    argument : conversion supplied
C:\ADVWIN\IMAGE2\TIF_DIR.C(833) : warning C4035: 'TIFFFreeDirectory' : no
    return value
C:\ADVWIN\IMAGE2\TIF_DIR.C(865) : warning C4035: 'TIFFDefaultDirectory' :
    no return value
C:\ADVWIN\IMAGE2\TIF_DIR.C(878) : warning C4035: 'setString' : no return
    value
C:\ADVWIN\IMAGE2\TIF_DIR.C(888) : warning C4135: conversion between
    different integral types
C:\ADVWIN\IMAGE2\TIF_DIR.C(888) : warning C4061: long/short mismatch in
    argument : conversion supplied
C:\ADVWIN\IMAGE2\TIF_DIR.C(889) : warning C4135: conversion between
    different integral types
```

```
C:\ADVWIN\IMAGE2\TIF_DIR.C(889) : warning C4061: long/short mismatch in
    argument : conversion supplied
C:\ADVWIN\IMAGE2\TIF_DIR.C(890) : warning C4035: 'setCurve' : no return
    value
C:\ADVWIN\IMAGE2\TIF_DIR.C(909) : warning C4135: conversion between
    different integral types
C:\ADVWIN\IMAGE2\TIF_DIR.C(909) : warning C4061: long/short mismatch in
    argument : conversion supplied
C:\ADVWIN\IMAGE2\TIF_DIR.C(950) : warning C4018: '==' : signed/unsigned
    mismatch
C:\ADVWIN\IMAGE2\TIF_DIR.C(950) : warning C4135: conversion between
    different integral types
C:\ADVWIN\IMAGE2\TIF_DIR.C(953) : warning C4071: 'function through ptr'
    : no function prototype given
C:\ADVWIN\IMAGE2\TIF_DIR.C(958) : warning C4135: conversion between
    different integral types
C:\ADVWIN\IMAGE2\TIF_DIR.C(958) : warning C4061: long/short mismatch in
    argument : conversion supplied
C:\ADVWIN\IMAGE2\TIF_DIR.C(959) : warning C4135: conversion between
    different integral types
C:\ADVWIN\IMAGE2\TIF_DIR.C(976) : warning C4071: 'setString' : no
    function prototype given
C:\ADVWIN\IMAGE2\TIF_DIR.C(1020) : warning C4135: conversion between
    different integral types
C:\ADVWIN\IMAGE2\TIF_DIR.C(1039) : warning C4136: conversion between
    different floating types
C:\ADVWIN\IMAGE2\TIF_DIR.C(1043) : warning C4136: conversion between
    different floating types
C:\ADVWIN\IMAGE2\TIF_DIR.C(1048) : warning C4135: conversion between
    different integral types
C:\ADVWIN\IMAGE2\TIF_DIR.C(1056) : warning C4136: conversion between
    different floating types
C:\ADVWIN\IMAGE2\TIF_DIR.C(1060) : warning C4136: conversion between
    different floating types
C:\ADVWIN\IMAGE2\TIF_DIR.C(1068) : warning C4071: 'setCurve' : no
    function prototype given
C:\ADVWIN\IMAGE2\TIF_DIR.C(1138) : warning C4135: conversion between
    different integral types
C:\ADVWIN\IMAGE2\TIF_DIR.C(1138) : warning C4061: long/short mismatch
    in argument : conversion supplied
C:\ADVWIN\IMAGE2\TIF_DIR.C(1232) : warning C4135: conversion between
    different integral types
C:\ADVWIN\IMAGE2\TIF_DIR.C(1235) : warning C4135: conversion between
    different integral types
C:\ADVWIN\IMAGE2\TIF_DIR.C(1312) : warning C4035: 'TIFFGetField1' : no
    return value
C:\ADVWIN\IMAGE2\TIF_DIR.C(1326) : warning C4035: 'TIFFgetfield' : no
    return value
C:\ADVWIN\IMAGE2\TIF_DIR.C(1384) : warning C4071: 'function through
    ptr' : no function prototype given
C:\ADVWIN\IMAGE2\TIF_DIR.C(1386) : warning C4071: 'function through
    ptr' : no function prototype given
C:\ADVWIN\IMAGE2\TIF_DIR.C(1546) : warning C4018: '==' : signed/un-
    signed mismatch
```

```
C:\ADVWIN\IMAGE2\TIF_DIR.C(1585) : warning C4051: type conversion -
    possible loss of data
C:\ADVWIN\IMAGE2\TIF_DIR.C(1643) : warning C4135: conversion between
    different integral types
C:\ADVWIN\IMAGE2\TIF_DIR.C(1645) : warning C4018: '==' : signed/un-
    signed mismatch
TIF_DIR.C - 0 error(s), 73 warning(s)
```

Wading through all these diagnostics is no fun at all, but that's what you get when you try to port code from a sloppy Unix program written in K&R C. The rest of the TIFF routines are not quite as bad, but there's no guarantee at all that they work.

It might be worthwhile to examine each source line that generates a warning. It might also be worthwhile to run LINT on the whole project and plow through all diagnostics generated (there will be hundreds). After cleaning up the source as much as possible, it'll be time to break out the debugger again.

I'm going to leave the joy of finding the rest of the TIFF-reading code errors to you: it's a challenging debugging task that will sharpen your skills enormously. You'll find plenty of sample TIFF files on the diskettes; start by putting a break point at **tiffview** in tiff.c. You'll need to look all the way down into the PTIFF structures to make sense of what is coming in from the files, how the TIFF tags are set up, and how the program deals with what it reads.

Happy hunting.

Common Windows Program Bugs

Invalid Pointer

Description: the program uses a memory pointer that is not valid.

Causes: allocation failure, lock failure, forgetting to lock memory block before use, overwriting pointer, failing to detect a discarded block, allocating sizeof(pointer type) instead of sizeof(object).

Symptoms: in real mode, weird delayed symptoms (the program is unstable after doing a certain operation); in protected mode, a trap either to the Unrecoverable Application Error (UAE) routine or the FatalExit routine.

Cures: debug this in protected mode (standard or enhanced), using the debugging kernel; make sure a current symbol file resides in your program's directory. The stack traceback will tell you which of your routines has the problem. You can then usually find the problem in the source code; if not, add a **DebugBreak** in the suspect routine, recompile with full debugging symbols, and step through the routine with a debugger. It may be useful to put a watch point on the pointer.

Invalid Handle

Description: the program uses a memory handle that is not valid.

Causes: allocation failure, object has been discarded, handle has been overwritten.

Symptoms: in the retail kernel, may be symptom-free except that something does not display as expected, or may cause an UAE. In the debugging kernel, there will normally be a UAE or FatalExit with traceback.

Cures: if the object is discardable (for instance the hourglass pointer) reload it before use. Otherwise, isolate the problem with debugging kernel stack trace, and further isolate by stepping through the offending routine. A watch point on the handle might be useful.

Resource Not Released

Description: a system resource has been allocated but not freed.

Causes: forgetting to free resource, handle invalid before object freed, more than one exit from a subroutine, inadequate error handling, spelling error.

Symptoms: if the resource is a device context, after the offending action is performed five times the program ends with a UAE or the system crashes. Other resources may cause free system resources or free memory to decrease with time.

Cures: monitor system resources and memory during operation (with hDC memory viewer, any of a number of shareware memory displays, or the program manager About box). Check the global heap, user heap, and GDI heap at key points during your program's execution using HeapWalk. If you can identify the kind of object left lying around, grep through your source code for places that create and destroy that type of object. Otherwise, isolate the problem with debugging kernel stack trace, and further isolate by stepping through the offending routine. A watch point on the object handle may be useful.

Stack Too Small

Description: the application needs more stack than was allocated.

Causes: recursive functions, large automatic structure or vector variables, complicated **printf** and **scanf** calls, failure to estimate stack requirements.

Symptoms: variables in local heap corrupted after a specific function call, a return statement or function end fails to bring control back to the calling routine.

Cures: monitor SS:SP with a debugger. Check SS:SP values in a Dr.

Watson log. Try changing stack allocation in the program's DEF file.

Local Heap Too Small

Description: the sum of the stack, all static variables, and locally allocated variables exceeds 64K.

Causes: the local heap shares a single data segment with the stack and variables declared **static** or **global**. You may have too many big program variables lying around, or be using too big a stack.

Symptoms: link error, **LocalAlloc** calls fail.

Cures: move global and static variables to the local or global heap. Use Window words. Use multiple local heaps.

Callback Function Not Exported

Description: a function that needs to be called by Windows, such as your WinMain, window procedure, or dialog procedure, did not have its symbol exported, so that Windows did not fix up its prologue.

Causes: failure to mention the procedure in the EXPORT section of the DEF file or failure to declare the function **_export**.

Symptoms: function not reached at all, function reached but data segment not set, function faults as soon as it tries to use a static or global variable, static or global variables appear to be filled with garbage.

Cures: run **FIXDS** on EXE file. Alternatively, add the **_export** keyword to the function declaration, or list the function in the EXPORT section of the program's DEF file.

MakeProcInstance Not Called for Callback Function

Description: a dialog procedure or other callback function in an EXE file that should be passed as an instance thunk doesn't have one or is passed as a function pointer. (Note: functions in DLLs do not need instance thunks.)

Causes: passed function pointer (**FunctionName**) rather than **Make-ProcInstance(FunctionName)**.

Symptoms: function not reached at all, function reached but data segment not set, function faults as soon as it tries to use a static or global variable, static or global variables appear to be filled with garbage; function success or failure may be sensitive to code discarding, loading, and motion history.

Cures: run **FIXDS** on EXE file, or call **MakeProcInstance** when necessary. Alternatively, restrict your application to protected mode.

In which we learn how to subclass and superclass controls, using the multiline edit control as our starting point. We will learn how to do field validation and how to activate the built-in clipboard functionality of the edit control.

Custom Edit Controls

· ·

Some how we never seem to outgrow using a computer for data processing. Data processing requires you first to get the data into the computer, which usually means that somebody has to do some typing.

Mainframe and minicomputer programs have evolved, slowly, from key-punch data entry to interactive data entry using a terminal. The data entry operator usually works with an on-screen form, and fills in the blank fields to complete the record.

Program designers have built all sorts of data validation functions into these programs to help prevent the most common sorts of errors. Our highly advanced Windows environment has dialog boxes instead of forms, and edit controls, check boxes, and so on instead of fields. But where are the data validation functions? The edit control doesn't have them: we'll have to build them in, or use a library that supports them.

About Edit Controls

The edit control is one of the most useful, and most complicated, standard window classes. As Microsoft tells us:

An edit control is a rectangular child window in which the user can enter text from the keyboard. The user selects the control, and gives it the input focus, by clicking the mouse inside it or pressing the TAB key. The user can enter text when the control displays a flashing caret. The mouse can be used to move the cursor and select characters to be replaced, or to position the cursor for inserting characters. The BACKSPACE key can be used to delete characters.

Edit controls use the fixed-pitch font and display ANSI characters. They expand tab characters into as many space characters as are required to move the cursor to the next tab stop. Tab stops are assumed to be at every eighth character position.

The edit control has a number of possible styles, which can be adjusted to give it a variety of behaviors. Setting **ES_MULTILINE** defines a multiline edit control; the Windows NOTEPAD application, the Petzold POPPAD sample, and the Windows SDK MULTIPAD sample demonstrate the power of the multiline edit control. The principal deficiency of the multiline edit control is that it is limited to 32K characters: you can't use it to edit large files without quite a bit of work.

Setting **ES_READONLY** (new for Windows 3.1) keeps the user from modifying the text in an edit control. If you combine **ES_MULTILINE** and **ES_READONLY**, you have a text browsing window. The table of edit control styles below is worth some study:

Style	Meaning
ES_AUTOHSCROLL	Automatically scrolls text to the right by 10 characters when the user types a character at the end of the line. When the user presses the ENTER key, the control scrolls all text back to position zero.
ES_AUTOVSCROLL	Automatically scrolls text up one page when the user presses ENTER on the last line.
ES_CENTER	Centers text in a multiline edit control.
ES_LEFT	Aligns text flush left.
ES_LOWERCASE	Converts all characters to lowercase as they are typed into the edit control.
ES_MULTILINE	Designates multiple-line edit control. (The default is single-line.) If the ES_AUTOVSCROLL style is specified, the edit control shows as many lines as possible and scrolls vertically when the user presses the ENTER key. If ES_AUTOVSCROLL is not given, the edit control shows as many lines as possible and beeps if ENTER is pressed when no more lines can be displayed.
ES_MULTILINE with ES_AUTOHSCROLL	If the ES_AUTOHSCROLL style is specified, the multiple-line edit control automatically scrolls horizontally when the caret goes past the right edge of the control. To start a new line, the user must press ENTER.
ES_MULTILINE without ES_AUTO HSCROLL	If ES_AUTOHSCROLL is not given, the control automatically wraps words to the beginning of the next line when necessary; a new line is also started if ENTER is pressed. The position of the wordwrap is determined by the window size. If the window size changes, the wordwrap position changes, and the text is redisplayed.
ES_MULTILINE and scroll bars	Multiple-line edit controls can have scroll bars. An edit control with scroll bars processes its own scroll-bar messages. Edit controls without scroll bars scroll as described above, and process any scroll messages sent by the parent window.

ES_NOHIDESEL	Normally, an edit control hides the selection when the control loses the input focus, and inverts the selection when the control receives the input focus. Specifying ES_NOHIDESEL deletes this default action.
ES_OEMCONVERT	Text entered in the edit control is converted from the ANSI character set to the OEM character set and then back to ANSI. This ensures proper character conversion when the application calls the AnsiToOem function to convert an ANSI string in the edit control to OEM characters. This style is most useful for edit controls that contain filenames.
ES_PASSWORD	Displays all characters as an asterisk (*) as they are typed into the edit control. An application can use the EM_SETPASS–WORDCHAR message to change the character that is displayed.
ES_READONLY	Prevents the user from entering or editing text in the edit control.
ES_RIGHT	Aligns text flush right in a multiline edit control.
ES_UPPERCASE	Converts all characters to uppercase as they are typed into the edit control.

You'll note that there are three possible text alignments in an edit control: **ES_LEFT**, **ES_CENTER**, and **ES_RIGHT**. There are three possible capitalizations: no change, **ES_UPPERCASE**, and **ES_LOWERCASE**. There is no built-in option for proper capitalization, such as you'd want for a city field (i.e., *Andover*, not *andover* or *ANDOVER*). You can keep characters from displaying in a simple edit field with the **ES_PASSWORD** style.

There are no **ES_NUMERIC** or **ES_ALPHAMERIC** styles, nor are there styles for **ES_DATE**, **ES_TIME**, or **ES_CURRENCY**. You can't easily supply a picture format to be used by an edit field, although we can build in such a capability by subclassing.

You can create an edit control as a window of class "**edit**"; this is what Petzold does in his POPPAD example. But most often you see edit controls in dialog boxes.

About Dialog Box Procedures

A quick review: a dialog box is a rather special kind of window. Ordinary windows have window procedures; dialog boxes have dialog box procedures. Ordinary windows may have child windows; dialog boxes have special child windows called controls along with support for moving the focus from control to control.

Dialog boxes can be modal or modeless. Modal dialog boxes grab the focus and automatically disable their parent window; modeless dialog boxes leave their parent window enabled. You create a dialog box with one of the functions in the following table:

Function	Action
CreateDialog	Creates a modeless dialog box.
CreateDialogIndirect	Creates a modeless dialog box.
CreateDialogIndirectParam	Creates a modeless dialog box and passes data to it when it is created.
CreateDialogParam	Creates a modeless dialog box and passes data to it when it is created.
DialogBox	Creates a modal dialog box.
DialogBoxIndirect	Creates a modal dialog box.
DialogBoxIndirectParam	Creates a modal dialog box and passes data to it when it is created.
DialogBoxParam	Creates a modal dialog box and passes data to it when it is created.

A disproportionate number of the defined messages in Windows have to do with dialog boxes and controls. Each dialog procedure is, in a sense, a subclass of the great dialog procedure in the sky: any messages not handled by the private dialog procedure need to be sent to **DefDlgProc**. **DefDlgProc** acts like a subclass of the generic window, and passes any messages that it doesn't handle to **DefWindowProc**. The source for **DefDlgProc** and **DefWindowProc** is supplied with the Windows SDK, and should be in your **windev-\samples\defprocs** directory. It is well worth the time spent to read and understand **DefDlgProc** and **DefWindowProc**.

The **WM_INITDIALOG** message is sent to a dialog procedure just before a dialog box is displayed. You should do your control initialization in the context of the **WM_INITDIALOG** message, as well as any subclassing you want for specific controls. The **TRUE** or **FALSE** return value from **WM_INITDIALOG** indicates whether or not the input focus should go to the default control passed to the dialog procedure in **wParam**. The application has to explicitly set the input focus to another control to safely return **FALSE** from **WM_INITDIALOG**. The effect of returning **FALSE** without setting the focus is to give you a totally messed-up dialog box display.

The **WM_GETDLGCODE** message is sent by Windows to an input procedure associated with a control. Normally, Windows handles all arrow- and tab-key input to the control. By responding to the **WM_GETDLGCODE** message, an application can take control of a particular type of input and process the input itself. The return code from a **WM_GETDLGCODE** message specifies what messages the dialog control wants to capture.

Although **DefWindowProc** always returns zero in response to the **WM_GETDLGCODE** message, the window functions for the predefined control classes return a code appropriate for each class. The **WM_GETDLGCODE** message and the returned values are useful for user-defined dialog controls and for standard controls modified by subclassing. The possible return codes from **WM_GETDLGCODE** are:

Return code	Meaning
DLGC_DEFPUSHBUTTON	Default push button.
DLGC_HASSETSEL	EM_SETSEL messages.
DLGC_PUSHBUTTON	Push button.
DLGC_RADIOBUTTON	Radio button.
DLGC_WANTALLKEYS	All keyboard input.
DLGC_WANTARROWS	DIRECTION keys.
DLGC_WANTCHARS	WM_CHAR messages.
DLGC_WANTMESSAGE	All keyboard input (the application passes this message on to control).
DLGC_WANTTAB	TAB key.

The **WM_CTLCOLOR** message is sent to the parent of a control or message box when the control is about to be drawn. In the context of a **WM_CTLCOLOR** message, the **wParam** parameter contains a handle to the device context of the control to be drawn; the low-order word of the **lParam** parameter contains a handle to the child window; and the high-order word of the **lParam** parameter contains a flag to indicate the kind of control being drawn.

The return value from **WM_CTLCOLOR** is either a handle to the background brush to be used, or **NULL**. Don't return **TRUE** and expect good things to happen. Returning a background brush handle is necessary, but not sufficient for some controls. For instance, to change the background color of a single line edit control, you need to set a brush handle in response to *both* the **CTLCOLOR_EDIT** and **CTLCOLOR_MSGBOX** message codes, *as well as* calling the **SetBkColor** function in response to the **CTLCOLOR_EDIT** code. You can also call **SetTextColor** in response to **CTLCOLOR_EDIT** to set the foreground text color for an edit control.

This example (from the Microsoft SDK help) creates a green brush, and passes the handle of the brush to a single-line edit control in response to a **WM_CTLCOLOR** message:

```
static HBRUSH hbrGreen;

switch(msg) {
    case WM_INITDIALOG:
        /* Create a green brush */
        hbrGreen = CreateSolidBrush(RGB(0, 255, 0));
        return TRUE;
    case WM_CTLCOLOR:
```

```
switch(HIWORD(lParam)) {
    case CTLCOLOR_EDIT:
    /* set the background color to green */
        SetBkColor((HDC) wParam, RGB(0, 255, 0));
        return hbrGreen;
        break;
    case CTLCOLOR_MSGBOX:
     /*
      * For single-line edit controls, we must also process
      * this code so that the background color of the format
      * rectangle will also be painted with our color.
      */
        return hbrGreen;
    }
    return (HBRUSH) NULL;
```

You can't set the color of a push button by returning a brush from **WM_CTL-COLOR**; instead you need to give the push button the **BS_OWNERDRAW** style; the button's parent will then receive a **WM_MEASUREITEM** message when the button is created, and a **WM_DRAWITEM** message when a visual aspect of the button has changed. Buttons need to be owner-drawn rather than handed a brush because of their three-dimensional look; the button needs to be drawn with highlight and shadow colors as well a face background and text color.

Buttons are not the only controls that can be owner-drawn: list boxes, combo boxes, and menus can also be owner-drawn. In all cases the **WM_MEASUREITEM** and **WM_DRAWITEM** messages are sent to the control's parent window.

You needn't draw three-dimensional buttons (which is a fair bit of work) if you don't want to: you can easily draw flat colored buttons, or put a bitmap on a button. For instance, the following code fragment (generated by DialogCoder, a source code generator for dialog boxes produced by The Software Organization, Inc.) correctly draws a flat green button with blue text. More code would be necessary if there were multiple owner-drawn controls in the dialog box.

```
case WM_DRAWITEM:
/* Draw the owner draw item(s) */
lpDraw = (LPDRAWITEMSTRUCT)lParam;
switch( lpDraw->itemAction )
{
   case ODA_DRAWENTIRE:
       FillRect( lpDraw->hDC, &lpDraw->rcItem, hGreen );
       SetBkColor( lpDraw->hDC, RGB(0,255,0) );
       SetTextColor( lpDraw->hDC, RGB(0,0,255) );
       DrawText( lpDraw->hDC,  "HI!", -1, &lpDraw->rcItem,
             DT_CENTER | DT_VCENTER | DT_SINGLELINE );
       break;
   case ODA_SELECT:
       InvertRect( lpDraw->hDC, &lpDraw->rcItem );
       break;
   case ODA_FOCUS:
```

```
        DrawFocusRect( lpDraw->hDC, &lpDraw->rcItem );
        break;
```

Putting a bitmap on a button is not that much harder. This code was also generated by DialogCoder:

```
case WM_DRAWITEM:
/* Draw the owner draw item(s) */
lpDraw = (LPDRAWITEMSTRUCT)lParam;
switch( lpDraw->itemAction )
{
  case ODA_DRAWENTIRE:
  /* Display bitmap via Owner Draw button selection */
      hBitMap = LoadBitmap(
            GetWindowWord( hDlg, GWW_HINSTANCE ), "mybitmap" );
      if( hBitMap != NULL ) {
          hDC = lpDraw->hDC;
          hMemoryDC = CreateCompatibleDC( hDC );
          SelectObject( hMemoryDC, hBitMap );
          GetObject( hBitMap, sizeof( BITMAP ), (LPSTR)&bm );
          pt.x = bm.bmWidth; pt.y = bm.bmHeight;
          DPtoLP( hDC, &pt, 1 );
          BitBlt( hDC, lpDraw->rcItem.left, lpDraw->rcItem.top,
              pt.x, pt.y, hMemoryDC, 0, 0, SRCCOPY );
          DeleteDC( hMemoryDC );
          DeleteObject( hBitMap );
          }
      break;
  case ODA_SELECT:
      InvertRect( lpDraw->hDC, &lpDraw->rcItem );
      break;
  case ODA_FOCUS:
      DrawFocusRect( lpDraw->hDC, &lpDraw->rcItem );
      break;
```

The **OK** and **Cancel** buttons (defined by default as controls 1 and 2) generate **WM_COMMAND** messages to the dialog box with their ID in **wParam**. If you've allocated any memory or resources in the context of **WM_INITDIALOG**, you should free them on the **ID_OK** or **ID_CANCEL** commands. Note that automatic variables survive only for the context of a single message; to have values last from message to message within the life of a dialog box, you need to keep them in static or global variables, keep them in window words, or allocate space for the values dynamically.

Verifying Field Entries

There are several strategies we can take to verify that the contents of an edit field are valid. We can check the field for validity after every keystroke or mouse action in the field, check it when the user tried to switch to another field, or check it when the user clicks OK.

There are a number of things we can do about an invalid field, too. We can beep at the user, disable the OK button, bring up a message box flagging the error, and/or move the input focus back to the invalid field. If we set the focus back to the invalid field, we might want to automatically delete the invalid characters, or perhaps select the problem characters, or maybe just put the caret at the first problem character.

One preventative measure we can take is to limit the length of the allowed text in an edit field. You do this by sending the control an **EM_LIMITTEXT** message. The following example sets the control **IDD_EDIT_INFO** to the current value of structure field **acctrec.acct_info** and limits the text entered to the size of the variable:

```
SetDlgItemText(hWndDlg,IDD_EDIT_INFO,acctrec.acct_info);
SendDlgItemMessage(hWndDlg,IDD_EDIT_INFO,EM_LIMITTEXT,
        sizeof(acctrec.acct_info),0L);
```

If the user tries to enter more text than would fit in the variable, the edit control will beep and will not accept any more characters. That may not be sufficient for a field that expects a numeric value, however.

In the code above we sent the control a message using the **SendDlgItem-Message** function. If we had multiple messages to send to the control, we probably would have gotten the control's window handle with **GetDlgItem**, and then sent the messages with **SendMessage** or **PostMessage**.

You can extract the contents of an edit field with **GetDlgItemText**, or, if the field is supposed to be an integer, with **GetDlgItemInt**. For verification purposes, **GetDlgItemText** is a better choice even if the value is an integer: **GetDlgItemInt** will return an integer value without checking for nonnumeric characters in the edit control. We can retrieve the contents of the field we set above with:

```
GetDlgItemText(hWndDlg,IDD_EDIT_INFO,acctrec.acct_info,
        sizeof(acctrec.acct_info));
```

Once we have the string, we can verify its validity with a simple parser, such as you can find in any elementary book on C programming. Now let's explore *when* to verify the field.

When the user tries to leave an edit field, it notifies its parent with an **EN_KILLFOCUS** message. This is one good time to verify that the contents of the edit field are valid, and verifying after the user is through won't slow down the user's typing. It is possible that the user will pass through the field often without changing it; in this case it would be better to know if the field has changed before doing anything with it.

When an edit field has changed its content, it notifies its parent with an **EN_CHANGE** message. Intercepting this message won't interfere with the use of arrow keys, but it will cause some overhead after every keystroke that inserts or deletes a character. In many cases intercepting **EN_CHANGE** for field verification will cause more slowdown than intercepting **EN_KILLFOCUS**.

You can reduce the overhead quite a bit if you query the status of the edit control in the context of an **EN_KILLFOCUS** message. You can do this by sending the edit control an **EM_GETMODIFY** message.

The least overhead is introduced if you defer validation until OK is pressed—which is the normal time you'd retrieve all the field contents. Unfortunately, this can leave the user rather frustrated, since she might have long since forgotten about the field that is incorrect. "Why couldn't the computer have told me when I was making the mistake?" she'll wail.

We already know how to make the computer beep with **MessageBeep**, and how to use the **MessageBox** function. Disabling the "**OK**" button is just a matter of calling **EnableWindow** with the parameter **FALSE**; reenabling the button is the same thing, except with the parameter true:

```
EnableWindow(GetDlgItem(hWndDlg,IDOK),FALSE);    //disables OK
EnableWindow(GetDlgItem(hWndDlg,IDOK),TRUE);     //enables OK
```

We can change the focus to another control in the dialog using the **WM_NEXTDLGCTL** message. This was implemented primarily so that user-defined controls that want tab keys can pass the tab off to the next or previous control in the dialog box. Before **WM_NEXTDLGCTL** was introduced in Windows 3.0, the best such a control could do was **SetFocus**, but that didn't take care of boxing default buttons. Note that you should use **PostMessage** to send **WM_NEXTDLGCTL**, not **SendMessage** or **SendDlgItemMessage**.

One problem with both **SetFocus** and **WM_NEXTDLGCTL** is that they won't necessarily update the caret in the edit control to which they switch. You can fix this by explicitly doing a **CreateCaret**, then a **SetCaretPos**, and finally a **ShowCaret** in the edit window.

In fact, you can do "good enough" field validation for an edit control without resorting to subclassing. But for the best results with the least total work, you'll have to subclass your edit controls if you want to validate them.

We learned how to subclass way back in Chapter 1. To review, the concept of subclassing is that we can create a window procedure that intercepts only certain messages for the window, and passes the rest of the messages to the normal window procedure for the class. Instead of intercepting a bunch of edit notify messages for each edit control we want to verify, we create one new window procedure that intercepts the equivalent window messages to do what we want, and subclass each edit control to use our new window procedure.

In theory, subclassing can be quite simple. In practice, it takes quite a bit of code to do a thorough job. For instance, the subclassing code used by DialogCoder to handle numeric, alphabetic, and picture fields amounts to some 700 lines of C source. A more ambitious library, WM_CONTROL by Millennium Software, has some 4,000 lines of C source. (The code in WM_CONTROL, a forms-type library, is not directly comparable with DialogCoder, which is more of a CASE tool. You'd probably use them for different purposes, but you also probably wouldn't want to mix the two in a single project.)

A Date Field

Let's examine the specific case of a date field. We can do this without subclassing if we want, but we'll have to write a conversion function for date strings. This is a little harder than it sounds: we need to handle international date string formats, and we need to represent the date in the computer as a number—the Julian date.

First, let's get the international settings from win.ini:

```
char sDate [2], sTime [2], sAMPM [2][5];
int iDate, iTime;
char Today[9];

void SetInternational (void)
  {
  static char cName [] = "intl" ;

  iDate = GetProfileInt (cName, "iDate", 0) ;
  iTime = GetProfileInt (cName, "iTime", 0) ;

  GetProfileString (cName, "sDate",  "/", sDate,     2) ;
  GetProfileString (cName, "sTime",  ":", sTime,     2) ;
  GetProfileString (cName, "s1159", "AM", sAMPM [0], 5) ;
  GetProfileString (cName, "s2359", "PM", sAMPM [1], 5) ;
  _strdate(Today);
  }
```

The **iDate** and **iTime** values from win.ini represent how to present date and time strings. If **iDate** is 0, the U.S. MM/DD/YY convention is used; if 1, the European DD/MM/YY convention; and if 2, the YY/MM/DD convention. If **iTime** is 0, we want a 12-hour clock, and if 1 a 24-hour clock. Note that we're not as flexible as we might be: the **iDate** and **sDate** settings are holdovers from Windows 2.x. There is a newer **sShortDate** setting that specifies the date format as a picture. Nevertheless, what we're doing works.

Now we need a way to convert from a Julian date to a meaningful string. This will of course depend on the international settings. We'll offset the date from January 1, 1980 in order to be able to store it in a short integer.

```
void date_to_string(int date,char *string)
{
        int mm,dd,yy;
        long jul1,jul2;
        char temp[20];
```

```
        if(date<0) {
                lstrcpy(string,"");
                return;
                }
        jul1=julday(1,1,1980);
        jul2=jul1 + date;
        caldat(jul2,&mm,&dd,&yy);
        yy %= 100;
        switch(iDate) {
                case 0:
                                itoa(mm,temp,10);
                                lstrcpy(string,temp);
                                lstrcat(string,sDate);
                                itoa(dd,temp,10);
                                lstrcat(string,temp);
                                lstrcat(string,sDate);
                                itoa(yy,temp,10);
                                lstrcat(string,temp);
                                break;
                case 1:
                                itoa(dd,temp,10);
                                lstrcpy(string,temp);
                                lstrcat(string,sDate);
                                itoa(mm,temp,10);
                                lstrcat(string,temp);
                                lstrcat(string,sDate);
                                itoa(yy,temp,10);
                                lstrcat(string,temp);
                                break;
                case 2:
                                itoa(yy,temp,10);
                                lstrcpy(string,temp);
                                lstrcat(string,sDate);
                                itoa(mm,temp,10);
                                lstrcat(string,temp);
                                lstrcat(string,sDate);
                                itoa(dd,temp,10);
                                lstrcat(string,temp);
                                break;
                }
}
```

The **caldat** function comes from *Numerical Recipes in C*, by Press et al., Cambridge University Press, as does its inverse, **julday**. The value **IGREG** represents October 15, 1582, the day the Gregorian calendar was adopted. For more information on these functions, I refer you to the source.

```
#define IGREG 2299161
void caldat(long julian,int *mm,int *id,int *iyyy)
{
        long ja,jalpha,jb,jc,jd,je;
```

```
        if (julian >= IGREG) {
             jalpha=((float) (julian-1867216)-0.25)/36524.25;
             ja=julian+1+jalpha-(long) (0.25*jalpha);
             }
        else
             ja=julian;
        jb=ja+1524;
        jc=6680.0+((float) (jb-2439870)-122.1)/365.25;
        jd=365*jc+(0.25*jc);
        je=(jb-jd)/30.6001;
        *id=jb-jd-(int) (30.6001*je);
        *mm=je-1;
        if (*mm > 12) *mm -= 12;
        *iyyy=jc-4715;
        if (*mm > 2) —(*iyyy);
        if (*iyyy <= 0) —(*iyyy);
}
#undef IGREG
```

Of course, we also need to go the other way. Again we must look at the several possible international formats.

```
int string_to_date(char *string)
{
        int mm,dd,yy;
        long jul1,jul2;
        char temp[20],*p;

        if(lstrlen(string)==0)
                return(-1);
        lstrcpy(temp,string);
        p=strtok(temp,sDate);
        switch(iDate) {
                case 0:
                                mm=atoi(p);
                                p=strtok(NULL,sDate);
                                dd=atoi(p);
                                p=strtok(NULL,sDate);
                                yy=atoi(p);
                                break;
                case 1:
                                dd=atoi(p);
                                p=strtok(NULL,sDate);
                                mm=atoi(p);
                                p=strtok(NULL,sDate);
                                yy=atoi(p);
                                break;
                case 2:
                                yy=atoi(p);
                                p=strtok(NULL,sDate);
```

```
                              mm=atoi(p);
                              p=strtok(NULL,sDate);
                              dd=atoi(p);
                              break;
        }
        if(yy<80)
                yy += 2000;
        else if(yy<1980)
                yy += 1900;
        jul1=julday(1,1,1980);
        jul2=julday(mm,dd,yy);
        return((int) (jul2-jul1));
}
#define IGREG (15+31L*(10+12L*1582))

long julday(int mm,int id,int iyyy)
{
                long jul;
                int ja,jy,jm;

                if (iyyy == 0) iyyy=1989;
                if (iyyy < 0) ++iyyy;
                if (mm > 2) {
                                jy=iyyy;
                                jm=mm+1;
                } else {
                                jy=iyyy-1;
                                jm=mm+13;
                }
                jul = (long) (floor(365.25*jy)+
                        floor(30.6001*jm)+id+1720995);
                if (id+31L*(mm+12L*iyyy) >= IGREG) {
                                ja=0.01*jy;
                                jul += 2-ja+(int) (0.25*ja);
                }
                return jul;
}
#undef IGREG
```

Given the functions above, you'll find it easy to have date fields in your dialog boxes. I leave a full-blown validation of the date as an exercise for the student. You'll find it a much simpler problem than the actual conversion. You'd combine the string-to-date conversion functions given above with **Get-DlgItemText** and **SetDlgItemText** and your date format and date range validation functions to produce **GetDlgItemDate** and **SetDlgItemDate**.

You might also be interested in time fields. This is a much simpler conversion problem than date fields, although you'll still have to deal with international format issues. You'll find **time_to_string** and **string_to_time** functions included with the functions above in fieldfns.c on the companion disks.

Float, Decimal, and Long Fields

The following functions, simple as they are, will make writing dialog box procedures for numeric fields a little easier. It's up to you to add field validation if you need it.

```
float GetDlgItemFloat(HWND hWnd, int ID)
{
        char szTemp[40];
        float fn;
        double dn;

        GetDlgItemText(hWnd, ID, (LPSTR)szTemp, sizeof(szTemp));
        dn=atof(szTemp);
        fn=dn;
        return(fn);
}

void SetDlgItemFloat(HWND hWndDlg, int iD, float ValueToDisplay)
{
        char szBuffer[40];

        sprintf(szBuffer, "%g", ValueToDisplay);
        SetDlgItemText( hWndDlg, iD, (LPSTR)szBuffer );
}

int GetDlgItemDec(HWND hWnd, int ID)
{
        float fp;
        int dd;

        fp=GetDlgItemFloat(hWnd,ID);
        dd=(int)(fp*10.0f);
        return(dd);
}

void SetDlgItemDec(HWND hWndDlg, int iD, int ValueToDisplay)
{
        char szBuffer[40];
        float fp;

        fp=(float)ValueToDisplay/10.0f;
        sprintf(szBuffer, "%g", fp);
        SetDlgItemText( hWndDlg, iD, (LPSTR)szBuffer );
}

long GetDlgItemLong(HWND hWnd, int ID)
{
        char szTemp[40];
        long ln;

        GetDlgItemText(hWnd, ID, (LPSTR)szTemp, sizeof(szTemp));
        ln=atol(szTemp);
        return(ln);
```

```
}

void SetDlgItemLong(HWND hWndDlg, int iD, long ValueToDisplay)
{
        char szBuffer[40];

        sprintf(szBuffer, "%ld", ValueToDisplay);
        SetDlgItemText( hWndDlg, iD, (LPSTR)szBuffer );
}
```

Note that the decimal field defined above is an integer with one implied decimal place. You might be interested in expanding this into a family of decimal fields with different numbers of implied decimal places.

Updating One Field from Others

Many times when designing a dialog box you have redundant fields. For instance, a rectangle has a height, width, and area. It would be perfectly reasonable to let the user fill in two of the three, and automatically calculate the third.

To do this in a timely manner we either need to subclass the fields and intercept all keystrokes, or simply intercept **EN_CHANGE** for each field. The code would look like the following, using the latter approach, assuming the **IDD_EDIT_WIDTH** and **IDD_EDIT_LENGTH** fields are decimal and the **IDD_EDIT_AREA** field is long.

```
case IDD_EDIT_WIDTH:
case IDD_EDIT_LENGTH:
    if(HIWORD(lParam)==EN_CHANGE
        && !Initializing) {
        temp1=GetDlgItemDec(hWndDlg,IDD_EDIT_WIDTH);
        temp2=GetDlgItemDec(hWndDlg,IDD_EDIT_LENGTH);
        ltemp=(long)temp1 * (long)temp2 / 100L;
        SetDlgItemLong(hWndDlg,IDD_EDIT_AREA,ltemp);
        }
```

You may wonder why the test for **!Initializing** is necessary. In the course of initializing the dialog box, the various fields are set to their current values. Setting text into the edit controls generates the **EN_CHANGE** notification. So we inhibit the automatic updating in the course of initializing the dialog box:

```
case WM_INITDIALOG:
    Initializing=1;
    SetDlgItemDec(hWndDlg,IDD_EDIT_WIDTH,roomrec.room_width);
    SetDlgItemDec(hWndDlg,IDD_EDIT_LENGTH,roomrec.room_length);
    SetDlgItemLong(hWndDlg,IDD_EDIT_AREA,roomrec.room_area);
    Initializing=0;
    break;
```

Controlling Fonts in Edit Controls

You can have any one font and point size displayed in a normal edit control. By default, the edit control will use the system font, which is proportional. You may prefer to have a fixed-width font if your edit control contains material that should line up in columns. The following code (used in the context of **WM_INITDIALOG**) sets an array of edit controls numbered 10 to 49 to all use the system fixed font. The method is simply to send the font handle to each control using the **WM_SETFONT** message.

```
hFontEdit=GetStockObject(SYSTEM_FIXED_FONT);
for(i=10;i<50;i++)
 SendDlgItemMessage(hWndDlg,i,WM_SETFONT,hFontEdit,FALSE);
```

It is not necessary to destroy the font afterwards, since we are using a stock object. If we actually created a font to use the edit boxes, we'd need to free it before destroying the dialog box.

Making Clipboard Functions Work for Multiline Edit Controls

Multiline edit controls have a lot of functionality above and beyond what you get in single-line edit controls. It's fairly obvious what to do to make multiline edit controls do their thing as windows; all the relevant commands can be put on menus, and in fact are normally assigned to the Edit menu.

It is conceptually more difficult to deal with multiline edit controls in dialog boxes, since dialog boxes, especially modal dialog boxes, don't normally have menus. But they can have push buttons—and you can subclass the edit control to recognize control-key combinations.

To get an edit control to copy the current selection, send it a **WM_COPY** message. To get it to cut the current selection, send it a **WM_CUT** message. To tell it to paste from the clipboard, send it a **WM_PASTE** message; to have it undo its last action, send it a **WM_UNDO** message. The code below relies on having buttons in the dialog box with identification numbers **EDIT_MENU_COPY**, **EDIT_MENU_CUT**, **EDIT_MENU_PASTE**, and **EDIT_MENU_UNDO**. It further relies on these numbers being set the same as the equivalent window messages.

```
#define EDIT_MENU_COPY    WM_COPY              //make button id's same as
#define EDIT_MENU_PASTE   WM_PASTE  //  message to send
#define EDIT_MENU_UNDO    WM_UNDO
#define EDIT_MENU_CUT     WM_CUT
...
DemonstrationDialogProc(
...
     case EDIT_MENU_UNDO:
     case EDIT_MENU_CUT:
```

```
case EDIT_MENU_PASTE:
case EDIT_MENU_COPY:
    hwndMEC = GetDlgItem(hDlg, IDD_ML_EDIT_CONTROL);
    if ((wParam == EDIT_MENU_CUT)
    || (wParam == EDIT_MENU_COPY)) {
        lSelection = SendMessage(hwndMEC, EM_GETSEL, 0, 0L);
        if (LOWORD(lSelection) == HIWORD(lSelection)) {
            MessageBox (hDlg, "No selected text",
                    NULL, MB_ICONEXCLAMATION | MB_OK);
            break;
            }
        }
    SendMessage(hwndMEC, wParam, 0, 0L);
    SetFocus(hwndMEC);
    break;
```

If the four **#define** statements did not apply, then you would need extra code to translate from **wParam** to a suitable message value.

Note that you want to send **WM_COPY** and **WM_CUT** messages only when there is a valid selection. A nicer way to handle the condition of no valid selection than putting up an error message box would be to enable or disable the relevant Copy and Cut buttons as the selection changed. You can find out if there is a selection using the **EM_GETSEL** message. It might be enough to update the buttons every time your dialog procedure gets an **EN_CHANGE** from the edit control; you might do better by subclassing the **EM_SETSEL**, mouse, and arrow-key handling of the edit window.

You'd probably want to send **WM_PASTE** messages only when there is **cf-Text** posted on the clipboard. You could check this every time your main window procedure receives a **WM_DRAWCLIPBOARD** message, by using the **IsClipboardFormatAvailable** function. To get on the clipboard chain and receive **WM_DRAWCLIPBOARD** messages, use the **SetClipboardViewer** function. Gray the Paste button by disabling its window.

You should only send a **WM_UNDO** message when the edit control has something to undo. To find out whether or not there is something to undo, use the **EM_CANUNDO** message. It should be sufficient to check whether the edit control has something to undo on receiving an **EN_CHANGE** message; use the result of the **EM_CANUNDO** query to enable or disable the Undo button.

To change the way the edit control responds to editing keystrokes, subclass the edit control and intercept **WM_CHAR** messages. You'll find that Del and Backspace delete characters in pretty much any edit control. You can easily make Ctrl-Del delete the current word, Shift-Del cut the current selection, Ctrl-Ins copy the current selection, Shift-Ins paste, and Alt-Backspace undo the last change by including their cases under **WM_CHAR** in the subclassed edit window procedure. The action for Shift-Del, for instance, would be to discard the **WM_CHAR** message and send a **WM_CUT** message in its place.

There's lots more we can accomplish by subclassing edit controls. But we can't easily make the standard edit control display more than one font and pitch: it operates on pure text data. To edit rich text—that is, text with font, style, and size changes—we'll have to write our own window class.

8

In which we reimplement the multi-line edit control, adding the capability to deal with multiple fonts and multiple point sizes. Our final control can be used as the basis of a simple WYSIWYG word processor.

A Rich Text Edit Control

• •

Every time I use a Windows word processor—with WYSIWYG display of multiple fonts, multiple type sizes, bold, italic, and so on—I wish I could incorporate a modest subset of that capability into my own applications. The image-processing application we've been working on is no exception—I'd like to be able to add text to pictures.

Of course, we can always use another program. Windows Paintbrush, for instance, can read most BMP files written by Image2, and can add text to the pictures. Paintbrush can also paste DIBs copied from Image2, although there's a trick to getting the whole image on a big picture: in Paintbrush, zoom out and then paste twice. (I'm not sure if this is considered a bug or a feature.) The Windows 3.1 version of Paintbrush can also act as an OLE server.

Paintbrush can only deal with one font, pitch, and style at a time. You can put multiple fonts on an image, but only by placing each bit of text separately. It's no fun at all trying to create even a modest, uncomplicated piece of rich text with Paintbrush. Imagine trying to add a simple copyright notice to a picture, something like this:

Copyright © 1991, Martin E. Heller. *All rights reserved.*

There are are two problems trying to do this with Paintbrush. One is finding the copyright symbol—which is entered as Alt-0169 using the numeric keypad.

The other is getting the italic part lined up with the roman part. It sure would be nice if we could either paste rich text from a Windows word processor, or edit rich text ourselves.

Rich Text Format

The Rich Text Format (RTF) specification, currently documented in the Word for Windows Technical Reference (and included on the companion disks), was first published in the March 1987 issue of Microsoft Systems Journal. At that time, there was no standard way to transfer formatted text among Windows or Macintosh applications. IBM's DCA (Document Content Architecture) was available, but Microsoft felt that DCA lacked a good font strategy and was not efficient for transferring short strings.

Microsoft wanted a standard that could handle both entire documents and short formatted strings; Charles Simonyi, then Microsoft's chief architect of applications, came up with RTF, a 7-bit ASCII format with control words specified in the form:

```
\lettersequence<delimiter>
```

If the delimiter is a digit or a hyphen, another parameter follows. RTF uses braces to mark groups of text, such as footnotes, headers, and titles.

RTF has several hundred standard keywords, which specify everything from the document's character set, stylesheets and fonts through the section- and paragraph-level specifications, down to the format of individual characters. RTF, like Word documents, assumes that smaller pieces inherit the properties of larger pieces unless specific properties are overridden. There are small exceptions to the rule: footnotes, headers, footers, and annotations don't inherit the formatting of the preceding text.

The listing that follows illustrates RTF format. It represents the text of the previous few paragraphs. I've cleaned up the line breaks a bit for readability.

```
{\rtf1\ansi \deff0{\fonttbl{\f0\froman Tms Rmn;}{\f1\fdecor Symbol;}
{\f2\fswiss Helv;}{\f3\froman NEWS SERIF;}{\f4\fswiss SANS;}
{\f5\fmodern COURIER;}{\f6\froman ITC GARAMOND;}}
{\colortbl;\red0\green0\blue0;\red0\green0\blue255;
\red0\green255\blue255;\red0\green255\blue0;
\red255\green0\blue255;\red255\green0\blue0;\red255\green255\blue0;
\red255\green255\blue255;}
{\stylesheet{\s253\sb120 \b\f4 \sbasedon0\snext0 heading 2;}
{\s254\sb240 \b\f4\fs32 \sbasedon0\snext0 heading 1;}
{\f3\fs20 \snext0 Normal;}
{\s2\qj\fi260\sl260 \f6\fs21 \sbasedon0\snext2 Body;}
{\s3\qj\sb160\sl259 \f6\fs21 \sbasedon2\snext2 Body First;}}
{\info{\author Martin Heller}
{\creatim\yr1991\mo9\dy17\hr15\min37}{\version1}{\edmins1}
```

```
{\nofpages1}{\nofwords0}{\nofchars0}{\vern8368}}
\widowctrl\ftnbj \sectd \linex0\endnhere \pard\plain
\s254\sb240 \b\f4\fs32 Rich Text Format
\par \pard\plain \s3\qj\sb160\sl259 \f6\fs21 The Rich Text Format
(RTF) specification was first published in the March, 1987 issue of
Microsoft Systems Journal.
{\pard\plain \s3\qj\sb160\sl259 \v\f6\fs21 {\xe {\v Rich Text Format}}}
 At the time, there was no standard way to transfer formatted text
among Windows or Macintosh applications. IBM's DCA (Document Content
Architecture) was available, but Microsoft felt that DCA lacked a good
font strategy and was not efficient for transferring short strings.
\par \pard\plain \s2\qj\fi260\sl260 \f6\fs21
Microsoft wanted a standard that could handle both entire documents
and short formatted strings; Charles Simonyi, then Microsoft's chief
architect of applications,  came up with RTF, a 7-bit ASCII format
with control words specified in the form:
\par {\b\f5 \\lettersequence<delimiter>}
\par If the delimiter is a digit or a hyphen, another parameter fol-
lows. RTF uses braces to mark groups of text, such as footnotes,
headers, and titles.
\par RTF has several hundred standard keywords, which specify every-
thing from the document's character set, stylesheets and fonts
through the section- and paragraph-level specifications, down to the
format of individual characters. RTF, like Word documents, as
sumes that smaller pieces inherit the properties of larger pieces
unless specific properties are overridden. There are small exceptions
to the rule: footnotes, headers, footers, and annotations don't
inherit the formatting of the preceding text.
\par }
```

Aren't you just dying to implement a reader for RTF? Neither am I. Maybe if there was a library I could call to parse RTF into some sort of rational data structure, I'd use it. But for the purpose of annotating DIBs, RTF is far too complicated to consider implementing in full. Instead, let's consider a simpler format.

Data Structures to Represent Rich Text

What are the essential things we need to know to implement our own, simplified rich text display? First, let's list our goals, remembering that we basically want to add captions and credits to pictures.

- Specify and display font and point size of characters
- Specify and display superscript and subscript characters
- Specify and display bold, italic, and underlined characters
- Rotate text to any angle
- Display text in any foreground or background color
- Copy and paste text using clipboard
- Paste bitmap and DIB of text image to clipboard

Our goals are actually quite different from the goals of a word processor. We'll have to think through what it will take to implement each goal.

For an internal data structure, we'll need an array of (Token, Position) pairs. The tokens specify what to do—change font, change size, group text, and so on—and the positions specify where in the text string to apply the action of the tokens. For instance:

```
enum TOKEN {
      NULL_TOKEN = 0,
      SUPERSCRIPT,
      SUBSCRIPT,
      LEFT_BRACKET,
      RIGHT_BRACKET,
      BOLD,
      ITALIC,
      UNDERLINE,
      ANGLE,
      TEXT_COLOR,
      BACKGROUND_COLOR,
      FONT,
      SIZE,
      END_OF_TEXT
      };
struct Lex {
      enum TOKEN token;
      short position;
      };
#define vLexLen 60              //maximum tokens in a line of text
static struct Lex vLex[vLexLen];
```

Once we have the internal lexical-scanning data structures, we need to decide on an external representation. Rather than adopt the RTF standard—our implementation of which would be woefully incomplete—let's adapt an older standard, the "@" command used in Scribe, Scribble, FinalWord, and Sprint.

Command	Meaning	Example
@+	Superscript	E=mc@+{2} E=mc^2
@-	Subscript	M@-{12} M$_{12}$
{	Left Bracket	@c{Plain@b{Bold}}
}	Right Bracket	@s{10}@i{@b{Hello}}
@b or @B	Bold	@b{Bold} **Bold**
@i or @I	Italic	@i{Italic} *Italic*
@u or @U	Underline	@u{Under} Under
@a or @A	Angle	@a{90}
@tc, @TC, @tC, or @tC	Text Color(R,G,B)	@tc{0,0,255}
@bc, @BC, @bC, or @Bc	Background Color	@bc{0,127,0}
@f or @F	Font	@f{Courier} Courier
@s or @S	Size	@s{12} 12 Point

We'll allow only one- or two-letter mnemonics following the "@" sign, and we'll require curly braces to avoid losing the use of parentheses and square brackets in text. The mnemonics won't be sensitive to case. Unrecognized control strings will be printed as entered.

We'll need three functions to implement this scheme: **ParseText**, **Get-ParsedTextExtent**, and **ParsedTextOut**. The first will be a simple lexical scanning routine, consisting mostly of nested **switch** statements. The second will duplicate the functionality of **GetTextExtent** for parsed (rich) text. And the third will mirror **TextOut** for parsed text.

"Logical Twips" Mode

To be able to specify a point size, we need to understand our mapping mode and how it relates to point size. Petzold describes a "logical twips" mode that is a variation on Windows' **MM_TWIPS** mapping mode; I have my own variation that turns out to display more quickly.

As you undoubtedly know, *twip* is a fabricated word describing a unit equal to 1/20 point, and a point is a standard printer's measure equal to about 1/72 inch. These measures apply to the size of the type on paper. We are going to apply them to the *logical* size of the type on the screen.

You'll recall that Windows has **LOGPIXELSX** and **LOGPIXELSY** indexes to the **GetDeviceCaps** API, each of which represents the number of horizontal and vertical pixels in a *logical inch*—the inch on some sort of ideal display. Real displays worth looking at usually display a logical inch larger than a physical inch; otherwise, you'd have trouble reading displayed type. Remember, the 96-dpi logical resolution of a VGA is pretty poor compared to the 300-dpi physical resolution of a typical laser printer. On my 16-inch monitor using an 800x600 pixel Super-VGA driver, Word for Windows' ruler is enlarged about 30 percent—that is, a ruler section displaying a nominal 100 points measures out at about 130 points using a type ruler pressed against the screen.

In **MM_TWIPS** mapping mode, each logical unit represents physical inches in device coordinates, and the coordinate system goes right and up. In **MM_TEXT** mapping mode, each logical unit represents one pixel, and the coordinate system goes right and down. Petzold's "logical twips" mapping mode has each logical unit representing *logical* inches, with a coordinate system that goes right and up. He sets the mode thus:

```
SetMapMode(hDC, MM_ANISOTROPIC);
SetWindowExt(hDC, 1440, 1440);
SetViewportExt(hDC,  GetDeviceCaps(hDC, LOGPIXELSX),
                     GetDeviceCaps(hDC, LOGPIXELSY));
```

This works fine, but drawing can be slow since the logical units are smaller than the physical screen units (pixels). All GDI functions that draw lines eventually generate individual points based on the logical units: many more points are generated in Petzold's "Logical Twips" mode than can be displayed on the screen.

To get around the speed problem while still displaying type at the expected size, I take the burden for calculating size translations away from Windows, and put it on my program: the logical size translation goes into a global variable, **float SizeFactor**, which I use to convert sizes given in points into the correct value for a logical font height:

```
SetMapMode(hDC, MM_ANISOTROPIC );
SetWindowOrg(hDC, 0, 0);
SetViewportOrg(hDC, 0, 0);
SizeFactor=GetDeviceCaps(hDC,LOGPIXELSY)/72.0f;    // logical points
SetWindowExt  (hDC, 32767, 32767);                 // max resolution
SetViewportExt(hDC, 32767, 32767);                 // same as above
...
logfont.lfHeight=Size*SizeFactor; //convert to logical pixels
logfont.lfWidth=0;
```

In practice, this turns out to be much quicker than using Petzold's trick, while accomplishing the same objective. The anisotropic mapping modes with window extents equal to viewport extents incur no noticeable mapping overhead—they are as fast as **MM_TEXT** mode.

The choice of 32767 for an extent size is appropriate for programs that need to maintain good integer range to do placement calculations. If you used a coordinate system of, say, 640x480 (the **MM_TEXT** coordinate system for VGA screens) to do calculations, you'd lose precision, and wind up with annoying 1- or 2-pixel variations in things that should line up exactly.

Any choice of extent that is the same for the window and the viewport will preserve the magical properties of our **SizeFactor** value. We could actually choose **GetDeviceCaps(hDC, HORZRES)** and **GetDeviceCaps(hDC, VERTRES)** for our horizontal and vertical extents, to get a mapping mode just like **MM_TEXT**. The fact is, we can even use the default **MM_TEXT** mode—any mode that doesn't enlarge or reduce the viewport relative to the window will work.

One additional note: If we set **logfont.lfWidth=0** and **logfont.lfHeight = Size*SizeFactor**, as above, we are actually asking for the *leading* to be **Size** points. If we really want the *type* to be **Size** points, we should ask for a negative height, e.g.:

```
logfont.lfHeight = -Size*SizeFactor.
```

Displaying Multiple Fonts in a Window

There is no more magic needed to get a font, beyond what I've already shown you. You use **CreateFont** or **CreateFontIndirect** to specify what you want, and then **SelectObject** to put it into the device context. The simplest form of this is:

```
SelectObject(hDC,CreateFontIndirect(&lf));
```

There remains the problem of restoring the previous font when we're done with the current font. Because we allow nested brackets, we have to allow for a stack of such actions.

```
HANDLE hArray[vLexLen];
...
<process a token>
    hArray[iFont++]=SelectObject(hDC,hDefaultFont);
    GetObject(hArray[iFont-1],sizeof(LOGFONT),&lf);
    <change current specification as desired>
    SelectObject(hDC,CreateFontIndirect(&lf));
...
<restore previous font after drawing text>
    if(iFont>0)
            DeleteObject(SelectObject(hDC,hArray[--iFont]));
...
```

Enumerating Fonts and Point Sizes

One of the new common dialogs in Windows 3.1 lets the user choose a font. Like all the common dialogs, **ChooseFont** is a function that your program calls with a structure that specifies initialization information for the dialog box; on return, the structure holds the information about the font the user chose. The calling sequence is:

```
BOOL ChooseFont(LPCHOOSEFONT lpcf);
```

where the **CHOOSEFONT** structure has the form:

```
typedef struct {     /* cf */
    DWORD      lStructSize;
    HWND       hwndOwner;
    HDC        hDC;
    LPLOGFONT  lpLogFont;
    int        iPointSize;
    DWORD      Flags;
    DWORD      rgbColors;
    DWORD      lCustData;
    FARPROC    lpfnHook;
    LPSTR      lpTemplateName;
    HANDLE     hInstance;
    LPSTR      lpszStyle;
    WORD       nFontType;
    int        nSizeMin;
    int        nSizeMax;
} CHOOSEFONT;
```

ChooseFont returns **TRUE** if the function is successful or **FALSE** if an error occurs.

The following code fragment (from the SDK documentation) initializes a **CHOOSEFONT** structure, then creates a font-selection dialog box:

```
HDC hdc;
LOGFONT lf;
CHOOSEFONT chf;

hdc = GetDC(hwnd);
chf.lStructSize = sizeof (CHOOSEFONT);
chf.hwndOwner = hwnd;
chf.hDC = hdc;
chf.lpLogFont = &lf;
chf.Flags = CF_SCREENFONTS | CF_EFFECTS;
chf.rgbColors = RGB(0, 255, 255);
chf.lCustData = 0L;
chf.lpfnHook = (FARPROC) NULL;
chf.lpTemplateName = (LPSTR) NULL;
chf.hInstance = (HANDLE) NULL;
chf.lpszStyle = (LPSTR) NULL;
chf.nFontType = SCREEN_FONTTYPE;
chf.nSizeMin = 0;
chf.nSizeMax = 0;
ChooseFont(&chf);
ReleaseDC(hwnd, hdc);
```

Prior to Windows 3.1, to choose a font you had to build a dialog box (or control bar) with list- or combo-boxes for the font name and point size. You'd use **EnumFonts** and a callback function to fill arrays for the list boxes, thus:

```
char FAR *FontList[MAXFONT];
BYTE CharSet[MAXFONT];
BYTE PitchAndFamily[MAXFONT];
short FontTypes[MAXFONT]
int FontIndex = 0;
int SizeList[MAXSIZE];
int SizeIndex = 0;
int CurrentFont = 0;
int CurrentSize = 0, Size=12;
FARPROC lpEnumFunc;

void GetFonts( HWND hWnd )
{
        HDC hDC;

        FontIndex = 0;
        SizeIndex = 0;
        hDC = GetPrinterDC();
        if (hDC == NULL)
                return;
        lpEnumFunc = MakeProcInstance(EnumFunc, hInstEnPlot);
        EnumFonts(hDC, (LPSTR) NULL, lpEnumFunc, (LPSTR) NULL);
```

```
              FreeProcInstance(lpEnumFunc);
              DeleteDC(hDC);
}

void SetDefaultSizes(void)
{
        int i;

        for(i=0;i<10;i++)
                SizeList[i]= 6 + i*2;
        SizeIndex=10;
}

void GetSizes( HWND hWnd, int CurrentFont )
{
        HDC hDC;

        SizeIndex = 0;
        hDC = GetPrinterDC();
        if (hDC == NULL)
                return;
        SetMapMode(hDC,MM_TWIPS);
        lpEnumFunc = MakeProcInstance(EnumFunc, hInstEnPlot);
        EnumFonts(hDC,FontList[CurrentFont],lpEnumFunc,(LPSTR) 1L);
        FreeProcInstance(lpEnumFunc);
        if(SizeIndex<=0)
                SetDefaultSizes();
        DeleteDC(hDC);
}


int _export FAR PASCAL EnumFunc( LPLOGFONT lpLogFont,
        LPTEXTMETRIC lpTextMetric, short FontType, LPSTR lpData )
{
switch (LOWORD(lpData)) {
  case 0:
      if (FontIndex >= MAXFONT)
       return (0);
      if(FontIndex>0 &&        //suppress duplicates
       lstrcmp(FontList[FontIndex-1],lpLogFont->lfFaceName)==0)
       return(FontIndex);
      lstrcpy(FontList[FontIndex],lpLogFont->lfFaceName);
      CharSet[FontIndex] = lpLogFont->lfCharSet;
      PitchAndFamily[FontIndex] = lpLogFont->lfPitchAndFamily;
      FontTypes[FontIndex] = FontType;
      return (++FontIndex);
  case 1:
      if (SizeIndex >= MAXSIZE)
       return (0);
      SizeList[SizeIndex] = lpLogFont->lfHeight / 20;
if(SizeIndex>0 && SizeList[SizeIndex]==SizeList[SizeIndex-1])
       return(SizeIndex);
      else
       return (++SizeIndex);
       }
}
```

As you can see, the common dialog is a lot less trouble. If you need to make your program backward-compatible with Windows 3.0, you can still use the common dialogs: you just have to ship **commdlg.dll** with your application. If your application has to run in real mode, you'll have to use **EnumFonts** instead.

Handling Superscripts and Subscripts

There are no built-in superscript or subscript font attributes in Windows: we need to roll our own. Basically, superscripts are smaller than body type and sit above the line; subscripts are smaller than body type and sit below the line.

The code shown below has been tuned to look pleasing on the page, although such things can be very much a matter of taste. The font height and width are each divided by 1.5. Superscripts are raised by a quarter of the current character height, and subscripts are lowered by half the current character height. Note that we handle only 90° rotation increments for superscripts and subscripts. As an exercise, you might want to figure out how to handle superscripts and subscripts at arbitrary angles.

```
Partial=Extent=GetTextExtent(hDC,lpString,vLex[0].position);
i=0;
while(vLex[i].token!=END_OF_TEXT) {
        j=vLex[i].position;
        switch(vLex[i].token) {
        case SUPERSCRIPT:
                if(hDefaultFont==NULL)
                        break;
                hArray[iFont++]=SelectObject(hDC,hDefaultFont);
                GetObject(hArray[iFont-1],sizeof(LOGFONT),&lf);
                lf.lfHeight /= 1.5;
                lf.lfWidth /= 1.5;
                SelectObject(hDC,CreateFontIndirect(&lf));
                extra = -1;
                switch(nOrientationToSet) {
                case 0:
                        Y += extra*(HIWORD(Partial)/4);
                        break;
                case 900:
                        X += extra*(LOWORD(Partial)/4);
                        break;
                case 1800:
                        Y -= extra*(HIWORD(Partial)/4);
                        break;
                case 2700:
                        X -= extra*(LOWORD(Partial)/4);
                        break;
                        }
                j += 3;
                k=0;
                i++;
                ExArray[iExtra++]=extra;
```

```
                        break;
            case SUBSCRIPT:
                    if(hDefaultFont==NULL)
                            break;
                    hArray[iFont++]=SelectObject(hDC,hDefaultFont);
                    GetObject(hArray[iFont-1],sizeof(LOGFONT),&lf);
                    lf.lfHeight /= 1.5;
                    lf.lfWidth /= 1.5;
                    SelectObject(hDC,CreateFontIndirect(&lf));
                    extra = 2;
                    switch(nOrientationToSet) {
                    case 0:
                            Y += extra*(HIWORD(Partial)/4);
                            break;
                    case 900:
                            X += extra*(LOWORD(Partial)/4);
                            break;
                    case 1800:
                            Y -= extra*(HIWORD(Partial)/4);
                            break;
                    case 2700:
                            X -= extra*(LOWORD(Partial)/4);
                            break;
                            }
                    j += 3;
                    k=0;
                    i++;
                    ExArray[iExtra++]=extra;
                    break;
```

Handling Bold, Italic, and Underlined Text

There *are* attributes in Windows to handle bold, italic, and underlined text. They can be set in the logical font structure for a **CreateFontIndirect** call, or in parameters for a **CreateFont** call.

By the way, **CreateFont** is something of a misnomer. What the call actually does is to cause Windows to *select* the font that best matches your specifications from the pool of available fonts.

The **nWeight** parameter to **CreateFont** and the **lfWeight** field in the **LOGFONT** structure passed to **CreateFontIndirect** should be set to 400 for a normal font, and 700 for a bold font. You can use the predefined mnemonics **FW_NORMAL** and **FW_BOLD** if you wish.

The **cItalic** parameter and **lfItalic** field specify an italic font if set nonzero, and a roman font if set to zero. Similarly, the **cUnderline** parameter and **lfUnderline** field specify an underlined font if set nonzero, and a plain font if set to zero. The **LOGFONT** structure also contains an **lfStrikeout** field; we aren't supporting it here, but you could easily add it if you wanted to display struck-out text.

Note that there is no **LOGFONT** field to control whether white space is underlined. If you want word underlining, print spaces and tabs without underlining; if you want continuous underlining, print all characters underlined.

Rotating Text

You can display rotated text, in some circumstances, by setting the font's orientation and escapement attributes when you specify the font for **CreateFont** or **CreateFontIndirect**. The **lfOrientation** field or **nOrientation** parameter controls the angle of each character's baseline relative to the horizontal; it is specified in tenths of a degree, counterclockwise from the x-axis. The **lf-Escapement** field or **nEscapement** parameter controls the angle of the escapement vector, which is drawn between the origins of the first and last character in a line. Like **lfOrientation**, **lfEscapement** is specified in tenths of a degree, counterclockwise from the x-axis.

Not every font can be rotated on every device. One thing you can do is to check the device's text capabilities with **GetDeviceCaps(hDC, TEXTCAPS)**. The value returned is bit-encoded. Bit 3, if set, indicates that the device can do 90-degree character rotation. Bit 4, if set, says that the device can do any character rotation. The mnemonic for bit 3 is **TC_CR_90** and for bit 4 is **TC_CR_ANY**.

Vector fonts can be rotated on any device, no matter what the device capabilities. What happens inside GDI when you go to print a vector character is that the printer driver bounces the call back to the screen driver; the screen driver converts the vector character to a series of line segments. Note that vector fonts don't look as good as outline or bitmapped fonts—they're really for pen plotters. The Windows vector fonts—Roman, Modern, and Script—were derived from A.V. Hershey's plotter fonts, produced more than 30 years ago at the U.S. National Bureau of Standards.

Normally, the screen device context reports no character rotation capabilities. Adobe Type Manager (ATM) changes that: when ATM is installed and active, both the **TC_CR_90** and **TC_CR_ANY** bits will be set. If you rely totally on device capabilities, you might be fooled: ATM can only rotate PostScript outline fonts. If you have ATM active but select a bitmapped font, it will not rotate correctly.

Windows 3.1 includes TrueType, and several TrueType fonts. These can also be rotated. You can tell if TrueType is available and active using the Windows 3.1 **GetRasterizerCaps** function. Don't try calling **GetRasterizerCaps** in Windows versions below 3.1.

If TrueType is active, you might want to use the Windows 3.1 function **EnumFontFamilies** rather than **EnumFonts** to find out what fonts are present on the system. The new **EnumFontFamilies** function retrieves style names associated with a TrueType font and returns extra information on the font type in the **nFontType** parameter to its callback routine. **nFontType** has three bit-encoded fields: **DEVICE_FONTTYPE**, **RASTER_FONTTYPE**, and **SCALABLE-_FONTTYPE**. Of these, only the **SCALABLE_FONTTYPE** field is new in Windows 3.1; the other two fields are reported by **EnumFonts**.

The **DEVICE_FONTTYPE** field is 1 for a device-based font, and 0 for a GDI-based font. TrueType fonts have **SCALABLE_FONTTYPE** 1 and **RASTER-_FONTTYPE** 0; bitmapped fonts have **SCALABLE_FONTTYPE** 0 and **RASTER-_FONTTYPE** 1; and vector fonts have both fields 0.

You can identify ATM fonts in the same way, but you don't need, and can't depend on the **SCALABLE_FONTTYPE** field. Using either **EnumFonts** or **Enum-FontFamilies**, ATM fonts will show up as vector device fonts: that is, they'll have **RASTER_FONTTYPE** 0 and **DEVICE_FONTTYPE** 1.

To summarize, we can rotate vector GDI fonts on any device, and device fonts on any device that has **TC_CR_90** and/or **TC_CR_ANY** set in its text device capacities. ATM fonts fall under both rules. We can also rotate TrueType fonts if they are available and active and enabled for the device. If TrueType fonts are not enabled for the device, we won't see them when we enumerate fonts. We cannot rotate raster GDI fonts on any device.

Scrolling Efficiently

The problem of scrolling text efficiently with known line breaks is relatively simple, but it still confuses beginning Windows programmers. The problem of scrolling rich text efficiently is more difficult, and still confuses developers of widely sold word processing programs.

Petzold covers the simplest case in Chapter 2 of *Programming Windows*. In his SYSMETS3 example he lays out the logic needed to use the **ScrollWindow** and **UpdateWindow** to scroll already-displayed text, as well as the logic needed to minimize the number of **TextOut** calls made in response to a **WM_PAINT** message.

You may find that a line-by-line **ScrollWindow** / **UpdateWindow** / **Text-Out** sequence is still too slow for your own purposes. For instance, a terminal emulator that needs to keep up with a 38,400 bps connection would have a hard time using that strategy. The coarser your scrolling, the faster it will go: if you have three lines of text in your buffer to display, try scrolling the window up three lines at once instead of one line at a time. You'll scroll fastest by not scrolling at all: jump up a full window at a time.

There are numerous complications introduced by allowing multiple fonts and sizes. You might have to adjust the vertical size of each line to allow for the maximum font size per line as well as superscripts and subscripts. You may have to word-wrap text to make it fit in the space available. You might even have to allow for angled text. Can you think of a way to scroll text that goes at different angles that is more efficient than repainting the Window?

Your best friends for word-wrapping are **GetTextExtent**, **GetTabbed-TextExtent**, and **GetTextExtentEx**. Your best friend for justification is **SetTextJustification**. Note that you'll need to use these functions for each run of a single font at a single size.

We won't need to implement scrolling for our rich-text edit control right away: the first step will be to make it work as a single-line control. A parsed-text multiline edit control is something you can take on as a project if you like: let me know if you come up with something that's better than Windows Write.

Handling Large Files

We discussed how to implement multiple local heaps in Chapter 1. If you try to write an edit control (whether or not it supports rich text of any sort) that handles arbitrary files you'll run into the 64KB limit on a single local heap, or the 8192 selector limit on the global heap, and pretty much have to resort to global heap suballocation of one sort or another. You'll find multiple local heaps nearly as efficient as any suballocation scheme, save perhaps the suballocation method used in **smalloc** on the companion disks.

There are a number of ways you could structure memory to work efficiently in an edit control for large files. You can allocate space for each line of text—this strategy works best for a line-oriented editor, such as a programmer's editor. Or you can allocate for each paragraph—which would make sense for a word processor. You could even allocate space for the whole document in one huge lump, but you'd find out soon that huge pointers are deadly slow compared to near pointers.

You can keep your line or paragraph pointers in an array, or in a linked list. The array is simpler and faster, but will impose some size limits. The linked list is more complicated and slower, but will handle any number of pointers. If you do implement a linked list, consider adding auxiliary data structures for bookmarks, previous positions, and section boundaries: this will speed up movement in the document. You might even want to think about making line-jumps and word-searches efficient by building B-tree, ISAM or hashed data structures.

Parsed Text Display

Our parsed text display functions follow. Note that they require **SizeFactor**, **hDefaultFont**, and **hPrimaryFont** to be set before any of the functions are called. Also note that **ParseText** has to be called for each string before either **GetParsedTextExtent** or **ParsedTextOut** is called for that string.

```
#include <windows.h>
#include <string.h>
#include <stdlib.h>
#include <math.h>
#include "debugfns.h"
#include <assert.h>
extern int xChar, yChar, xChar0, yChar0;
extern HANDLE hDefaultFont;
extern HFONT hPrimaryFont;
extern LOGFONT logfont;
extern float SizeFactor;
enum TOKEN {
      NULL_TOKEN = 0,
      SUPERSCRIPT,
      SUBSCRIPT,
      LEFT_BRACKET,
      RIGHT_BRACKET,
      BOLD,
      ITALIC,
      UNDERLINE,
      ANGLE,
      TEXT_COLOR,
      BACKGROUND_COLOR,
      FONT,
      SIZE,
      END_OF_TEXT
      };
struct Lex {
      enum TOKEN token;
      short position;
      };
#define vLexLen 60              //maximum tokens in a line of text
static struct Lex vLex[vLexLen];

lstrpbrk(LPSTR lpString, LPSTR lpChars) {
      register int i, j;

      for (i = 0;  lpString[i] != NULL;  i++)
            for (j = 0;  lpChars[j] != NULL;  j++)
                  if (lpString[i] == lpChars[j])
                        return (i);
      return (-1);
 }


/************************************************
Command                         Meaning
@+                              Superscript
@-                              Subscript
{                               Left Bracket
}                               Right Bracket
@b or @B                        Bold
```

```
@bc, @BC, @bC, or @Bc       Background Color
@i or @I                    Italic
@u or @U                    Underline
@a or @A                    Angle
@tc, @TC, @tC, or @tC       Text Color(R,G,B)
@f or @F                    Font     @f{Courier}
@s or @S                    Size     @s{12}
************************************************/

short ParseText(LPSTR lpString, short nMaxCount){
      short nCount, i, j, next = 0, nest = 0;
      static char set1[] = "@", set2[] = "@}";
      char *pC;

      // init structures
      for (i = 0;   i < vLexLen;   i++)
            vLex[i].token = vLex[i].position = 0;
      nCount = min(lstrlen(lpString), nMaxCount);

      // scan string for special characters
      if ((i = lstrpbrk(lpString, "@")) == -1)
            goto alldone;

      // something found — do lexical scan
lex:
      switch (lpString[i]) {
  case '@':
      switch (lpString[i + 1]) {
        case '+':                           //SUPERSCRIPT
            vLex[next].token = SUPERSCRIPT;
            vLex[next++].position = i++;
            break;
        case '-':                           //SUBSCRIPT
            vLex[next].token = SUBSCRIPT;
            vLex[next++].position = i++;
            break;
        case 'f':
        case 'F':                           //FONT
            vLex[next].token = FONT;
            vLex[next++].position = i++;
            break;
        case 's':
        case 'S':                           //SIZE
            vLex[next].token = SIZE;
            vLex[next++].position = i++;
            break;
        case 'B':
        case 'b':                           //BOLD
            if (lpString[i + 2] == '{') {
                  vLex[next].token = BOLD;
                  vLex[next++].position = i++;
                  }                         //BACKGROUND_COLOR
            else if (lpString[i + 2] == 'c'
```

```
                      || lpString[i + 2] == 'C') {
                    vLex[next].token = BACKGROUND_COLOR;
                    vLex[next++].position = i++;
                    i++;
                    }
            break;
        case 'I':
        case 'i':                          //ITALIC
            vLex[next].token = ITALIC;
            vLex[next++].position = i++;
            break;
        case 'U':
        case 'u':                          //UNDERLINE
            vLex[next].token = UNDERLINE;
            vLex[next++].position = i++;
            break;
        case 'A':
        case 'a':                          //ANGLE
            vLex[next].token = ANGLE;
            vLex[next++].position = i++;
            break;
        case 'T':
        case 't':                          //TEXT_COLOR
            if (lpString[i + 2] == 'c'
              || lpString[i + 2] == 'C') {
                    vLex[next].token = TEXT_COLOR;
                    vLex[next++].position = i++;
                    i++;
                    }
            break;
        default:
            goto get_next_token;
            }
        if (lpString[i + 1] == '{') {        //LEFT_BRACKET
            vLex[next].token = LEFT_BRACKET;
            vLex[next++].position = i++;
            nest++;
            }
        else {                              //token invalid
            —next;
            }
        break;

case '}':                                  //RIGHT_BRACKET
    vLex[next].token = RIGHT_BRACKET;
    vLex[next++].position = i;
    --nest;
    break;

default:
    goto get_next_token;
    }
```

```
get_next_token:
      pC = nest > 0 ? set2 : set1;
      if ((j = lstrpbrk(lpString + i + 1, pC)) != -1) {
            i = j + i + 1;
            goto lex;
            }
      vLex[next].token = END_OF_TEXT;
      vLex[next].position = nCount;

alldone:
      if (nest) {
      DebugToFile((PSTR) "ParseText> Warning: unmatched {} %d\n%s",
                  nest, lpString);
            MessageBeep(0);
            }
      return nCount;
      }

DWORD NEAR ParsedTextWork(HDC hDC,short X,short Y,
                  LPSTR lpString, short nCount, BOOL bOut) {
      BOOL bFlag;
      HANDLE hArray[vLexLen];
      short ExArray[vLexLen];
      short iFont = 0, i, j, k, extra, iExtra = 0;
      short nDevCaps=0,R,G,B;
      int nOrientationToSet=0;
      DWORD Extent, Partial;
      LOGFONT lf;
      static char delim[]="{,}";
      char pString[256],*pC;

      if (vLex[0].token) {  // any lexical tokens?
      // yes, do the ganze megillah
       lstrcpy(pString,lpString);
       if(bOut) {
        bFlag = TextOut(hDC, X, Y, lpString, vLex[0].position);
        SetTextColor(hDC,RGB(0,0,0));
        SetBkColor(hDC,RGB(255,255,255));
        }
       Partial = Extent = GetTextExtent(hDC, lpString,
            vLex[0].position);
       i = 0;
       while (vLex[i].token != END_OF_TEXT &&
             vLex[i].token != NULL_TOKEN) {
            j = vLex[i].position;
            switch (vLex[i].token) {
              case SUPERSCRIPT:
                    if (hDefaultFont == NULL)
                          break;
                    hArray[iFont++] = SelectObject(hDC,
                          hDefaultFont);
                    GetObject(hArray[iFont - 1],
                    sizeof(LOGFONT),(LPSTR)&lf);
```

```
            lf.lfHeight /= 1.5;
            lf.lfWidth /= 1.5;
            SelectObject(hDC, CreateFontIndirect(&lf));
            extra = -1;
            switch (nOrientationToSet) {
              case 0:
                    Y += extra * (HIWORD(Partial) / 4);
                    break;
              case 900:
                    X += extra * (LOWORD(Partial) / 4);
                    break;
              case 1800:
                    Y -= extra * (HIWORD(Partial) / 4);
                    break;
              case 2700:
                    X -= extra * (LOWORD(Partial) / 4);
                    break;
                    }
        j += 3;
        i++;
        ExArray[iExtra++] = extra;
        break;
    case SUBSCRIPT:
        if (hDefaultFont == NULL)
                break;
        hArray[iFont++] = SelectObject(hDC,
                hDefaultFont);
        GetObject(hArray[iFont - 1], sizeof(LOGFONT),
                (LPSTR)&lf);
        lf.lfHeight /= 1.5;
        lf.lfWidth /= 1.5;
        SelectObject(hDC, CreateFontIndirect(&lf));
        extra = 2;
        switch (nOrientationToSet) {
          case 0:
                Y += extra * (HIWORD(Partial) / 4);
                break;
          case 900:
                X += extra * (LOWORD(Partial) / 4);
                break;
          case 1800:
                Y -= extra * (HIWORD(Partial) / 4);
                break;
          case 2700:
                X -= extra * (LOWORD(Partial) / 4);
                break;
                }
        j += 3;
        i++;
        ExArray[iExtra++] = extra;
        break;
    case BOLD:
        if (hDefaultFont == NULL)
```

```
                    break;
            hArray[iFont++] = SelectObject(hDC,
                    hDefaultFont);
            GetObject(hArray[iFont - 1], sizeof(LOGFONT),
                    (LPSTR)&lf);
            lf.lfWeight = 700;
            SelectObject(hDC, CreateFontIndirect(&lf));
            extra = 0;
            j += 3;
            i++;
            ExArray[iExtra++] = extra;
            break;
    case FONT:
            if (hDefaultFont == NULL)
                    break;
            hArray[iFont++] = SelectObject(hDC,
                    hDefaultFont);
            GetObject(hArray[iFont - 1], sizeof(LOGFONT),
                    (LPSTR)&lf);
            j = vLex[++i].position + 2;  //left bracket
            k = vLex[++i].position - j;  //right bracket
            assert(k>0);
            strncpy(lf.lfFaceName, pString + j, k);
            lf.lfFaceName[k] = '\0';
            SelectObject(hDC, CreateFontIndirect(&lf));
            j = vLex[i].position + 1;
            extra = 0;
            ExArray[iExtra++] = extra;
            break;
    case SIZE:
            if (hDefaultFont == NULL)
                    break;
            hArray[iFont++] = SelectObject(hDC,
                    hDefaultFont);
            GetObject(hArray[iFont - 1], sizeof(LOGFONT),
                    (LPSTR)&lf);
            j = vLex[++i].position + 2;  //left bracket
            k = vLex[++i].position - j;  //right bracket
            assert(k>0);
            lf.lfHeight = (int)(atoi(pString + j) *
                    SizeFactor);
            SelectObject(hDC, CreateFontIndirect(&lf));
            j = vLex[i].position + 1;
            extra = 0;
            ExArray[iExtra++] = extra;
            break;
    case LEFT_BRACKET:
            DebugToFile((PSTR) "ParsedTextWork Error: "
                    "LEFT_BRACKET not eaten");
            j++;
            i++;
            break;
    case RIGHT_BRACKET:
```

```
                extra = ExArray[-iExtra];
                if (iFont > 0)
                        DeleteObject(SelectObject(hDC,
                                hArray[-iFont]));
                Partial = GetTextExtent(hDC, "]", 1);
                switch (nOrientationToSet) {
                  case 0:
                        Y -= extra * (HIWORD(Partial) / 4);
                        break;
                  case 900:
                        X -= extra * (LOWORD(Partial) / 4);
                        break;
                  case 1800:
                        Y += extra * (HIWORD(Partial) / 4);
                        break;
                  case 2700:
                        X += extra * (LOWORD(Partial) / 4);
                        break;
                        }
                j++;
                break;
        case ITALIC:
                if (hDefaultFont == NULL)
                        break;
                hArray[iFont++] = SelectObject(hDC,
                        hDefaultFont);
                GetObject(hArray[iFont - 1], sizeof(LOGFONT),
                        (LPSTR)&lf);
                lf.lfItalic = 1;
                SelectObject(hDC, CreateFontIndirect(&lf));
                extra = 0;
                j += 3;
                i++;
                ExArray[iExtra++] = extra;
                break;
        case UNDERLINE:
                if (hDefaultFont == NULL)
                        break;
                hArray[iFont++] = SelectObject(hDC,
                        hDefaultFont);
                GetObject(hArray[iFont - 1], sizeof(LOGFONT),
                        (LPSTR)&lf);
                lf.lfUnderline = 1;
                SelectObject(hDC, CreateFontIndirect(&lf));
                extra = 0;
                j += 3;
                i++;
                ExArray[iExtra++] = extra;
                break;
        case ANGLE:
                if (hDefaultFont == NULL)
                        break;
                nDevCaps=GetDeviceCaps(hDC,TEXTCAPS); //future
```

```
                hArray[iFont++] = SelectObject(hDC,
                        hDefaultFont);
                GetObject(hArray[iFont - 1], sizeof(LOGFONT),
                        (LPSTR)&lf);
//should check font type to see if it can be rotated
// ...future... see discussion in text
                j = vLex[++i].position + 2;  //left bracket
                k = vLex[++i].position - j;  //right bracket
                assert(k>0);
                nOrientationToSet = atoi(pString + j) * 10;
                lf.lfOrientation = lf.lfEscapement =
                        nOrientationToSet;
                SelectObject(hDC, CreateFontIndirect(&lf));
                j = vLex[i].position + 1;
//Ideally we should make sure that a rotated font was
//actually obtained ...future... see discussion in text
                extra = 0;
                ExArray[iExtra++] = extra;
                break;
        case TEXT_COLOR:
                j = vLex[++i].position + 2;  //left bracket
                k = vLex[++i].position ;     //right bracket
                assert(k>j);
                R = G = B = 0;
                *(pString+k)='\0';
                pC = strtok(pString + j, delim);
                if(pC)
                        R = atoi(pC);
                pC = strtok(NULL, delim);
                if(pC)
                        G = atoi(pC);
                pC = strtok(NULL, delim);
                if(pC)
                        B = atoi(pC);
                j = vLex[i].position + 1;
                if(bOut)
                        SetTextColor (hDC,RGB(R,G,B));
                break;
        case BACKGROUND_COLOR:
                j = vLex[++i].position + 2; //left bracket
                k = vLex[++i].position ;     //right bracket
                assert(k>j);
                R = G = B = 255;
                *(pString+k)='\0';
                pC = strtok(pString + j, delim);
                if(pC)
                        R = atoi(pC);
                pC = strtok(NULL, delim);
                if(pC)
                        G = atoi(pC);
                pC = strtok(NULL, delim);
                if(pC)
                        B = atoi(pC);
```

```
                 j = vLex[i].position + 1;
                 if(bOut)
                         SetBkColor (hDC,RGB(R,G,B));
                 break;
           default:
                 j++;
                 DebugToFile((PSTR)"ParsedTextWork> Warning:"
                         " unknown token %d %c",
                         vLex[i].token, lpString+j);
                 break;
                 }
  k = vLex[++i].position - j;
  if(k>0) {
   switch(nOrientationToSet) {
   case 0:
    if(bOut)
         bFlag=TextOut(hDC,X+LOWORD(Extent),
                          Y,lpString+j,k);
     Partial=GetTextExtent(hDC,lpString+j,k);
     Extent=MAKELONG(LOWORD(Extent)+LOWORD(Partial),
         HIWORD(Extent));
     break;
    case 900:
     if(bOut)
         bFlag=TextOut(hDC,X,Y-HIWORD(Extent),
                          lpString+j,k);
     Partial=GetTextExtent(hDC,lpString+j,k);
     Extent=MAKELONG(LOWORD(Extent),
         HIWORD(Extent)+HIWORD(Partial));
     break;
    case 1800:
     if(bOut)
         bFlag=TextOut(hDC,X-LOWORD(Extent),
                          Y,lpString+j,k);
     Partial=GetTextExtent(hDC,lpString+j,k);
     Extent=MAKELONG(LOWORD(Extent)+LOWORD(Partial),
                 HIWORD(Extent));
     break;
    case 2700:
     if(bOut)
         bFlag=TextOut(hDC,X,Y+HIWORD(Extent),
                          lpString+j,k);
     Partial=GetTextExtent(hDC,lpString+j,k);
     Extent=MAKELONG(LOWORD(Extent),
                 HIWORD(Extent)+HIWORD(Partial));
     break;
   default:
     if(bOut)
         bFlag=TextOut(hDC,X+LOWORD(Extent),
                 Y+HIWORD(Extent),lpString+j,k);
     Partial = GetTextExtent(hDC, lpString + j, k);
     Extent = MAKELONG(LOWORD(Extent)+LOWORD(Partial),
                 HIWORD(Extent)+HIWORD(Partial));
```

```
                  break;
                } //switch (nOrientation)
              } //if k>0
            } //while token to process
          } //if any tokens in string
      else if(bOut)
        bFlag = TextOut(hDC, X, Y, lpString, nCount);
      else
        Extent = GetTextExtent(hDC, lpString, nCount);

      while (iFont > 0)
        DeleteObject(SelectObject(hDC, hArray[-iFont]));

      if(bOut)
        return (DWORD)bFlag;
      else
        return Extent;
}

DWORD GetParsedTextExtent(HDC hDC, LPSTR lpString, short nCount) {
      return ParsedTextWork(hDC,0,0,lpString,nCount,FALSE);
}

BOOL ParsedTextOut(HDC hDC, short X, short Y, LPSTR lpString,
                      short nCount) {
      return (BOOL)ParsedTextWork(hDC,X,Y,lpString,nCount,TRUE);
}
```

I've built a little test program, **testpar1,** that lets you enter a text string and interprets it using the parsed text functions. The interface is minimal: it brings up a dialog box for the text string in response to a menu item. The text parsing and display happens in the program's paint procedure, and pressing OK in the dialog box generates an **InvalidateRect** call. For coding speed, I generated the program's outline with QuickCase:W, then added the extra code and debugged using QuickC for Windows.

```
/* QuickCase:W KNB Version 1.00 */
#include "TESTPAR1.h"
#include "parsed.h"
#include "debugfns.h"

float SizeFactor;
float Size;
char szText[80]="";
LOGFONT logfont;
HFONT hPrimaryFont,hDefaultFont;
TEXTMETRIC tm;
int xChar,xChar0,yChar,yChar0;
char szFaceName[80]="";

int PASCAL WinMain(HANDLE hInstance, HANDLE hPrevInstance, LPSTR
```

```
lpszCmdLine, int nCmdShow)
{
 MSG   msg;    /* MSG structure to store your messages          */
 int   nRc;    /* return value from Register Classes            */

 strcpy(szAppName, "TESTPAR1");
 hInst = hInstance;
 if(!hPrevInstance)
   {
/* register window classes if first instance of application */
   if ((nRc = nCwRegisterClasses()) == -1)
      {
/* registering one of the windows failed            */
      LoadString(hInst, IDS_ERR_REGISTER_CLASS,
            szString,sizeof(szString));
      MessageBox(NULL, szString, NULL, MB_ICONEXCLAMATION);
      return nRc;
      }
   }

 /* create application's Main window                    */
 hWndMain = CreateWindow(
            szAppName,            /* Window class name   */
            "Parsed Text Test",/* Window's title        */
            WS_CAPTION          /* Title and Min/Max     */
            WS_SYSMENU          /* Add system menu box */
            WS_MINIMIZEBOX  |   /* Add minimize box      */
            WS_MAXIMIZEBOX  |   /* Add maximize box      */
            WS_THICKFRAME   |   /* thick sizeable frame*/
            WS_CLIPCHILDREN |
                        /* don't draw in child windows areas */
            WS_OVERLAPPED,
            CW_USEDEFAULT, 0,  /* Use default X, Y     */
            CW_USEDEFAULT, 0,  /* Use default X, Y     *
            NULL,          /* Parent window's handle   */
            NULL,          /* Default to Class Menu */
            hInst, /* Instance of window */
            NULL);  /* Create struct for WM_CREATE */

 if(hWndMain == NULL)
      {
      LoadString(hInst, IDS_ERR_CREATE_WINDOW, szString,
            sizeof(szString));
      MessageBox(NULL, szString, NULL, MB_ICONEXCLAMATION);
      return IDS_ERR_CREATE_WINDOW;
      }
 ShowWindow(hWndMain, nCmdShow);    /* display main window      */
 while(GetMessage(&msg, NULL, 0, 0))  /* Until WM_QUIT message  */
      {
      TranslateMessage(&msg);
      DispatchMessage(&msg);
      }
```

```
 /* Do clean up before exiting from the application          */
 CwUnRegisterClasses();
 return msg.wParam;
} /*    End of WinMain                            */

LONG FAR PASCAL WndProc(HWND hWnd, WORD Message, WORD wParam,
      LONG lParam)
{
 HMENU hMenu=0;          /* handle for the menu   */
 HBITMAP hBitmap=0;      /* handle for bitmaps    */
 HDC hDC;                /* handle for the display device */
 PAINTSTRUCT ps;         /* holds PAINT information   */
 int nRc=0;              /* return code  */
 int ilen;
 DWORD Extent;

 switch (Message)
  {
 case WM_COMMAND:
/* The Windows messages for action bar and pulldown menu items */
/* are processed here.                                    */
  switch (wParam)
  {
     case IDM_G_TEST:
 /* Place User Code to respond to the                      */
 /* Menu Item Named "&Test..." here.                       */
     {
     FARPROC lpfnENTERMsgProc;

     lpfnENTERMsgProc = MakeProcInstance((FARPROC)ENTERMsgProc,
           hInst);
     nRc = DialogBox(hInst, (LPSTR)(DWORD)toparse, hWnd,
           lpfnENTERMsgProc);
     FreeProcInstance(lpfnENTERMsgProc);
     }
     if(nRc)
           InvalidateRect(hWnd,NULL,TRUE);
     break;

     default:
      return DefWindowProc(hWnd, Message, wParam, lParam);
  }
  break;                  /* End of WM_COMMAND              */

 case WM_CREATE:
     break;             /*  End of WM_CREATE         */
 case WM_MOVE:          /*  code for moving the window      */
     break;
 case WM_SIZE:          /*  code for sizing client area */
     break;             /* End of WM_SIZE                   */
 case WM_PAINT:         /* code for the window's client area  */
/* Obtain a handle to the device context */
/* BeginPaint will send WM_ERASEBKGND if appropriate */
```

```
        memset(&ps, 0x00, sizeof(PAINTSTRUCT));
        hDC = BeginPaint(hWnd, &ps);
//——   Code for displaying szText as parsed text ——
        ilen=lstrlen(szText);
        if(ilen>0) {
         SetBkMode(hDC, OPAQUE);
//#define ANI
#ifdef ANI
        SetMapMode(hDC, MM_ANISOTROPIC );
        SetWindowOrg(hDC, 0, 0);
        SetViewportOrg(hDC, 0, 0);
        SetWindowExt  (hDC, 32767, 32767); // max resolution
        SetViewportExt(hDC, 32767, 32767); // same as above
#endif
        SizeFactor=GetDeviceCaps(hDC,LOGPIXELSY)/72.0f; //logical pts
        Size=14;
        logfont.lfHeight=(int)(Size*SizeFactor); //convert to pixels
        logfont.lfWidth=0;      //use default character aspect ratio
        logfont.lfPitchAndFamily=FF_ROMAN;
        hPrimaryFont=CreateFontIndirect(&logfont);
        if(hPrimaryFont==NULL)
         hDefaultFont=NULL; // couldn't create primary
        else
         hDefaultFont=SelectObject(hDC,hPrimaryFont);
        GetTextMetrics (hDC, &tm);
        xChar = tm.tmAveCharWidth;
        xChar0= (tm.tmMaxCharWidth+3*xChar)/4;
        yChar = tm.tmHeight + tm.tmExternalLeading;
        yChar0 = tm.tmHeight;
        GetTextFace (hDC, sizeof szFaceName, szFaceName) ;
        ParseText(szText,ilen);
        Extent=GetParsedTextExtent(hDC,szText,ilen);
        ParsedTextOut(hDC,10*xChar,10*yChar,szText,ilen);
        if(hDefaultFont)
         DeleteObject(SelectObject(hDC,hDefaultFont));
        }
//————————————————————————

/* Inform Windows painting is complete      */
        EndPaint(hWnd, &ps);
        break;          /*  End of WM_PAINT */

 case WM_CLOSE:  /* close the window       */
/* Destroy child windows, modeless dialogs, then, this window */
        DestroyWindow(hWnd);
        if (hWnd == hWndMain)
          PostQuitMessage(0);  /* Quit the application */
        break;

 default:
/* For any message for which you don't specifically provide a */
/* service routine, you should return the message to Windows  */
/* for default message processing.                        */
```

```
            return DefWindowProc(hWnd, Message, wParam, lParam);
         }
 return 0L;
 }      /* End of WndProc  */

BOOL FAR PASCAL ENTERMsgProc(HWND hWndDlg, WORD Message, WORD wParam,
LONG lParam)
{
 switch(Message)
 {
   case WM_INITDIALOG:
        cwCenter(hWndDlg, 0);
        /* initialize working variables      */
        SetDlgItemText(hWndDlg,IDEDIT,szText);
        SendDlgItemMessage(hWndDlg,IDEDIT,EM_LIMITTEXT,
                    sizeof(szText)-1,0L);
        SetFocus(GetDlgItem(hWndDlg,IDEDIT));
        return FALSE; //because we set the focus to the edit control
        break; /* End of WM_INITDIALOG*/
  case WM_CLOSE:
/* Closing the Dialog behaves the same as Cancel */
        PostMessage(hWndDlg, WM_COMMAND, IDCANCEL, 0L);
        break; /* End of WM_CLOSE*/
  case WM_COMMAND:
   switch(wParam)
   {
        case IDEDIT: /* Edit Control */
          break;
        case IDOK:
          GetDlgItemText(hWndDlg, IDEDIT, szText, sizeof(szText));
          EndDialog(hWndDlg, TRUE);
          break;
        case IDCANCEL:
   /* Ignore data values entered into the controls */
   /* and dismiss the dialog window returning FALSE */
        EndDialog(hWndDlg, FALSE);
          break;

   }
   break;          /* End of WM_COMMAND */

 default:
   return FALSE;
 }
 return TRUE;
} /* End of ENTERMsgProc */

int nCwRegisterClasses(void)
{
 WNDCLASS wndclass;    /* struct to define a window class */
 memset(&wndclass, 0x00, sizeof(WNDCLASS));
 /* load WNDCLASS with window's characteristics */
 wndclass.style = CS_HREDRAW | CS_VREDRAW | CS_BYTEALIGNWINDOW;
 wndclass.lpfnWndProc = WndProc;
 /* Extra storage for Class and Window objects */
```

```
  wndclass.cbClsExtra = 0;
  wndclass.cbWndExtra = 0;
  wndclass.hInstance = hInst;
  wndclass.hIcon = LoadIcon(NULL, IDI_APPLICATION);
  wndclass.hCursor = LoadCursor(NULL, IDC_ARROW);
  /* Create brush for erasing background    */
  wndclass.hbrBackground = (HBRUSH)(COLOR_WINDOW+1);
  wndclass.lpszMenuName = szAppName;   /* Menu Name is App Name */
  wndclass.lpszClassName = szAppName; /* Class Name is App Name */
  if(!RegisterClass(&wndclass))
        return -1;
  return(0);
} /* End of nCwRegisterClasses */

void cwCenter(hWnd, top)
HWND hWnd;
int top;
{
  POINT       pt;
  RECT        swp;
  RECT        rParent;
  int         iwidth;
  int         iheight;

  /* get the rectangles for the parent and the child */
  GetWindowRect(hWnd, &swp);
  GetClientRect(hWndMain, &rParent);

  /* calculate the height and width for MoveWindow */
  iwidth = swp.right - swp.left;
  iheight = swp.bottom - swp.top;

  /* find the center point and convert to screen coordinates */
  pt.x = (rParent.right - rParent.left) / 2;
  pt.y = (rParent.bottom - rParent.top) / 2;
  ClientToScreen(hWndMain, &pt);

  /* calculate the new x, y starting point */
  pt.x = pt.x - (iwidth / 2);
  pt.y = pt.y - (iheight / 2);

  /* top will adjust the window position, up or down */
  if(top)
        pt.y = pt.y + top;

  /* move the window  */
  MoveWindow(hWnd, pt.x, pt.y, iwidth, iheight, FALSE);
}

void CwUnRegisterClasses(void)
{
  WNDCLASS     wndclass; /* struct to define a window class */
  memset(&wndclass, 0x00, sizeof(WNDCLASS));
  UnregisterClass(szAppName, hInst);
}        /* End of CwUnRegisterClasses*/
```

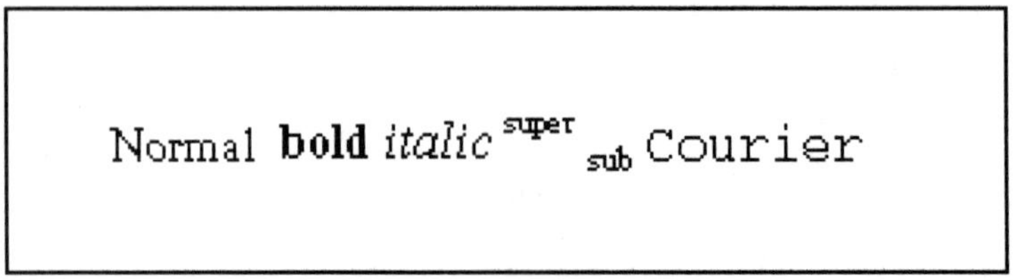

Normal **bold** *italic* ^{super} _{sub} Courier

Figure 8.1. Parsed text displayed by TESTPAR1

You'll find that this test application works fine, as shown by Figure 8.1. You won't much like the interface, though. The next step would be to put the input edit control right in the main window and to get rid of the dialog box. You'd update the main window display any time you got an **EN_CHANGED** message from the edit control.

After trying that, you'd want to eliminate the edit control entirely and accept characters directly into the main window, displaying the string as soon as it is typed. You'd want to add control-key combinations to set character attributes, which would insert the "@"-commands (or even update the **vLex** structure) behind the scenes. In addition, you'd want menu items for the character attributes, and perhaps buttons for convenience. You'd have to add selection logic so that you could apply an attribute to the current selection.

You'd go on from there to support multiple lines of text, word wrapping, and so on. And finally you'd turn the window procedure we developed into a custom control, as outlined in Chapter 1.

In which we use the rich text edit functions from the previous chapter in our bitmap editing program, to add image annotation capability.

Titling a Bitmap

. . . .

We may not have finished turning the parsed-text functions into a decent edit control, but we do have enough to use. Our goal is to be able to put one line of rich text at a time into an image.

Adding Annotation Capabilities to the Image Application

We need to steal hunks of our parsed text test program and add them to Image2. The bulk of the changes will go in **menucomm.c**. We'll add a new item under the edit menu, and assign it to **IDM_RICHTEXT**. The new menu item of course requires a change to **Image2.rc**, and a new **#define** in **Image2.h**. We'll have to add **parsed.obj** to **makefile**, for Microsoft C; for QuickC or Borland C++, add **parsed.c** to the project.

    Don't forget to export the dialog function for text entry: I did. Embarrassing, that. It took me about twenty minutes to debug to the point where I was sure **DS** wasn't being set right in the text entry dialog procedure; then I knew that I had either forgotten to **MakeProcInstance** the dialog procedure (I hadn't) or export it (I had).

```
float SizeFactor;
float Size;
static char szRichText[128]="";
```

```
LOGFONT logfont;
HFONT hPrimaryFont,hDefaultFont;
TEXTMETRIC tm;
int xChar,xChar0,yChar,yChar0;
char szFaceName[80]="";
BOOL _export FAR PASCAL ENTERMsgProc(HWND hWndDlg, WORD Message,
                           WORD wParam, LONG lParam);
...
  case IDM_RICHTEXT:
       //bring up dialog box to enter text string
       nRc = fDialog(toparse, hWnd, ENTERMsgProc);
       ilen=lstrlen(szRichText);
       if(ilen==0 || nRc==0) {
              MessageBeep(0);
              break;
              }
       //write parsed text into bitmap
       StartWait();
       hdc1 = GetDC(NULL);
       hDC  = CreateCompatibleDC(hdc1);
       ReleaseDC(NULL, hdc1);
       SizeFactor=GetDeviceCaps(hDC,LOGPIXELSY)/72.0f;
                                           // logical points
       Size=14;
       logfont.lfHeight=(int)(Size*SizeFactor);
                                           //convert to logical pixels
       logfont.lfWidth=0;
       logfont.lfPitchAndFamily=FF_ROMAN;
       hPrimaryFont=CreateFontIndirect(&logfont);
       if(hPrimaryFont==NULL)
              hDefaultFont=NULL;
                             // couldn't create primary — use default
       else
              hDefaultFont=SelectObject(hDC,hPrimaryFont);
       GetTextMetrics (hDC, &tm);
       xChar = tm.tmAveCharWidth;
       xChar0= (tm.tmMaxCharWidth+3*xChar)/4;
       yChar = tm.tmHeight + tm.tmExternalLeading;
       yChar0 = tm.tmHeight;
       GetTextFace (hDC, sizeof szFaceName, szFaceName) ;
       ParseText(szRichText,ilen);
       Extent=GetParsedTextExtent(hDC,szRichText,ilen);
       dx=max(LOWORD(Extent),yChar0); //just in case!
       dy=max(HIWORD(Extent),yChar0);
       hbm=CreateCompatibleBitmap(hDC,dx,dy);
       hbmOld=SelectObject(hDC,hbm);
       hpalT = SelectPalette(hDC, hpalCurrent, FALSE);
       RealizePalette(hDC);
       PatBlt(hDC,0,0,dx,dy,WHITENESS);
       //The starting point of 0,0 is only valid for 0 degrees
       //Need a switch statement for other angles
       ParsedTextOut(hDC,0,0,szRichText,ilen);
       if(hDefaultFont)
```

```
                    DeleteObject(SelectObject(hDC,hDefaultFont));
        SelectObject(hDC,hbmOld);
        SelectPalette(hDC, hpalT, FALSE);
        DeleteDC(hDC);
        EndWait();
//now the logic is just like paste clipping, but no palette merge
        if(!IsRectEmpty(&rcClip) &&
                (rcClip.bottom-rcClip.top  > 2) &&
                (rcClip.right -rcClip.left > 2))
                fStretchClipping=TRUE;
        else
                fStretchClipping=FALSE;
        BackupCurrentDIB();
        h=DibFromBitmap(hbm,BI_RGB,0,hpalCurrent);
        DragTheClipping(hWnd,h,hbm,hpalCurrent,fStretchClipping);
        StartWait();
        hdibCurrent=MergeImages(hdibCurrent,h,hpalCurrent,
                                rcClip,fStretchClipping);
        EndWait();
        if (hdibCurrent) {
                bLegitDraw = TRUE;
                lstrcpy(achFileName, "<Annotated>");
                hbiCurrent = hdibCurrent;
                SizeWindow(hWnd);
                }
        else {
                bLegitDraw = FALSE;
                ErrMsg("Image Annotation Failed");
                }
        break;
...
BOOL _export FAR PASCAL ENTERMsgProc(HWND hWndDlg, WORD Message,
                            WORD wParam, LONG lParam)
{
 switch(Message)
        {
        case WM_INITDIALOG:
        /* initialize working variables      */
                SetDlgItemText(hWndDlg,IDEDIT,szRichText);
                SendDlgItemMessage(hWndDlg,IDEDIT,EM_LIMITTEXT,
                        sizeof(szRichText)-1,0L);
                SetFocus(GetDlgItem(hWndDlg,IDEDIT));
                return FALSE;
                break; /* End of WM_INITDIALOG */
        case WM_CLOSE:
        /* Closing the Dialog behaves the same as Cancel */
                PostMessage(hWndDlg, WM_COMMAND, IDCANCEL, 0L);
                break; /* End of WM_CLOSE */
        case WM_COMMAND:
                switch(wParam)
                    {
                        case IDEDIT: /* Edit Control */
                          break;
```

```
                    case IDOK:
                        GetDlgItemText(hWndDlg,IDEDIT,
                                    szRichText,sizeof(szRichText));
                        EndDialog(hWndDlg, TRUE);
                        break;
                    case IDCANCEL:
   /* Ignore data values entered into the controls */
   /* and dismiss the dialog window returning FALSE            */
                        EndDialog(hWndDlg, FALSE);
                        break;
                }
            break;   /* End of WM_COMMAND */
        default:
                return FALSE;
        }
   return TRUE;
} /* End of ENTERMsgProc */
```

That'll do (see Figure 9.1), as long as you are content to have text at the normal orientation and are satisfied with the interface. To make text display correctly at a 90° angle, you'll have to change the starting point for **ParsedTextOut** to (0, -dy) instead of the (0, 0) point used at 0°. I'll let you figure out what to do at other angles.

You might want improve the interface for editing rich text by beefing up the dialog box. Consider adding an edit field for the initial angle, and pushbuttons for italic, bold, and underlined text. Pushbuttons could bring up the color selection common dialog for text and background colors. Another pushbutton could bring up the font selection common dialog, or you could use the code in Chapter 8 to fill drop-down combo boxes with font names and sizes.

If you've already written a rich text control as outlined at the end of Chapter 8, you could substitute it for the plain edit control in the dialog box and get WYSIWYG editing of parsed text. In fact, there are hundreds of things you could do to improve Image2: it's a useful program, but it's nowhere near being what I consider a shippable application. Enough, though: you're ready to take it from here.

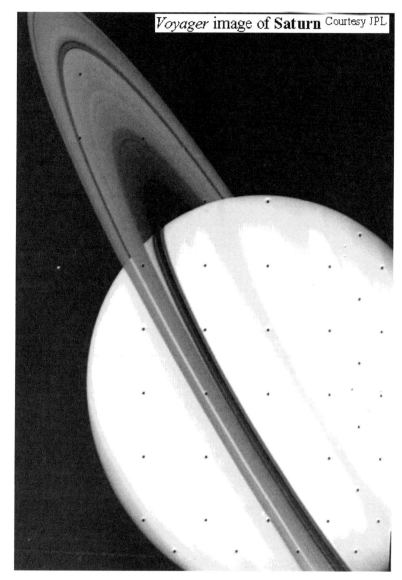

Figure 9.1. Annotated image of Saturn

10

In which we learn how one might port a Windows program to other environments, and explore the strengths and weaknesses of various porting techniques.

Porting

. . . .

Windows is hot now, but you never know which way the wind will blow tomorrow. Let's consider, briefly, how we'd move a Windows application to other platforms without having to rewrite it from scratch. While we're at it, we can also look at moving from other platforms to Windows.

Porting to OS/2 Presentation Manager

The most obvious target for porting from Windows is OS/2 Presentation Manager. If you just want your Windows program to run in OS/2 2.0, you don't have to do anything: OS/2 2.0 includes support for Windows binaries in standard mode. OS/2 1.3 can run Windows 3.0 in a DOS box, but only in real mode.

To take a Windows program to OS/2 1.3 and have it run in protected mode, you need to port it, but there are tools that make this fairly easy. To take it to OS/2 2.0 and have it run in 32-bit protected mode, you need to port it, but there are no tools: you'll have to bring it across by hand.[1]

If you convert by hand, you'll have to fight with all the subtle and not-so-subtle differences between PM and Windows. PM is a preemptive multitasking system that directly supports multiple threads of execution; Windows is a cooperative multitasking system without thread support.

---

[1] At the time this book went to press, a 32-bit version of Mirrors was introduced for OS/2 2.0.

319

The Windows graphics system, GDI, is considerably simpler than the PM graphics system, GPI. GPI resembles the mainframe GKS and GDDI graphics standards as much as it does GDI: it has *segments* like GKS, it has *paths*, it has *presentation bundles*. There's also an annoying sign reversal: Windows has the origin at the top of the screen, and PM has the origin at the bottom of the screen.

Don't underestimate the effort needed to port from Windows to OS/2 by hand: it is significant. On the other hand, porting with a compatibility library like WLO or Mirrors is relatively easy. Still, the execution speed of a program ported with WLO or Mirrors won't be as good as a program that is carefully hand-ported.

Porting by Relinking with WLO or Mirrors

The Microsoft Windows Library for OS/2 (WLO) and Micrografx Mirrors library both purport to let you bring a Windows program over to OS/2 1.x protected mode simply by relinking the application. I don't have Mirrors; I understand that it is similar to WLO.

The WLO kit can be used for development under DOS or OS/2; it requires the Windows 3.0 SDK, MSC 5.1 or 6.0, and OS/2 1.21 or later. You need to test your converted application under OS/2.

The WLO link libraries and DLLs have the same names as their respective Windows counterparts: GDI, USER, and so on. If you simply relink your Windows application with the WLO libraries, you *should* have an executable that will run both under Presentation Manager and Windows in protected mode.

For the record, I did attempt to port Image2 to OS/2 with WLO 1.0 by simply relinking. It didn't quite work: I'd try to start Image 2, and after a long pause, I'd get a message from the printer driver about an unknown job; when I cancelled the job, the Image2 window would come up. As soon as I tried to change directories from the open file dialog box, the application would have a GP fault and die. I didn't pursue the source of these problems in any depth, although I suspect both could easily be corrected.

If you have an in-house Windows application, a straight relink with WLO might be enough to satisfy your OS/2 users (assuming it worked properly). For a commercial program, you'll need to take a few more steps.

To begin with, you'll have to modify your setup program. The WLO Development kit includes a Wloinst program that will install the WLO DLLs on the destination OS/2 system as well as installing your program files. You might also have to modify your installation strategy for OS/2: the environment is quite different. Be aware of LIBPATH and the \OS2\DLL directory; be aware that INI files will be binary, not ASCII; don't try to look for WIN.INI or KERNEL.EXE or \WINDOWS.

You'll also need to convert your application icon. PM icons have a different format from Windows icons. Use the WLO **Convicon** tool or design a new icon using the OS/2 Icon Editor. The converted icon needs to be attached to the relinked EXE file as an .ICON extended attribute (EA); you can do this with the OS/2 File Manager or with **Wloinst**.

If you have DLLs in your application, you not only have to relink them with the WLO libraries, you need to change the source code. Once modified and relinked, the DLLs will be binary compatible with both Windows and PM. The WLO **Convdll** tool adds code to the beginning of the DLL to make the register environment in PM look just like the Windows register environment. You'll need to modify your **LibEntry** code to **INCLUDE CONVDLL.INC** immediately after the **proc** statement or between the **cProc** and **cBegin** lines. You'll have to run **Convdll** after reassembling and relinking.

If your application has its own Windows fonts, convert them to PM fonts with the WLO **Convfont** tool. If you use the **EnumFonts, CreateFont** or **CreateFontIndirect** Windows functions, you may have to modify your code for WLO: the Windows font mapper will only give you fonts that match the device resolution, but the PM font mapper expects you to check font resolution against display device resolution yourself.

You debug WLO applications using OS/2 debuggers. You can use the protected-mode version of CodeView, although you should not try to run CodeView in a window on a single-monitor system; run CVP in a full-screen session with the "Screen Swap" switch turned on. Don't try to switch out of CodeView at a breakpoint; it'll crash OS/2. You can also use MultiScope for OS/2, the OS/2 kernel symbolic debugger, or any other OS/2 debugger that supports PM executables.

The WLO libraries come in both retail and debugging versions. The WLO debugging versions will send messages to a debugging terminal, much like the Windows debugging kernels.

Limitations of WLO 1.0

Not all printer escapes are supported in the WLO mapping layer: if you use printer escapes in your program they may not work. Also note that output from Windows and OS/2 on the same printer might look different because of the different device drivers and presentation models. You'll also notice minor display differences at the pixel level because of differences in the way GDI and GPI work.

DOS TSRs and device drivers aren't supported by WLO; neither are Windows device drivers. You can't call system interrupts directly from PM; you can change **int 21h** instructions to **Dos3Call** function calls, or to equivalent C runtime or OS/2 functions. You can replace network-related interrupts with the **NetBiosCall** function. Note that not all DOS system calls are supported, and that there is no support for NETBIOS callback functions.

If your program uses **in**, **out**, **cli**, or **sti** assembly instructions, you'll have to modify your source. WLO doesn't support exported memory segment selectors (e.g., **__B800h**), EMS memory, or XMS memory. If you depend on having multiple instances of your application that share data, you might find that WLO doesn't do what you want, either—WLO applications always get a NULL previous instance handle.

There are limitations on hook functions under WLO, and on **CF_OWNER-DISPLAY** formats on the clipboard. **AnimatePalette** is not supported, although other palette mangement functions from Windows are simulated by the WLO layer. Palettes are not directly supported by OS/2 1.x.

Not all ROP codes are supported by OS/2—you can depend on having only 6 of the possible 16 ROP2 codes. Region functions are limited to rectangular regions, and **FrameRgn** is not supported. **FloodFill** and **ExtFloodFill** are not supported.

The **SetTextAlign** function is unsupported in WLO. Text in metafiles is limited to 512-character strings; some other functions that work in Windows metafiles (including several important DIB, palette, and region functions) don't work in PM metafiles.

The Windows segment functions (**AllocCStoDSAlias**, **AllocSelector**, **ChangeSelector**, **DefineHandleTable**, and **GetCodeInfo**) are not supported by WLO, according to the WLO 1.0 documentation. (A text file supplied with the kit indicates that **AllocCStoDSAlias** might actually be supported.) None of the Windows sound functions are supported by WLO; neither are any of the Windows 32-bit memory management functions.

Adding OS/2-Specific Features

If you want the maximum performance from applications converted with WLO, you should add additional OS/2 functionality. The most important feature you might want to add is multiple threads of execution.

There are conflicts between OS/2 and Windows include files. You can isolate OS/2 functions in their own source modules, or hand-prototype OS/2 functions needed in a module that uses Windows functions. You may even want to build your OS/2-specific functions into an OS/2 DLL.

Using Threads

Threads can make an enormous difference in the performance of a PM program. You need to keep the message queue moving in both Windows and PM; in

Windows you do so by calling **PeekMessage** loops during long operations. (See the discussion of **SpinTheMessageLoop** in Chapter 3.)

In PM you more often have a main thread that processes the message queue, and additional threads that do the time-consuming work. Individual threads are synchronized with semaphores.

You can get away with doing a WLO port without adding threads: your **PeekMessage** loops will work. However, if your program has time-consuming tasks that should be done in the background (such as repaginating a word-processing document), you should strongly consider adding threads. You can also get up to a factor of two performance improvement by putting I/O- and CPU-intensive operations in separate threads.

The WLO floating-point emulator, WIN87EM.DLL, doesn't support multiple threads. You might be able to use it if only one thread does floating-point calculations. Otherwise, you'll need to use the alternate floating-point library instead of the emulation library.

There are other restrictions on threads in WLO applications. Secondary threads can't call any Windows API functions with the exception of **Post-Message**. Of course, **PostMessage** gives you a mechanism for asking the primary thread to do things. If you want to call C runtime library routines from a secondary thread, the code needs to be in a separate OS/2 DLL. Secondary threads shouldn't call OS/2 API functions, such as **DosCreateThread**, **DosOpen**, **DosRead**, and **DosWrite**.

What *can* you do in secondary threads? You can have a thread always waiting to repaint the screen, to keep the overhead of screen repaints out of the main message-queue thread. You can have a thread doing CPU-intensive chores, like spreadsheet recalculations. You can have a thread doing housekeeping tasks in the background at low priority.

Handling Long Filenames and EAs

OS/2's high-performance file system (HPFS) supports free-format filenames of up to 260 characters; the FAT file system, by contrast, supports filenames of eight characters plus a three-character extension. OS/2 also supports extended attributes (EAs) for files on either file system.

You should really make your WLO application aware of long filenames and EAs. You'll need to allocate more space for filenames and paths; **DosQFile-Info** will tell you how much space. You'll also need to mark your application as being aware of long filenames: use the **NEWFILES** directive in your DEF file or mark the application **-lfns** with **Markexe** or **Markwlo**.

Be careful to preserve EAs when you move or copy files; use the OS/2 **DosCopy** function, and/or the **DosQFileInfo** and **DosSetFileInfo** functions, to handle EAs properly.

There are parsing issues that arise if your program tries to separate the path from the proper filename and assumes the FAT 8.3 format. HPFS files can have embedded spaces and multiple dots. You might find it useful to parse the name from the end rather than the beginning.

Porting to OS/2 can be an adventure. With the advent of OS/2 2.0 with its binary support of Windows applications, it may be less important to port your Windows program to OS/2 1.x than it is to make sure your Windows program runs well in OS/2 2.0. On the other hand, the speed improvement you'll get from the judicious use of threads could make the difference between a program that feels sluggish under PM and one that seems sprightly.

Porting to DOS

On occasion, it becomes important to take a program from Windows to DOS. It may be that the target audience needs to use older 8088-based machines, or that screen speed is important to the end users, or that the program needs to run in a restricted amount of memory.

It may also be necessary to add the functions of a Windows program to the functions of an existing DOS program. For instance, EnPlot is a Windows program that can create and display graphs; MatDB is a DOS program that needs to be able to display EnPlot graphs, as well as perform many character-oriented operations that are quicker under DOS.

MEWEL and WINDOWS.TXT are text-mode DOS libraries that emulate Windows. Both also include tools for porting Windows resources to DOS and creating resources for DOS. These libraries give you the SAA/CUA look of Windows with the speed of character-mode DOS, but they don't do anything for graphics.

You can port GDI graphics to DOS using a graphics library. While you can certainly use the graphics libraries that ship with the various compilers, you may find that a third-party graphics library such as Essential Graphics, MetaGraphics, or Halo supports more of the Windows GDI primitives and constructs. You may find distinguishing factors in the way libraries support patterned lines, in how they support fonts, and in their execution speed.

If you don't want the exact emulation of Windows provided by MEWEL or WINDOWS.TXT, you might want to consider porting your Windows menu and dialog box system to a DOS menu and forms system like Vermont Views. You could also consider porting from Windows to a multiplatform library; then you might wind up with a single set of sources from which you could generate Windows, DOS, PM, and X programs.

Porting from DOS to Windows

Going from DOS to Windows is technically easier than the reverse, although the process can be painful for the DOS developer who overestimates his knowl-

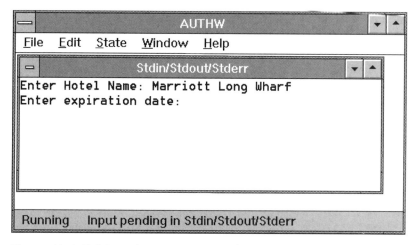

Figure 10.1. DOS application converted to Windows with QuickWin

edge of Windows. While it isn't all that hard to cut up a DOS program and paste the bits into the correct message contexts of a Windows program, it can still be a lot of work.

Most compiler vendors now ship a library you can use for quick-and-dirty ports from DOS to Windows. The Microsoft DOS-compatibility Windows library is called QuickWin; the Borland library is called WinCrt. Zortech's library is called WINC. Another standard C function library for Windows, WINIO, is available for free: WINIO was written by Andrew Schulman and David Maxey, and the full source code was published in the July 1991 issue of Microsoft Systems Journal.

I've used QuickWin from QuickC for Windows: take a stream-oriented C program, tell QuickC to link it with QuickWin, and it just works. Figure 10.1 shows such an application.

Porting to the Macintosh

I don't have any personal experience porting Windows code to the Macintosh or vice versa. There are some issues I should bring up, however.

Most Windows programs are written in C; most Macintosh programs are written in Pascal. On the other hand, writing Mac programs in Lightspeed C is not hard or unusual, and you can easily write Turbo Pascal for Windows.

Macintosh memory handles are doubly-indirect pointers; dereferencing them is an implicit operation. You have to lock Windows memory handles to dereference them. In addition, the near and far pointers of the Windows environment are alien to the flat memory structure of the Mac.

Both environments use resources, menus, dialog boxes, fonts—and these days many of the same utilities and fonts are available on both platforms.

Nevertheless, you shouldn't underestimate the effort involved in this port. Note that you can write a single set of XVT sources (see the section on XVT below) that will work on both of these platforms, or you can write a common set of platform-independent "core" sources and two sets of platform-dependent "edge" sources. Typically, 80 percent of the application will be common to both platforms.

Porting to Unix

My general comments about core and edge sources in the Macintosh section apply equally well to Unix. There isn't, however, one Unix to rule them all and in the darkness bind them. No, there are Unixes of every color and stripe.

Right now, the major Unix Graphical User Interfaces are Open Look and OSF/Motif. Open Look uses NeWS and Display Postscript for drawing; Motif uses the X-Window system.

XVT supports X-Window/Motif applications along with Windows, PM, Mac, and character-mode applications. Another way to get from Windows to Motif is the Wind/U API library, available from Bristol Technology Inc., Weston, CT.

I don't know of any library or porting tool to get from Windows to Open Look. That may indicate that Motif is "winning," or that Open Look is too hard a target for a viable porting library.

Other Approaches to Portability

Beyond segregating system-dependent code from system-independent code, there are several methodologies for smoothing the transition between operating systems. The two major approaches are CASE tools and system-independent libraries.

CASE tools or program generators that support multiple platforms can move the user interface portion of an application very quickly, but don't help with other parts of the application. Computational code usually ports with little effort; graphics code may require a great deal of rewriting. CASE tools generate native user-interface code that usually runs as fast as hand-written user-interface code.

Multiplatform libraries, on the other hand, let you write a single set of sources that will work unchanged on all supported target platforms. The advantage of such a library is you should need to rewrite little or no source code for a port if you were careful when writing for your first platform. The disadvantage is that the library adds a layer between your application and the system that increases the size and slows the speed of the final applications.

All the product-specific information that follows is subject to change. If you are interested in using any of these products, I suggest that you contact the vendor directly for updated information.

CASE:W Corporate Edition, a prototyper and code generator from Case-Works of Atlanta, Georgia, generates decent Windows user-interface code and has a compatible twin, CASE:PM, for Presentation Manager. Versions of CASE:W exist to generate C code and also to generate C++ code compatible with CommonView. Versions of CASE:PM exist to generate C, C++, Fortran, and Cobol. There is also supposed to be a Motif/X-Window version of this product. CASE:W uses a knowledge-based system to generate code from a design and to regenerate a design from edited code. I have used only the Windows/C versions of CASE:W. Note that a stripped down version of CASE:W, QuickCASE:W, is shipped with Microsoft Quick C for Windows.

WindowsMaker Professional, a similar product from Candlelight Software, seems a little quicker and easier to use than CASE:W, although the C source generated is somewhat idiosyncratic. WindowsMaker doesn't regenerate code; instead, it supplies hooks to separate files of user code. WindowsMaker is supposed to have versions for Windows, PM, New Wave, MEWEL, and Motif. I have used only the Windows version.

GPF, from Microformatic, is a somewhat more capable (and somewhat more expensive) prototyping and code generation tool for Presentation Manager. It is supposed to have a Windows version sometime soon; I have used only the PM version.

XVT, from XVT Software of Boulder, CO, is a multiplatform GUI library for C and C++. XVT has Windows, Macintosh, X/Motif, PM, and character-mode versions. Portability is XVT's sole *raison d'être*; it does a good job of it without adding too much overhead. However, to use XVT you'll have to write to the XVT API, which is rather different from the Windows API. I have used only the Windows version of XVT.

C++/Views, from CNS Inc., is a C++ class library that implements a Smalltalk-like Model-View-Controller model on top of Windows. CNS has plans to port C++/Views to PM and Motif; I have used only the Windows version.

CommonView, from Glockenspiel Inc. of Dublin, Ireland, is the granddaddy of portable GUI class libraries for C++. There are supposed to be versions of CommonView for Windows, PM, and Motif; I haven't used any of them.

Zinc is a newer C++ user interface class library for DOS and Windows. I have seen a demo of the DOS version switch nicely among various character-mode and graphics-mode screen resolutions; I haven't seen the Windows version of Zinc at all, and haven't tried to use Zinc for development.

I'm sure there are more CASE tools and libraries that might be of use for writing portable GUI code; I've listed only the tools that I know support Windows in C or C++. In following this field, I've found that products and companies come and go on a monthly basis; if and when you go looking for a portable development environment, you should check both the ads and articles in the current issues of magazines that cover programming—*Byte, Dr. Dobb's, Programmer's Journal, Computer Language,* and so on.

11

A Concluding Unscientific Postscript

. . . .

In every real programming project, there are inevitably compromises and tradeoffs to be made. The projects in this book are no exception: there are over a hundred things I would have liked to add. I've written up several of these as exercises (see Appendix 1) and mentioned several others in the text.

There are also many things I would change about the book were I starting now to write it again. Too late: it is written. But I can dream . . . .

The Road Not Taken

One thing I might do differently now would be to abandon real mode. While I was deep into writing the book and had already finished the discussion of memory management, Microsoft decided to remove real mode support from Windows 3.1. Most developers favored the move; still, some end-users may not let go of Windows 3.0a because they can only run in real mode for some reason.

I might also want to jump into Windows 3.1 with both feet. Mostly, what I've covered in the book will work both in Windows 3.0 and Windows 3.1. I wrote the few things that are version-dependent (such as free system resource checking) with conditional code for each version. There are a lot of useful new functions in Windows 3.1; if I was sure that Windows 3.0 will go away when Windows 3.1 ships, I would use more of them. As it is, I have consciously chosen the more compatible path rather than the more adventurous one.

The multimedia extensions to Windows finally shipped as I was finishing the writing of this book; as I was preparing galley proofs, Steve Ballmer decided to include the multimedia extensions in Windows 3.1. I had a beta Multimedia Development Kit (MDK) all along, but didn't feel I could fairly assume that all readers would have access to the MDK. One improvement in the MDK that would have helped in writing image-processing code is the ability to use a DIB as a device context. Plain Windows can open a memory device context and work with a device-dependent bitmap in that device context; to get from DDB to DIB you have to do some work. In multimedia-extended Windows you can use GDI functions to directly modify a DIB: imagine how much simpler that would make DIB editing!

The pen extensions to Windows were in development simultaneously with Windows 3.1. I chose not to cover them in this book primarily because a developer doesn't have to do anything significant to get the pen handwriting and gesture recognizer to work in a Windows application. Most pen support is automatic—it'll work everywhere you use an edit control. Discussing more complete pen support would amount to a digression that might have taken away from rather than added to the overall value of the book.

I would dearly have loved to cover Win32 and NT: image-processing pretty much cries out for 32-bit support. The HUGE pointer arithmetic we had to do when dealing with gray-scaling and color-adjustment for true-color DIBs is slow and buggy—it would be totally unnecessary in a 32-bit environment. If I ever turn Image2 into a commercial application, you can bet it will have a 32-bit version.

Along the lines of preparing you for 32-bit Windows, I would have liked to cover and use the "Message Cracker" APIs. These were introduced with the "strict" version of **WINDOWS.H** in beta 2 of Windows 3.1; I didn't really understand the need for them until Kyle Marsh of Microsoft called me and explained. Once I had the Win32 documentation, it became obvious.

Briefly, in 32-bit Windows handles are 32 bits wide; in Windows as we now know it handles are 16 bits wide. Windows messages have the additional message parameters **wParam** and **lParam**; **wParam** is currently 16 bits and **lParam** is 32 bits. In Win32, *both* **wParam** and **lParam** will be 32-bit values.

Now, some Windows messages pack a handle and some other value into **lParam**; some Windows messages pass a handle in **wParam**. In Win32 a handle will fill either **lParam** or **wParam**—there is no room to pack additional parameters. For example, in Windows 3.x **WM_COMMAND** passes a window identification number in **wParam**, and the window handle and command number packed in **lParam**. In 32-bit Windows, **WM_COMMAND** will have to dedicate **lParam** to the window handle, and pack the window id and command into **wParam**.

You could write code to deal with such differences using **#ifdef** clauses, but you wouldn't like it. To let you write one clean set of sources for both Windows 3.x and Win32, Microsoft came up with message crackers. The **ON_WM_???** macros go inside the standard window procedure switch statement; they handle a particular message by calling your message handler function. The **FORWARD_WM_???** macros let you forward messages and their parameters through **DefWindowProc**, **SendMessage**, or **CallWindowProc**.

For example, we currently handle mouse movements with:

```
switch(msg) {
...
    case WM_MOUSEMOVE:
    <some code>
    break;
...
    default:
    return DefWindowProc(hwnd,msg,wParam,lParam);
    }
```

With message crackers, we'd do things a little differently. The code with message crackers isn't really any more readable, but it is type-safe and portable:

```
VOID MyProg_OnMouseMove(HWND hwnd, POINT pt, WORD keyFlags);
...
switch(msg) {
...
    ON_WM_MOUSEMOVE(MyProg_OnMouseMove, hwnd, wParam, lParam);
...
    default:
    return DefWindowProc(hwnd,msg,wParam,lParam);
    }

VOID MyProg_OnMouseMove(HWND hwnd, POINT pt, WORD keyFlags) {
    <some code>
    }
```

Note that the **MyProg_OnMouseMove** procedure is declared with typed parameters that reflect the information being passed, rather than with generic **WORD wParam** and **LONG lParam** parameters. The unpacking and casting operations are buried in the **ON_WM_MOUSEMOVE** macro, which in turn is kept in **WINDOWS.H**.

I didn't have anything like the time needed to rewrite all the code in this book to use message crackers—I got the information as the book was going into production. I'll have to go through the exercise myself when I port to Win32. There is no Appendix entitled "exercises for the author": it would never be complete.

Lessons Learned

The primary goal of *Advanced Windows Programming* is to help you get from the point of being able to read and write toy Windows programs to the point of being able to read and write real programs. People have complained that I didn't sugar-coat the enormous block of code listings in Chapter 3: that was deliberate. How are you going to learn to read real programs? By reading a real program.

By the same token, how are you going to learn to write real programs? First of all, by learning to extend real programs: hence, the exercises for the student. You might object to my leaving you the job of debugging the TIFF code, arguably the most complicated part of Image2: but how else are you going to learn to debug complicated code, other than by having complicated code to debug? I've simplified the problem a bit by giving you test cases that reproduce all the known problems and telling you roughly where to look; in *real* life users will call you with problems they haven't isolated and can't reproduce, expecting you to fix them using your powers of clairvoyance and telekinesis.

I hope you've understood most of the technical issues I've raised and tried to explain. If you've understood only that the issues exist, you're ahead of 67 percent of the people claiming to be Windows programmers; if you understand the explanations as well, you're ahead of 86 percent of them. If you caught the flaws in the explanations and know what *really* goes on, you're ahead of 99 percent of *hoi polloi.*

In certain chapters you may find that I introduce a subject and then perhaps go on to another subject before you're completely satisfied that I've covered the subject: in many cases this was deliberate. Some programming and debugging skills come most easily with practice: my goal was to give you the information you need to start using the tools, in the hope that the details will register as you practice. In that sense, writing a book about programming is as futile as writing a book about playing the violin: ultimately, reader must become doer, or all is in vain.

The Lure of Objects

Throughout this book I've written all my code in C. I made a valiant attempt to reuse code from various sources, but it was an uphill battle all the way.

The gurus of object-oriented programming claim that organizing code in class hierarchies makes it inherently easier to reuse. Meanwhile, several vendors are busy developing C++ class libraries that shield you from the details of the Windows API.

Of course, I remember that in past decades structured programming was going to save us. Now object-oriented programming is going to save us. Maybe some people are easier to save than others.

I find the idea of reusing code more easily quite attractive. I have mixed feelings about being shielded from the system, however. On the one hand, such shielding should relieve you from many of the details of Windows programming. On the other hand, getting the details right makes all the difference in programming. As long as the details are right underneath the hood, you don't need to worry too much about them. But when they aren't right, you'd better know how to open up the hood and fix the engine.

I've looked at a lot of C++ compilers and class libraries: I'm still looking. Maybe for my *next* project I'll take the leap of faith and work in C++, if it's a project in which the risk can be controlled and for which the benefits of C++ appear to outweigh the costs.

Thoughts for Future Development

Many of my ideas for extending Image2 are found in Appendix 1, *Exercises for the Student.* Many more ideas can be found scattered through the text; you'll find me picking up ideas and putting them down again in favor of other efforts.

Given unlimited time and effort, Image2 could become any number of things. Most obviously, it could become an image-processing program for scanned images. Less obviously, it could become a painting program, a drawing program, a word processor, or all of the above rolled into one. It could also evolve in the direction of OLE, fissioning into several small, specialized programs that can deal with each other's data in interesting ways.

Add in the multimedia extensions and some extra hardware, and the program could evolve in totally different directions: video image capture and image processing, video image editing, animation; it could assign hotspots to parts of an image that would cause sounds to play (click on the lion's mouth and he roars); it could have hotspots to bring up animations or video clips.

Or, Image2 could lose its identity and become part of another program. Your own multimedia authoring program might need a component that could read a variety of bitmapped graphics formats and display them in a window. Your desktop publishing program might need a component that could change the palette of an image.

This can go on all day. The directions are limited only by your own imagination. The next version of Image2 shouldn't be called Image3: it should be called Imagine. Go, now, and dream it up.

1

In which we pose windows programming problems for use both in
the classroom and by the professional programmer who wants to
sharpen his or her skills.

Exercises for the Student

. . . .

1. Write a macro or program for your favorite editor or string language to customize a windows template program. The template should be left untouched in its original directory; the macro should create a new subdirectory, copy all the files, then rename all the functions and resources. Start with **GENERIC**; you should be able to finish with **MYPROG** by typing a single command like **makenew myprog**.

2. Add support for interlaced GIF files to the Image2 program.

3. Add palette ripple to the Image2 program. Try out your palette ripple with some Mandelbrot generated by FRACTINT or any other fractal genera- tion program.

4. Add line-drawing capability to the Image2 program. Allow the lines to be dotted or straight. Let the user control the width and color of the line, too. Implement copy, cut, paste, delete and undo for lines.

5. Add box-drawing capability to the Image2 display program. Allow the user to choose the box color and whether the box is filled. Allow the box to be transparent and let the user select the percent transparency. Imple- ment full editing for boxes. Generate new palette colors if needed when

combining a transparent box with the underlying image. Deal with running out of palette slots. Allow the user to undo the last box.

6. Add a freehand drawing capability to the Image2 program. Allow dotted lines as well as solid lines. Try drawing the line segments with **MoveTo()** and **LineTo()**. Do dotted lines look right with this method? Try using **Polyline()**. What is the difference? Is the difference something you would have expected after reading the documentation for **LineTo** and **Polyline**?

7. Add a color quantization function to IMAGE. Use the Gervautz Octree Quantization Algorithm to select the best n (default:256) colors from a 24-bit image. After selecting the colors, realize the DIB in 8-bit RLL format. How much space does this procedure save? If you have access to a 24- or 16-bit display, compare original 24-bit images with their 8-bit reductions. Can all images be color-quantized without loss of quality? Why?

8. Debug IMAGE's reading of TIFF files. Keep thorough notes about what problems you find and how you fixed them. What debugging techniques worked for you? What techniques turned out to be a waste of time? Would it have been easier to rewrite the code from scratch? Why or why not? How much do you think a fully debugged TIFF reader for Windows that handles all TIFF classes, tags and compression schemes should be worth?

9. Write **GetDlgItemDate** and **SetDlgItemDate** functions using the date-to-string conversion functions given in Chapter 7. Add date format validation and date range validation. Write an edit field subclass for validated dates.

10. Turn the parsed text functions of Chapter 8 into a "rich" edit control, with multiline support. Make the control usable in the dialog editor. Parallel the functionality of the standard edit control as much as possible. You can gain some of the functionality by superclassing if you can figure out how. Otherwise, you'll have to reinvent the code for all the basic operations.

11. Turn the parsed text functions of Chapter 8 into a real word processor that can handle files of arbitrary size. You can build from the "rich" edit control of the previous problem if you wish, but you'll have to modify the memory management to use multiple local heaps.

12. Turn the parsed text functions of Chapter 8 into a syntax-sensitive programmer's editor with formatting that reflects the programming language. Pick a language and assign different text attributes to keywords, comments, strings, numbers, constants, global variables, automatic variables, and so on. Add automatic indenting as well if you can. Try to make the program fast enough to be usable for day-to-day editing. Integrate the editor with a compiler; use the compiler's browse database if it has one.

2

Using Zortech C++

. . . .

Zortech C++ 3.0 supports both C++ and C code generation for Windows. The Zortech command line compiler, ZTC, has a number of switches appropriate for compiling Windows applications:

Switch	Meaning
-b	Run the "big" compiler.
-br	Run the 286 DOS-extended compiler.
-bx	Run the 386 DOS-extended compiler.
-bw	Run the Windows-compatible compiler (runs *only* under Windows).
-c	Compile only; do not link.
-g	Include debug information.
-ms	Compile for small memory model.
-mm	Compile for medium memory model.
-ml	Compile for large memory model.
-mw	Assume SS != DS (for a DLL).
-mu	Load DS for each function call.
-o	Optimize.
-W or -W1	Generate full function prologs and epilogs for all far functions.

-W- or -W0	Do not generate prologs and epilogs (for DOS programs).
-W2	Generate reduced function prologs and epilogs for nonexported far functions; generate full function prologs and epilogs for exported far functions.
-W3	Generate smart function prologs and epilogs for exported far functions. A smart prolog loads the DS register from the SS register; use only if DS == SS. Don't use -W3 for a DLL.

Zortech C++ has its own MAKE, resource compiler (ZRC), linker (BLINK) and Windows debugger (ZBDW). ZRC seems to be identical to Microsoft's RC for all practical purposes. BLINK supports command line switches and DEF file statements compatible with Microsoft's LINK. Zortech C++ also includes a copy of Microsoft's HC help compiler.

I've built a make file for building Image2 with Zortech C. Unfortunately, Zortech C doesn't completely support huge pointers. Therefore, much of the DIB code in Image2 will not even compile. The solution to this is apparently to rewrite some of the code to use Zortech's runtime library functions for huge pointer manipulation. There was no clean way to do this while maintaining compatibility with the other compilers supported, so I haven't supplied the modifications.

3

Using Borland C++

. . . .

Borland C++ Version 3.0—one of the fastest compilers around—has a highly interactive Windows-hosted environment, TCW. I've built a project file for Image2, Image2.prj (included on the companion disks), that should let you build the Image2 application without much trouble using TCW.

If you don't have version 3 or want to build your own Image2 project file, start by adding all the C files to the project. Add Image2.def, dlgopena.obj and Image2.res as well. You may have to build Image2.res and Image2.hlp from the DOS command line: the commands are `rc -r image2` and `hc image2.hpj`. Choose a Windows EXE for your target, medium memory model, smart callbacks, floating point emulation, and non–case-sensitive links.

I did have to spend a day massaging the Image2 sources to compile correctly with Borland C++; most of the things I had to fix reflected only the different predefined symbols in Microsoft and Borland C. The final sources seem to work, up to a point, with both compilers.

You might encounter a few problems in the Image2.exe as built by Borland C++ that I haven't mentioned as bugs in the version built with Microsoft C. Try displaying all the supplied image files; you'll find out quickly where they are. You shouldn't have any trouble debugging and fixing them: I left them in because they illustrate problems you'll encounter often when porting between the Microsoft and Borland compilers. If you don't find any such problems, it means that Borland has improved their compatibility since I checked it.

If you choose to build a make file for a DOS command line version of Borland C++, you'll need to understand the compiler switches and the difference between Borland **MAKE** and Microsoft **NMAKE**.

If you have a new enough version of BC++, you'll find that Borland **MAKE** supports a superset of Microsoft **NMAKE** directives. Otherwise, you'll have to change **!IFDEF** lines to **!if $d** and change the syntax used to generate Image2.lnk to **ECHO** lines as I've done in **makefile.ztc**. You'll be able to simplify the make file significantly by turning on automatic dependency checking.

For compilation speed, you'll want to enable the use of precompiled headers with the **-H** switch. You might also want to experiment with fast huge pointer arithmetic; enable it with the **-h** switch. Compile Image2 using the medium model, **-mm**, and with smart callbacks, **-WS**. For debugging, turn source debugging on with **-v** and perhaps turn on line numbers with **-y** as well. The switch to suppress linking after compilation, **-c**, is the same as in Microsoft C.

I've found Borland C++ a more than viable alternative to Microsoft C for developing Windows programs. If you take the great leap forward to C++, make sure you look at the OWL libraries: you'll find them a big time-saver compared with trying to build your own class hierarchies.

In which we discuss porting our code
from Microsoft C to Watcom C.

Using Watcom C

· ·

Watcom C 8.5 is a 16-bit optimizing compiler that supports Windows as well as DOS and OS/2. A companion product, Watcom C/386 8.5, generates 32-bit Windows code as well as 32-bit executables for extended DOS, NetWare, QNX, and OS/2 2.0. Watcom C requires you to have the Microsoft Windows SDK; you'll need to use the SDK resource and help compilers, and to construct a special library from the SDK import libraries for use with the Watcom linker.

I've written a make file you can use to build Image2 with Watcom C; it is named **makefile.wcc**. You notice that the syntax for **wmake** is a little different from the syntax for **nmake**: the most noticeable change is in the way you generate external files from the make file.

Watcom has three drivers for its compiler: **wcl**, **wcc**, and **wccp**. The first is a compile-and-link driver that can invoke either of the others, the second the bound compiler driver that can be run on any DOS or OS/2 system, and the third is a protected-mode compiler driver that can be run on any 80386 or 80486 DOS system. For generality, I wrote the **make** file to build Image2 with **wcc**; you'll find that certain functions won't be fully optimized if you compile this way under DOS, for lack of memory. If you have a 386 or 486 system and compile under DOS you might want to change the compilation rule to use the extended **wccp** compiler.

Watcom's command-line option for controlling optimization is of the form **/o<flags>**. I set up the production options to be **/ols**, which optimize loops and favor size over speed. The debugging option **/d2** generates all possible debugging information and additionally disables optimization unless you override the optimizaton settings. You should also generate Windows prologues and epilogues with the **/zw** option and remove stack checks with **/s**. If you are building for protected-mode only you can add the **/2** switch to generate 80286 instructions.

The **wlink** linker has a keyword syntax that is quite different from the positional syntax used by Microsoft's **link**. In some ways, the Watcom linker makes more sense: the information in a wlink response file combines the information from a **link** response file and a **link** DEF file. I took advantage of Watcom's **ms2wlink** utility to help me convert my **make** file between the two formats.

I had only to make a few small changes in H files—similar to those needed to accommodate the Borland compiler—to make Image2 compile with Watcom C. There was one undefined symbol in the link; you can easily find this problem and cure it by rewriting one line of source code, should it still persist in your copy of the Watcom libraries. You can also force the linker to build an executable despite the undefined symbol by using the **undefsok** linker directive.

In which we discuss porting our code from Microsoft C to Quick C for Windows.

Using Quick C

. . . .

Microsoft's Quick C for Windows (QC/Win) is, as you might expect, largely compatible with Microsoft C. Of course, it doesn't optimize code; but the compilation speed is quite good. The QC/Win integrated environment works with projects, much like Borland's integrated environment. One difference is that QC/Win has a Windows-hosted debugger. Another is that QC/Win has a prototyping and code generation tool.

I've made a project file for Image2 for use with QC/Win: it's the file **Image2.mak**. QC/Win will find it and use it. Constructing the project file was a matter of adding all the C source, DEF, and RC files to the project list. I found it useful to add dependent files, such as **image2.h**, to the project: QC/Win doesn't do automatic dependency checking.

I had to change only two lines of code, both in an H file, to make my Microsoft C code work with QC/Win. The changes made no difference to other C compilers; they had to do with minor differences in some of the standard H file processing between QC/Win and MSC. I found no additional runtime errors in the QC/Win version of Image2 compared with the MSC version.

QC/Win shields you from the compiler command line, so I don't need to cover that here. It also has an "oldnames" library that lets you mix MSC-compiled and QC/Win-compiled modules in a single executable.

In general, you'll find using QC/Win a pleasant experience. When you start designing your own programs, don't neglect to try QuickCASE:W for prototyping and code generation.

Index